American Dionysia

Violence and tragedy riddle democracy – ironically because of its very design and success. To articulate this troubling claim, Steven Johnston explores the crimes of democratic founding, the brutal use democracies make of citizens and animals during wartime, the inevitable repercussions of majority rule, and the militant practices of citizenship required to deal with democracy's enemies. Democracy must take responsibility for the consequences of its success; politics that denies violence merely replicates it. Johnston thus calls for the development of a tragic democratic politics and proposes institutional and civic responses to democracy's reign, including the reinvention of tragic festivals and holidays, a new breed of public memorials, and mandatory legislative reparations sessions. Theorizing the violent puzzle of democracy, Johnston addresses classic and contemporary political theory, films, little-known monuments and memorials, the subversive music of Bruce Springsteen, and the potential of democratic violence by the people themselves.

Steven Johnston is the Neal A. Maxwell Chair in Political Theory, Public Policy, and Public Service in the Department of Political Science at the University of Utah. He is the author of *The Truth about Patriotism* (2007) and *Encountering Tragedy: Rousseau and the Project of Democratic Order* (1999). He has published articles in *Theory & Event*, *Contemporary Political Theory*, *Strategies*, *Political Research Quarterly*, and *Polity*. In 2013 he founded the Neal A. Maxwell Lecture Series in Political Theory and Contemporary Politics. He is a regular contributor to the academic theory and politics blog *The Contemporary Condition*.

For Judy, always

American Dionysia

Violence, Tragedy, and Democratic Politics

STEVEN JOHNSTON

University of Utah

CAMBRIDGE
UNIVERSITY PRESS

CAMBRIDGE
UNIVERSITY PRESS

32 Avenue of the Americas, New York, NY 10013-2473, USA

Cambridge University Press is part of the University of Cambridge.

It furthers the University's mission by disseminating knowledge in the pursuit of education, learning, and research at the highest international levels of excellence.

www.cambridge.org
Information on this title: www.cambridge.org/9781107496675

First published 2015

A catalog record for this publication is available from the British Library.

Library of Congress Cataloging in Publication Data
Johnston, Steven.
American dionysia : violence, tragedy, and democratic politics / Steven Johnston.
   pages   cm
ISBN 978-1-107-10060-2 (hardback) – ISBN 978-1-107-49667-5 (paperback)
1. Political violence – United States.   2. War and society – United States.
3. Democracy – United States.   I. Title.
HN90.V5J65   2015
303.6'60973–dc23   2014047367

ISBN 978-1-107-10060-2 Hardback
ISBN 978-1-107-49667-5 Paperback

Contents

Acknowledgments

This book would not have been possible without the invaluable contributions of a great many people. Thanks to Libby Anker, who read the manuscript in its entirety and provided feedback at once provocative, challenging, and constructive – in short, the very best kind. I am deeply grateful to Simon Stow for his remarkable grasp of tragedy and patriotism and for our (sometimes profound) disagreements. Simon is a thoughtful and generous scholar who often understands the arguments I am trying to make better than I do, perhaps especially when he thinks I'm wrong – which is not uncommon. The Friday afternoon theory sessions Char Miller and I have been holding for many years now have been especially fruitful – and flavorful. He has listened to every idea in this book and has forced me to sharpen each of them. Thank you, Char.

Toward the close of the book project, Libby Anker asked me to address her graduate seminar on post-9/11 political culture at the Pentagon Memorial in Arlington, Virginia. While I don't write about this memorial in the book, the classes have been a marvelous source of theoretical stimulation about civic space and public monuments, and I look forward to attending more of them in the years ahead. Also near the project's end, Char Miller invited me to direct a walking tour of the National Mall for his Monumental Politics class at George Mason University. Not only did the tour provide a captive, enthusiastic audience that converted itself into a formidable interlocutor; it gave me the opportunity to revisit the Vietnam Veterans Memorial complex and learn, thanks to Alexis Patullo, of Glenna Goodacre's original submission for the Vietnam Women's Memorial, which I discuss in Chapter 6.

My heartfelt thanks go to Matt Scherer for his timely invitation to me to give a public lecture at George Mason University on violence and democracy in the spring of 2014. The talk I prepared allowed me to extend, experiment with, and refine many of the themes crucial to Chapter 5. Thanks also to Michelle Clarke of Dartmouth College for asking me to participate in the conference "The Ethics of Patriotism" she organized in 2009. It was a fabulous event that afforded me the chance to investigate and develop the theme of animals in war, thereby providing a foundation for what became Chapter 3.

I would like to acknowledge a number of colleagues for serving on conference panels and various friends who have discussed the issues in the book with me, including Winifred Amaturo, Jane Bennett, Mark Button, William E. Connolly, Kennan Ferguson, Michaele Ferguson, Peter Funke, Luke Garrott, Michael Gibbons, Cheryl Hall, Bonnie Honig, Bill Jensen, Brenda Johnston, Jill Locke, Megan Munzert, Ella Myers, Laurie Naranch, Matt Scherer, Jade Schiff, Scott Solomon, and Simon Stow.

Finally, thanks to the three anonymous reviewers for Cambridge University Press whose comments, criticisms, and suggestions for revisions made this book much stronger than it otherwise would have been.

While working on the book in Washington, DC, I often enjoyed the hospitality of Locolat Café and Mintwood Place. Thanks to Niel and Ada Piferoen and Neill Blackwood and Ben Peres for running world-class restaurants with exquisite food and drink and offering convivial settings in which to work.

An earlier version of Chapter 1 appeared in *Contemporary Political Theory*, 8:3, August 2009; and an earlier version of Chapter 3 appeared in *Political Research Quarterly*, 65:2, June 2012. I thank the editors and publishers of these journals.

There is no better way to conclude the acknowledgments than to express my love and gratitude to Judy Gallant for our life together. Her unwavering faith, support, and encouragement are sources of both wonder and strength. Everyone should be fortunate to have such a kind, generous, loving person in their life.

Introduction

There Will Be Blood: Antinomies of Democracy

> Democracy is the pride and the hope of modernity. It also contains danger.
> The danger does not flow merely from forces hostile to democratic institu-
> tions. It resides within the ideal itself.
>
> William E. Connolly, *Politics and Ambiguity*

> Ours is essentially a tragic age, so we refuse to take it tragically.
>
> D. H. Lawrence, *Lady Chatterley's Lover*

Democracy engenders magical thinking. It suggests a world (to be) transformed. It empowers people to create and recreate the world in their
own image. Nothing seems to lie beyond their demiurgic reach. Calls for
freedom, justice, equality, fairness, and dignity must remain unfulfilled in
its absence. In democracy, dreams can and do come true. Democracy is
associated with life and its possibilities.

Ironically, democracy rarely leaves people satisfied, let alone pleased.
If anything, the introduction of democracy signals the onset of new predicaments as much as the redress of prior dilemmas. Violence, exclusion,
injury, sacrifice, and cruelty abound in democracy. It tends to subvert,
from inception, its founding norms and principles, its fundamental goals
and purposes, its own feats and creations, including when it claims to be
introducing, pursuing, or defending them. In short, democracy promises
much, but faced with its exacting standards and open-ended imperatives,
it cannot deliver what it promises. This is one reason democracy seems to
specialize in resentment, perhaps the most common good among citizens.
Democracy is linked, rightly so, to limitations, to violence, to death –
especially its own.

I

Tragically, democracy starts killing itself at birth, and the killing continues throughout its lifetime. These deaths, large and small, often go unrecognized – but not unfelt. Promises broken, possibilities obstructed, and injustices inflicted generate disaffection, anger, perhaps violence, each directed at democracy itself. In a sense, people must perpetually hope for and mourn the democracy (always being) taken from them. Political loss, in other words, necessarily shapes the democratic experience: power taken; sovereignty denied; values profaned; faith undermined.[1] Democracy thus loses, on a regular basis, precisely what it can never lose, which means its legitimacy – and viability – always seems at stake.

Can democracy amount to more than the return of the same political story: failure, defeat, death? Yes. Democracy's self-inflicted deaths also provide opportunities from which renewed life can spring. The successful practice of politics, in other words, comes with serious costs attached (lives damaged, interests ignored, beliefs trampled), yet these costs, if taken seriously, can be converted into openings, even welcome obligations, and furnish the raw material of a revivified politics. Democracy is always in position and enjoys the ability to reanimate itself. Reanimation, in turn, comes with its own tragic price, for some of the political practices, including democratic violence by citizens, required for democracy's restoration and rejuvenation simultaneously can tarnish it.

Do people expect too much from democracy? Yes, but this does not mean that people are wrong to expect it, let alone complain (or worse) about its myriad infirmities. Democracy itself is to be assigned responsibility for the troubles it faces. Given commitments to mutual self-rule, equality before the law, respect for difference, openness to plurality, public responsibility, and shared duty, democracy suggests a brand new day in politics. It inspires. It inspires because it promises a system of rule of, by, and for the people themselves in which violence is said to have no proper place in the common life; the security and dignity of citizens against instrumentalization and disposability are guaranteed through basic rights and liberties; robust discourse, contestation, and opposition enable truth and candor rather than official stories and self-serving fictions to circulate and flourish; abuses or injuries suffered due to political institutions are considered incidental, regrettable, and correctible; and constitutional mechanisms are provided that ensure formal public accountability regarding the exercise of power in the name of basic foundational values.

Still, democracy routinely undertakes courses of action and generates results through its customary workings that ought to be considered problematic at best. Yet these results are understood, experienced, and considered acceptable thanks in part to democracy's reigning principles, practices, and understandings, perhaps especially its procedural norms. We are told that a law, policy, or issue can always be revisited and subjected to revocation or alteration. Fortunes can be reversed by winning the next election – or the one after that. Citizens can appeal to the media or take to the streets to advocate peacefully for change. Nothing need be permanent in a democracy, unless the people will it – and not even then.

Democracies also produce highly dubious outcomes in emergency circumstances or extraordinary times, though citizens often seem less concerned about such developments given a perceived sense of necessity or inescapability. Shortcuts would not be tolerated when times are good, they tell themselves, but expediency is often required in times of crisis. This doubles democracy's troubles, again indicating that it constitutes its greatest adversary. Democracy tells a number of stories that enable it to gloss over or cover up its evident deficiencies, which in turn serve to perpetuate and prolong them, much to its detriment and discredit. Democracy can show signs of health and vigor though it is in fact already dead or dying.

Democracy, then, finds itself in need of a tragic sensibility so that it can appreciate the ways in which it enacts and thereby deconstructs itself. It is both life-giving and death-inducing. It must rededicate itself to giving life precisely because it engenders extensive death. It must acknowledge death in life. It must discern life in death. Democracy excels at celebrating itself. It needs to learn to reproach itself with equal skill. Most of all, it needs to learn the art of reanimation, including through violence, to make the potential real. A tragic ethos can both capture the agonizing dilemmas a democracy occasions and proffer creative responses to them. Tragedy, understood in Nietzschean fashion, does not entail resignation, a docile acceptance of damnable results. Rather, it fosters new bursts of innovation that previously escaped the imagination.[2] It can also trigger a spirit of daring and adventure against the odds, perhaps involving forms of democratic violence by citizens, not because we believe ourselves masters of our fate but precisely because we know otherwise. We act knowing that success *and* failure await us – at least to some degree and to some extent. The two cannot be separated. Brilliant failure defines democratic aspiration. It suggests that great things can happen. Think of the young Oedipus who leaves his home in Corinth determined to defy the gods and cheat death. Along the way, he dispenses life – and thus more death. Apollo's prophecy may have come true, but only in part. Oedipus also beat it, if only in part. A democracy, then, must have grand pretensions even though it knows, sooner or later, that they will be punctured – a comeuppance is always waiting.

A tragic sensibility entails, accordingly, a newfound approach to remedial action and responsibility – a capacious sense of responsibility. Rooted in a deep sense of duality, this notion starts with the assumption that doing well in politics, with the best of intentions, offers no immunity from doing harm. To have a tragic sense of action and responsibility is to assume that democratic life involves taking on what I call the burden of success.[3] Insofar as victory represents the general goal of political undertakings, it does not mean the end of politics for the victor, even when it's the people themselves. We cannot rest on our laurels, however well-deserved they may appear to be. Just the opposite – success mandates the immediate continuation of politics. Obligations ensue from winning. Why must this be the case? The short answer: victory is made possible by those who suffer defeat, loss, injury, and death insofar as they accept and absorb their costs and consequences.[4] Political success, then, is rife with ambiguity. Those who lose (often) deserve better than what they get. Even if the fabled rules of the democratic game allow for or even guarantee losers, this does not mean contentment should follow achievements – not in a democracy, anyway. It cannot, in good political conscience, ignore the pain for which it is responsible. Nor can it resort to and rest content with Rousseauean bromides (to vote against the general will is to be mistaken). Alas, democracies do not tend to understand themselves as tragic endeavors, informed by misfortune, suffering, and damage. This needs to change. And in order to change it, democracy must be forced to reflect on itself, which can be fostered, as I argue in the chapters to come, through the introduction of new public rituals (an American Dionysia), novel civic commemorations (Admission Day, Democracy Day, and Resistance Day), alternative monuments and memorials (a redesigned Vietnam Memorial complex), and augmented political institutions – all of which address democracy's self-induced tragic ambiguities.

Tragedy, then, seems ideally suited to democracy. It can recognize, acknowledge, and accommodate democracy's character, including its inherent failures, without bad faith. Tragedy does not seek to put a happy face on democratic realities. Rather than mollification, it is a discourse of candor and respect – for hard truths regarding life and world, which democracy requires given its (often) unbearable combination of commitments made and failures produced, good realized and harm inflicted, justice delivered and injustice secured. Democracy can endure absent a tragic public philosophy, but it cannot flourish. Reanimating democracy entails confronting its perverse, morbid, at times warlike character. Let us think of democracy as a double – not alternately, episodically, covertly but concurrently, persistently, conspicuously.

What might it mean to imagine democracy as a double, a self-creating, self-consuming regime? On the one hand, democracy is the warp of life: it executes its ambitions, mobilizes its citizens, protects its people, and defends its principles to great effect. On the other hand, democracy is the woof of death: it executes its ambitions, sacrifices its citizens, harms its people, and violates its principles to great effect. At its best, democracy blooms and in doing so kills itself. It dies, if a little, with every move it makes. Democracy, then, cannot be what we want it to be, nor what we think it could be (if only), nor what it tells us it might be at its finest. Bonnie Honig conceives of democracy through a modern Gothic lens, featuring "a mood of ... unease, suspicion, and mistrust." On this reading democracy's identity is undecidable, perhaps a regime of freedom, perhaps a regime of newfound domination: "We may passionately support certain heroes (or principles or institutions) in political life while also knowing that we ought not take our eyes off them for fear of what they might do to us if we did." [5] Honig's concern is well placed. Yet, on a tragic reading of democracy as a double, the undecidability fades and it does not matter whether democracy remains under the people's steady surveillance. Democracy is going to do both substantial good and serious ill – because *it cannot not* do so. Certainty replaces suspicion. Nevertheless, democracy seduces through its notable successes. We fall for it – rightfully so. It has its moments. And then it disappoints, that is, kills – again. Democracy's reanimation requires taking life (back) from death, to act with an urgent sense of necessity coupled with a chastened sense of possibility in the face of political realities indifferent, often resistant to our best efforts. Ironically, reanimation also involves death, a turn to violence, the production of loss. The tragedy of democratic politics, however, can save us from its truth. We cannot dwell in death and still live democratically.

HOW GREEK DO WE NEED TO BE?

Democracy conveys, perhaps summons, a tragic perspective, but such a political sensibility seems more or less absent from or even alien to the contemporary scene. How can this make sense? How is the tragic not a part of everyday democratic life and discourse? The short answer is that a tragic sensibility would place considerable demands on polity and citizen, and neither seems aware of, let alone ready for, the challenge, especially with a beguiling alternative present that obscures tragic necessities and disables tragic possibilities: patriotism. Patriotism lets democratic polities off the tragic hook with a network of ready-made collective narratives, understandings, and attitudes that tell us all is well in *our* democracy, if not now, then one day. Patriotism also relies on a web of institutional commitments, communal rituals, commemorative ceremonies, and architectural forms that reiterate the same message, even if they no longer serve democratic purposes (assuming they once did). The old ways (accountability through voting; change via electoral, legislative, and judicial mechanisms; unity by virtue of holidays such as Independence Day, Memorial Day, Veterans Day, etc.) do not work and need to be recovered or replaced.

Patriotism is not an intermittent problem, confined to elections or wartime when vehement passions, both volatile and manipulable, emerge. Patriotism creates problems permanent and deep-seated. It stands in the way of a tragic sensibility. Some might claim that it exemplifies such a sensibility given its own preoccupation with sacrifice and death (freedom is not free, as one popular patriotic mantra proclaims), but patriotism is in love with death as the fount of meaning and significance in life, which is why it is not, ultimately, tragic. If anything, patriotism insulates democracy from the panoply of tragic phenomena it would otherwise have to address while enabling it, brilliantly, to tell itself it confronts hard social and political truths. This is the artificial need patriotism fills for democracy. On the reading offered here, patriotism regularly disrupts democracy and tragedy's creative synergy – hence it must be perpetually revisited, including by those who think they have dealt with or might be immune to it. Patriotic culture is omnipresent, and we all tend to be patriots, whether we recognize it or not. As George Kateb claims, "almost no one can help being a patriot of some kind and to some degree."[6] Kateb makes the claim to disconcert. And it does disconcert – not so much because one might wave a flag on the Fourth of July; sing the Star-Spangled Banner at a football game; cheer American athletes in the Olympic; cry at a national monument or memorial ceremony; or (not so) secretly root for American troops at war – even in a dubious military enterprise. Rather, Kateb's claim disconcerts because patriotism can insinuate itself into our consciousness of ourselves as citizen-subjects. We can unwittingly possess the romanticized sensibility that is patriotism. We find ourselves moved by its code of sacrifice, especially the ultimate sacrifice, death. We posit a gap between what is and what ought to be and struggle to close it, experiencing pride and gratification as we proceed even if we know the gap can never be fully closed. We believe movement, however, is a sign of progress and greater things to come. We live with an unarticulated yet profound sense of affinity for our country given the power and possibility it signifies, though both may regularly misfire. Love of country, whether active or dormant, enables a political culture not only to explain, ignore, deny, rationalize, contextualize, or obfuscate a seemingly endless litany of national shortcomings but also to accept and affirm them. Kateb argues that patriotism appeals to people because it helps them, thanks to group membership, "carry the burdens of selfhood, of individual identity. The greatest part of the burden is the quest for meaningfulness, which is tantamount to receiving definition for the self."[7] Patriotism also appeals to people because it helps them carry another load as citizens, namely, the burdens of democracy, including in particular the web of immorality, violence, and tragedy in which it necessarily implicates them. Thus, even if patriotism assumes a somewhat more critical form, it still allows a country, in advance, to forgive, forget, and move beyond its deficiencies, however grave. If anything, a partial or provisional acknowledgment of deficiencies can actually foster self-celebration. It may even enhance it. Shortcomings can range from institutional inadequacies to imperial atrocities. Any country, it is said, combines good and ill, but good, in the long run, far outweighs ill. No country is perfect, it is said, and perfection is a perpetual project anyway. Just as we embrace family and friends despite or even because of their obvious faults, we ought to align ourselves to country, appreciating its ambiguous character. To be drawn to such views, which implicitly deny democracy as a double, is what it means to be a patriot – not a tragedian.

Patriotism, then, might appear sophisticated, worldly, in a word, tragic, insofar as it acknowledges ambiguity and confesses ambivalence. Does this self-consciousness suggest that patriotism amounts to a tragic sensibility and thus the kind of ethos democracy requires? I do not think so. Still, it is important to articulate the reasons why patriotism cannot fill the tragic bill. Patriotism might flirt with the tragic, but, in the end, it scorns consummation. Patriotism can accommodate an initial sense of ambiguity about country. To be compelling, patriotism must skirt naiveté or innocence about a country's identity. It even benefits from a country's troubled past and marred present, both of which give patriotism something to struggle with and against. An initial affirmation of ambiguity can make love more mature but also more intense, more concentrated. Nevertheless, if ambiguity means something can be understood in more ways than one, patriots will always fasten on a favored interpretation, what they take to be – beyond this or that mere appearance – the true picture of their country. The country to be loved is not – not *ultimately* anyway – indistinct or indecipherable. Exit ambiguity – and tragedy.

Ambivalence poses greater difficulties than ambiguity. Isn't it a tragic affect par excellence? Didn't Athens's City Dionysia embody precisely this emotional complexity, a volatile combination of excessive celebration and stinging critique? Perhaps, but patriotic love, as I mentioned, is permanent and perpetual, not intermittent, let alone optional. Regardless of evidence (evidence misses the point), patriotism does not allow for a stance that might *eventually* move from conflict, equivocation, or uncertainty to rejection. Ambivalence is unstable. It names an affect that might turn decisively to repudiation. For patriotism there is always something about a country that can be recuperated or redeemed – that can save it from rejection. If all love is about the art of illusion, love of country may be the fancy that perfects the practice. No patriot is ambivalent – *not in the end*. This outcome is lethal to a tragic sensibility.

THE TRAGEDY OF DEMOCRATIC POLITICS

Democracy cannot be neatly severed from patriotism, as if the latter were separate and distinct from, even alien to it. Democracy cultivates and exploits patriotism as it struggles to conceal alarming truths about its own identity. Thus, democracy must confront its tragic character, which patriotism works to obscure and thereby aggravate and accentuate.[8] Democracy requires a tragic perspective, in short, to address and resolve its demons, including patriotism. Resolution, though, remains partial, incomplete, in need of reiteration. After all, democracy's constitutive tragedies would perdure in the absence of patriotism. Admittedly, a tragic sensibility needs to work some of the same ground as patriotism, not only to contest its efforts to colonize the political life-world for its own narcoticizing purposes but also to develop alternative democratic possibilities – oftentimes from the same political matter. It is easy to misunderstand the dangers patriotism poses, especially if it is divorced from democracy. Compelling apologias have been made on patriotism's behalf, making it appear vital to democracy. Still, it is democracy's exceptionalism that is at issue. It is *in democracy* that patriotism honors and celebrates a code that sanctions the elimination of other peoples, even other species, in the name of freedom. While marking sacrifice, patriotism invariably situates it within a broader context informed by pride. This enables democracy to make war against its own citizens as it conducts particular wars such as Vietnam and against all manner of animals as it wages war generally, the subjects of Chapters 2 and 3. It is *in democracy* that patriotism can re-cover anything – however horrific – and make it noble, beautiful, glorious. The National September 11 Memorial and Museum in New York is but the latest example, as seen in Chapter 6. Democracy, the double, cheers as patriotism adds to democracy's inherent violence by cultivating an ethic that affirms killing and death, especially its own, regardless of scale. This provides democracy with political license – encouragement it cannot resist and does not need. Insofar as tragedy and patriotism traverse and excavate much of the same political terrain, however, tragedy possesses the resources to contest it. To cultivate a tragic ethos in democratic politics is to be entangled with patriotism, at least initially. It is also to take from patriotism precisely what it seeks to monopolize, namely life, violence, and death.

The elaboration of a tragic sensibility cannot wait. Democracy's vaunted self-conception needs to be challenged given its tendency to induce complacency. Violence, Machiavelli and Weber noted, is an ineliminable part of politics. It takes many forms. Running counter to the Rousseauean tradition, the subject of Chapter 4, democracy's everyday injustices and cruelties need to be pinpointed and owned, not rationalized, denied, or evaded. Candor and repair are the least that democratic citizens ought to expect. A tragic sensibility entails attentiveness to grievance, maltreatment, suffering, and damage, but it also resists and refuses, unlike patriotism, to moralize the pain endemic to democratic political life. Moralization is inappropriate insofar as injury is both inevitable and unavoidable. Injury does not necessarily result from bad or interested actors with questionable intentions. It flows from the incompatibility of equally worthy goals. It flows from the clash of competing forms of life. It flows from the injustice that justice often entails. It flows from the unpredictable character of action-in-concert. It flows from the stubborn nature of things. Moral self-restraint is essential to minimize resentment and backlash, predictable reactions when a polity's self-understandings

are subjected to pressure. To identify and decry shortcomings can easily be confused with simple condemnation. Democracy, however, is an
ambiguous regime with multiple sites and sources of agency and action. It
cannot be all things to everyone. It specializes in both the marvelous and
the ugly, the desired and the unwanted. It is double. A tragic sensibility
thus entails a commitment to action rooted in a cheerful yet defiant resignation, which might seem paradoxical given tragedy's understanding of
action as fraught. A tragic approach to action folds an appreciation for
limits and consequences into its ethos. Democracy has to act – at times
through the state, at other moments through democratic citizens pursuing their own initiatives. It has to act, to whatever extent possible, to be
able to affirm, in the greater fullness of time, what it has done, what it has
achieved, what it has brought into being for good and ill. When a democracy acts it has to assume it is about to cause harm and make amends
if possible – if not now, then perhaps later. At its best it anticipates the
harm it is about to cause and addresses it, in some fashion, in advance.
A reactive politics, however finely tuned, is necessary but not sufficient.
Thus tragic action continually attends to its ledger. A tragic sensibility is
always anxious, unsettled, dissatisfied.

A tragic sense of responsibility befitting a democracy runs counter to
the ethos of sacrifice at the heart of patriotism. Tragic responsibility flows
from the generosity that can, if cultivated, accompany success, especially
given the compromised character of (so many) political achievements.
And generosity flows from gratitude, not just the gratitude of success but
also from knowing how contingent things are. They might have turned
out otherwise – soon they will. Tragedy, then, pulls on us. It spurs us on
to become worthy of an accomplishment, to become equal to its greatness and terribleness. Rousseau may not have pursued this duality, but
he devised institutions that can be supplemented to address it, as seen
in Chapter 4. Democracy does not honor or celebrate itself as it enacts
such an ethos, however. It is a debt incurred and imposed, willed and
mandated. It is a debt of necessity. Yet the debt is not to be invoked
to justify debt ad infinitum. The wounds, injuries, sacrifices, and deaths
that democracy wreaks are not to be instrumentalized, reduced through
glorification to political tools for political purposes. Instrumentalization
strips death of its tragedy and finality. Death cannot be redeemed, but
this does not mean a kind of atonement is not called for. Democracy's
death-dealing enables and engenders its reanimation.[9]

To illustrate the distinctiveness of a tragic sensibility, consider
Athens's Great Dionysia. Before the city's dramatic competition began,

it conducted several patriotic ceremonies celebrating the city, its accomplishments, and citizens who made noteworthy contributions to it the prior year. The most affectively moving of these rituals was the official presentation of war orphans raised by the city after their fathers died in battle for Athens. A herald reviewed each father's exploits and then the boys, now men and citizens, dressed in full body armor, swore allegiance to the city by vowing to do for Athens what their fathers had done before them. They too would sacrifice everything for the city: death trumps life as life exists for death. Athens may have invented tragedy, but did it necessarily possess a (full-blown) tragic sensibility? It certainly possessed a patriotic sensibility.[10]

What if the Dionysia's opening ceremonies proceeded along tragic lines, making democracy a question and putting it at risk rather than safely contextualizing it through patriotic ritual? What if a poet rather than a general presided, declaring that no generation is entitled to claim, as a matter of course, the allegiance of subsequent generations, regardless of the sacrifices (ostensibly) made on their behalf? What if the city formally apologized to the war orphans it raised, promising them that they do not necessarily have to follow in their father's necrotic footsteps rather than celebrating and guaranteeing their willingness to do so? Do citizen-fathers die just so their sons can die, too? If so, sons would be deprived first of their fathers and then of their own lives – perhaps before they have truly begun. What if the war orphans-cum-citizens, likewise, dressed in civilian garb, did not offer their lives automatically to the city? What if they expressed a certain enmity to the city that takes so many fathers from their sons and families? What if they mourned the loss, however necessary, of their fathers, and insisted that Athens is best served by a commitment to life rather than death, that perpetual preparation and readiness for war only makes it more likely war will come? What if they challenged the city to prove itself worthy of their (always qualified) allegiance, something to be earned or won recurrently? Death can make life possible, but it should not be treated as the glorious prelude to more death. No city should kill itself in the name of death. Insofar as death produces debt, payment cannot be directed to the dead, as patriotism insists. Indebtedness to the dead is boundless and can justify anything, including more death, so that previous sacrifice shall not be in vain. From a tragic perspective, debt must be to the living, to what can be created, especially since creation is always marked by the destruction it entails. Death needs to be put in its place rather than given free reign. Sacrifices can be acknowledged and addressed but ultimately they need to be left behind, "forgotten," even if forgetting is a conceit to prevent an ethic of sacrifice from, well, sacrificing everything to its own ideal. This is an example of what it means not to dwell in death but to reanimate democracy courtesy of the opportunities it provides – to take life back from death.[11]

POLITY AND COSMOS

To reflect on democracy's tragic possibilities is also to reflect on the relationship between the political order and the cosmos. In *The Gay Science* Nietzsche speaks of the world in terms of chaos, which means we should not only beware of but also resist the temptation to describe it in terms that succumb to what he calls "aesthetic anthropomorphism." The world contains any number of necessities, Nietzsche argues, but comforting notions such as beauty, law, order, harmony, and balance do not pertain to it. This is the maelstrom into which we humans are thrown from the beginning.[12]

It might be best, then, to say that the world is indifferent to human being. This is a contestable presumption, of course, but no more so than the friendlier ontologies that undergird, say, much liberal and communitarian political thinking. What social, moral, and political implications follow from a presumption of indifference? It's not as if the world does not impinge on us no matter where we turn. It does. The danger here is that the claim of indifference might lead to a profound misunderstanding. Indifference is not meant to suggest that we can proceed through life unimpeded and unimpaired, as if the world, unconcerned or looking away, is available to be mastered. The world is not a disinterested spectator without effect on human being. It is difficult, forbidding, uncertain, volatile, resistant, dangerous, and lethal. The idea is not to judge or ascribe intent to it but to recognize the vortex in which we (always already) find ourselves – and to which we make our own contribution since we are also a fundamental part of it. A world so composed must be navigated with care and concern, and we democrats must adopt and affirm a particular disposition to it, a disposition at once modest, forbearing, wary, even resigned, but also sovereign, insistent, daring, occasionally ruthless – in a word, tragic.

What might the ancient Greeks contribute to the question of our relationship to the cosmos? William E. Connolly notes a point of contention in Greek culture regarding the gods, which means regarding the incredible acts, events, and happenings engulfing, often besetting, the world. Were the gods to be understood as beings or figures? Each possibility poses its own set of problems. If acknowledged as beings in which people believe, the gods frequently seem hostile to person and polity, perhaps unduly narrowing the space of human initiative. If understood as figures or forces that encroach on the core of human existence, the outlook does not necessarily improve. Connolly writes:

> As figures, the gods suggest a world composed of diverse forces that do not always harmonize. The world is unbalanced. These forces periodically enter into conjunctions and collisions. The array of forces can include a variety of human doctrines, the volatility of individual and group passions under stress, the dearth of wise judgment or readiness to hear it at key moments, the break-out of a plague, an invasion, a triumph that encourages overstepping, an earth-quake, a radical change in climate, a swarm of locusts, an asteroid shower, and other forces yet.[13]

Connolly's depiction of a tragic world disturbs and surprises – disturbs given its perilous details, surprises given that the narration accompanying it seems to understate or underplay (deliberately? for political reasons?) the difficulty of the situations and circumstances in which humankind finds itself. The tragic vision I pursue presumes a world that not only is unbalanced but also has many elemental parts that are fundamentally, irreconcilably at odds with each other. Not only do the forces impinging on human life not always harmonize; they also constitute a condition in which strife, struggle, enmity, and death predominate. What if, then, we were to think of the gods as if they were both beings and figures – that is, as if the world consists of a web of potencies, energies, influences, and intentions that combine to act in ways that result in antipathy toward human life and projects, especially democratic ones? This way of thinking might help account for a world in which institutions designed to serve human purposes and interests exceed anyone's control or understanding; in which projects earmarked to succeed fail and good intentions consti-tute not just a handicap but also a provocation, even offense, to others; in which alternative or contrary possibilities are assumed to be limited, unrealistic, utopian, or nonexistent; in which enmity is always close at hand and some constituencies seek to oppose and destroy others regard-less of the consequences, including if it means harming or destroying themselves. The world is not just unbalanced but also misaligned, per-verse, malignant.

The way in which I construe a concatenation of forces somewhat differently than Connolly can have significant political implications. The opportunities for political movement and response may be nar-rower, and they may counsel, at times anyway, a darker, dicier kind of engagement, one that involves democratic political violence. *If* mine is a grimmer, more foreboding, and perhaps less cheerful tragic vision, in which obstacles are more substantial, resistance more intransigent, enmity and enemies more resolute, the combination of forces more lethal, and thus the world even less hospitable and susceptible to intervention, whether in terms of negotiation, compromise, or peaceful coexistence, it suggests that results will come at a greater cost. These themes are pursued in Chapters 4 and 5 through considerations of, respectively, Bruce Springsteen's bacchanalian embrace of violent street justice in response to democracy's neoliberal depredations and constitutional patriotism's militant flirtations with violence in response to democracy's endangerment that more radical constituencies unimpressed by the sanctity of nonviolence would find disappointing.

This is a political vision contemporary democratic theorists tend to find uncomfortable. Consider Stephen White's recent contribution to the specter of tragedy in democratic politics. He finds Chantal Mouffe's agonistic ambition to combine a Schmittian politics of friend and enemy with liberal pluralism untenable. According to White, Mouffe's political subject is implausible. How can it assert fundamental antagonism at one moment and extend generosity and legitimacy to its deadly foe the next? If situated in a weak political position and on the defensive, Mouffe's recommended liberal ethos would be a tactical move, meaning it is performed in bad faith. If situated in a strong political position and on the offensive, such an ethos will be discarded whenever it proves to be inconvenient. White cannot imagine where Mouffe will find the resources, affective and otherwise, she needs for such an ethos.[14]

One possible answer: Greek tragedy. The world and its constituents are a lot messier, a lot uglier than White's account seems to suggest. Ontologically we live in a world informed by turbulence, where forces mix and clash in precarious combinations with results both generally predictable and individually novel. Politically we live in a world that encourages sovereign pretensions, where incommensurable conflicts seem gratuitous and subject to mastery, especially given an institutional context designed to house and channel them. Autoimmunity in its various guises can be prevented, deflected, cured many want to say, with perseverance. Not so with Mouffe, whose Sophoclean agonism resists romanticization and accords enemies the respect they deserve (have earned) as enemies – of alternative faiths, rival political creeds, religious tolerance, the working poor, people of color, pluralism, democracy itself. She does not necessarily seek to democratize them.

For Mouffe, enemies are multifaceted. Stressing an ineliminable element of conflict in politics need not "[open] out onto a fascist vista."[15] Pace White, a democratic Schmittian politics starting with the premise that political identity is constituted by difference does not necessarily "construe difference in a way that *continually* enhances hostility and conflict."[16] It depends. As White argues in connection with Connolly's purportedly superior version of agonism, "the kinds and degrees of conflict in a given society are dependent on how pliant or resistant citizens are to a whole set of 'temptations' or 'pressures' to fundamentalize the play of identity and difference."[17] I do not believe Mouffe would disagree. Either way, White's formulation seems to belie a tragic appreciation of life, as if one could imagine a world in which the play of identity and difference unfolds absent fundamentalization (if not for certain responsible agents), thereby making for a more agreeable polity and cosmos. For some moral and political agents, however, fundamentalization is part and parcel of identity and difference and does not pose a problem – anything but. It is to be affirmed, cultivated, and lived, a reflection of the order of things. In such circumstances Mouffe might invoke a fugitive antagonism in which moments arise where the Schmittian ethos is apt, especially insofar as an adversary or opponent turns itself into an enemy, in which case even a tempered agonism is unwise, possibly objectionable.[18] Even if an adversary is heterogeneous, it may contain undemocratic or even anti-democratic aspects that cannot be rendered "just another legitimate perspective" in the cacophony that is democratic pluralism. When an adversary seeks to seize control of politics and the state and subvert, damage, or eliminate the demos, it may be considered in that respect an enemy – not just to be defeated and kept at bay, at least for now, but also to be removed from the field of play or destroyed. For Mouffe democracy cannot be used to destroy itself. No doubt this is true for Connolly and White as well.[19] The Greeks appear pertinent here since they understand certain struggles to be incommensurable and violence inevitable. This does not mean they were simply resigned to such strife or discord. As Bonnie Honig's initial reading of *Antigone* indicates, Greek partisans were prepared to articulate and defend a way of life.[20] There is supposed to be winning and losing in politics, and the loser suffers accordingly. As Aeschylus revealed, the winner suffers also – a valuable palliative, but violence still informs life.

Mouffe can theoretically combine Schmittian enmity and a democratic pluralist ethos given the movement or fluidity that a tragic politics requires. Presumptive generosity may be called for in an agonistic politics – except when it is not. Yes, one can always issue an invitation, in Nietzschean fashion, to an adversary-cum-enemy to revisit and rethink fundamentals, but one must also make a judgment as to when this might be impossible or unwise and when another tack must be taken altogether – if democracy or life itself is at stake. Mouffe asks, "Can all antagonisms be transformed into agonisms and all positions be accepted as legitimate and accommodated within the agonistic struggle?"[21] For her the answer is no, a no that comes *sooner* than White's or Connolly's, which is why a tragic politics in defense of democracy, while hard, is no vice. This is not to say that it is without responsibilities.

WE ARE OEDIPUS

Thanks to the Greeks, a notorious monarchical stage figure can illuminate the dilemmas a democracy faces, including impossible situations and choices. Tragic theater afforded democratic Athens the annual opportunity to reflect critically on itself, safely, at a distance. The city could identify with its culture's boldest, most brilliant, daring characters, those who performed memorably under extraordinary circumstances but who also experienced disaster because of their boldness, brilliance, and daring. On this register Oedipus is a first among equals. In Sophocles's *Oedipus the King* he makes a name for himself as the detective who hunts for an unknown criminal to save his kingdom and does not relent until completion – not after being discouraged and warned by others, and not even after he starts to suspect that he is tracking himself. The life of the city requires that the investigation conclude no matter the eventual results. This is the well-known Sophoclean Oedipus, a distinctive figure of knowledge, rationality, insight, and power as well as ignorance, impulsiveness, blindness, and cruelty. The two sets of characteristics are inseparable, symbiotic.

Another Oedipus also lurks in the pages of *Oedipus the King*. As Bonnie Honig proposes a new *Antigone*, I propose something of a new Oedipus, focusing on Corinth's heir apparent as a model for democratic political action and also to unpack the vexed combination of possibilities, risks, and limitations democracy necessarily entails.[22] Honig ingeniously calls on readers of Greek tragic poetry to look to its dramaturgy rather than focus unduly on its arguments and ideas.[23] Accordingly, what matters here in *Oedipus the King* is not what Oedipus says but what he does, and what he does is leave Corinth. Rather than resign himself to an already existing trajectory, he charts an alternative course. Oedipus performs a sovereign act in nonsovereign circumstances. The question for democracy then becomes how it succeeds and fails. And given the human predicament, it undeniably does both – but perhaps in more ways than is commonly appreciated.

Oedipus surrenders and recovers sovereignty, acknowledging its absence along one dimension but then affirming its potential for new beginnings along another dimension. He is aware of forces beyond human control, to the limitations informing the power at our disposal, limitations to be respected if not treated as sacred. Most of all, perhaps, he is aware of the toll action takes, the price it exacts – soundness of intention, nobility of goal notwithstanding. The young Oedipus appears only briefly in the play, in retrospect. When Oedipus learns the geography of Laius's killing, he is shaken. He knows he may be responsible for the beloved king's death. This prospect leads Oedipus to reveal (to Jocasta) the details of his departure from Corinth and why he suspects his guilt. At a banquet a drunken partygoer proclaimed he was not Polybus and Merope's son. The doubt surrounding his parentage could not be assuaged. Though reassured by his parents, Oedipus is nonetheless compelled to consult the Oracle at Delphi for assistance. Denied the answer he sought, he nonetheless receives an unnerving prophecy – of terrible violence and transgression in a world where horrific things are all too common. Oedipus's response to it signals a complex disposition to life and its contingencies.

Respecting the god's power to work his will but simultaneously refusing to submit to its inevitability, Oedipus vows to leave home and never return. If he abandons Corinth, he cannot sleep with his mother or kill his father. The only sure guarantee, it seems, would be to take his life, but this Oedipus does not consider. It may be said that he refuses the comforts of suicide, which in itself suggests sovereign defiance. Oedipus might remain in Corinth convinced that no circumstances could arise in which he would commit such heinous acts, especially since he enjoys foreknowledge. Apparently the young Oedipus is too modest for such a stance. Again, while he acknowledges and pays respect to limits, he does not meekly submit to them. They can be probed, tested, pushed. Oedipus surrenders a life of certain power and privilege for an uncertain life on the road, in exile, homeless. His parents will not live forever, of course. Oedipus might well outlive and outlast them and thus defeat the god's ill will for him. Either way, Oedipus found himself in a situation not of his making where, finally, a decision was called for and made knowing full well it would carry decidedly mixed consequences. It was also made over or despite objections his parents would have raised. Oedipus could do right (protect his parents and Corinth) only by also doing wrong (harming his parents, himself, and possibly Corinth, which would lose its prince, the next in line to the throne). A violent prophecy is met with a response that is also laden with injury. Nevertheless, the impossibility of one life and world, the most desired life and world, does not mean other lives and worlds are not desirable or possible.

With time, however, the specter of prophecy fades. The role of the gods in life cannot be known with any certainty. Nor does everyone believe in them, as Jocasta's invocation of chance indicates. Oedipus admits to being afraid and running, always running, but he does eventually stop and settle down in a new land. Loss of one life lived can also mean opportunity and great adventure in another. Oedipus in no way thinks his life is over, even if the gods appear to have made things distinctly difficult for him, even if it appears unusually circumscribed and already damaged by terror. Though he believes he is doing the best he can to protect his parents, the choice also involves serious risk, for as long as he lives he remains in position, even if he cannot imagine it, to fulfill the prophecy. Oedipus builds a new, successful life in a foreign city, bringing him glories it would have taken much longer to achieve in Corinth had he stayed and waited his turn to take the throne.

As it turns out, life is more complicated than Oedipus realized. Determined to avoid the horrors prophesied for the house of Cadmus, the preemptive action he takes actually helps bring about their (partial) realization. Yet this is not a question of unmitigated horror. Yes, Oedipus may subsequently be treated as a pariah, but he is also a savior. For one thing, it could be argued that Oedipus killed a man, Laius, who very much needed killing. Not only was Laius the kind of man not only prepared but also inclined to deploy lethal violence for a triviality, namely, to declare and enforce a presumed right of way on a public road. Laius also ordered the murder of his infant son because he was frightened by a Delphic prophecy for his own transgressions. If he had learned his son had been spared or met him on his travels, he would no doubt have ordered him killed again. Laius, in other words, was no ordinary killer. He recognized no apparent human boundaries. Nor did he possess the integrity or courage of the son he tried to eliminate. Laius's first thought was of himself. Oedipus's first thought was of others. What kind of ruler could Laius have been? He had no solution to the Sphinx. As soon as Oedipus arrives, solves the riddle, and assumes the throne, Laius is quickly forgotten. Laius was not his son's father.

At the end of *Oedipus the King*, Oedipus punishes himself for his cosmic offenses, but in addition to holding Laius accountable for his crimes – one directly (the incident on the road), one inadvertently (the decision to kill his newborn son) – he also spared his (other) parents. After all, Oedipus had two mothers and fathers. Apollo did not specify which parents were the subject of his prophecy, and the play makes it clear that Polybus loved his son regardless of his bloodline. And the city of Corinth did too, for it seeks out Oedipus to ask him to assume the throne following Polybus's death. Oedipus's love for Polybus and Merope is also beyond question, given the life-affirming sacrifice he makes for them. Laius and Jocasta could not be saved, but Polybus and Merope met with no harm from Oedipus, who becomes the figure of an ambivalent, ambiguous sovereignty. Apollo may have damned Oedipus, but Oedipus also bested Apollo.

Insofar as *Oedipus the King* illuminates the dynamics of political creation and destruction and their fallout, it contributes to a distinguished theoretical tradition speaking to the tragic character of politics. Moreover, Oedipus's self-sabotage, his self-mutilation, models an exercise of sovereignty from which democracy might benefit. Oedipus's blinding can be read as recognition of the dangerous, often violent powers at sovereignty's disposal, which call not just for self-restraint but also for diminution. Sovereignty must deny to itself some of its prerogatives precisely because it can, by definition, exercise them only imperfectly, even unwillingly. Oedipus, recall, left home alarmed by the violence he might do but all too soon finds himself in a life-and-death struggle with a stranger. He not only matches the stranger's presumptive arrogance. He also escalates the violence and exacts bloody revenge for the offense. The gratuitous violence also puts him in position to refound Thebes, of course. Things rarely move in one direction.

By play's end Oedipus has compiled a remarkable record of achievement-cum-failure. He has saved Thebes – twice. He also has blood, death, and incest on his ledger. Oedipus surrenders political power. He is to become an exile – again. For Thebes abdication is supposedly best. The plague should lift. It also portends serious trouble given the thorough mediocrity of Oedipus's successor. Nevertheless, it is the Oedipus who refuses to follow the example of Jocasta who merits emulation. He reappears after Jocasta's death and refuses to kill himself for the crimes for which he is responsible, if not to blame. In that refusal, which constitutes an affirmation that he is also responsible for much good and that the cosmos is replete with tragic possibilities, he is a figure of life, of resilience, of reinvention. When he walks back into the royal house, one can only hope that he will reassert his rightful claim to the throne and continue to rule Thebes. Blind, he now possesses the tragic sensibility needed to rule. He is exemplary not despite his ambiguous record but precisely because of it. Sovereignty, the creative power of which cannot be disavowed, is partial, fraught, compromised, unstable, even, at times, self-denying – that is, tragic.

THERE WILL BE BLOOD

In addition to the Introduction, *American Dionysia* consists of six chapters and a conclusion.[24] Chapter 1, "American Dionysia," re-covers a minor tradition of tragic reflections in the history of western political thought, turning to thinkers such as Machiavelli, Nietzsche, Weber, and Camus. They understand the conduct of politics – from founding to a polity's conclusion – involves the employment of dubious means, including violence, and the production of problematic consequences to achieve ends that are, in turn, affected by them. This is the tragic dynamic at the heart of democratic politics. This discussion is the prelude to an argument for an American civic film festival to be held annually on July Fourth on the Mall in Washington, DC. The American Dionysia would enact a tragic cinema and in doing so reinvent a quintessentially patriotic space and sensibility. The idea is based on Athens's City Dionysia. To exemplify the kind of film appropriate to such a festival, I reconstruct John Ford's *The Man Who Shot Liberty Valance*, presenting it as a tragic meditation on democratic politics, that is, a politics that simultaneously achieves and annihilates its designs. Ransom Stoddard (Jimmy Stewart) models a tragic sense of political action and responsibility from which democracy can profit. An education in the tragic enables Stoddard to enter politics with enthusiasm and build a career on a murder and a lie after he learns the truth of the killing that made him famous. For Stoddard death spurs new life and creation but not its own celebration. Death, then, spurs action even as it is (ostensibly) left behind. This is not the end of the story, however.

Interpretations of *Liberty Valance* tend to focus on Stoddard's spectacular entry into politics rather than his long political career, which is usually ignored, except to note the immense rewards he reaped from a murder and its cover-up. It is easy to ignore, of course, since the film is told in flashback and we see nothing of Stoddard in the contemporary political arena. Still, I treat it as a mystery in need of a solution. He was supposed to secure statehood and return to Shinbone. He did not. Stoddard's career, I argue, points to the tragic burdens – and thus also possibilities – that political success entails. Stoddard assumed a lifelong career in politics not only to take responsibility for and become worthy of a founding crime but also because of the recurrent crimes a democratic order commits – again, as a sign not of failure but of its very success. Success does entail failure, but failure affords (great) opportunity. Stoddard represents a democracy's struggle to become equal to its crimes, something that can be achieved, *if at all*, only after the fact.

Chapter 2, "Democracy at War with Itself: Citizens," explores a tragic dynamic in which democracy sacrifices its ideals and betrays its responsibilities as it enacts and defends them. More specifically, democracy does well in mobilizing citizens to sacrifice on its behalf in wartime. This success, in turn, engenders social and political complications it cannot handle. It may not even address them. Democracy could better position itself to identify and negotiate this dynamic if not for patriotism and its narrations on the one hand and several political imperatives to which democracy seems prone on the other. Among other things, democracy suffers from a kind of teleological compulsion according to which it can and must always be greater than it is (more free, more inclusive, more open, more tolerant, etc.).[25] Democracy also welcomes competition with other political regimes against which it must constantly prove itself. The competition often takes military or security form: democracy must demonstrate to itself and to the world that its strengths are not weaknesses, that its ideals can be tempered by realism, and that it is as capable of exercising the awesome power at its disposal as well as any nondemocratic regime. Democracy's own inherently anxious identity prompts it to take actions contrary to its ideals and become other to itself, become something more closely resembling its enemies.

Democracy's doubled character can be revealed by re-presenting one of its classic figures, the citizen-soldier, through the lens of Gothic horror, more specifically what Mark Edmundson calls apocalyptic Gothic. The genre-switching in this chapter informs, initially, an encounter with Simon Stow's tragic patriotic approach to democratic politics and citizenship and then provides the occasion to revisit Richard Rorty's traditional patriotic vision. The result is a new understanding of both. Mary Shelley's *Frankenstein* (along with Sophocles's *Ajax* and *Philoctetes*) is also deployed to expose democracy's production of monsters of its own creation that come back not only to haunt it but also to threaten its very existence. A reading of *First Blood*, an underrated political jeremiad from the Reagan years, illuminates democracy's monster-making practices. John J. Rambo (Sylvester Stallone) is a figuration not just of Frankenstein's fiend but also of *democratic achievement*, the citizen who does everything his country asks but also the citizen the country irreparably scars and then abandons as a result of his loyal service. He thus represents what democracy does to its young and what they, in turn, ultimately do to it. At best Rambo is reduced to a homeless noncitizen. At worst he becomes the enemy within who would destroy the democracy that destroyed him – a tragic case of mutually assured destruction.

Ironically, *First Blood* carries a life-affirming alternative to the resentment-driven rampage it champions. At the film's conclusion Rambo, exhausted and broken by his nihilistic revenge campaign, experiences a moment in which the audience can see the indispensability of separation and distance, if not quite divorce, from a once-beloved polity drenched in death. The conclusion recalls the opening sequences in the film that present Rambo with a democratic bent: independent, questioning, ambivalent about national identification, skeptical of state authority, hesitant (but ready) to turn to violence to defend basic rights and ideals. This is a figure that grew out of (in both senses of the term) a patriotic culture and enterprise (war). Democratic life emerged, if briefly, from death.

Following the proposal for an American Dionysia, democracy's war against its own citizens leads to a proposal for Admission Day, a new tragic democratic ritual in which the polity acknowledges the offenses it routinely commits against them, perhaps the most dramatic instances of which occur during and after war. Admission Day thus reverses the script performed at Athens's Great Dionysia – which celebrates citizens for services rendered to the city. Democracy, like Oedipus, should be wary of enhancing its own power and cultivate ways to chasten it instead.

Chapter 3, "Democracy at War with Itself: Animals," continues to trace democracy's doubled character as it articulates and enacts its values in war – this time along a new dimension, the use of other species to defend its freedom and way of life. Once again, democracy suffers from internal pressure to treat its values as dispensable in the very effort to protect them. Again, it's as if democracy must prove to the world and thus to itself that its strengths do not render it impotent or ineffective at critical historical moments, especially World Wars I and II – the first to make the world safe for democracy, the second to save it for democracy. More specifically, the chapter dissects the Animals in

War Memorial in London, which opened in 2004. Designed as a tribute to animals that have "served" in war and "contributed" to human freedom, it presumes animals (especially dogs, horses, and donkeys) to be mere equipment. It looks as though it might offer a tragic take on the use of animals in war (one inscription reads, "They Had No Choice"), but animals, so the argument goes, want to serve their human masters and even benefit from their so-called service. The latter claim is embodied in the sculptural figures and layout of the memorial, suggesting that service in war leads to their happiness. What the memorial leaves unsaid is that democracies, to prosecute a war successfully, would render extinct entire animal species. Many millions of horses were killed in WWI, for example, and if every horse on the planet had to die to win the war, they would have died. It might be the democracies that (somehow) had no choice

Either way, democracy here does not so much create its own monster (Rambo) as become monstrous, threatening life itself in the process. The threat takes particularly brutal forms, namely, the eradication, by whatever means necessary, of the resistance animals offer to training and their destruction if they do not take to it. If animals cannot be converted into "soldiers," they are assigned responsibility for failure. They are also assigned responsibility for their own subsequent liquidation. The political example and lesson that animal resistance might have offered to the polity is lost. From a tragic democratic perspective, I sketch a discordant memorial to animals in war suggestive of the limits a democracy needs to respect, especially during wartime. Democracy, then, proves its commitment to its values not by sacrificing them but by refusing to compromise them under pressure, even if, tragically, this also puts them in great (or greater) danger.

Chapter 4, "Forcing Democracy to Be Free: Rousseau to Springsteen," turns to Rousseau, especially to *On the Social Contract*, to delineate the violence inherent in democracy from the founding moment until it expires from internal rot. The original figure of this violence is the Legislator, which, despite or even because of Rousseau's best efforts at denial, must resort to force to bring the polity into being. The place of violence continues well into the republic's life. For example, the will of citizens must be made to conform to majority legislative decisions informed by the general will. Citizens who do not conform can be punished accordingly for the good of the community and for their own good as well. Rousseau's respect for the sanctity of majority rule effectively denies the (potential) violence of everyday politics, a result the continuing influence of which haunts contemporary democratic theory.

Nevertheless, Rousseau's thought contains resources from which a tragic alternative can be pursued. These resources can be extracted from *On the Social Contract*'s institutional designs. Citizens enjoy their finest political hour when they rush to the assembly to conduct the official business of politics. This is an idealized account of life in a republic, which points to an uncomfortable political truth, namely, citizens cannot necessarily be trusted to fulfill their civic obligations. Thus Rousseau mandates regular legislative sessions to be convened on a given date that nothing can alter, abolish, or postpone – not even the people themselves.[26] This is one of the ways Rousseau forces the people to be free. They must convene as a show of (their) sovereign authority and deter any who might usurp it. Rousseau, I argue, did not go far enough. In the same spirit, a democracy needs to establish, by date alone, legislative reparations sessions dealing exclusively with the costs of its prior legislative efforts. No new legislation can be introduced that is not a direct response to the harms and injuries previously inflicted. The voice of those injured, excluded, and silenced is to prevail, and the session cannot end without remedial action being taken. Mandatory reparations sessions are designed to temper democracy's sovereign pretensions and foster a sensibility that presumes that even great political triumphs are also to be regarded as failures.

Finally, the chapter turns to Bruce Springsteen and Danielle Allen. In 2012's *Wrecking Ball*, Springsteen's anti-heroic characters resort to violence in desperate times as their democracy works to destroy them. Their resistance can serve as a tragic democratic political example. While Springsteen continues to present his music as the interventions of an angry patriot, his songs work to defeat this purpose and point to a tragic democratic perspective, embodied by his characters: they turn to violence to secure the equality, freedom, and justice otherwise refused them. It is a question of necessity. They act where democracy cannot or will not act, but they act in a way that reveals the need for democracy to take seriously the conditions necessary for its exercise. That is, democracy can fold the results of the violence that select citizens perpetrate into its basic institutional structure – which, of course, does not render the violence moot. Rather it points to a polity's persistent need for (at least the possibility of) democratic violence, a disconcerting claim developed in greater detail in Chapter 5.

Like Springsteen, Danielle Allen posits a gap between democratic promise and performance and addresses the tragic outcomes democracies routinely produce (though she eschews the language of tragedy). She notes that the pursuit and realization of general goods in a democracy result in harm to (some) others. Allen seeks to smooth these inconvenient results with a conception of political friendship, but this move can only work, I argue, against a strong patriotic backdrop. Thus, following Ralph Ellison, she calls for political sacrifice to be democratized and commemorated, prized and honored just as military service is currently prized and honored. Allen, again like Springsteen, approaches democracy from a critical angle only to pull back, thus blunting the force and potential effect of her critique, including the possibility of a tragic democratic alternative that would emphasize democracy's successes and destructive trajectories while also de-moralizing them (to address the persistent problem of ressentiment in democracy). Democracy need not apologize for its successes, but it does have to be responsible for them. Allen's work, then, inadvertently reminds us of the difficulties facing the articulation of a tragic public philosophy and politics.

Chapter 5, "Two Cheers for Democratic Violence," critiques the promising political alternative known as constitutional patriotism. Given its commitment to militancy (democracies must admit they have enemies and be prepared to engage them), constitutional patriotism might seem like an apt form of citizenship for modern, pluralistic democracies. Yet contemporary democratic theorists (Patchen Markell and Jan-Werner Müller, for example) worry insofar as constitutional patriotism necessarily turns to "supplements of particularity" to foster the affect it needs. These supplements, in turn, which derive from traditional patriotic cultures, may subvert the better instincts of constitutional patriotism. It is a high-wire act with great risks. What about rewards?

Constitutional patriotism receives sustained critical attention in Markell's treatment of Habermas's democratic activism of the early 1990s in response to neo-Nazi violence against immigrants in various German cities. The German state was slow to respond, and democrats were becoming increasingly frustrated. The organizers of Munich's huge street protest, for one, appeared to make some ominous threats expressive of their democratic militancy, but these threats eventually came to nothing. In the face of the potential need for democratic violence on behalf of the constitutional order, they seemed to blink. This not only suggests the limits to constitutional patriotism's militancy. It also indicates its difference from a tragic democratic perspective, where the necessity of violence, under certain circumstances, is affirmed.

Following the encounter with constitutional patriotism, the chapter explores the protean work of John Keane and John McCormick, contemporary theorists thinking seriously about violence and conflict in democracy. Keane recognizes that there may be circumstances in which violence is legitimate, but he argues they should be thought of as rare, exceptional, and eliminable. McCormick would like to enhance and radicalize the institutionalization of conflict in democracy, but he stays aloof from the question of violence. Both theorists advance the discussion of violence in democracy though each pulls back from exploring a question central to this book: does democracy necessarily rely on the very violence (or at least potential for violence) that it also disavows? This can take both problematic and productive forms. To explore both simultaneously, I dissect a 2013 film, *The East*, which follows a militant environmental group as it conducts violent counterattacks against deadly corporate malfeasance and criminality. These attacks are justified in terms of necessity, deterrence, and justice when the state is compromised. The film suggests that while one might not be exactly for violence, one is not necessarily always against it either. The film also suggests that democracy relies on a violence it formally rejects, a duality that is part and parcel of the American political tradition. Witness the founding, where citizens' capacity for violence was indispensable to the revolution, and more recently the Civil Rights Movement, where the threat of violence made nonviolence possible. This dynamic can also be seen in the work of republicans such as Machiavelli, something that McCormick's work points to but does not pursue. The fraught success of the democratic militants in *The East* suggests that democratic citizens need to be able to practice violence thoughtfully and well if democracy is going to have any chance of belonging to the people themselves.

Chapter 6, "New Tragic Democratic Traditions," addresses America's dominant public commemorative rituals and civic memorial architecture in the late twentieth and early twenty-first centuries. Not surprisingly, the September 11, 2001, attacks and the Vietnam War preoccupy the country. Democracy, however, suffers from these preoccupations. First, the chapter reconstructs official tenth anniversary events for the so-called 9/11 strikes, and, second, it analyzes the new memorials in Shanksville, Pennsylvania, and New York City "commemorating" them. These events and structures excel at recreating the horrors of September 11 without serious regard to their effects on democracy. Victimization and the cultivation of enmity provide the narrative framework. Thus occasions that might reanimate the polity in democratic directions instead contribute to the narcissism of a democracy obsessed with its exceptionalism. The forty people of United 93 who found themselves trapped in the global war of contending terrorisms, for example, were posthumously converted into frontline soldiers willing to sacrifice themselves for the greater good, proving that democracies possess the right stuff to defeat their enemies even and especially as one of them seems brought to its knees.

Nevertheless, September 11, now known as Patriot Day in the United States, affords opportunities for tragic democratic countering. Thus, in line with suggestions in earlier chapters for an American Dionysia and an Admission Day, I propose that September 11 be renamed Democracy Day in order to address issues of political violence, enmity, and resilience in self-consciously Greek fashion. It would consist of three different odes: an Ode to Democracy, an Ode to the Enemy, and an Ode to Life Itself. Here I engage, among other texts, the sublime oration delivered by Martin Luther King, Jr. at Riverside Church in New York City in 1967, which teaches democracy how to encounter an enemy. King treats the enemy, in this case Vietnam, as an occasion for democratic self-overcoming rather than as a cause for existential dread, resentment, and deadly violence. We treat the other as a spur to create a world in which the ideology it espouses and alternative it proposes would find no foothold. We preempt their calls for freedom, justice, and equality with our own initiatives. The goal may be impossible, but as an aspiration it does not directly foster violence. Translating King's ethos into architectural form, I also propose that America's sacred civic monuments and memorials on the Mall in Washington, DC, incorporate the perspective of the enemies who inspired them or even a memorial designed by the enemy itself, looking to the John McCain Memorial and the Thuy Bo Memorial, both in Vietnam, for tragic inspiration.

The chapter concludes with Barack Obama's 2012 Memorial Day Address, which launched the newly minted fiftieth anniversary of the Vietnam War at the Vietnam Veterans Memorial (Maya Lin's wall). This dangerous, even repugnant speech reflected and reinforced democracy's practice of denial regarding the damage it unleashes against its own citizens during wartime in the guise of welcoming them home. Obama's unthinking patriotism makes it more rather than less likely that America's democracy will continue to treat its young men and women as resources to be used at the military's disposal and also points to the need for Admission Day, introduced in Chapter 2. Obama appears to be a friend of democracy but comes out of the closet as a rhetorical revanchist, and his refusal to confront what the country required of its soldiers and what those soldiers in turn inflicted on Vietnam and the Vietnamese represents another lost opportunity for tragic reflection. He converts the apocalyptic tragedy of the Vietnam War – an instance of a democracy destroying itself at home as it sought to defend, solidify, and expand its ideals abroad – into an occasion for Athenian-like self-celebration – with its attendant blindness and ugliness. At the close of the chapter, therefore, I extol the little-known May 4 Memorial at Kent State University, which, dedicated to the gift of life rather than a cult of death, serves as a vital response to democracy's horrors without denying, glorifying, or contributing to them – as more traditional war memorials do, including even Maya Lin's fabled Vietnam Veterans Memorial wall. I thus propose May 4 as Resistance Day, to foster the political sensibility perhaps most important to democracy.

In the conclusion, I turn to another western, *Shane*, to explore tragic democratic possibilities. Joe Starrett, not Shane, emerges as the figure of a new politics thanks to a tragic conflict. Though subjected to ritual humiliation in and by the film, Starrett, much like Ransom Stoddard in *Liberty Valance*, displays visionary credentials and ambitions from the get-go, combining a capacity for political creation, including the use of violence, with great hesitation and caution, knowing the terrible damage acting in concert in the world routinely entails. This reading complements but also runs counter to interpretations of the film that tend toward the romantic. Democracy is a high-stakes wager that combines risk and reward, success and failure. And it is success that a democracy has to confront and find a way to live with ethically. Shane departs at film's end, free from responsibility for the violence he has unleashed as well as its implications. For Starrett, however, there is no exit, no turning back. Shane cannot live with the ambiguity of the founding achievement, though he prefers to wrap it in nobility, while Starrett must find a way to address it and the other tragedies certain to come, the mark of a tragic comportment to life and politics.

I

American Dionysia

It would appear that in human affairs ... there is ... this difficulty: that, when one wants to bring things to the pitch of perfection, one always finds that, bound up with what is good, there is some evil which is so easily brought about in doing good that it would seem to be impossible to have the one without the other.

Niccolò Machiavelli, *The Discourses*

We are faced with conflicting values; the dogma that they must somehow, somewhere be reconcilable is a mere pious hope; experience shows it is false. We must choose, and in choosing one thing lose another, irretrievably perhaps.

Isaiah Berlin, *The Crooked Timber of Humanity*

If these are democratic times, then they are also violent times. Violence is not incidental or external to democracy, self-image notwithstanding, but fundamental to and constitutive of it. Formally democracy's relationship to violence alternates between regrettable, unavoidable, and unacceptable. In critical respects, however, violence is not only indispensable to democracy but also welcome in it – because it is exhilarating, empowering, and productive. Democracy, it might be said, thrives on violence and reaches a kind of pinnacle when it can be claimed, if only in retrospect, that violence exercised by that great figure, the people themselves, established, upheld, defended, or enhanced democratic principles and purposes. Democracy is thus an inherently risky, even deadly proposition, which is one reason why it requires a distinct public philosophy to articulate itself.

Pluralism, thanks to William E. Connolly, Isaiah Berlin, Chantal Mouffe, and others, has enjoyed a theoretical renaissance and might be considered the likely designee, especially given its compatibility, even implicit solidarity, with a tragic understanding of life and politics.[1] At its best, a pluralist democracy provides a hospitable setting for the ineradicable presence of competition and conflict, manifested in mortal struggles over the identity and status of basic political values; hard, even impossible choices between equally worthwhile principles and goals; harms imposed and losses suffered in the pursuit of common ambitions and commitments; and ideals punctured at the peak of their success by virtue of that success. This is the stuff not only of violence but also of tragedy, which in a pluralist context is commonplace. It is not the privilege of a heroic few doing battle in uniquely hostile milieus where their destruction is all but assured. The everyday workings of democracy suffice for tragedy to flourish. Pluralism presumes tragedy and the merits of a pluralist political order depend, in part, on its ability to negotiate the tragic element it reflects and fosters. By all indications, then, pluralism itself reveals tragedy's dominant place in political life and its suitability for the role of bona fide public philosophy of pluralist democracy.

What resources are available to think about tragedy? The concept tends to elude capture. As Terry Eagleton argues: "no definition of tragedy more elaborate than 'very sad' has ever worked."[2] Regardless, I turn initially to Camus to provide some preliminary theoretical bearings. I then summon Machiavelli, Nietzsche, and Weber to sketch a political conception of tragedy that includes an appreciation of what is often considered, however precipitously, democracy's nemesis, namely violence. Finally, I propose an American Dionysia as a ritual practice of pluralist democracy and call on an underappreciated classic of American cinema, John Ford's *The Man Who Shot Liberty Valance*, to demonstrate tragedy's critical potential and elaborate further a tragic conception of democratic politics and citizenship.

ON MODERN TRAGEDY

Camus, in a 1955 lecture in Athens, explored the possibility of modern tragedy. Noting that great tragic art has flourished but twice in Western history – once in ancient Greece and then again in Europe from Shakespeare to Racine – he analyzed these periods to identify its conditions of possibility. Historically, the world must be in flux. Poised on the edge of transition, a dynamic present kindles an unknown future. Peoples and civilizations find themselves engulfed by energies both creative and destructive. Tragedy flourishes amid upheaval and turbulence. War is especially productive. Ontologically, Camus narrates a cosmic face-off between a divine order and concrete individuals bucking it. Human beings emboldened by the power of reason are no longer content to fold themselves into a world of sacred signs, concepts, and systems. The stage is thus set for an epic engagement as predetermined answers yield to relentless questions and new arrangements. Ironically, these very same creatures, once they become independent and self-sufficient, kill tragedy by razing the very world that made it possible.[3] On Camus's understanding, tragedy must be short-lived.

Nevertheless, Camus, like several of his contemporaries, would revive tragedy by an act of artistic will. Thus, to do tragedy is to resurrect it, and the world is replete with promising material. "Our age is extremely interesting, that is to say, it is tragic."[4] Though Camus provides few details for his contention, the specter of nuclear annihilation could spawn a rebirth of tragedy. At the same time, he denies the idea of an atheistic tragedy, insisting that if humans lacked a divine check, they would "simply" find themselves alone in the world, adventurers perhaps but hardly tragic figures.[5] Tragedy, the argument goes, requires a transcendental context to materialize. Yet why cannot radical conflict, for example, assume immanent rather than transcendental form? Why assume that the conditions prevailing when tragedy previously flourished constitute necessary conditions?

Camus's willfulness, if not his political theology, offers inspiration for a this-worldly tragic vision. It starts with the notion of a contingent (read: uncreated) world indifferent not only to human ambitions but also to human being itself. Absence of a divine order does not translate to a world open to human intervention, subject to whatever we might want to make of it – just the opposite. An uncreated world means a world resistant to human designs. As a matter of course we find ourselves face to face with limits, complications, and impediments that, in turn, induce messy consequences. Cosmic homelessness animates a tragic vision of life – even though there is nothing tragic about homelessness per se. Tragedies unfold in the movement from the ontological to the empirical. Projects initiated beget their own flaws, trigger their own opposition, and compromise their own endings. This is not to suggest they just fail – far from it. Success entails ambiguity – achievement, yes, but also defeat, loss, and injury. Politically, this involves basic values subordinated, undermined, or jettisoned; vital interests ignored, thwarted, or denied; a way of life altered, damaged, or lost.

A tragic vision, then, accents the contradictory nature of things, which often issues in the worst that people and polity must face in the complex project of living together. It seeks, therefore, to cultivate an affirmative mode of being reflective of a kind of wisdom and care that ensue from encounters with life's terrible quandaries. When Camus declares modern tragedy possible, he adopts a gratuitous cause. Tragedies abound. We live them. This is true of founding, ordinary lawmaking, elections, judicial decisions, military actions, public policies, state practices, and citizen action, among other things. Tragedies compose the very stuff of political life. As such they can energize, spur, and elevate – thanks to a tragic vision.

George Steiner provides a cautionary theoretical lesson. For Steiner, tragedy in its "pure or absolute mode ... is a dramatic representation, enactment, or generation of a highly specific world view" captured neatly by Theognis's judgment, "It is best not to be born, next best to die young." This assessment suggests, according to Steiner, that "human life per se, both ontologically and existentially, is an affliction." Not only are "non-existence or early extinction ... urgent desiderata"; our "presence on this earth is fundamentally absurd or unwelcome," which means "our lives are not a gift ... but a self-punishing anomaly."[6] While Steiner's characterization of life resonates, Theognis's appraisal effectively reduces it to its most insufferable aspects. Yes, life can be afflicting given, among other things, its ability to frustrate and defeat our best-laid plans and all-important designs. Life so understood and experienced might lead to hopelessness and capitulation. It can also be conceived, perhaps especially in politics, as the greatest of challenges. After all, every success tempts us to believe that we can master and be at home in the world even if we also know and affirm this to be impossible.

A MINOR TRADITION OF POLITICS

Think of Machiavelli, Nietzsche, and Weber as charter members of a modern tradition of tragic thought, a tradition from which contemporary democracies can learn how to conduct and comport themselves. A tragic faith starts with the assumption that we find ourselves deposited in a world apathetic to human life and to what might be made of it. Insofar as social and political communities were not meant to live one theoretical ideal, moral code, or constitutional creed rather than another, collective projects simultaneously enable and frustrate, fulfill and deny, realize and suppress, unite and fracture.[7] Conflict and antagonism become routine. Finitude, moreover, informs life's unfolding. Not only do rot and termination await social and political endeavors, mocking any pretensions to permanence. Defects and failures also reveal themselves to be constitutive of success no matter how well conceived or executed something (a constitution, law, policy, or practice) may be. A tragic vision of politics revolves around the necessarily self-frustrating, self-subverting character of life, where goods secured entail noteworthy loss, including harm. And what is lost is precisely what is valued most. This dynamic cannot be adequately addressed by noting that nothing is perfect or invoking the legitimate exercise of power. A tragic sensibility affirms and takes responsibility for the troubled character of life, for its ineliminable hardness, its perversity. This means democratic political orders in particular find themselves trapped in reapings at once vicious and sublime.

Let's start with Machiavelli. He celebrates politics, the realm of singular actors and exceptional deeds. Human being's creative powers achieve their fullest and finest expression in politics, which offers the possibility of great accolades and unsurpassed glory. It also furnishes far-reaching reproofs and grave punishments. Without these dual possibilities, politics would not be worth the considerable investment in toil and trauma it exacts. If success were guaranteed beforehand rather than slated for distress, its prestige would suffer. Given the presence of fortune, however, politics routinely encounters (and engenders) trial and tribulation. Fortune signifies a contingent, grief-stricken world. Politics thus requires flexibility and a spirit of experimentation to handle a fluid environment as the world flaunts its ability to foil even immaculate conceptions. A world animated by fortune guarantees a world of tragedies.[8]

For Machiavelli, founding a republic represents the consummate political challenge: "it should be realized that taking the initiative in introducing a new form of government is very difficult and dangerous, and unlikely to succeed."[9] What makes founding special? A paradox: the introduction of law cannot be secured legally, which would require the prior existence of the very institutions to be fashioned – hence the indispensability of violence. And while founding may settle things, it does not resolve them once and for all. Violence leaves scars and memories behind. From inception to maturity in the life of a republic, conflict is an inescapable aspect of politics. A republic requires mechanisms and practices to productively channel the rhythms and energies (both good and ill) circulating in society. However generative, conflict still comes with serious costs attached to it, including violence and death, something Machiavelli's readers do not usually emphasize.[10]

In this regard, consider Machiavelli's commendation of Rome's dualistic legislative arrangements and its juridical machinery of public indictment for their ability to preserve and protect the common liberty. The struggle between the Senate and the Tribunate checks the nobles' unquenchable desire to dominate and protects the people's desire not to be dominated – if the nobles can be made to adhere to the rules when necessary. As for the court, the people need recourse to a permanent legal outlet for their anger and grievances, the products of unrelenting class warfare. Otherwise factions may form or foreign forces might be invited to set wrongs right. Machiavelli's preferred legislative and judicial apparatuses would not necessarily eliminate violence. While designed to preempt resort to "abnormal means," they would actually concentrate and minimize violence. Thus, even when the court gets things wrong, system-threatening disorder would prove unlikely. Deem it the lesser of "evils."[11]

Machiavelli, then, affirms the ambiguity marking a republic and its basic institutions: what is essential is also inimical; what is meant to protect the order also jeopardizes it. Elaborate safeguards can manage ambiguity but they do not and cannot eliminate it.[12] Though a rendezvous with death awaits it, a republic's life can be prolonged if it is well designed – and with luck. Still, even at its best, violence haunts its every move, a stalking rarely acknowledged. Bonnie Honig's exemplary treatment of Machiavelli's agonistic politics, for example, apparently omits the potential for blood on which it rests. Discussing Machiavelli's admiration of Rome's institutional discord, she cites his rebuke to critics who focus not on the good effects produced for liberty but on the "cries and the noise these disturbances occasioned in public places."[13] Even so, isn't it possible to appreciate good effects and also address the noise and cries? What kind of casualties did the maintenance of liberty produce? What, if anything, is owed liberty's sacrificial victims? Thus, when Honig invokes Machiavelli's praise for political tumult, she notes his insistence that "the republic's 'agitations' caused no 'exiles nor any violence prejudicial to the general good.'"[14] Rather, "they empowered the republic," which means their suppression would have been unwise. Again, while the violence involved may not have compromised the general good, the spilling of blood should not be overlooked – unless some can be sacrificed for the benefit of the rest, a utilitarian calculus with which most democracies profess discomfort. For Machiavelli, democratic violence and its perpetual possibility seem to be precisely the "guarantees" needed to inaugurate and sustain free political institutions, which separates him from (some) contemporary agonists indebted to his political schematics.[15]

Nietzsche, too, believes creation presupposes destruction. Erecting a new idol involves the elimination of a predecessor that may not wish to go gently into history's good night. This dynamic operates at the founding of a polity, a sequence of events Nietzsche takes to be violence-laden rather than the result of a social contract.[16] Not only is a contract a piece of political mythmaking. It is poor mythmaking. Who would be inspired by reason and logic at such a decisive historical moment? What's more, violence invariably continues in the post-founding world. Politics institutionalizes and channels enmity, and while new battles ordinarily predominate, old struggles resurface, including foundational struggles unforgotten by history's losers. Still, Nietzsche deems enmity to be of great worth, essential not just for a polity's self-preservation but also for its political prosperity.[17]

Thus Nietzsche, as Honig argues, is a more complicated figure than critics often recognize, possessing, among other things, a "reverence for institutions."[18] He valorizes the Greek notion of contest, a form of discord in which political actors duel in public to develop their skills and attain civic glory through their contributions to the greater good. Here no one must be allowed exclusive title to rule. The proscription of political domination underwrites the apparently paradoxical practice of ostracism, which is designed to preserve and promote the sanctity of the contest and thus the health of democracy by sending into exile those political actors who might acquire, even legitimately, undue power.[19] By safeguarding the contest, politics and thus freedom perdure – though the tragedies (exclusion, violence, suffering, etc.) thereby produced are not necessarily acknowledged, let alone addressed. Failure to secure the contest may result in domination, but what of the citizens whose expulsion makes the preservation of the contest possible? What, if anything, is due them? Can a democratic polity rest content once it has removed them? Or has its responsibility just begun? Insofar as exile (excommunication from the polis and its life-affirming activities) constitutes a fate worse than death, the annihilation in which it results means that the distinction between agonism and antagonism fades. It is not just that the former might degenerate into the latter, as Stephen White fears, but also that there may be little, if any, difference between the two, at least on many occasions.[20] Like Machiavelli on discord, Nietzsche's embrace of enmity does not intimate lawlessness. It is a sign of an order's strength. He once mischievously suggested that the definitive mark of a just society – a society to come – would be its ability to dispense with violence as it responds to its assailants: "It is possible to imagine a society flushed with such a sense of power that it could afford to let its offenders go unpunished."[21] In the meantime, as the world refuses to conform to the heart's desire, Nietzsche assumes we must act knowing that to affirm one thing is to forego other admirable possibilities.[22] In politics, to privilege one form of life, one regime of truth is to deny, refuse, silence (or worse) alternatives. The legitimate exercise of power can obscure its own violence. It cannot erase it. This aspect of politics, especially in a democracy, may be lamentable, objectionable, or unacceptable, but depending on circumstances it might also be invigorating and a catalyst to fundamental achievements.

Following in this line of thinking, Weber argues that the art of politics must include in its repertoire the exercise of violence. This is not due to some failing or shortcoming. Politics is an endeavor rooted in force. Among other things, it requires the use of questionable means in the service of good ends. Weber rejects as naïve the charges that good can originate only from good and that evil begets nothing but more of itself. He insists that anyone familiar with history (or everyday experience) recognizes these claims to be fallacious. It's not that ends will not be affected by means. Rather, politics is tragic phenomenon because it must be conducted regardless of its damnable dynamic.[23] Good intentions provide no guarantees, nor can the world be blamed for what we must do. To indulge in moral misgivings and spurn the political world would amount not to an unaffordable luxury but to moral cowardice. Knowing that the consequences of action may involve evil requires fortitude and courage. We injure ourselves as we harm others. At the same time, politics cannot write itself a blank check resigned to violence's inevitability. This would be tantamount to callous disregard for life. Our hands are always dirty. And there are few, if any, guideposts for action. "From no ethics in the world can it be concluded when and to what extent the ethically good purpose 'justifies' the ethically dangerous means and ramifications."[24]

As Weber notes, the tragic cannot be reduced to a question of dubious means. Democratizing sovereignty, for instance, legitimizes the source of political power, but difficulties continue to beset its exercise. Just political outcomes can be achieved through appropriate means and yet the results can be problematic, meaning that they can mar, deform, and ruin lives.

Bracing candor notwithstanding, Weber's reflections on politics reinforce but might not further the minor tragic tradition of political thought when it comes to democracy. They might even be read as a step in the wrong direction. As Dana Villa notes, while there are a number of striking parallels between Weber and Machiavelli, perhaps especially regarding the beneficial effects conflict can have on liberty, the differences may be more important – in the end. Weber seeks not only to cool political passions. Given his unflattering assessment of the people, he pursues a brand of politics rooted in an elite exercise of leadership.[25] Ordinary citizenship is not his concern, much to the detriment of democratic action.

Weber excels at delineating the political condition of modernity, characterized by plurality, conflict, struggle, and, eventually, the need for ungrounded choice. In the contest between contending political visions, the intensity of which flows from their origins in rival existential faiths, there are always going to be winners and losers – and the winners lose as well. Among other things, the conduct of politics cannot hope to avoid injustice or violence. That said, it must do all it can to avoid what Villa calls "excessive violence." Under these conditions, the vocation of politics as a calling is not for the faint of heart. Politics can crush the souls of people given what it requires them to do, not just to others but also, in the process, to themselves. The realization of the common good must trump the pursuit of their own interests, moral and political. Thus the survival, intact, of one's personality is by no means guaranteed. Neither the best of intentions nor virtual success removes the burdens of responsibility for what we must do.

Insofar as Weber focuses on the moral integrity of leaders as a means to ennoble or redeem politics, what kind of person should be at the helm of government? Who can bear the *moral* burdens of politics? Who has the inner strength to remain whole? Weber wants to know, but as Peter Euben argues, "there is no formulaic answer to these questions."[26] More importantly, *pace* Weber, Villa, and Euben, these may not be quite the right questions. It might be more pertinent to ask, who can bear and meet the *political* challenges of politics? Who has the creative imagination to envision the possibilities tragic situations engender? Who can get things done when politics seems to have concluded or been exhausted? In short, it is not enough to be *aware* of the consequences, real or potential, of one's decisions and actions. It is not enough to be *aware* that one may not even know the consequences, real or potential, of one's decisions and actions. It is not enough to *experience* serious *angst* as a result of the obligations politics entails or to assume personal responsibility for what has been done. These reactions may be valuable, but even in combination they do not meet the requirements of political responsibility. What Weber needs to ask is what the political leader is to *do* in the *aftermath* of the actions he must take and the consequences they necessarily generate.[27]

A TRAGIC PUBLIC PHILOSOPHY

Stanley Cavell posits the idea of a doubled world, a split between life as it is and what it might (one day) become. The energy generated by disappointment in such doubling can be mobilized to pursue an idea of transfiguration – not toward an ultimate perfection but toward something new, something else, something other.[28] Like Cavell, a tragic ethos affirms a politics of becoming, but such a politics cannot erase the world's flaws as such. Rather, it must displace or reconstitute them. A tragic vision suspects that we always end up, in some sense, where we began. It refuses the alluring notion that there is a gap to be closed between what is and what can be imagined with unwanted features removed in progressive fashion until they disappear altogether and desired features introduced until they are fully installed. Taking tragedy seriously means to live necessarily, not contingently, in a complicated, compromised singularity.

A tragic perspective proceeds with the recognition, routinely confirmed by experience, that politics entails limits. Conflicts, enmities, and antagonisms over normative visions, constitutional principles, legislative agendas, and moral values that do not necessarily admit mutual accommodation or peaceful coexistence bedevil social and political life. They may not monopolize politics, but they can preoccupy, even dominate it. This pertains not only to minority projects that seek to impose their will but majoritarian impulses that seek institutional expression. Political accomplishments regularly rack up credit for an array of injustices, many knowingly committed. To do and do well, then, is also to do ill, to fail, not incidentally but elementally. Despite the backlash produced by efforts to bend the world to will, it does not defy creative intervention per se. A tragic sensibility cultivates the discipline necessary to recognize the difference and to live creatively in the space it opens.

Given a world rent by tragic dynamics, certain features of political life seem irresistible – for example, the repetition of unscripted or unintended consequences. Thanks to tragedy's reliable patterns, however, there is also ample opportunity to maneuver – thus the regular production of tragedies in the world need not lead to resignation and withdrawal. Though the harm political action routinely inflicts cannot be avoided, *the aftermath* affords new opportunities for initiative. It also serves as a reminder that the concerns governing action remain in play. The persistence of tragic results acts as a spur. Notwithstanding Steiner's insistence that "tragedy is irreparable" and defies "just compensation," it makes for an inherently tense, turbulent condition that calls for perpetual tending.[29] While Steiner claims tragedies start from "the fact of catastrophe" and "end badly," the fact of catastrophe depicts a narrow class of tragedies which, generally speaking, do not actually end – not really. However horrific things get, there is always an aftermath that is part and parcel of the tragic equation demanding that something be done, something not merely gestural. A tragic frame enables a people to pursue, as Cavell recommends, questions of who they are and what they aspire to be, which involves a society always making and remaking itself because it can never be quite what it claims or would like to become.

A tragic perspective, accordingly, involves several strictures. Care is to be taken to avoid hubris, no small accomplishment in politics, for if the powers at a democracy's disposal are great – as sometimes they are – and if the achievements of a democracy are equally great – as sometimes they are – the will to impose our will on the world can be dangerously seductive. Do not make Oedipus's Corinthian mistake and assume problems enjoy neatly corresponding solutions. Rather, start with an assumption of harm. Good intentions offer no guarantees. We can succeed exactly as planned and still, perhaps especially, find serious reason for reproach.[30] We may have to employ disagreeable, even objectionable means to attain a desired outcome, which is itself thereby altered, if still worthwhile. We can be constitutionally sound and normatively solid and yet produce laws and policies that result in something problematic.[31] But if we begin with Machiavelli's dictum that the response or "solution" to one problem in turn generates another problem itself in need of response, we can appreciate the tragic bind-cum-challenge of politics.[32] The production of regrettable or deplorable by-products, then, is not a reason to resist or refuse action on moral grounds – politics in this case would become impossible. Rather, responsibility must be taken for the consequences of success. A tragic politics thus involves its own ethos of commitment. Failure and wrongdoing invariably demand explanation and accounting. Success does, too. These obligations point to the prolific and self-subverting dimensions of political life and action. Name a greater test than designing a constitution, law, or policy with responses – likely to be inadequate – already built in to address its ramifications.

Temporal acuity thus informs a tragic perspective. Rather than look backward and bemoan the past in a spirit of regret and recrimination. Rather than imagine a future in which previous mistakes can be eliminated once and for all thanks to the accumulation of knowledge and experience. A tragic sensibility counsels that we live in an ever present aftermath, a temporal loop where the past haunts and inspires us and the future promises an eternal return of the same. Affirming that to act amid plural values, interests, and agents means that we do harm as we do good, we search for ways in which we can become worthy of the price paid for making a mark in the world. It would be understandable, once the multifarious consequences of action are reckoned, if passivity or paralysis set in when faced with the need to act. In a pluralist democracy, where respect and dignity are to be accorded persons, how can we proceed with a course of action when we know, whatever good it does, that it will also do distinct harm? To cite the majority will, a rational consensus, expert knowledge, or emergency circumstances cannot make these existential infelicities disappear. To proceed in politics means that we have to reply to what we have (just) done. We cannot rest, recline, and marvel at the success of our efforts, however undeniable they may be in certain respects. This doubles the burden of action. Success entails the certainty of failure (in some respects), which means that success has spawned a new obligation to act. We may have thought that once it was completed our work was done. If so, we were mistaken. Completion is largely an illusion.

A finely tuned tragic perspective, if adopted as the public philosophy of a pluralist democracy, can attenuate the will to blame, assign responsibility, and punish. We affirm that the mainsprings of democratic politics presuppose and engender impossible situations in which right and wrong go hand in hand – not because of malice of forethought but given the bounded character of life and action. The conduct of politics in a pluralist setting exemplifies circumstances that fit Nietzsche's call for a spiritualization of enmity. We have a symbiotic relationship with our enemies. They deserve consideration and respect precisely because they are our enemies and we need them as such, but also because they have suffered defeat at our hands. We are uncomfortably like them. In the course of their defeat we have damaged ourselves and our cause. If victory is (supposedly) shared, loss needs to be held in common, too. Success creates indebtedness to those defeated, for they have paid a price for our victory and made it possible. Magnanimity and generosity emerge as the best ways to acknowledge triumph and its attendant costs. One day (soon), the positions will be reversed.

Tragedy, then, would seem to place substantial burdens on a democratic polity and its citizens, especially regarding the question of responsibility. If democracy requires a tragic public philosophy and sensibility, how might it be cultivated? Can the "we" that I keep invoking as an invitation materialize?

AN AMERICAN DIONYSIA

In the United States, the Fourth of July commemorates America's revolutionary spirit and independence. As John Schaar noted, however, America's great patriotic holidays have become little more than administratively manipulated occasions for extended weekends and surplus consumption.[33] Imagine the Fourth of July, then, as a day the country is assigned a civic task and pleasure. Insofar as a tragic dynamic permeates life and yet suffers from collective thoughtlessness (think of how the word tragedy is invoked ad nauseam in the news media), tragedy calls for a space where it can be the subject of reflection. The space would operate as a site of democratic citizenship. If all polities necessarily work to create citizens appropriate to them, the National Mall in Washington, for example, might be reconfigured as a performative, space for the cultivation of a tragic sensibility. While the Mall's patriotic monuments and memorials prefer to deflect and deny America's ambiguous historical legacy, they cannot erase it altogether, which means the seeds of a tragic public space already exist.[34]

Imagine the Fourth of July as the occasion for a tragic cinema. Visualize the Mall with a string of amphitheaters and movie screens strategically positioned from the Lincoln Memorial to the Capitol. Following Athenian tradition, assign Bill Gates, Warren Buffet, the Koch brothers, Sheldon Adelson, Michael Bloomberg, various members of the Walton family, and other billionaires the annual honor of funding the costs of the film festival. Gates, for one, spends copious amounts of money abroad to promote the health and well-being of those in desperate need. Let him spend some of his resources at home for democracy's health and well-being, also in desperate need of assistance. Billionaires should be required, in the name of freedom, to devote some of their fortunes to serve rather than subvert democracy.

Given the tragic ironies informing America's founding, the Fourth of July lends itself to a national political festival designed to facilitate common meditation on the meanings and costs of the sacred triad, "life, liberty, and the pursuit of happiness." After all, the nation-to-be acquired its territory through dispossession and displacement of Native peoples and secured its freedom thanks, at least in part, to weapons purchased by the wealth slavery generated. In short: without ethnic cleansing, no country; without slavery, no independence.[35]

The idea of an American Dionysia draws on Athens's City Dionysia, a civic festival informed by patriotic and military imperatives.[36] Besides recognizing citizens who made noteworthy contributions to Athens, the festival introduced a privileged segment of the city's next generation, namely war orphans, boys whose fathers had been killed in battle and subsequently raised by the city. Athens seized the sacred occasion not only to display its new cast of citizen-soldiers. It paid tribute to itself for educating, training, and molding them. The ceremony signaled the regard in which the boys were held. Outfitted in military gear, they were released from state tutelage to assume the formal duties attending membership. With the military component of citizenship emphasized, the city effectively announced a new line ready to die for the greater good and glory of Athens – just as their fathers had been ready to die, just as generations of fathers before them had been ready to die, too. Athens's civic death logic thereby confirmed and consolidated itself: death can be honored only through sacrifice, meaning more death, which, in turn, demands its own lethal payment.[37] Patriotic celebration and affirmation framed the tragic theater to follow. While not negating the critical nature of the plays, the patriotic trappings of the Dionysia provided a safe, secure affective environment in which they could be delivered and their results monitored. Plays that stirred to excess the emotions of the people could be banned and their authors fined (though this seems to have been rare).[38]

What kind of film might succeed at an American Dionysia? What existing genres, if any, might be apt? Or must a new category of film, the tragic, be self-consciously invented? Drawing on America's rich film history, I treat John Ford's dark epic, *The Man Who Shot Liberty Valance*, as a tragic rendering of the paradoxes attending the birth of a political order. Just as Greek tragic dramas offer a boundless resource for political reflection, American westerns constitute a tragic cinematic canon. Like their Greek ancestors, westerns rely on a well-worked stock of stories and legends allowing for innumerable narrative variations that can address the difficult questions polities prefer to duck.[39] The violent origins of democracy is one such question, especially insofar as founding signals the permanent place of violence in the order of things.

ONCE UPON A TIME IN THE WEST

Founding reinvents life. It involves not creation ex nihilo but fabrication from turmoil, which poses much greater architectonic challenges. The power deployed at the birth of a polity is limited and contested. As a result, founding cannot be pure or pristine. It is a dirty affair. But insofar as it promises a new, better way of life, it must be seen to adhere to accepted principles and standards. Otherwise the community introduced arrives stillborn. The story of Founding reduces complex events to a single wondrous moment of arrival that reverberates throughout a polity's lifetime. Citizens have deep affective needs for founding to be miraculous and wondrous, which means a polity can feed on its beginnings, if well attested, for generations to come, to "remote futurity." Thanks to selective remembering and timely forgetting, founding tends to be a retrospective phenomenon. It relies on the willing (if also unknowing) suspension of political disbelief. A distinctive, distinguished political event, it offers fertile ground for a tragic vision.

The Man Who Shot Liberty Valance enacts a founding drama in the late 1870s American west. Via flashback decades after the fact, it tells the story of Shinbone, a small town with a large ambition: to become part of a new state in an expanding nation. All of Shinbone favors statehood. To them it means progress, prosperity, a future secured. Without it, they must suffer a world governed by contingency in which life is fragile and cheap. The territory's cattle interests prefer the continuation of an open range and bitterly oppose statehood. Though vastly outnumbered, they feel sovereign, having conquered and settled the land, thereby 'opening' it to others, those who now seek statehood. While a process has been instituted to decide the statehood question, there appears to be no prior agreement that legitimizes it, a key narrative detail the film does not pause to consider. If anything, the procedure designed to resolve the statehood conflict decides it in advance. Numbers win. The film tends to hold the cattle interests responsible for the founding violence, but the film also presents a prepolitical condition in which violence is inescapable.[40] Either way, the cattle ranchers refuse to be relegated to the sidelines; so they turn to that original creative force, violence. Guns can make things happen – or not happen.[41]

Liberty Valance features two reluctant "heroes" who embody Machiavelli's and Nietzsche's dictum that to create is to destroy, and who, if hesitantly, take responsibility for articulating and implementing a new form of life. When Ransom Stoddard (Jimmy Stewart) arrives in Shinbone, he is moving west to make a name for himself. He lands in Shinbone apparently by accident, the victim of a brutal stagecoach robbery. *Liberty Valance*'s early scenes establish the oppositions that govern the film: community versus anarchy, law versus illiteracy, discourse versus violence, strength versus machismo.[42] Stoddard represents the drive to realize the first term in each of these pairs, which can achieve fulfillment only at the expense of the second. The film tells a story of necessary overcoming.

Thanks to Tom Doniphon (John Wayne), Stoddard learns the identity of his attacker, Liberty Valance (Lee Marvin). He also learns that Valance is well known to Shinbone. Yet he enjoys free rein to terrorize at will. The town's passivity regarding Valance baffles Stoddard. He wonders (aloud) what kind of community he has stumbled upon. The norms of civilization Stoddard represents must defeat the resistance their potential introduction fosters – not just from those opposed to but also those ostensibly in favor of them.

Some months later, Shinbone holds an election to send delegates to the territorial convention that will decide the question of statehood. When Valance, the cattlemen's hired gun, attempts to steal the election and suffers humiliating defeat instead, he presents Stoddard, one of the delegates elected, with two options: leave town or face him on the street. Statehood hangs in the balance. Politics and violence merge as forms of life collide.

Stoddard finds himself in a terrible bind. If he honors his commitment to statehood and faces Valance in a showdown, he compromises the rule of law and surely dies – and statehood with him. If he leaves town, statehood still dies and, unwilling or unable to match deed to word, he suffers existential death. This is Stoddard's defining moment, which diverts attention from the problematic nature of the election just conducted. Advertised as democratic, it amounted to an exercise in confirming publicly a truth unanimously held. Or so we are supposed to believe – but the film's refusal to give (or allow) authentic voice to opposition cannot erase it.

Valance effectively makes Stoddard's decision for him by nearly beating to death his closest friend, Dutton Peabody (Edmond O'Brien), the town's newspaper publisher who recently disclosed one of Valance's crimes.[43] In an act of privatization, Stoddard disregards the rule of law and, ironically, orders the town marshal to call Valance to the street to meet him. No one challenges the propriety of Stoddard's move: privatization can vindicate itself. He turns to the kind of evil Machiavelli and

Weber identified as the hallmark of politics. To do what is morally right, which is to render law something more than words on paper, he must contravene the law. The way of life he would establish must be violated at its very core for it to come into being. Stoddard suspected this paradox early on and started secretly practicing with a pistol in anticipation of a showdown, a tacit admission that law alone cannot bring itself into being, and a stunning repudiation of his prior and proud insistence that he would not resort to violence in order to stay in Shinbone and deal with Valance.

Stoddard's about-face also reveals the feral underside of civic virtue. He acts for the greater good but also to sate a visceral need for vengeance.[44] The prospect of death may scare Stoddard but it also inspires him. He wants to kill Valance. It would feel good. It would do great public good. And it would render the privatization of violence moot. It would be converted into public service, valorized, and forgotten. In the meantime, Stoddard's evident trepidation, shared by the entire community, signals democracy's anxieties about its identity and its capabilities. Does it have what it takes to defend itself against its enemies? Can it match their ruthlessness if and when necessary? Democracy's credibility is on the line. For democracy, credibility is always on the line, a theme taken up in Chapters 2 and 3.

When Valance and Stoddard finally meet, Valance toys with him in a cruel parody of the western faceoff. Determined to torment and humiliate Stoddard before killing him, Valance's delay proves costly. Stoddard lands the perfect kill shot. Instant admiration and celebrity follow his virtuoso performance, the fairytale heroics of which virtually guarantee statehood for the territory. *The Man Who Shot Liberty Valance* appears to be an inspirational, legendary tale for a democratic age.

Legends are made not born, of course; Stoddard's great deed requires dissemination, not to mention official confirmation. At the territorial convention, Mr. Peabody places Stoddard's name in nomination for Congress. As a prelude, he offers a genealogy of the west. He applauds the daring pioneers, the cattlemen, who subdued the land and opened it for development. Their ambition dictated the use of violence. Alas, their era has passed. Just as they forced Indians to cede their rightful claims, the cattlemen must accept an identical fate: erasure. They are owed respect, here paid by acknowledgment, but nothing more. In Nietzschean fashion, Peabody understands that building something new entails removing something (now) old. This is no cause for regret, let alone recrimination. It is called progress. Stoddard embodies the new west. Teacher, lawyer, and

champion of justice, he put his life on the line to eliminate a longstanding public evil. The violence he deployed – incidental, unavoidable – lost
any potentially problematic quality through its noble purpose. Peabody's
celebratory narrative leaves no room for tragic possibilities. The past, a
mere footnote in Peabody's speech, can be momentarily remembered and
then safely forgotten.[45]

SUPPOSING THE TRUTH WERE A LIE

Stoddard's nomination, not surprisingly, spawns vehement opposition.
The cattlemen's spokesperson charges him with hypocrisy. The great
champion of law and order appointed himself judge and jury and turned
to the gun in a quest for vengeance. His only qualification for office: "he
killed a man." The truth in the accusation stings and Stoddard exits the
convention hall determined to return east. He cannot abide the idea that
violence might produce good. Statehood seems doomed.

Doniphon intervenes. He mocks Stoddard for his fit of conscience
and then discloses, with considerable scorn, that he did not kill Valance
after all (as if the mere idea of it was ridiculous). Stoddard is dumb-
struck – as is the audience (on a first reading). In a flashback within
a flashback, Doniphon reveals that he murdered Valance from a dark
alley. Doniphon's stealth killing combines two refusals: to see his "friend"
killed; to become involved in territorial politics. Doniphon insists that *he*
can live with the consequences of his decision, as if they bear no personal,
let alone political ramifications. This amounts to false bravado and a
bluff – though Stoddard appears convinced and heads back, with enthusiasm, to the convention hall to accept the nomination. Doniphon and the
way of life he represents – independent, self-reliant, isolated, precarious,
dangerous – disappear from the face of the earth. Where does the sudden
reversal leave us?

The founding of the political community impeaches itself. It reflects
the workings of justice. It also rests on a crime, an act of violence, specifically murder (Doniphon's description is "cold-blooded murder").
Nevertheless, Stoddard's belated confession at a moment in the forward
march of progress when no one cares to hear it makes genuine public
revelation unthinkable. Apparently great political achievements – and the
men who deliver them – are marked in ways that cannot be acknowledged.[46] In *Liberty Valance*, official representatives of the generations
subsequent to founding insist on burying the truth that lives at the heart
of things. In this respect, *Valance* can be placed in the Rousseauean

tradition, as we will see in Chapter 4. Maxwell Scott, the newspaper editor to whom Stoddard has been telling his founding tale, declares what he takes to be self-evident: "This is the west, sir. When legend becomes fact, print the legend."[47] Scott not only declines to run the "tabloid" story. He destroys the written evidence of it (the notes taken by his reporter). Scott's civic patriotism implicates the audience, which now bears the guilty knowledge and concurs.[48] Our affirmation of the conclusion confers legitimacy on Doniphon and Stoddard's decision to keep silent and effectively erases the crime. Fictions make life possible. The loyalty, commitment, and devotion of citizens find perpetual sustenance in Stoddard's legend. It would be sheer recklessness to tamper with the keystone of a magnificent political edifice.[49]

Thus, while *Liberty Valance* might appear to be an exposé, it serves as a warning against disclosure. It conveys resignation to truths that need not, should not, and even cannot be told. We (now) know there are secrets to be kept – hence the discrepancy between the problematic story the film reveals and its comportment to it. In other words, while the film appears to debunk nation-building myths, as Michael J. Shapiro argues, its own commentary encourages the audience to take a dispassionate stance toward the morally fraught tale just recounted.[50] Doniphon's demise becomes a mere byproduct of a naturally progressing order of things – no need to give it a second thought. In short, *Liberty Valance* reveals awkward truths at one level and counsels the adoption of a worldly resignation and silence at another.[51]

How is it, though, that Stoddard returns to the convention hall to accept the nomination?[52] Valance's death may not be lamented, which neatly disposes of the cattlemen, but can Doniphon's destruction (and the admirable way of life he represented) be ignored? Stoddard faced what Bernard Williams describes as a tragic choice. No matter what course of action he chose (or chose him) he would feel, in some profound way, a deep sense of regret.[53] Machiavelli and Weber stress the need to come to terms with the existential burdens politics entails, which includes the ability to accept that doing good requires doing ill, and that the ill done is not changed by its welcome purpose. Following Doniphon's confession, Stoddard could return east, but return would negate Doniphon's sacrifice, made at such high price. Doniphon saved Stoddard's life and in doing so effectively completed the destruction of the very world in which he flourished. Stoddard would thereby refuse the founding gift to which his friend's deed amounts. It would surely derail the statehood movement and kill the hopes and dreams of friends, neighbors, and countless people in the territory. Stoddard would commit private and public harm. If he accepts the nomination, of course, this virtually guarantees statehood, an undeniable good, but it also amounts to building a life on both murder and deception, which is immoral. When Stoddard asks Doniphon rhetorically, "Isn't it enough to kill a man without trying to build a life on it?" the answer is no, it is not nearly enough. One must build a life on it. There is no choice. Stoddard must become an accomplice to Tom's crime and, worse, self-destruction. Keeping Doniphon's secret guarantees his downward spiral into oblivion. Though Tom claims he can live with cold-blooded murder, the claim amounts to sheer bluster. He cannot live with it. It is killing him.[54] The violence that thrills some destroys others.

Recall the sequence of events. Following (what appeared to be) Stoddard's heroics, Doniphon goes on a drunken binge, capped by deliberately setting fire to his house and a resigned suicide attempt. As Doniphon's house roars in flames (the loudest moment and most terrifying image in the film), the action shifts abruptly to Capitol City, the site of the territorial convention. The cross-cut drives home a brutal truth about the symbiotic relationship between creation and destruction, which the very structure of the film forces us to acknowledge and promptly ignore: Ransom Stoddard's ascent requires Tom Doniphon's demise. And what a demise it is.[55]

It culminates with Stoddard, renowned United States Senator, arriving in Shinbone unannounced. That he has returned to attend a funeral prompts the local newspaper editor to ask in bewilderment: who died? The answer given, Tom Doniphon, does not register. The film, then, becomes a western mystery. Who was Tom Doniphon? Revolving around this question, the film's mood disconcerts. Not only does death demands its due. Something about this particular death haunts people. Hallie Stoddard recoils in horror at the sight of the plain, crudely built wood box that holds Doniphon's corpse. A pauper's anonymous burial awaits him. There is no funeral. Inspecting the body, the Senator notices, much to his outrage, that the dead man has been stripped of his boots. He orders them returned. No respect for the downtrodden dead.

For a tragic vision of life and politics, things fall into place. If Machiavelli, Nietzsche, and Weber are right that creation presupposes destruction, destruction enables lasting creation. Is this an intrinsic feature of life for which no apologies need to be made? Or are matters more complicated? Stoddard's career can be read as the democratically necessary response to Doniphon's criminal self-sacrifice. A life devoted to public service can become worthy of founding crimes, in this case a murder, and its subsequent cover-up.[56] Given Stoddard's legal ambitions, he could have returned to Shinbone following statehood and resumed his law career. He did not. In fact, he does not return until Doniphon's death. We learn that Stoddard has been a Congressman, multi-term governor, multi-term United States Senator, as well as Ambassador to Great Britain. The past thirty to forty years of his professional life have consisted of nothing but distinctive public service.[57] A revered figure with a national profile, the Vice Presidency is his, if he wants it.

How should Stoddard's career be interpreted? Even too much service is not enough. Doniphon himself suggested the model of tragic citizenship and responsibility Stoddard's career enacts. Rather than convince Stoddard to accept the nomination, Doniphon, having destroyed the way of life he loved on behalf of Stoddard's more civilized world, commands him: "You taught [Hallie] to read and write. Now give her something to read and write about." Doniphon's demand is temporally sophisticated. He tells Stoddard to give Hallie something to read and write about "now." This suggests that shooting Valance does not count. He must do something else, something more. He must build a life on a killing, but he cannot rest content with the killing. He cannot allow his life to be reduced to a killing. Thus Stoddard's public career represents singular dedication to an ideal of political action and responsibility that flowed, ironically, from a mantra that attached itself to his name, "Nothing's too good for the man who shot Liberty Valance."

At the film's close, with Doniphon's death marked, Stoddard informs Hallie that he'd like to quit politics and return to Shinbone to restart the law practice he abandoned with his rise to political stardom. Return would close the circle of his public life. Could it be argued that he has done enough to honor his friend's gift and redeem the order? It might be best to resist a definitive conclusion. Perhaps such a debt cannot be paid. Still, Stoddard, now an elder statesman, effectively declines to make any further payments. Though it occasionally pains him to live with the perpetual applause generated by a lie, formal atonement ceases – though the cost, if not quite the debt, remains. Stoddard, moreover, may believe, like Oedipus, that he needs to make the final payment of his debt by terminating his political career as it is about to peak. Surrendering power at the veritable summit amounts to a kind of political self-castration, an act that would match Doniphon's founding gesture.[58]

NECESSARY REVELATIONS

The film's conclusion insinuates that Stoddard's legend, though fabricated, captures the essence of things better than the actual truth. Silence is thus a decision without cost, without remainder. It is no decision at all, really. Why, then, press for full disclosure? Why tamper with congealed truths?

With *Liberty Valance* exposure illuminates the reality of creative destruction. A story of overcoming and achievement coexists with a hidden history containing a ruthless instrumental ethos: by any means necessary. The terror of Doniphon's murder exceeds the savagery of Valance's depredations. At least he committed his crimes out in the open, face-to-face.[59] Doniphon's covert execution of Valance anticipates, even models the monopoly on violence to be enjoyed and exercised by the state. Against it, one has no chance. Valance's death signals that Doniphon's private brand of violence can be co-opted exclusively for public use, making it even more formidable. The Senator's friendly, good-natured, folksy demeanor belies the face of Leviathan. Shinbone, once a town bustling with energy and vitality, becomes peaceful and quiet, sedate and bland. It has been tamed and democratic citizenship pays the price. Order, even lifelessness prevail – prosperity notwithstanding. The very people who once fought a sheep war, defeated the cattle interests, and secured statehood render themselves incapable of duplicating the kind of feat that set them free. Democratic violence may have eliminated aristocratic violence but this victory may also have unintended consequences, as we will see in Chapters 4 and 5.

Revelation of a founding's flip side, then, might prove catalytic. As the Stoddards depart, Hallie proudly notes Shinbone's conversion from wilderness to garden. The great civic achievement, however, harbors ambiguities. Reams of black smoke spew out of the train that brought them to Shinbone. This political paradise contains more than its fair share of ruin. The very power to dominate and control nature, to bend it to an aesthetic will, cannot elide its own poisonous contributions to the landscape. Yet people in the train see nothing but beauty. Those who do violence to the world and live with the damage every day cannot necessarily see it. They are too close. Unless articulated and acknowledged, the costs of statehood can accumulate until it is too late to respond to them in meaningful fashion. Insofar as a democratic political community must inspire affection and commitment among all citizens and not just those who tend to identify with it because of the general prosperity it brings, it cannot afford to ignore, let alone deny, the wounds it delivers.

TRAGIC AFFIRMATIONS

The Man Who Shot Liberty Valance enacts the tragic nature of founding and thus the "evil" that Machiavelli, Nietzsche, and Weber identify as constitutive of political creation. It also reveals the criminal underside of American civic virtue. A democratic society establishes itself by eradicating, without regret, other peoples and other modes of being in the world. Once installed, democracy tallies additional costs. Paradoxes operative at the founding continue throughout the life of the order. What, then, might a tragic ethos affirm and not just reveal?

A tragic vision affirms the coexistence of promise and risk. Insofar as few, if any, political ambitions can be realized without serious consequences, they might foster a sense of license. Since violence plays an inescapable role in politics, and politics offers perpetual opportunities for redemption, what risk would not be worth running, what sacrifice (especially of others) would not be worth imposing?[60] A democratic political community might satisfy itself by invoking necessity, making apology, and offering symbolic compensation. Recognition that violence is inexorable and invaluable opens the world of politics to dangerous possibilities of abuse. The resources at a democracy's disposal make it easy to forget that the world does not lend itself to human fashioning, even though achievement often seems to suggest otherwise. It can become tempting to portray the costs attending politics as incidental or insignificant, or to label those adversely affected as marginal and thus merely unfortunate. Ressentiment also lurks here. The inability to succeed as planned can frustrate and anger political actors. Politics can seem interminable, incapable of bringing something to fruition. Someone must be to blame for this kind of "failure." Those on the margins or in the minority can become prime targets, especially if they are deemed willful, defiant, or obstructionist, or perverse, dangerous, or evil. Any (problematic) measures taken to achieve this or that goal can then become occasions for triumphant self-celebration and applause.

A tragic sensibility, which presumes democratic politics cannot avoid injustice, counsels respect, even honor for hard choices made, sacrifices assumed, and losses suffered. The injustices part and parcel of democratic life are not necessarily the product of ill will or bad intent, recognition of which can defuse otherwise politically destructive passions.

Nevertheless, justice necessarily animates a tragic vision. To keep the troubled results of political endeavors publicly visible and the subject of contestation counters the tendency to treat the world as fashionable and to become complacent with accomplishments that realize a common good or express a majority will. Tragedies circulate in political life, rendering one and all susceptible to them. They must but cannot be overcome – this makes them a perpetual project. To harness political forces, then, a tragic vision issues an Oedipean challenge: anyone can succeed, but whose successes can simultaneously fail with grandeur, that is, with generosity? Since success and failure are twins, style matters. The calling of politics, ironically, is to be a magnificent failure. A tragic vision thus might invoke Beckett: "Ever tried. Ever failed. No matter. Try again. Fail again. Fail better."[61]

At the close of *The Man Who Shot Liberty Valance*, the Stoddards return east. The train conductor makes every effort to pamper the Senator, who cannot enjoy it insofar as the conductor insists that "nothing's too good for the man who shot Liberty Valance." Stoddard knows the tragedy in which he played a critical role. The conductor lives in ignorance. The film ends on this grim conversational note, suggesting the power of one moment frozen in time. Stoddard not only believes that Tom Doniphon rightly deserves to be considered the man who shot Liberty Valance. Regarding the tragic, Stoddard himself does not recognize the character or appreciate the implications of his long, distinguished political career. The popular demand for a heroic narrative featuring a legendary figure makes such recognition and appreciation of the ordinary calling of politics hard-won achievements.

Stoddard is haunted not only by misattribution but also celebration. While he can accept the necessity of killing Valance, glorifying it remains vile. Necessity cannot induce morality. Shooting Valance may not have been wrong, a judgment with which Stoddard has always been able to live, however uncomfortably ("Isn't it enough to kill a man?"), but he cannot consider it a foundation for politics. Stoddard's pursuit of a political career following Doniphon's confession can thus be understood as Stoddard embracing tragic political imperatives. The legend may be a lie, but it can and must be made democratically productive. Stoddard's career is tantamount to a performance of a political ethos, namely, tragic responsibility. As with Oedipus's departure from Corinth, the meaning of Stoddard's political odyssey cannot be known in advance. He must begin it *now* to be able, *one day*, to give an account of it, which can then be judged. Stoddard's commitment to statehood must morph into a larger undertaking. Doniphon activated a considerable debt, but the debt must be paid elsewhere, to others, as it were. There is nothing to be done for Doniphon – there never was. More importantly, the tragic is not exceptional. Doniphon is not unique. Not limited to the birth of a political order, the tragic is a routine part of politics, which amounts to a trap sprung by each initiative pursued and each obligation assumed. Perez argues that "the best rhetorical card [Stoddard] can play is the act of violence that has won him fame. When he finds out that it is Tom who has blood on his hands, he realizes that he, too, must get his hands dirty, if only in rhetoric." Yet it's more than a question of rhetoric. The difference between Tom and Ranse dissolves with Stoddard's ascendancy. Initially Ranse may "steal" Tom's force – ultimately he owns it.[62] The violence of politics is real; Stoddard's hands get dirty. In a democracy success cannot be had without cost and debt cannot be expunged through a single payment. Payments need to be made in perpetuity and distributed widely.

Stoddard retires from politics, but democracy's debts continue. He has been accumulating them on behalf of the order, even if, perhaps especially if, citizens live in ignorance of them. The figure of Stoddard embodies the ethos of tragic responsibility even if Stoddard himself lives in ignorance of it. After all, he stops the story he narrates in the film at the moment he returns to the convention hall and effectively sanitizes his own career by reducing it to five words, "well, you know the rest," as if everything has been irreproachable despite a shaky beginning. When Stoddard returned to the convention hall, he embraced the mantle of contemporary hero, a legend in the making. A society without legends, Pippin writes, raises "questions about its sustainability as a political enterprise. But the passion for something more – more glorious, larger than life, mythic, a common destiny, a world historical mission – is, I would suggest, treated here as the greater danger."[63] While Pippin's suspicion about "the greater danger" is arguable, political legends do pose dangers precisely because their protean capacities guarantee both world historical creation and concomitant horror. Yet isn't this what it means to be a democracy?

2

Democracy at War with Itself

Citizens

But the one thing I always begged for was never given: Safe passage home. No, I've been here for ten years now, wasting away, suffering starvation and misery, feeding my flesh to this insatiable sickness. This is what the sons of Atreus and Odysseus have inflicted on me. May the Gods on Olympus one day make them suffer for what they did.

Sophocles, *Philoctetes*

The democratic citizen ... is less willing than members of other societies to be a mere stone in an edifice.

William E. Connolly, *Politics and Ambiguity*

If democracy bends toward the tragic, patriotism leans toward the Gothic. As democracy's agent, patriotism draws on horrific events, construed in ghoulish terms, to service democracy's need for love, fealty, and tribute. Democracy seems content, even pleased, to allow patriotism free reign insofar as patriotism obscures the tragic dynamics that bedevil it, including practices best characterized as prejudicial, even suicidal, to democracy. Patriotic culture, of course, understands itself differently. As far as it's concerned, patriotism reminds citizens that democracy, a uniquely vulnerable kind of polity, faces lethal enemies and imminent threats, a judgment that many citizens have no desire to challenge, let alone reject. For circumstances often dictate that a democracy mimic its enemies to protect itself against them, to fully prepare for the danger sure to materialize. As democracy's servant, patriotism happily plays its supporting role, but it also frequently assumes center stage.

Though democracy is well-advised to explore a tragic political sensibility, it prefers a patriotic comportment instead. Patriotism, it must be remembered, likes to sound warnings (urgent, dire) and demand remedies (bold, dramatic) on behalf of the democracy it ostensibly serves. It's all quite exciting, romantic, and a bit melodramatic.[1] But not unsurprising. Democracy apparently creates an unacknowledged need for patriotism and its bedazzlements. Nietzsche argued that killing God was a deed too great for its authors to abide. Likewise, democracy may find living in a world beset by its own tragedies too terrible to admit.

In a democracy patriotism can induce unthinking acceptance of otherwise problematic features of social, political, and economic life. To read patriotism as democracy's Gothic production, then, is to put citizens, ordinarily somnambulant, on notice regarding the everyday pieties they encounter and imbibe – not just about perils supposedly present in the world but also about the character of their own polity. Democracies impose on their citizens any number of responsibilities, obligations, necessities, inevitabilities, and results that harm, injure, wound, and even kill them. This is true not only in zones of democratic life that one might expect, such as military service during wartime. It is also true in areas of democratic life that might be thought immune from such affliction, such as politics.

This reading of democracy encourages a tragic political awakening as it lays before citizens the dark realities of politics hiding in plain sight. How does democracy reveal and conceal simultaneously? For one thing, it deploys patriotism as a political horror show, *its* political horror show. Democracy, that is, enlists patriotism as its accomplice *after the fact* in the production and circulation of spectacles of war and the sideshows commemorating them thanks to which national loyalty and love monopolize public attention and govern political discourse rather than democracy's constitutive failings, which are assigned to external causes.[2] Patriotism, as a result, saves democracy from having to confront uncomfortable truths about itself. But the reputed rescue mission eventually backfires to the detriment of democracy – even life itself. Democracy unleashes patriotism as a golem in the political world that defies containment and control, poised to devour everything in its path, more or less blind to its destructive, terrifying furies.

Democracy, however, is in position to reanimate itself thanks to the culture of violence and death enlisted to serve it. From the ill, then, comes the corrective. Some of democratic life's most horrifying moments, which signal patriotism's self-induced exhaustion and death, suggest, even demand a tragic approach to politics. These twin dynamics can be seen at work in the Reagan-era classic *First Blood*, a revenge fantasy for disgruntled patriots, and, more specifically, in the liminal figure of John J. Rambo. *First Blood*, the reputation of its pornographic sequels notwithstanding, is best read as a tragic horror film illuminating, first, democracy's self-destructive propensities, especially toward its own citizens, and, second, democracy's possibilities for civic renewal.

PATRIOTISM'S BLOODY MASQUERADE

Commemoratively speaking, democracy's deployment of horror can pass unnoticed, especially insofar as a banal vocabulary of tragedy enjoys wide distribution. According to the patriotic calendar, for example, September 11, 2009, marked the eighth anniversary of al-Qaeda's successful attacks on New York City and the Pentagon and its failed assault on Washington, DC. Commemorative events mimicked prior anniversaries: ceremonial bells rung, moments of silence observed, victims' names recited, eternal remembrance sworn, and civic adulation professed. As Simon Stow argues, patriotic affairs prefer to be, even privilege, thoughtless occasions. To affirm traditional identities and consolidate dominant norms, death receives special preference, and melodramatic forms often work best for these political tasks. There is no need for reflection, let alone critical thinking. Just the opposite: each is unwelcome.[3]

President Barack Obama, speaking at a Pentagon ceremony, reflected and reinforced democracy's unthinking habits. The private ritual, reserved for victims' families, concentrated and intensified the lethal emotions in play. Obama would freeze death and its agonies in perpetuity through an event most in the United States consider an epic tragedy: "Eight Septembers have come and gone. Nearly three thousand days have passed, almost one for each of those taken from us. But no turning of the season can diminish the pain and the loss of that day. No passage of time and no dark skies can ever dull the meaning of this moment."[4] A performance such as Obama's becomes self-fulfilling practice, for death's pain ordinarily eases over time – unless it is nurtured and tended. And there is no reason to nurture and tend horror unless the "tragedy" it names warrants it – except, that is, for political purposes. Democracy, therefore, works the grounds of death to consolidate dominant national self-conceptions and disseminate common political truths. Patriotism and tragedy would seem to merge.

Thus, the Port Authority of New York and New Jersey has been distributing September 11 debris across the country (and abroad) in the name of memorialization. To further its efforts, the Port Authority conducted a national media campaign to relocate some two thousand pieces of steel it has lovingly housed for years. If a city, town, state, museum, corporation, government agency, or even foreign nation asks for rubble, the request will almost certainly be granted, assuming the entity making it can pay the freight to have it transported. Between the seventh and eighth anniversary celebrations, twenty-five requisitions were granted. A dozen more awaited approval. Architectural pieces scarred by death serve the cause of "patriotic awareness."⁵

Patriotic awareness tends to be narrowly construed. In 2009 September 11 was named a National Day of Service. People were encouraged to do something worthwhile in their local communities – from beach cleanup to park repairs. Objections were immediate and vehement. The rhetorical character of the objections revealed, however inadvertently, patriotism's connection, even addiction, to death and, more disturbingly, its antipathy to life. Debra Burlingame, sister of the pilot whose jet struck the Pentagon, ridiculed it as some kind of "Earth Day where we go and plant trees." Right-wing ideologue Matthew Vadum derided the idea of service for its emphasis on things such as "food banks and community gardens."⁶ Befitting a tragedy, death must remain the centerpiece.

What, then, might constitute a more fitting September 11 tribute? What about a warship, namely, the U.S.S. New York? Made in part from seven and one-half tons of World Trade Center steel, it "came to life" on November 7, 2009. Mere debris, thanks to the newly sacred ground that provided it, morphs into precious military metal ready to defend democracy. Suffused with death, the warship is a veritable floating cemetery. Once commissioned those citizens whose remains partly compose the ship's materials would become posthumous patriots, finally serving their country. A status that eluded them in life, despite the best of ceremonial efforts, would finally be theirs. Material that amounted to the remains of death at home now projects and wields deadly force abroad. The U.S.S. New York is at once the object that imbibes death and the subject that imparts it, each indispensable not only to patriotism's necrotic circle but also to democracy's hard-edged self-image. A warship so composed suggests that September 11 is something more than a traditional patriotic occasion. It is also a day on which democracy can celebrate the people themselves, who also die for country. Although there is never a shortage of warriors in uniform who fall, democracy also calls on ordinary citizens to do or suffer its dirty work. The latter is its true sign of political greatness.

Sacrifice and death anchor September 11, 2001, anniversaries, which otherwise make for a strange, somewhat awkward subject of democratic national memorialization. Not only is the day not comparable (patriotic fantasy aside) to another infamous surprise attack, December 7, 1941. In addition, the events known as 9/11 do not signify any actual achievement or success (valiant rescue efforts notwithstanding). If anything, contrary to other celebrated national events, they have led only to disastrous wars and destructive assaults on the Constitution. The principal war, the "War on Terror," cannot even be won. September 11, 2001, more than anything else, epitomizes a day of contingent victimization. In New York people who happened to be in the wrong place at the wrong time were killed. They did not give their lives to a grand, national cause. They were not asked to make a sacrifice. They did not volunteer. They were not drafted. The World Trade Center was not a battlefield, though subsequent memorialization renders it one. Nor was it an American political symbol of freedom, equality, or justice. It stood, if it stood for anything other than architectural malfeasance, for global capitalism. The first responders who perished trying to save people from more than ninety countries, including the United States, were also contingent victims – including of an antiquated communications system. They died as consummate New York City professionals doing their jobs under terrifying circumstances – not as American patriots heading into the breach in the name of democratic freedom against a known enemy. They are to be saluted for their efforts, but those efforts and their deaths could be recognized independent of the democracy in which they happen to live.

Nevertheless, in the United States, September 11 signifies an identity crime with America's democracy as the casualty. Democracy was attacked because of the freedom that defines it. Rather than provide an occasion for (an imperial) democracy to exercise critical self-scrutiny, death vindicates it. It is in death that democracy truly comes to life. President Obama, mourner in chief, cannot let the pain diminish or dull. The strategy is straightforward. To commemorate September 11 is, among other things, to activate and mobilize images of falling buildings and plunging bodies, images worthy of a horror show. Death alone is not quite sufficient to democratic commemoration – only horror, it seems, can complete and perfect it. In this regard, September 11 is still nothing but commonplace. Perhaps, then, it's time, as with all childish things, for democracy to put patriotism aside and move on to a tragic understanding.

WHY WE CAN'T BE TRAGEDIANS

George Kateb argues, with deliberate understatement, that patriotism is a mistake.[7] Whether ideal or practice, it constitutes an affront to Enlightenment values to which one and all should aspire: independence of mind, refusal of fanaticism, and disdain for idolatry, group idolatry in particular.[8] Kateb also argues that patriotism "is an inevitable mistake. It cannot be avoided; almost no one can help being a patriot of some kind and to some degree." In democratic politics, sacrifice of life signals the greatest civic commitment. Among citizens, soldiers receive the greatest praise, respect, and tribute; of holidays, none can match the affective intensity of Memorial Day, Veterans Day, or Patriot Day; in public space, monuments to war dominate sacred ground. Democracy, aided by patriotism, feeds on a steady diet of death, always on guard for new sources of sustenance.

Democracy is committed to patriotism in some form. Assume for a moment that patriotism helps provide democracy with a loyalty, sense of duty, and civic commitment that it might otherwise lack. What happens to democracy when it treats patriotism as a valued political partner? What happens to democracy when patriotism as an alleged tonic produces ills greater than or even destructive of the benefits it supposedly provides? Given patriotism's devotion to sacrifice, especially death, and given democracy's eagerness to embrace it, what happens when the combination of democracy and patriotism turns out to be not just dangerous to democratic politics but also dangerous in a more fundamental way?[9] What happens when it becomes antithetical to life itself? Can tragedy sever and save democracy from its lethal relationship to patriotism?

To answer these questions, I take inspiration from Bonnie Honig and ask: Does a patriotism-suffused democracy have a genre?[10] Or, better, what genre should be assigned to patriotic democracy? That is, rather than assuming there is a right answer to the question of democracy, patriotism, and genre, I explore whether thinking of democracy and patriotism in terms of genre can make a productive contribution to democratic thought and practice. Might framing the exploits of patriotic democracy in the right generic terms enable thinking about politics in a tragic mode?

Those who pair democracy and patriotism, exemplified by Richard Rorty, gravitate toward a romanticized narration. Governed by profound feelings of pride, adoration, devotion, and fidelity – in a word, love – patriotic democracy projects the best possible face onto the polity. Not whether it deserves it or not. It always deserves it. Patriotic democracy as romance promises a long, rewarding bond between citizen and order, one not without its difficult and trying moments, but one always well worth them.

Admittedly, romantic accounts of democracy and patriotism contain flashes of critical insight, suggesting the possibility of an ambiguous narration of this hybrid that appreciates its lurid character. Still, a romantic appreciation for ambiguity is always limited, to be resolved in favor of patriotic democracy's greater goodness. Thus, a Gothic frame – more specifically, what Honig calls modern Gothic – might prove more contributive. It could expose and accentuate the doubled character of patriotic democracy – that which fosters pride, commitment, and sacrifice also engenders chauvinism, zealotry, and hatred. As Honig might say, don't turn your back on it – not for long, anyway.[11]

While tempting, I do not think modern Gothic, despite its attractions, can sufficiently capture patriotic democracy's dangers. While democracy and patriotism might appear to combine elements at once beneficial and detrimental, leaving its identity productively unstable and undecidable, patriotic democracy is best understood as an untenable fabrication born of combustible materials that render it, in the end, antithetical to democracy, even to life itself, which makes it incompatible with the tragic sensibility pursued here. Patriotic democracy's ambiguity, then, practices to deceive. Treated instead as a specimen of apocalyptic Gothic, a form of horror crystallized in the figure of Frankenstein's monster, patriotic democracy necessarily turns back on itself and reaps violence, destruction, and nothingness. Unlike Dr. Frankenstein, we democrats, patriotism's authors, may not fear it, but we should. Democracy makes it more, not less, dangerous.

APOCALYPTIC GOTHIC

A Gothic vision, which specializes in all manner of horror, highlights the underside of life.[12] However picturesque the world appears on the surface, it is replete with dangers, perils, traumas, and terrors. Despite the undeniable beauty and wonder of nature, the allure and attractions of civilization, the charms and seductions of people, things are not always what they seem and cannot be taken at face value. Threats inherent in the world can suddenly erupt, providing abundant cause for not just anxiety but also fear. If anything, the calm and serenity of everyday life induce a false sense of security. Moreover, life is not only layered but also temporally dense. The past bedevils the present.[13] While the world is reputed to be rife with opportunities for new beginnings and second chances, there is no escape from crimes committed and wrongs perpetrated in the past. Life is not unencumbered. It unfolds in a vast indecipherable web of prior decisions that imprisons and haunts us all. There is always a price to be paid, often recurring, for actions once taken.

In apocalyptic Gothic, one of three forms discussed by Mark Edmundson in *Nightmare on Main Street,* society finds itself the subject of menace.[14] Mary Shelley's *Frankenstein* effectively inaugurates and exemplifies the genre. In it, human being seeks to penetrate and unravel the mysteries of life and death and endow itself with unlimited creative power. We seek, in short, to become godlike, for what cannot be accomplished if sufficient time and energy are devoted to a project, any project? Once free from the decay, decline, and death that inform existence, for example, human being could enjoy immortality, able to generate life on command. The Cartesian dream can be realized as humans become the "masters and possessors of nature."[15]

The project of mastery and possession, however, can turn out to be not just illusory but also ruinous. Apocalyptic Gothic issues warnings about the self-destructive bent of grand human projects, that is, about limits (such warnings might be especially apt for politics and war, as we will see below). Among other things, humans cannot necessarily control the product of their labors, however extensive, which routinely turn back on them, generating results exactly the opposite of those desired. Yet, as *Frankenstein* suggests, the warnings sounded may not be heard. Human being is flush not only with scientific learning and technological prowess. It is also filled with good, even noble intentions. Projects for betterment abound. Mistakes are always made, but failure is considered the condition of advancement. In the end, ambition and outcome can be brought into alignment with unintended, unwanted consequences removed. Dr. Frankenstein might seem to take human aspiration to its logical extreme, but if he achieves his goal, it establishes itself willy-nilly as the standard to be overcome. Something else, something more, something new, something better can always be conceived and implemented. Or so it is assumed.

Revisiting some of the details of Shelley's narrative reveals disconcerting parallels between a scientist's construction of a new being and a democratic polity's manufacture of a patriotic culture and citizen (to be explored in the next three sections of the chapter). The recipient of a first-rate scientific education, Frankenstein represents one of Europe's best and brightest minds. At his university he pursues a distinct path of intellectual investigation: life and its secrets. Years of work and devotion finally pay off as the world appears susceptible to his epistemological endeavors. To put his precious acquisition of knowledge to the test, Frankenstein famously patrols charnel houses, dissection rooms, and slaughterhouses to assemble the parts he requires to build a brand "new" being, that is, to bestow animation on lifeless matter.[16] He is on the verge of turning the world upside down. Borders will be crossed, frontiers conquered.

Frankenstein's project, however, is fatally flawed. Human knowledge and technical power suffer from limits that cannot be identified, and the material (nature) with which humans work does not simply cooperate with the desire to fashion it, at least not according to plan. Death, for one, defies the human drive to redeem it. It cannot serve as the fount of life. Thus Frankenstein's moment of ostensible triumph is actually a moment of abject horror: he realizes that he has produced something monstrous. Frankenstein flees from his creation. It may live, but Frankenstein recognizes it as death's handiwork. It cannot surmount the constitutive elements of its being. He has let loose on the world something terrible. Composed of detritus, it is drawn ineluctably toward death.

The monster, of course, possesses a different self-conception. It merely wants to be at home in the world. It reaches out, first, to its "father" and then, when that fails, to humanity, convinced that people will be able to overlook its appearance and embrace it for the sensitive and caring creature it knows itself to be. Despite repeated efforts, it cannot make itself understood or welcome. The emotions (from a feeling of rejection to self-loathing to contemptuous rage) this engenders in it prove overwhelming. It cannot negotiate them. Stung by its creator's and the world's revulsion, hell-bent on making both suffer reprisals, it "declare[s] everlasting war against the species."[17]

Simultaneously, the monster demands that Frankenstein design a mate for it, which will cure its intolerable loneliness and the uncontrollable fury that accompanies it. The monster has killed and promises to kill again if Frankenstein does not accede to its wishes. If anything, it claims, this is Frankenstein's responsibility, his debt, thus his obligation. It did not ask to be born.

Moved, Frankenstein lets the monster persuade him.[18] To correct his first mistake, then, he agrees to repeat it. The perverse irony is due not just to Frankenstein's vanity and ego. It is also due to the scientific and cultural logic governing the enlightened age. The solution the monster proposes affirms our place and power in the grand scheme of things. It is virtually irresistible to someone such as Frankenstein. It confirms rather than challenges human self-conceptions. What masquerades as a remedy is to be found in the ill, both of which are of our own making. We remain in charge of the world rather than defeated by it.

Frankenstein ultimately recognizes the folly of proceeding with a second creation before he finishes it, admitting the unpredictable consequences of his decision. It is impossible to know what effect introducing a second being of this kind might have on the world. There is certainly every reason to fear the worst.[19] The reversal further incenses the monster and leads to more (and more awful) deaths. The monster is blessed with superhuman powers, both mental and physical, and exacts a serious toll on its creator.

Even so, Frankenstein repeatedly underestimates the dangers the monster poses.[20] It's as if experience is irrelevant in the face of presumptions to knowledge and control. Frankenstein spends what remains of his life hunting down the demon – to no avail. Ultimately he is no match for his monster, who seems to relish the chase, and the good doctor kills himself executing his self-assigned task. Yet Frankenstein, too, found himself energized by the hunt.[21] In pursuit of the monster, he seems to have become one – or revealed one within – himself.

How different is Frankenstein from his hideous creation? The monster looms as his double, our double. Don't we turn to violence when our values or interests, however we define them, are threatened? Don't we believe we can control the violence we deploy? Don't we possess the ability to justify otherwise horrific deeds by the invocation of what is right and just? Thus *Frankenstein* suggests there are certain powers that should not be exercised or indulged, certain projects that should not be pursued, precisely because we believe, wrongly, that we can control our constructs. In retrospect, Frankenstein (and we) should have seen this all along. If things could not have turned out differently, why can't we see the implications of our actions beforehand? Why are they always seen only in retrospect?

Thanks to its sensitivity to darkness, a Gothic frame, ironically, proves illuminating. It can puncture a society's self-conceits and deflate the self-serving, self-congratulatory stories it likes and needs to tell (about) itself. A Gothic reading offers a contrapuntal vision of common norms, traditional understandings, and historical practices, pinpointing not just their constitutive ambiguities but also their fatal failings. It functions as exposé, revealing and calling attention to aspects of things that might otherwise go unnoticed – because they reflect an order's common sense, conventional wisdom, or self-evident truths. Though brimming with confidence, democracy may be deceiving itself. Apocalyptic Gothic refines and intensifies the revelations produced by modern Gothic. If successful, it renders previously ambiguous political phenomena lucid. That which appeared multifaceted and complicated now betrays dominant features that not only characterize but also master it, allowing for a new critical assessment. Our comportment moves from ambivalence to refusal. More specifically, patriotic democracy, nominal attractions notwithstanding, can be experienced as monstrous.

PATRIOTIC DEMOCRACY AND GENRE

Richard Rorty loved his democracy, America. It might also be said that Richard Rorty was in love with America, a romance for the ages. Critical to a project of political rejuvenation, Rorty advocated the telling of great patriotic tales showing America at what he took to be its democratic best.[22] It didn't matter whether these stories might be nothing more than partial (and thus contestable) truths. What did matter was whether they were politically effective, that is, inspirational – leading people to commit themselves, practically, affectively, to the urgent business of reform. The narrative resources available were abundant, for American history is littered with accomplishments and triumphs that generation after generation could deploy to serious civic purpose. Pericles once advised Athenians to fall in love with their city. Rorty aspired to a similar feeling for America and its citizens and believed the United States possessed the godlike power to induce it. Insofar as democracies depend on citizens for success, Rorty's recommendations seem tactically sound, bound to work. Yet patriotic democracy was not just a question of tactics for Rorty. It was also a question of identity, something that had to be created and recreated, invented and reinvented.

Rorty's romance with America did not lack for occasional disillusionment. He was familiar enough with American history to know that the country had much to be ashamed of – slavery, wars of conquest, vast inequality – but moral stain is not mortal sin, and no failing could be considered permanent. Wrongs can be righted – or at least not repeated in the future. The beloved democracy can always make good on its promises, both to itself and the world, more closely approximating the political ideals that inform and animate its existence. This is a labor of love, the task of generations, with no preset end date. It gives meaning to politics.

Rorty thus flirts with – but never quite consummates – a politics of ambiguity, meaning that his American democracy dallies with Gothic elements. The country capable of unadorned good also finds itself committing inexplicable, indefensible acts of evil. In Rorty's narrative hands, pride in democracy enjoys an impressive adaptability. It is "compatible with remembering that we expanded our boundaries by massacring the tribes which blocked our way, that we broke the word we had pledged in the Treaty of Guadalupe Hidalgo, and that we caused the death of a million Vietnamese out of sheer macho arrogance."[23] What is to be made of this disconcerting combination of good and evil? Does it render Rorty's romance with America's democracy modern Gothic, a tale bringing together necessarily ambiguous elements? Or is such a reading something he would almost certainly resist insofar as it might unduly complicate or endanger a politics of hope?[24] Or do the details Rorty provides about his love affair suggest another Gothic form altogether?

Rorty's narrative nonchalance is noteworthy. *Achieving Our Country*'s presentation of America both accepts and deflects moral responsibility for its history, reducing it to the realm of memory alone and thus irrelevant to the present. That is, for Rorty no remedial action is required. Rorty's patriotic democracy effectively resigns itself to the inevitability of violence in politics. This is the way of the world. It may be cause for (some) lament, but any lament would necessarily have to be limited. In short, the greater achievements of which these unfortunate events form a part must be privileged. Any other disposition would amount to self-laceration, a masochistic sensibility rooted in some notion of irredeemable sin. Rorty will have none of it. It risks not just self-loathing but also political paralysis, and in America there is (always) work to be done.

Yet to First Peoples, Mexicans, Vietnamese, and America's young soldiers, among others, Rorty's apparently candid but always forgiving account would likely prove horrific. Peoples of color find themselves deemed unworthy of life on equal terms with those who massacred them or "caused their death" (the latter a more benign phrase suggesting inadvertence). Rorty's reference, in a sequence of American crimes, to the Treaty of Guadalupe Hidalgo seems particularly odd. Why cite violation of the treaty America imposed on Mexico, adding insult and injury to insult and injury, but not America's imperial war of aggression and acquisition itself? Would the catalogue of violence otherwise become unduly heavy? Would the pattern of imperial racial violence across centuries defy democratic reappropriation? And what about the cost of America's imperial adventure in Vietnam? What kind of destruction did the American

democracy unleash on a generation of young men and women in uniform? This last question will be addressed directly when we turn to *First
Blood* later in the chapter.

Rorty's narrative cannot accommodate the presence of a political monster let loose first on the continent and then across the world, devouring anything it desired. This monster, recall, was cheered and celebrated
by an adoring mob of supporters believing in their own exceptionalism,
able to countenance reprehensible actions taken in their name as long
as goods both political and economic were ultimately delivered. Now
Rorty's characterization of America, "the first nation-state with nobody
to please but itself – not even God," takes particularly ominous shape,
for unaccountable creative power vented in and on the world necessarily brings with it a corresponding destructiveness. Politically Rorty's
America aspires to create a world with "less unnecessary suffering,"
though his great democracy can live with the troubling or problematic
consequences accompanying its efforts. This is what makes it great. "We
are the greatest poem because we put ourselves in the place of God ...
We redefine God as our future selves." Other peoples will not simply bow
down before this self-creating divinity, of course, but bow eventually they
must. Ironically, Rorty accuses American leftists of possessing a Gothic
view of the country, believing that change is impossible because of the
specters haunting it. As Honig argues, Rorty effectively demonizes those
he charges with demonizing America.[25] Yet the specter haunting Rorty's
democratic imaginary is not the American Left but America itself: the
country has been at war, including a large number of wars of choice,
nearly in perpetuity since its birth, which Rorty's encomiums acknowledge and then work to obscure.

Nevertheless, Rorty's cheerful narrative of American democracy contains a confessional moment of apocalyptic Gothic proportions. The New
Left does not fare well under Rorty's critical gaze, but even his withering
assessment concedes that it was responsible for ending the Vietnam War
(a shameful episode in America's history) by taking to the streets. Rorty
then avows that if the New Left had not interceded, the country could
still, decades later, be sending young people off to die in the jungles of
Vietnam in an unwinnable war, shredding the country's constitutional
democracy in the process.[26]

Rorty's counterfactual horror story requires an explanation. What
could make such a perverse vision come true, in which no scale of collective murder-cum-suicide-cum-murder could derail a needless war? Given
Rorty's contextualization of Vietnam in a broader Cold War crusade for

freedom against Soviet evil, America's deployment of generation after generation after generation of citizens in an interminable conflict could be sustained only if it was suffering from chronic democratic credibility problems and shamed by a patriotic culture that enshrines sacrifice as its highest ideal. Each generation would honor the commitment of those preceding it. Anything other than staying the course would not only endanger democracy. It would also dishonor previous democratic citizen-sacrifice. This democratic-patriotic logic entails an infinite regress that cannot call a halt to needless slaughter because the country cannot recognize that little or nothing is actually at stake in the local incarnation of an ostensibly global struggle.

In Rorty's narrative hands, the American democracy could feed upon itself (sending successive generations to die in Vietnam) to the point of moral and political death while failing to realize the irreparable damage it was doing to itself. Patriotism makes such an apocalyptic fate thinkable, and democracy makes it possible. Rorty may even take pride in his democracy's ability to fight until literal exhaustion, with no ultimate purpose, until nothing is left. It speaks, if perversely, to the kind of capability democracy needs to defend itself in a world hostile to it. Democracy is always in search of its credibility. The prospect of America at war in Vietnam in the 1990s, at the very least, does *not* horrify Rorty.[27]

Nor does the larger Cold War narrative trouble him. He takes it for granted that American democracy was fighting the good fight. The United States and the Soviet Union squared off in a series of revolving proxy wars that ravaged countries and destroyed peoples from Southeast Asia to Africa to Central America. There seemed to be no limit to these conflicts or to the conventional resources that might be devoted to them. Regional hostilities were considered indispensable political outlets through which the world's two superpowers could safely vent not only their mutual competition for spheres of influence and material well-being but also their ideological contempt, hostility, and aggression without utterly destroying each other, to say nothing of the planet. Ironically, superpower competition presupposed, reinforced, and jeopardized a nuclear standoff that supposedly guaranteed conflict would not escalate. Yet if these regional conflicts did spiral out of control, the nuclear threshold would be crossed quickly. The United States, for example, supposedly limited its bombing in northern Vietnam in order not to provoke the Soviets into direct intervention. At the same time, Nixon and Kissinger did their best to create the impression that the president was mad and might resort to the nuclear option to keep the Soviets at bay.[28] Perhaps it is not surprising, then, that Rorty does not find the prospect of perpetual war in Vietnam horrifying. The larger cosmic engagement legitimizing it portended a level of violence threatening humankind's annihilation. Nuclear weapons could well turn back on their creators and plunge the earth into a nuclear winter from which it would never recover, perhaps the perfection of apocalyptic Gothic.

THE IMPOSSIBILITY OF A TRAGIC PATRIOTISM

Simon Stow also loves America. Contrary to Rorty, however, Stow refuses to romance his beloved democracy. Rather, he would bring a tragic perspective to bear on patriotic democracy, thanks largely to a detailed encounter with Thucydides (and thus Pericles). Stow may not consider patriotism an essentially natural phenomenon like John Schaar does, but he affirms love of country as a constitutive part of citizenship. Appreciative of America's ambiguous character, Stow, unlike Rorty, deems tragedy the appropriate frame to identify and navigate its virtues and vices. Might a critical or tragic patriotism, then, mount a serious challenge as democracy's public philosophy?

Stow pursues a critical, dialectical patriotism defined by balance. Athens's Festival of Dionysia provides a model. At this annual spring event, the city honored and celebrated itself; it also subjected itself to scrutiny. The self-examination included the production of tragedies, a prestigious dramatic competition judged by a select number of citizens in which dominant norms, practices, and conventions governing politics, leadership, loyalty, heroism, and glory received sustained, often unflattering attention. As detailed in the last chapter, prior to showing the plays, the city conducted important civic business. Leading military officials poured libations and made sacrifices. Citizens performing notable service or making an important contribution to the city were recognized. War orphans raised by the city who had come of age were introduced, taking their rightful place as citizens ready to make the same sacrifices as their fathers. It is precisely the dialectical combination of celebration and criticism – the contest of opposites in fruitful engagement – that Stow seeks to capture and recover. Celebration makes criticism possible by rendering it tolerable. Criticism, in turn, moderates celebration, insulating it from the dangers of excess.[29]

Hence the importance of Thucydides. Stow argues that Thucydides presents two Pericles, one *in* the *History of the Peloponnesian War* and one *of* the *History of the Peloponnesian War*. The Pericles in the *History* appears in the Funeral Oration. The Pericles of the *History* emerges in the report of the plague that immediately follows the Oration. In the first, Pericles pays tribute to Athenian dead. Athens invented the public oration honoring those who sacrificed their lives on behalf of the city. Courage in battle brings distinction of the highest kind. Military service furnishes the ultimate meaning a citizen can enjoy. Without the city, life is impossible. Tribute to the dead becomes the occasion to salute the greatness of the city itself. Pericles heaps lavish praise on Athens for its values: freedom, toleration, generosity, friendship, and virtue. Distinct from Sparta, Athens is nothing if not an example and education to the rest of Greece. The city's greatness flows from a way of life chosen by its citizens. Sparta's so-called achievements result from martial discipline imposed on its people. Pericles speaks of the dead, but his speech targets the living, not only families who lost loved ones but also citizens present and future who must not merely emulate but also exceed the accomplishments of their predecessors. Those who have given everything provide a legacy worthy of and calling for, even demanding, respect, something that can be demonstrated only by surpassing it. Gifts from the past cannot just be accepted. They must be augmented. To fail in this civic task would be tantamount to declaring that the dead died in vain – which is unthinkable. Citizens must meet their civic obligations and responsibilities, putting aside more personal causes and concerns. Pericles's oration is a call to action, a call to arms.

Stow argues that the Pericles in the Oration offers an idealized conception of Athens. The city could not live up to the excellence or perfection of the image. The blindness and arrogance such narration induces prove disastrous. Believing in its own exceptionalism, Athens cultivates attitudes (superiority, jingoism) and undertakes projects (war, empire) that are ultimately self-destructive. The kind of patriotic democracy expressed in Pericles's Oration can be unthinking, intemperate, narcissistic – and lethal.

Thucydides juxtaposes the Funeral Oration with an account of the plague that devastated Athens in the second year of the war. In it, we see Athens at its worst. Lawlessness is the norm. Believing death imminent, citizens eschew civic spirit and its traditions of service and sacrifice to indulge in delights of the moment. Little care is given to the sick or the dead. The city resembles an open-air cemetery. The creative-destructive will to power that once defined Athens, perhaps especially in the context of war, has been supplanted by a sense of powerlessness in the face of unrelenting disease. Epidemic has reduced Athens to the level of animality. The city is unrecognizable to itself, even its enemies. Stow writes: "In setting up this juxtaposition of the two Athens, Thucydides offers his readers the opportunity for critical reflection: the chance to experience dialectic. They move between two worlds, recognizing that neither presents Athens in her entirety, but that each is a partial perspective from which they should seek to construct a more-balanced picture. Thucydides offers a Dionysian perspective ... He seeks not to sway his readers with simple patriotism ... but instead offers them the possibility of a more-balanced, critical patriotism ..."[30]

Stow's astute reading of Thucydides contains both an oddity and an omission. First, the oddity: As Stow rightly observes, Pericles speaks to the living. The Oration is also an exhortation, not just to the young men who are or will one day be citizens but also to their parents. Mothers and fathers are advised to take great pride in their sons' exploits. Dying on behalf of the city is an occasion for happiness, not sadness (though brief mourning is understandably necessary). Men achieve a kind of immortality killing and being killed for the city. They will be remembered and revered by generations of Athenians to come, their lives invoked as examples. The dead will never be forgotten as long as the city lives on, and it will live on as long as more young men are prepared to sacrifice for it. While Pericles does not pretend that he can convince parents of these difficult social and political truths, he nonetheless urges them to have more children, that is, more sons, thus more bodies for the front lines. This constitutes their civic responsibility, a duty that cannot be ignored, evaded, or refused. The city depends on parents providing it with more citizens: sacrifice begets sacrifice; death begets more death. No one dies without purpose and meaning. No one can be allowed to die without purpose and meaning. The only guarantee against vain death is the logic of civic sacrifice.

Remember, this is Pericles's *idealized* vision of Athens, the identity to which the city should aspire. According to Stow, Thucydides offers partial perspectives of Athens, suggesting that while it does not fully embody Pericles's ideal, it also exceeds its conduct during the plague. Fair enough. But is the ideal worthy of democratic aspiration, let alone attainment? What does it mean to treat Pericles's ideal as such, even if it always already remains tantalizingly out of reach? Yes, the rhetoric moves, thrills, and inspires. Pericles draws on a wide range of emotions and dispositions that he, in turn, tends and cultivates, including despair, fear, respect, pride, and ambition. Assume Athens represents the finest achievement in the history of politics. What is the price of this achievement? Pericles intimates without fully articulating it when he addresses parents. At the close of the first year of what will be a long war culminating in the destruction of Athenian democracy, parents must conceive of themselves as breeders of soldiers, which simultaneously reduces children to the future honored dead. Athens may be idealized, but thanks to a democracy's patriotic ritual, it is a strange idealization, one in which the city becomes an insatiable military-political monster capable of consuming all that lives within its considerable reach, a monster equipped to feed and sustain itself indefinitely, in part by trying to grow and expand as it consumes. It feeds on life in the name of death. Death is what keeps it alive and eventually amounts to its reason for being. It cannot live without more and more death. Given this internal dynamic, life itself disappears, amounting to little more than a means to another end, no longer an end in itself. The Oration that starts as a heroic tale of derring-do converts itself into a horrific tale of never-ending, ever-escalating sacrifice. And this is before Thucydides turns to the plague. The horror is lodged inside the ideal, subverting and working to defeat the idealization containing it.[31] Pericles's figure of Athens is thus essentially unstable, the gradual elaboration of a contradiction in terms rather than a platform for dialectic.

Pericles's Funeral Oration is legendary, the stuff of democracy's patriotic lore. Yet the speech he delivers to Athens "after the second invasion of the Peloponnesians" and the outbreak of plague, a double dose of deprivation and suffering for Athenians, may be more disconcerting. At this point in the war, Pericles himself is in danger. Dispirited by military fortunes, Athenians vent their anger and rage at Pericles, their beloved leader, seriously diminishing his good standing and popularity. This turn of events comes as no surprise to Pericles, however. He even anticipated it. The twin disasters befalling Athens do not unduly concern him. Rather, he converts them into yet another occasion for civic encouragement and incitement. If anything, the unprecedented dangers now facing Athens offer it the greatest of opportunities for distinction. It stands to lose everything, and "it is more of a disgrace to be robbed of what one has than to fail in some new undertaking."[32]

Pericles thus appeals to the pride, even vainglory, of his fellow citizens. He reminds them of what they supposedly already know. Athens is a great city, and citizens bear responsibility for its health and well-being. A statement of civic duty may not be sufficient to motivate Athenians, so Pericles admonishes them. We look down on those who "pretend to a reputation to which they are not entitled." Even more distasteful and "equally to be condemned are those who, through lack of moral fibre, fail to live up

to the reputation which is theirs already."[33] Patriotic democracy entails
self-discipline and courage. Pericles expects (demands) nothing less.

Given the calamities facing Athens, some might wonder if the war can
be won and if it is best to continue fighting it. Things might deteriorate
further, and victory could prove elusive – at best. Pericles dismisses such
fears, insisting there are no good reasons for indulging them. On Pericles's
democratic-patriotic model, no argument can be made for ending (the)
war, thus for peace. Cessation does not fit within its conceptual frame.
The course must always be stayed. This is the Athenian way. It's a tradition not to be abandoned. "Remember, too, that the reason why Athens
has the greatest name in all the world is because she has never given
in to adversity, but *has spent more life and labor in warfare than any
other state*, thus winning the greatest power that has ever existed in history, such a power that will be remembered for ever by posterity ..."[34]
For Pericles, then, patriotic democracy does not admit of a scenario in
which defeat can be imagined or war might result in a Pyrrhic victory.
That is, the results do not necessarily matter. Thus, were Athens to suffer
decisive military defeat, were every solider to be killed or captured and
placed in bondage, the outcome could be recuperated for democracy's
purposes: old men, women, and children would proudly tell the tale of
Athenian heroism down to the last man. Should Athens suffer total annihilation, refusing to acknowledge a lost cause and fighting on until no
one remained alive, the city would live on in the minds and memories
of peoples everywhere, or so the patriotic democrat could envision. This
would not constitute an absurdity within Pericles's civic logic.[35]

Thucydides's presentations of Athens through the figure of Pericles do
not offer extremes in opposition suitable for dialectic. Each, in solidarity,
mimics the extremity of the other. They are identical. Each loves death. In
a democracy the worst that can happen to it is actually the best that can
happen to it: calamity provides the opportunity for love to experience its
fullest, finest expression. Thucydides's presentations thus lead not to a
more balanced love of democracy but to an appreciation of the absurdity
of such a comportment given the many apocalyptic horrors it necessarily,
even joyfully, entails.[36]

FRANKENSTEIN'S MONSTER IN AMERICA

Rorty, Stow, and Pericles do not offer their democratic visions as exemplary of political horror. Each, presumably, would resist such a characterization, though each understands that patriotic democracy must

inevitably trade in violence and death – at least to some extent. Still, an apocalyptic Gothic lens can offer a politically contributive take on their civic contributions, especially insofar as they assume patriotism can be made safe for democracy and productively employed by it. The first wager being made here is that the right Gothic lens enables a democratic community committed to patriotic blandishments to recognize and appreciate the unduly problematic character and cost of its affirmations, as if for the first time. The second wager being made is that an apocalyptic Gothic perspective can contribute to a tragic sensibility.

Rorty, as we have seen, loved America's patriotic democracy. He also loved its war films, in particular those starring John Wayne. To highlight, dramatize, and re-cover the political logic at work in Rorty (and Stow and Pericles) and thereby reveal tragic dimensions of political life otherwise obscured, I turn not to Wayne but to Sylverster Stallone and the original production of what became an American and international cinematic franchise.

First Blood, a 1982 film about a Vietnam veteran, the war, and the country to which he returns, could be classified in several genres: action, adventure, drama, fantasy, mystery, science fiction, suspense, or war. It is tense, fast-paced, violent, heavy-handed, and manipulative. It also plays on notions of pride, innocence, victimhood, resentment, rage, and vengeance. Love it or hate it, find it righteous or absurd, deem it thrilling or ugly, *First Blood* refuses to be ignored. Given its politics, it can be considered a first-rate apocalyptic Gothic horror film, the brilliance of which stems from the normality of the world it presents, the dark underside just below the surface of life it reveals, the self-escalating logic of enmity it displays, and the predictable sequence of events, including a monstrous outcome, it narrates. Moreover, the terror it creates on screen and the satisfaction it elicits in the audience offer few, if any, real surprises. We welcome the first. We anticipate the second. And, politically, that is precisely the problem. A democracy's patriotic rage begets violence that begets destruction – until nothing is left. But does anyone notice the result, a tragic tale of Sophoclean proportions in which democracy digs its own grave and the gravediggers it employs ultimately kill and bury it?

First Blood symptomized the advent of Reagan. Crowned the year before, the perennial actor campaigned on a vehemently patriotic platform, seeking to restore not only America's place of prominence in the world but also its vaunted sense of democratic exceptionalism at home – no more Carter malaise. We can and should be proud of ourselves, candidate Reagan assured the country he would govern. A creature of

World War II and the new global order it spawned, Reagan believed in America's Cold War mission to police the planet and fight the evils of messianic communism. This included what he took to be a noble and criminally aborted effort in South Vietnam to preserve its indepen- dence. Rather than a source of guilt, let alone self-reproach, Reagan reconceived the American experience in Southeast Asia, folding it into the nation's founding commitment to freedom. (Rorty was nothing if not Reaganesque on Vietnam.) The war may have been lost, unnec- essarily of course, but defeat cast shame on the liberal Democrats, radical students, renegade priests, and other unpatriotic elements of American society responsible for it – not the country as a whole. For America to recapture its self-confidence and, consequently, its right- ful power and position in the world, the ghost of Vietnam had to be exorcised. Small, backward, ideologically handicapped societies do not defeat world-historical agents of the good. The country needed a dose of psycho-political therapy, and Reagan was just the former pitchman-turned-politician to administer it. At the same time, a cine- matic assist from Hollywood couldn't hurt.

First Blood unfolds in Hope, a small town in the Pacific Northwest, not long after Vietnam's shocking conclusion. Other than the opening sunbathed sequences in which John Rambo (Stallone) searches for a friend with whom he served in Vietnam and learns that he died from exposure to Agent Orange, the film's atmospherics are relentlessly over- cast, dominated by rain, cold, wet, clouds, shadows, darkness. For the next ninety-three minutes, nothing good can happen in Hope.

War lost, Rambo returns to the United States, but he has not come home, a common feeling among vets and a common accusation against the United States, as we will see again in Chapter 6 when analyzing Barack Obama on Vietnam.[37] *First Blood* portrays what democracies do to citizens who serve in war. Rambo lives everywhere and nowhere. Nomadic, homeless, he drifts from place to place. Though not abandoned on a remote island, he is as isolated and alone, as angry and abandoned, as Philoctetes. He has no possessions – just the clothes on his back, including an Army jacket embroidered with a faded American flag, and a sleeping bag. Also like Philoctetes, Rambo carries a weapon of war with him wherever he goes – not a magical bow, but a fearsome survival knife. It makes Rambo invincible. This deracinated citizen-soldier goes for days, even weeks, without speaking to anyone. With the last member of his unit killed by cancer, Rambo is a lone survivor. He appears zombielike, part of a special breed of walking dead. If nothing else, he wants to be left alone.

But, like both Philoctetes and Frankenstein's monster, he also seeks the home he believes is wrongfully denied him.

As Rambo wanders into Hope looking for something to eat, Will Teasle, the town's sheriff, "befriends" him. Disgusted by the mere sight of Rambo, Teasle, noting the provocative Army jacket, decides Rambo must go – and go now. Hope will not tolerate his presence – not for a single second. It might attract other "drifters." Delivering him to the town's limits, Teasle points the way to Portland and recommends that he take a bath. America is no longer a place for reinvention. It cannot even recognize a citizen-soldier who served it. Given Rambo's precipitous fall in status and standing since the war, this is no surprise.

After the Sheriff drives away, Rambo pauses. In the western tradition of Will Kane in *High Noon*, he heads back to town knowing, perhaps welcoming the reaction it will provoke. Is return a matter of principle ("Is there any law against me getting something [to eat] here?")? Is it that he's being made to "run" ("Why are you pushing me?")? Is it a matter of self-respect ("You know, wearing that flag on that jacket, looking the way you do, you're asking for trouble around here, friend ... We don't want guys like you in this town.")? Whatever the case, Rambo is no innocent. He knows what his decision means. We all do. Yet who in the audience doesn't want Rambo to return to vent his ressentiment? Who doesn't want to see the confrontation – followed by the comeuppance – that is certain to come? The film makes the audience well aware of its love affair with violence, which is also democracy's love affair with violence. Furious, Sheriff Teasle arrests Rambo, ready to employ deadly force if given the slightest pretext. The film's fuse has been lit. How slowly will it burn?

Small-town lawlessness by the law soon repeats itself. The sheriff orders his deputies to delouse the rank, unkempt Rambo to make him presentable for court. Like Philoctetes, Rambo smells bad. If anything, Rambo's stench may exceed Philoctetes's, for Rambo and his brethren committed a more serious act of sacrilege. However well they fought in Vietnam, they lost the war, America's first military defeat. Given the national, even international, humiliation this involved, nothing else matters. Defeat is a fact that colors every perception.

Rambo did not leave Vietnam unscathed. Briefly captured, the scars decorating his back and chest (signs the deputies refuse to acknowledge, let alone honor) confirm his heroic status. After beating Rambo and showering him with a fire hose, the deputies insist on shaving him with a straight razor. It is just a matter of time before Rambo responds.

At the sight of the blade, flashbacks intrude, not just of enemy capture but also of torture. Rambo suffers from post-traumatic stress disorder (PTSD). This is what the war they fought did to American soldiers.

Prompted by American torture, Rambo breaks free of police custody, leaving a handful of deputies beaten, broken, humiliated, and helpless in his wake. Fleeing the police station, he takes nothing but his survival knife. Like Philoctetes, he is identified with one simple but deadly weapon. Rambo's escape sets the stage for the remainder of the film, as the local authorities, soon joined by the state police and National Guard, hunt Rambo and Rambo finally, famously turns back on his pursuers. The film moves from action-adventure-drama to apocalyptic Gothic revenge picture. It proves quite horrifying. More than a few rogue cops are at risk. Hope, the stand-in for American democracy, sits on a self-made precipice. They don't know it, but we do.

First Blood, of course, is about something other than the petty tyranny of a small-town sheriff, his hooligans, and one man's refusal to kowtow to state power. *First Blood* is a meditation-cum-polemic on the Vietnam War, the meaning of patriotic democracy, and the country's (lost) moral identity. It is also a documentary about what democracies require of and do to their young citizens with little concern or remorse.[38] Rambo, one of many in his generation, fought a war with which he did not identify. Nevertheless, he performed his duty to the utmost, following even questionable orders and assignments. Colonel Trautman, Rambo's commanding officer, inadvertently confesses to the war crimes they committed in Vietnam: fighting to defeat a people's war requires killing the people themselves. The political class that drafted Rambo betrayed him, waging a war it did not need to fight and could not win. (Rambo would have fought in Vietnam indefinitely, the embodiment of Rorty's Gothic nightmare.) He and his friends sacrificed – and were sacrificed – for nothing. They remained loyal to their country and to one another. Their country deserted them. Worse, it subjected them to politics, a stinging form of rejection that transformed them into scapegoats for a lost war, the country's first. Once they were citizen-soldiers of distinction, trusted with great responsibilities. As the war effort collapsed, everything changed. Upon return, they were treated with contempt, derision – veritable pariahs in their homeland. After the fact, the country decided it never really wanted to fight the war in the first place. As casualties mounted, as repatriated body bags defined the war, and once the war became officially unwinnable, people turned on it. Eventually they wanted to forget it ever happened.

Thus America may think the war is over and behind it, but not those who fought in it. They were trained to serve their country. This requires converting citizens into soldiers, and the manufacturing process is terrible. Once completed, the effects cannot be reversed just because a peace treaty has been signed. Rambo remains what he was made, with scars more than skin deep to prove it. Yet the country does nothing to reintegrate soldiers into civilian life. Perhaps democracy's dirty secret is that they cannot be reintegrated into civilian life, not all of them, not reliably. Fortunately, soldiers can be disposed of once spent. Disowned by the military, Rambo cannot even get a job parking cars. Appearing in Hope, he is reduced to nothing – a drifter stripped of the prestige formerly his due. In fact, following his arrest, the deputies, noticing dog tags, learn that Rambo is a soldier. Given their own felt inadequacies, this piece of information actually incites them, spurring them on to greater acts of cruelty, especially when Rambo refuses to cooperate in his own submission. Local law enforcement enacts the hostile welcome "home" about which Rambo later complains.

Rambo, then, takes "mundane" police brutality and converts it into an occasion to "return" to the jungles of Vietnam (relocated in the Pacific Northwest) and demonstrate American expertise: controlled, precision violence on the one hand; wild, generalized destruction on the other. In relatively short order, Rambo morphs from quiet, polite, soft-spoken, mild-mannered ex-solider to traumatized veteran standing up for his rights against the state to angry, aggressive, apparently superhuman warmongering psychopath who annihilates everything in his sight. Like Frankenstein's monster, he cannot be defeated by mere humans. Hence Trautman's astonishing mission in Hope: not to save Rambo from local law enforcement personnel, but to save two hundred wide-eyed wannabe weekend warriors from Rambo. They have no chance against this otherworldly creation. Thus, following Rambo's escape from custody and as *First Blood*'s geography shifts from jail cell to mountain forest and, finally, back to Hope, the genre in which it should be read manifests itself: apocalyptic Gothic horror.

As befits a horror story, the audience is taken for quite a ride as the larger community, much like Dr. Frankenstein pursuing his monster, chases Rambo in a futile attempt to capture the creative-destructive force it created and unleashed in the name of democracy. As the sheriff and his deputies track Rambo, one of them realizes it's a grave mistake. They are not the hunters, but the hunted.[39] No one listens to the voice of reason, of course, because none of them understands the affective force with which they are dealing. Rather, the reluctant deputy is mocked for fearing the "boogeyman." One by one, however, Rambo wounds, injures, disables, and terrorizes the posse pursuing him. None of them sees him coming. Each is left screaming hysterically for the sheriff/father to rescue him.

Accompanied by bursts of thunder and lightning, the camera isolates each deputy; the isolation signals the target's demise. Rambo attacks from anywhere and nowhere: earth, sky, underbrush. Much like Frankenstein's monster, he is effectively invisible. He is seen only when he wants to be seen. The audience knows he is coming but cannot locate him. Rambo is one with nature, an apparition that stalks and haunts his prey. He could have killed them all, but Rambo is still a soldier. He will not needlessly kill his fellow citizens – it would be gratuitous. He tries to convince Teasle to stop chasing him, that is, to surrender, informing the sheriff that his writ does not extend to the wilderness where he, Rambo, is the law. "Let it go," Rambo advises him (with knife to throat), "or I'll give you a war you won't believe." Though reduced to tears, the sheriff cannot and will not submit. Having served in the (forgotten) Korean War and having missed Vietnam, he must prove his credentials, an opportunity he seems to relish. If anything, the sheriff undergoes welcome reanimation. The specter of patriotic democracy's apocalyptic brutality energizes and excites him. As it does Rambo, whose half-hearted effort early on to derail the cycle of escalation cannot be taken in good faith. He never had any intention of surrendering. It's not in the soldier's playbook. Even *First Blood*'s conceit that Rambo, despite the destructiveness he unleashes, kills no one only calls attention to the symbiotic relationship between patriotic democracy and death. Given the level of violence, Rambo must kill people, if only collaterally. This is where *First Blood* descends into camp.[40]

Rambo is portrayed as democracy's ultimate citizen-solider, but he is something more. As the sheriff retreats to organize reinforcements, he asks, "Whatever possessed God in heaven to make a man like Rambo?" Teasle knows what we all suspect, namely, that Rambo is not really a man at all but something else, something strange, something alien, something monstrous.[41] Enter Trautman, dressed in military suit and tie, taut beret, and a snug, fully buttoned trench coat, looking every bit the military mad scientist, who announces, "God didn't make Rambo. I made him. I recruited him. I trained him. I commanded him for three years in Vietnam. I'd say that makes him mine." Trautman, the figure of a larger military, political, and patriotic culture, made Rambo by subjecting him to highly specialized training, training which did not eschew but embraced pain, deprivation, suffering, and death.

Rambo was made by Trautman in another sense as well. Rambo displays a keen feel for American military history and political tradition. He knows what he's due: the honor, recognition, and commemoration of a country that takes sacrifice for granted. Rambo came to life on the graves of his uniformed predecessors, ready to follow them to their sacred destination six feet under at Arlington. Trautman may not have robbed the coffins of the nation's military cemeteries to build his ideal recruit, but Rambo's ethos springs from mass death just the same, from those who once upon a time threw themselves on a grenade or charged into withering enemy fire. Rambo would happily join them in the same revered resting place. To die serving the country is best. To be wounded serving the country is second best. It proves commitment (to dying), but life becomes something of a consolation prize, tolerated perhaps, but not embraced or celebrated. Rambo needs, even welcomes death to complete his service and home-going.

Trautman, accordingly, offers Teasle sound advice: arrange for Rambo to slip through the search perimeter – to defuse the situation (and him). Seize Rambo in Seattle in a couple of weeks without incident. As Trautman remarks later in the film, "God knows what damage he's prepared to do." Modeling any good horror victim, Teasle refuses his identity as such and scorns the idea of an unstoppable one-man, war-making force. Rather than accept Trautman's high praise of Rambo's death-laden talents, he mocks Trautman (who actually believes in monsters?) for trying to scare everyone to death, insisting that Trautman's only concern is to determine why one of his machines malfunctioned. Of course, there is no evidence that his machine, his scientific creation, is malfunctioning. This is the tragedy of the film. Democracy destroys its own as it defends and thereby destroys itself.

Either way, this machine cannot be deactivated upon command. Violence, killing, and death constitute a way of life for it. Trautman recognizes that he cannot control the force he's let loose on the world in the name of democracy. Rambo insists on prosecuting this war, his war, to its narcissistic conclusion. They drew first blood, he says. This time he'll "finish" what he didn't start (even if he can't win this war ultimately either). Like Ajax, he will destroy those who have wronged him, even if they are just surrogates for the greater wrongs he has suffered at the hands of American democracy. Rambo's real war is with the country that refuses to recognize his rightful standing as a warrior and – unable to reincorporate him into the very society for which he sacrificed everything – rejects him. For Rambo, much like Ajax, death is preferable to a civilian way of life, especially to a life lived in shame and dishonor. Tragically, the shame and dishonor have actually been earned. Through Trautman, as I previously mentioned, we learn that Rambo was guilty of war crimes (indiscriminate killing of civilians) while serving in Vietnam. His country placed him in a situation where it was unavoidable.

Mimicking good horror vehicles, *First Blood* pauses before the final fury erupts. After police pinpoint Rambo's location, toy soldiers fire a small rocket at his position in an abandoned mineshaft. Assuming they have killed him, they pose for photographs, Iwo Jima-style. Though presumed dead, democracy's monster child cannot be killed by a bunch of timid sunshine patriots in the boondocks. Rambo's preordained burial ground is Arlington National Cemetery, eternal home to (Congressional) Medal of Honor winners. Teasle admits to feeling cheated. He wanted the opportunity to kill Rambo himself, the so-called best of the best.

Rambo's "death," of course, gives him another chance to leave Hope. No one would know – except Rambo himself, which means the violence is not only about to resume but also escalate. Like Frankenstein's monster, Rambo is on a destructive mission that controls him as much as he controls it. He returns to Hope and lays waste to the town. Destruction is Hope's (America's) just desserts. Rambo may appear one with nature, but, like any good patriot, he proceeds with his secular crusade ignorant of and indifferent to its consequences for the natural and social worlds.

Rambo fixes on one political target: the police station. Taking his fight from countryside to city, the one and only bastion of nominal civilian control, Rambo mimics the Viet Cong enemy he once fought. With Hope's streets evacuated, he single-handedly assaults police headquarters. Armed with an M-60 machine gun, wielding it with one hand (more camp), Rambo disables electric transformers and plunges the town into darkness. More explosions, more damage. Rambo finally concentrates fire on the police station itself, slowly dismantling it. Teasle is crouched on the roof, clutching his gun in abject terror, reduced to a mere boy. Reanimation has its limits. Even prior to capture, Rambo has "won." The local tyrant has been deposed, humiliated. Rambo effectively destroyed the village to save it. And destroy it he did, callous to life and limb. Teasle, too, would have destroyed the town in order to save it. He just didn't get the chance. He is Rambo's lesser twin. Rambo did momentarily resurrect Teasle, rescuing him from a stultifying bourgeois life, but Teasle didn't have similar affective resources available to him. Korea is still buried, forgotten. Rambo's scars are fresh, visible, and raw. Teasle's are sealed, hidden, and dulled.

First Blood may be an apocalyptic Gothic horror story, but it's democracy's horror story (and a tragedy, too), which makes ending it complicated. Does Rambo live or die? If Rambo dies, what manner of death best suits him? Trautman materializes in the police station, having made no effort to halt Rambo's final fusillade, and orders him not to kill a badly wounded Teasle. At first, Rambo can only grunt a response, as if the faculty of speech has been lost in the orgy of violence. Soon enough, however, Rambo vents the postwar resentment festering inside him. Rejected by the democracy he served, he rejects anyone's right to criticize him ("Who are they ['all those maggots'] to protest me?"). A soldier surrounded by enemies, he cannot abide his fellow democratic citizens. They spat on him (*First Blood* reiterates one of the great myths of Vietnam betrayal), and he returns fire in his own distinct fashion – with the police, National Guard, and Hope serving as stand-ins. Traumatized in the retelling, Rambo collapses. He mimics Ajax crumpled on the floor of his tent surrounded by the entrails of the beasts he has tortured and slaughtered. Rambo sits in the midst of the debris of a once-functioning modern police station in the middle of what was once a vibrant small town. Trautman does his best to offer him, his sobbing monster, some physical comfort. No repulsion here. Perhaps Rambo was not so much persuaded to call off the violence as he was exhausted by its expression. He was running on affective fumes. Disillusionment with an ideal begets rage, which engenders violence, which in turn finds whatever fuel it needs to sustain itself. Thanks to Trautman's intervention (he appears as suddenly as Heracles does to induce Philoctetes to carry out his mission in Troy), Rambo departs in handcuffs, neatly disguised, destination Fort Bragg. Apparently, Rambo's "private war" (Trautman's description) carries no formal or official penalties. Demanding the respect due a war veteran, Rambo enacts a revenge most can only fantasize. Like Ajax, Rambo feels no remorse for the horrific violence he deployed against his "enemies." He is nothing if not certain of his moral credentials, even though, again like Ajax, he can persuade no one of his position. Back in the hands of its maker, who knows where this daemon might next surface in the name of democracy?[42]

There is an alternate ending to *First Blood* in which Rambo, following his diatribe against American democracy, commits suicide.[43] Admitting to Trautman the danger he represents, he asks his former commanding officer to kill him. Death would be preferable to a life spent in jail (this is another Ajax-like moment). Trautman trained him, made him. It's his obligation to kill him – the very least he's owed by his creator. Rambo grabs Trautman's pistol from its holster and hands it to him, imploring him again and again: "Do it." When Trautman balks, Rambo grabs his hand and pulls the trigger for (and with) him. It's a team effort.

Test audiences hated the suicide ending – it did not survive the final cut. It might, however, have rendered the tragic dimensions of the film undeniable. Ironically, Rambo's survival also seems fitting, a reflection of the country's inability to understand the Vietnam War or patriotism. The logic of patriotic narrative tends toward death, but the film refuses Rambo the patriot-hero's noble denouement and lets American democracy off the hook in the process. Rambo looks whole again as he leaves the police station calm and collected, which confirms that America remains ignorant of what it made Rambo do and what it did to him. *First Blood* thus feels rather unpatriotic. It doesn't have the full courage of its political convictions. Of course, the film doesn't imagine patriotic democracy to be an apocalyptic Gothic horror show.

Rather, for *First Blood*, moral victory in Hope redeems actual defeat in Vietnam – which wasn't a real loss anyway since the game was rigged ("somebody wouldn't let us win"). A lone citizen-soldier, however, imbued with monstrous power, proves what America's democracy can do when unhindered by military timidity or political calculation. Democracy may suffer from inherent anxieties, but they can be surmounted. For the already initiated and informed, Rambo's death would have confirmed patriotic democracy as indisputably good for the country. Rambo would make one final symbolic sacrifice, himself, to serve democracy by example. Death alone identifies the authenticity of the patriotic democrat: better to die on behalf of a noble ideal than capitulate to an ignoble reality. Perhaps this is an esoteric truth known only by the few. Suicide might also mark Rambo not so much a casualty of war but more a victim of democracy's need for violence, making it a self-consuming artifact that, having destroyed what it loves, finally must feed on itself. Not all horror films have a felicitous ending, I'm afraid.

Alas, *First Blood*, with the alternate ending, might have made a lasting contribution to tragic cinema and been a fitting entrant into an American Dionysia. The United States, like many democratic states, sends its young off to fight and die in horrific wars, wars that involve killing – sometimes unintentionally, sometimes not – innocent civilians. What these soldiers experience can render them unfit to return to the society they have "given" their lives to protect and defend. They suffer from all manner of post-traumatic stresses (a condition that long predates its official naming), which can lead to anything from simple depression to aggressive violence to suicide.[44] The country they love does not know what to do with them. They oftentimes cannot be made whole and fully repatriated. This is not a truth democracy wishes to advertise. If anything, it has every reason to conceal such tragic truths – to keep the war machine running. But if a democracy must defend itself, it also does so at an intolerable price. *First Blood* denies the price as Rambo walks off screen confidently, defiantly. It has a runtime of ninety-three minutes, at the end of which Rambo looks none the worse for war, despite the war he made on American democracy and the war America's democracy waged against him.[45]

TRAGEDY OR: LEAVING PATRIOTIC DEMOCRACY BEHIND

In the aftermath of *First Blood*, and insofar as democratic polities necessarily depend on their citizens for success, can patriotic democracy be considered a tragic good, something at once indispensable and inimical, both life-giving and life-threatening? After all, wouldn't such an approach to patriotic democracy be sensitive to the fundamental ambiguity at its heart, affirming its necessity but alert to its lethality?

This, as we saw earlier, seems to be Stow's position. It might be argued, for example, that the patriotic passion enabling citizens to rush to the selective service office to defend their country in time of crisis also raises the possibility of that very same passion being deployed to silence (or worse) those who might resist, protest, or refuse the call to arms. Likewise, the patriotic passion to participate in the institutional life of the country to realize fundamental values may foster hatred or contempt for those in opposition, rendering them subject to subordination, marginalization, and exclusion. Similarly, the patriotic democrat who passionately articulates, defends, and celebrates the country's core principles may, in times of emergency, be prone to conclude that those very same principles have to be curtailed, even suspended, to honor and protect the legacy inherited from ancestors who made such hard choices themselves. Finally, patriotic democracy's insistence on regular civic tributes to the country's greatness, cultivating a sense of pride and indebtedness, may also foster blindness, ugliness, and provincialism as the costs of its achievements receive short shrift or are denied altogether, thereby contributing to a distorted political culture. Patriotic democracy, it seems, combines strengths and deficiencies, virtues and infirmities, excellences and impairments. The good cannot be forsaken. The bad, therefore, must be accommodated – hence the tragedy. What, if anything, is wrong with this depiction?

Any project to save patriotic democracy and deliver it reborn to a democratic polity needs to address questions about its provenance before assigning it tragic status. Insofar as Stow, unlike Rorty, sees through patriotism's regulative fictions, what makes it a political ethos worth pursuing? One prong of Stow's productive dialectic, the idealizations that inspire, seems not just a wild exaggeration but also objectionable. The problem with patriotic ideals isn't that they are not or cannot be fully realized but that they might be. Either way, can't the affective commitment patriotic democracy signifies be otherwise secured from citizens?

Stow may conceive patriotism as a tragic necessity given the challenges, commitments, and threats democracies face in a complex, difficult, and hostile world. The claim is they cannot be met without the love that patriotic democracy mobilizes, channels, and deploys. If so, a critical or tragic patriotism, to be convincing, needs to make an argument for its necessity rather than presume or insinuate it. The role patriotic democracy may have demonstrably played in politics on prior occasions cannot suffice here. Of what precisely does patriotic democracy's necessity consist? For example, in wartime militaries excel at forging the dedicated, devoted soldiers they need to prosecute armed interventions. It doesn't matter how they get hold of them. Give them a quota of bodies and they'll do the rest. Democracies do not need people running to volunteer to have an effective military, as World War II proved in the United States. In peacetime, likewise, states routinely affect their citizens' lives through legislation, policies, programs, court decisions, and bureaucratic rulings, thereby making indifference or neutrality more or less impossible and passionate connection inevitable. Citizens always already find themselves deeply implicated, affectively speaking, with their polities, even if and when professing distance, disgust, and alienation. Democracies produce, thanks to the conduct of politics writ large, the citizens they need to make them flourish. Why, then, must citizens attend and relate to their polity through patriotic love, more specifically, love that enshrines sacrifice at its core, the only reliable proof of which is killing and dying?[46]

Perhaps *First Blood* intimates a way out of the self-destructive trap democracy springs on itself. Rambo made the decision to "return" to Hope knowing full well it would trigger an angry response. He might have walked away instead, ignoring the sheriff's insults. Rambo returned to Hope to resume the war, but he had options, unlike the democratic citizens who resist the order of things we will see in Chapters 4 and 5. As if an addict, Rambo needed a fix – of violence. The sheriff, for him, was not just a petty official invested with too much power who provoked retaliation for abusing it. He became the official representative of a democracy that lost its way and scapegoated and disowned those who served it – and paid a terrible, irreparable price in doing so. The sheriff had to be destroyed because the betrayal he represented had to be answered. When Rambo experienced an everyday democratic insult, as mentioned above, he could not abide the chastening delivered by a world that operates according to its own terms. He converted a not uncommon, if thoroughly unpleasant, encounter into a holy political cause. Democracy entails taking (rights, resources, opportunities, etc.), but given the power at the disposal of the people themselves, it also requires forbearing and, occasionally, forsaking. Power rightfully possessed should not necessarily be exercised, especially if it damages what it is meant to serve or if the consequences of its exercise cannot be justified.

Rambo's tirade at the end of the film includes a furious reminder that he did not volunteer for the war ("I didn't ask you; you asked me"), a war he never actually defends. Rambo embodies a second double. On the one hand, he is a patriot despite himself, the enraged veteran bent on recognition from and revenge against an ungrateful democracy. On the other hand, he is a democratic citizen reborn in the ashes of patriotic commitment, wary of state power and ready to resist it. Colonel Trautman's subject, despite careful construction, has imploded from the exercise of its brilliance. The Rambo who walked in and out of Hope is indignant; defiant; distrustful of authority; wise to the political fairytales countries, including democracies, like to tell themselves; and aware that the democratic state can consume everything in its path. Rambo finds himself in a position to leave patriotic democracy behind because he has lived through its perverse perfection – even before he gets to Hope. Thus, a democracy may devour its own people as it seeks to defend itself, but this tragedy can, with assistance, lead to a democracy less inclined to unwitting self-destruction thanks to the new citizens it has inadvertently forged. The same dynamic will be explored in Chapters 4 and 5, as neoliberal democracy gives birth to citizens with capacities not so much for destructive, totalistic revenge, as with Rambo, but for creative, targeted resistance that may also include the precise use of violence when the state is compromised.

How might democracy's self-defeating dynamic be countered? What kind of civic occasion can be imagined to address the likes of John J. Rambo? They would be honored guests on Veterans Day, of course, where tributes are paid to those who served in the armed forces. Rambo himself would be unlikely to attend such thanksgiving. It would not speak to his experience of war or its aftermath. Even if sincere, it would feel false and forced. If the old traditions will not work anymore, what new conventions might replace them? What kind of ceremony might complement the American Dionysia proposed in Chapter 1?

ADMISSION DAY

First Blood, read against the patriotic grain, points to the need for democracy to take stock of itself. If the film constitutes an informal confession of democracy's inherent villainy, what might formalize it? The answer: Admission Day. While many American states already observe such an occasion, it refers to the date they were admitted into the Union. I have something else in mind. Democracy needs to set a day aside when everything comes to a halt to acknowledge the damage it routinely wreaks on its citizens in war. *First Blood* reveals a truth already known but routinely evaded or denied: democracies send young men and women off to fight, and many of those who return are no longer fit to be citizens. They have been permanently damaged by war and pose a danger to themselves, to others, to society, to democracy. They cannot be repaired. They cannot be reintegrated. We are responsible for them. We inflicted this on them.

In *First Blood*, Rambo is celebrated for his killer expertise. He can deliver untold destruction with a knife, a gun, or his bare hands. His specialty: attrition. He has been "trained to ignore pain and weather." He can live off the land, "eating things that would make a billy goat puke." Not only are all of these skills irrelevant to civic life in democracy. They render him unfit for it. As Rambo declares, "you just don't turn it off." What is more, you hold responsible the community that forced you to serve and made you what you are: "there are no friendly civilians." Even Trautman, his one ally in the film, concedes that he has no idea what to do with Rambo, though he still insists that Rambo was "once very special" no matter what he has become. Trautman speaks for the military, which knowingly sends soldiers such as Rambo back into the world on their own. Rambo rejects civilian life as worthless. It has nothing to offer him, nothing to compare with the responsibilities he enjoyed during war, where he handled million-dollar equipment. Now he cannot even land menial work. Trautman made Rambo fit for war. He thus made him unfit for life in democratic society. Yet Trautman blames him for the destruction of Hope: "You did everything you could to make this private war happen."

An Admission Day would entail not only democracy's acknowledgment of decisions made, actions taken, and consequences reaped. It would also entail a confession of democracy's wrongdoing, an apology, and a plea for forgiveness. This is what we made you do. This is what we did to you. We knew what would happen to you. There is no way to compensate you for this. We wronged you. We harmed you. We ask your forgiveness. A democracy needs to cultivate a sense of pride and pleasure for its brilliance and creativity if it's going to make a unique mark in political life. It also needs to cultivate a sense of shame and remorse for its cruelty and destructiveness if it's going to distinguish itself from other political orders. Pericles would have Athenians fall in love with Athens through his Funeral Oration, doing his best to keep the imperial war machine running. Admission Day would enable citizens to hate their democracy, at least for a time, documenting the homelessness of veterans, the suicide rates of active duty personnel, damage done to marriages, domestic violence, unemployment, and alcohol and drug abuse. If Pericles would have imperial Athens serve as an education for Greeks, Admission Day would constitute an education for democracies.

Political ritual alone would not suffice. The American military publicly opposes the resumption of the draft. It prefers an all-volunteer professional force and does not want to return to the bad old days of the 1960s and 1970s of recalcitrant recruits, to say nothing of war resisters and the burning of draft cards. Yet that is why democracy should reinstate conscription, not so much to make sacrifice egalitarian by redistributing the burdens of citizenship but to fold the very possibility, even likelihood, of resistance into the decision to go to war. Democracy needs to be accountable, which means it needs to be made accountable. Citizens thus need to be put in a position where the consequences of passivity for them are real. John J. Rambo did not exist prior to Vietnam. He had to be made before he could fight in his democracy's global crusade. Imagine instead if democracy, when faced with a decision to go to war, especially a war of choice, had to address citizens who were already like the postwar John J. Rambo, distrustful of authority and capable of violence. It might think twice. It might even blink. Admission Day is not to be an occasion for righting wrongs, for trying to compensate or ameliorate the damage it has inflicted. Democracy should not aspire to let itself off the hook.

Admission Day requires an architectural counterpart in national public space. A memorial prototype already exists: the In Memory Plaque at the Vietnam Veterans Memorial complex. It reads: "In memory of the men and women who served in the Vietnam War and later died as a result of their service. We honor and remember their sacrifice." Though respect and remembrance are insufficient for Admission Day, the fourth Vietnam memorial, while taking traditional commemorative form, pays tribute to those who died as a result of PTSD (suicide) or exposure to defoliants, both of which point to the criminal nature of the war and the crimes we effectively forced our soldiers to commit. The plaque is not an apology, but its implicit logic suggests the need for one to make up for its own deficiencies – its own silences. Citizens can also lose their lives as a result of service in a war without being killed (PTSD again), which means they would not be eligible for inclusion on the Vietnam Veterans Memorial wall or be covered by the plaque. Democracy's living honored dead do not exist, acknowledgment of which presumes a development in memorialization yet to occur. "Casualties of war" is a broader category than states recognize. Death does not exhaust it. The official design of a new Admission Day memorial might also take inspiration from the Japanese American Memorial to Patriotism and read: "Here we admit the wrongs we commit in the name of democracy. We rededicate ourselves to a democracy that does not sacrifice its ideals in order to achieve or secure them."[47]

One of the ambitions behind Admission Day is to place democracy in an ambiguous position when it calls on citizens to serve it in some capacity, especially during war. It should never feel that it can take sacrifice for granted, even to defend the common way of life, which, after all, formally rejects the use of some citizens for the benefit of others. If this self-destructive dynamic becomes a source of shame, it might be preempted or minimized, even if it can't be eliminated. This might place democracy in an awkward, even potentially dangerous, position, but it might also force it to adhere to its ideals with greater integrity. There are no guarantees, of course, but a democracy that encourages skepticism, even anger from its citizens when it goes to war, citizens who can raise democracy's own record against it, may be a democracy worth defending.

3

Democracy at War with Itself

Animals

> For where animals are concerned there is always love.
>
> Jilly Cooper, *Animals in War*

> Dogs do not build monuments to their dead.
>
> William W. Putney, *Always Faithful*

> The greatness of a nation and its moral progress can be judged by the way its animals are treated.
>
> Mahatma Gandhi, *Selected Writings*

J'ACCUSE

On April 1, 2001, Richard Ben Cramer issued a polemic titled "They Were Heroes Too." Published in *Parade Magazine*, it reached an audience of millions.[1] Cramer intended to right what he deemed a conspicuous, longstanding wrong. When it comes to war, America's democracy has perpetrated its share of civic snubs against those who served it. On the Mall in Washington, DC, the nation's sacred symbolic space, the Vietnam Veterans Memorial, the Korean War Memorial, and the World War II Memorial pay tribute to veterans in wars that were, respectively, reviled, forgotten, and slighted. It might seem that the completion of Friedrich St. Florian's grandiose World War II design settled memorial accounts. Not so. A unique group of vets has not received its due. Advocates have pushed for, among other things, a national monument, a tree at Arlington National Cemetery, a commemorative postage stamp, and full inclusion in the National Museum of American History. Each effort resulted in failure, which does not mean efforts to secure recognition have ceased. Cramer assumes that if the country knew of the patriotic crime being committed against some of its most loyal denizens, surely a remedy would emerge. Hence the piece in *Parade Magazine* calling attention to this sorry state of affairs and detailing the heroics of an underappreciated band of brothers – dogs, the dogs we send to war to serve and die on our behalf.[2]

Cramer's reproach, whatever its merits, neglected recent memorial developments.[3] One example: on July 21, 1994, the fiftieth anniversary of Guam's invasion, the Marine War Dog Memorial was unveiled at the United States Marine Corps War Dog Cemetery on the island. The memorial salutes twenty-five dogs killed "liberating Guam in 1944." Featuring the life-size rendering of a Doberman (Kurt), the statue sits on a pedestal surrounded by the graves of twenty-five dogs killed in the name of democracy. Kurt is in the down position, relaxed but ready for action. Ears pointed, he is alert and forever on duty guarding his comrades, much as soldiers "patrol" the space in front of the Tomb of the Unknowns in Arlington National Cemetery. Reminiscent of the Vietnam Veterans Memorial wall in Washington, the names of the dogs (Kurt, Skipper, etc.) are inscribed on the side of the pedestal. The memorial inscription mimics tributes offered humans, invoking the idea of volunteered sacrifice in the name of freedom: "25 Marine War Dogs gave their lives liberating Guam in 1944. They served as sentries, messengers, scouts. They explored caves, detected mines and booby traps. SEMPER FIDELIS." Nevertheless, insofar as no single war dog memorial can be said to constitute a national memorial, the *story* of animals in war remains largely untold. To many animal lovers, this lack is a grave political injustice.

Any sense of injustice, however, seems misplaced, and with this suspicion in mind I plan to make democracy question itself and its commitments. This, in turn, means patriotism must be interrogated. But here patriotism is first and foremost democracy's stand-in or surrogate, thus providing it with much needed cover. Patriotism requires, even demands, public recognition of service to country, especially military service. The demand extends beyond citizens to animals. Ironically, democracy – and thus patriotism – reveals much about itself – no doubt more than intended – through the memorialization of animals. In short, when democracy tells war stories of animals, it backfires. It reveals, even exposes, democracy in a way that few other phenomena can do. To demonstrate and analyze this result, I explore the following questions: What might drive a democracy not only to disregard but also to breach its ethical-political core, thereby setting it on a path of potential self-destruction? Might there be a tragic logic or dynamic at work, and if so, what is it? Moreover, what happens when a democratic people do in fact sacrifice what they claim to love most, that which morally defines them, and celebrate the sacrifice? This involves not just families "giving" mothers and fathers, sons and daughters, and husbands and wives to military service. It also involves another intimate relationship, a unique emotional bond that transcends the purely human. It involves a democracy's readiness to bring even the nonhuman world into its moral and political orbit, cheered on by patriotism. As patriotic democratic culture remains on the alert for new memorial and monumental forms with which to sustain and solidify itself, "man's best friends" come to represent vital political matter. What, then, do the sacrifice of animals and its subsequent celebration signify? Democracy's constitutive attachment to sacrifice, especially death, through patriotism renders it dangerous not only to democratic politics but also in a more fundamental way. Democracy becomes antithetical to life itself insofar as it displays a tendency to do anything to defend itself. Once again, though, democracy can reanimate itself from the tragedies, here horrific, for which it is responsible.

LOVING ANIMALS TO DEATH

Civic memorials make the past present. They also render history an object of contestation that channels and galvanizes the politics of the present. Peoples invent and reinvent themselves in the course of erecting monuments to their triumphs, their tribulations, their achievements, their values. Commemoration and memorialization constitute an existential struggle in which rival political constituencies seek hegemony. Civic expressions of love seek interpretive unanimity – forced if necessary. But resolution or consensus amounts to wishful thinking regarding public architecture. The will to univocality engenders opposition and plurality, vivid evidence of which can be seen in the controversies surrounding design competitions governing public monuments and memorials.

Remarkably, then, politics seems absent in the memorialization of animals. Animals don't divide. They unite. Pet-loving nations that would honor them have no doubts about the legitimacy or necessity of this task. Given the wartime "service" rendered by animals, it would seem impossible not to acknowledge and recognize them in some fashion. Skeptics sometimes need to be educated about the role that animals play in wartime, or they might seek limits on the honors to be accorded them (do not bestow medals, for example) in order to preserve one dimension of the human/animal boundary, but they too wish to pay proper respects.

It is precisely the imperative surrounding animal memorialization that is of concern. What does it say about democracy that people feel compelled to honor animals in the first place? What does it say about democracies that they honor them in the way they do? What does it say about democracies that the following words are read as tribute but not also as self-condemnation: "For their contribution to the war effort, the dogs paid a dear price, but the good they did was still far out of proportion to the sacrifice they made"?[4] Animals cannot share in the fruits of victory. Animal survivors cannot appreciate the sacrifices they made or the tributes they receive. Bereaved animal parents cannot take solace in seeing their offspring's names inscribed in stone for all eternity. Future generations of animals cannot be inspired to match the exploits of their forebears. Animals do not visit sacred public spaces. Ordinarily they are not even allowed on memorial grounds. Memorials to animals, in short, necessarily raise questions about their reason for being. If anything, the very reasons given for honoring animals perform double duty: they simultaneously dishonor those bestowing it. Not only are animals subjected to the known horrors of war. War also turns inward on, even against, animals themselves. War consumes everything in its path, including the very beings that make that consumption possible. Think of war as cannibalization, a kind of killing field for animals (a theme elaborated in Animal Memorialization below).

Still, animal memorials have come to form a valued part of the civic memorial complex. As such, they purport to embody the love that humans and animals share, a love reaching its perfection in wartime. Democracies salute animals and, given the place that animals, perhaps especially dogs, occupy in the lives of human beings, they in turn salute us. It's a mutual admiration and affection society. Yet animal memorials also confirm, solidify, and expand democracy's perverse sanctioning of death in the name of self-defense. As seen in the last chapter, democratic societies feed on sacrifice, which leads to debt, which requires more sacrifice, which is to be redeemed by taking on additional debt, that is, more sacrifice. With animal memorials, democracy approves a new manifestation of sacrifice and a new class of "heroes" to enter the patriotic universe. With death resupplied, these memorials suggest that democracy, thanks in part to patriotism, but only in part, is hostile to life itself. They reveal that democracy, ultimately, respects no boundaries when it feels threatened. When sacrifice, in particular the sacrifice of what is most precious, is considered the condition of possibility of democratic life, a life designed for human beings, the use of animals belies the very notion of limits to sacrifice. Love deepens the greater the sacrifice made on its behalf. Love and cost are thus codependents. As cost rises, it proves love's conviction, which, in turn, makes what is most precious expendable. Democracy, then, exalts what ought to be unthinkable. The animal memorials it builds embody, while obscuring, practices worthier of disbelief and horror than celebration and respect. The democratic commitment that informs animal memorialization seems blind to its own narcissistic, life-denying character. If democracy is at stake, everything is permitted.

TAKE MY LIFE, PLEASE

Sameness informs animal war stories, which differ in one crucial respect from stories about two-legged soldiers. Animals that execute the everyday tasks assigned them become the subjects of heroization. Dogs, for example, are deployed in war for one reason: to save human lives. Anything they do that can be linked to such a result brings encomiums, including to the owners who volunteer them. Performance proves beyond doubt (if there was any doubt) that dogs are brave, loyal, and steadfast. The rigorous training forcibly imposed on them, with absolute obedience required for service, fades from view – even if success must be attained through the select application of pain. Likewise, if dogs cannot be trained, whether due to physical impairment, disease, or so-called character defect, they can and will be destroyed.[5]

What is it that dogs do? They assume many of the most dangerous assignments military forces prefer to spare human beings. Taking point on patrol, especially in jungle settings, is one of the riskiest combat assignments (along with landmine and booby trap detection). It not only exposes dogs to initial enemy fire. Military foes soon adapt to the combat roles dogs play and begin to target them individually, even, in the case of Vietnam, offering bounties for their execution, thereby effectively doubling the danger to which they are exposed.[6] Regardless, dogs are considered successful to the extent that they "alert" to enemy forces or draw fire and prevent the loss of human lives. Dog casualties are ultimately irrelevant. Human life saved means everything.

The United States military supposedly uses dogs for defensive rather than offensive purposes (a hard distinction to make, let alone maintain), since the latter supposedly leads to cruel and excessive treatment. Yet the

United States routinely experiments with – to determine the capabilities of – dogs (and other species). During World War II, for example, the Army attempted to train dogs to destroy enemy pillboxes. It ultimately abandoned the effort, but not because of moral concerns. It was abandoned because the suicide mission proved unworkable. The chaos and wreckage of the battlefield rendered dogs unreliable, even dangerous, to those on whose behalf they were directed to kill. Dogs might return to their handlers just as the explosives they carried were about to detonate. In short, the United States military has operated on the assumption that if dogs can perform a task, especially one considered highly dangerous or risky, they will perform it.[7]

The military starts training working dogs when they are young – between six months and two years. Most malleable in this period, some start as young as five days old.[8] This means that dogs, if we compare them to humans, are taken as "infants" or "children." The regimen forced upon them is difficult, as I indicated above. They must not only learn to obey commands without hesitation. They must also be able to function under circumstances that would ordinarily provoke paralysis or flight. It is critical, therefore, to expose and normalize dogs to battlelike conditions. Subjection to the repetitive sound of gunfire and the deafening, concussive experience of bombardment, both of which shock and horrify dogs, are key components of training. Unlike human soldiers, however, dogs do not understand the difference between appearance and reality. The terror inflicted on them cannot be dismissed or rationalized as a simulation. The suffering that dogs experience in so-called training thus anticipates the real thing more closely than their handlers apparently realize. Since the military ultimately considers dogs to be equipment no different than a machine, this treatment, "bordering on the inhumane," does not necessarily pose ethical problems.[9]

Treating dogs as equipment, the flip side of love, reached its grisly logical conclusion during the Vietnam War. Of the some five thousand military working dogs employed, roughly two hundred returned to the United States.[10] Combat deaths aside, thousands of survivors were left behind with the Army of the Republic of Vietnam. Most were euthanized. None returned to prewar life. Reintegration was deemed too difficult, meaning too expensive, thus making it logistically and fiscally convenient to continue to treat dogs as a species of military property despite the war's end, to be disposed of in whatever manner worked best, that is, posed the fewest problems.

The United States War Dog Association, an advocacy group launched by current and former handlers dedicated to spreading the gospel about military working dogs and securing proper recognition and memorialization for them, enacts the performative contradiction bedeviling animal lovers and animals in war. Though with love, it, too, considers dogs to be property. On the association's website, one finds its K-9 Wall of Honor, a tribute that lists dozens of dogs killed in action and describes the circumstances, invariably heroic, of their deaths. The Wall of Honor also includes the "K-9 promise," which involves people who love dogs most speaking on their behalf. Since animals cannot speak for themselves, one might think the association would deliver a skilled impersonation. Consider the following declaration: "My eyes are your eyes to watch and protect you and yours. My ears are your ears to hear and detect evil minds in the dark. My nose is your nose to scent the invader of your domain. And so you may live my life is also yours."[11] The dog, as it were, dissects and surrenders itself piece by piece to humans to use as they see fit without regard for its well-being – in short, to continue running their vast war machine. Despite the rhetoric of equality the military circulates about dogs as fellow soldiers, the possibility that dogs "in" the military might have needs or wants or interests of their own is here unthinkable. Any of these canine gifts, once taken, means the effective end of the dog's life. The pledge amounts to the dog surrendering its own life and welcoming, even inviting, its own death. For the dog soldier the injunction, "I was only following orders," which means becoming the extension of another's will, represents war's perfection rather than its perversion. Is it any wonder that dogs were made complicit in the torture of enemy prisoners, whether in Vietnam or Iraq?

DO WE LOVE OUR DOGS?

One might think that the use of animals, especially dogs, in war would pose serious ethical problems for the families who donate them, the experts who breed and train them, and the peoples who venerate them. One would be wrong. As nationally renowned dog breeder and self-styled patriot Arlene Erlanger put it after the United States entered World War II, *"the dog world must play its part* in this thing."[12] The imperative reveals human being's power to fabricate and then order the world while evading responsibility for converting one segment of it into standing reserve. Doubtless other so-called animal worlds can be called into being and pressed into service, too. The imperative also suggests democracy's utter ruthlessness when it comes to the conduct of war. Faced with enemies the likes of which the world has never before seen, democracy must not only prove it is equal to the task; it must convince itself that it is equal to the task. To say that the dog world – given life as such, as the dog world – must do its part is to say that dogs, too, must sacrifice and die. Democracy can match fascism deed for brutal deed, if that is what it takes to win the war. Democracy cannot allow its inherent self-anxieties to derail it. It does not enact its way of life only to have that life come back to haunt it at a moment of crisis. It cannot let its values be used against it, especially to destroy it. If this means acting like one's enemy, this is a sacrifice that it can afford to make. Democracy is not a suicide pact, and any suspicions to the contrary need to be dispelled – and during wartime, dispelled with a vengeance. Exceptionalism spawns exceptions.

Democracy's use of the dog world represents more than a free-floating resentment about assuming the burdens of citizenship during wartime. It suggests that death's creative reach can be extended in new, unexpected ways to bind the political order. Erlanger referred vaguely to "what the war means to dogs," which intimates new depths to democracy's narcissism and sense of vulnerability and enmity. Dogs, too, have a stake in "this thing." Life and liberty are at stake for us. Perhaps they are at risk for them, too, because our common enemy does not value life as we do. Either way, they can be "enlisted." They can be rendered part of us. To the objection that dogs are forced to serve in wars for which they are not responsible, the response is ready: this makes dogs no different than the average soldier, who is entitled to no such concern.[13] Apparently a democracy proves it is not a suicide pact by effectively committing moral, if not quite political, self-destruction. Democracy shows the rightness of its cause and the value of what it sacrifices by sacrificing, unbidden, what is most precious to it.

To appreciate the successful military use of animals, especially dogs, and its subsequent public affirmation through memorialization, I turn to Kennan Ferguson's superb essay on dogs and love. It illuminates the love people feel for dogs (and by extension other animals), which scrambles the traditional hierarchy governing human-animal relations. People often bestow not just special privileges but also unique status on pets. When making fundamental ethical decisions, people routinely prioritize dogs over human beings. But how? Doesn't this ranking represent a betrayal of humanity? Doesn't the betrayal, in turn, pose a problem for democratic citizenship and its presumptions of equality and solidarity? How can people choose dogs (or other animals) over their fellow human beings, especially their fellow citizens?[14]

People love dogs, but they love them individually. Specificity matters. People would opt to save their fellow human beings, generally speaking, rather than dogs, generally speaking. Yet people's love of their own dogs is different and undoes otherwise everyday ethical comportments. People and dogs satisfy mutual needs in one another, but "the emotional attachment is not reducible to those needs."[15] Owners would not hesitate to save their pet's life by paying for an expensive operation even if such money could be used to save the lives of other notional human beings. Abstract considerations cannot compete with the specificity of dog love.

Dogs figure as more than objects of care and concern. They can make us better, more fully human. Loving dogs, according to popular belief, indicates "a caring, kind, humane soul." People attain virtue as they transcend narrow self-interest and act on behalf of those "beasts [that] cannot even speak." As people care for dogs, they cultivate skills and aptitudes that redound to human relationships – parent-child, for one. Dogs have also served as role models ("virtuous actors rather than insensate embodiments of abstract virtues") for human beings to emulate. They have even been considered "morally superior to human beings," in part because they were naturally or inherently good and "did not need to remind [themselves] to be loyal and courageous, as did a man." Of course, we were responsible for this moral triumph, for human beings domesticated dogs and thereby expunged their ferocity.[16]

Ironically, the very love of dogs (and other animals) enabling humans to take decisive action on their behalf, to make sacrifices for them, governs the sacrifice that people make of these self-same dogs (and other animals) in wartime. As Ferguson notes, "the ideal canine is one with the human ideals of compassion, loyalty, and bravery." These are its "essential qualities."[17] Not surprisingly, then, dog owners in the United States, Great Britain, and elsewhere have rushed to volunteer their pets for war.[18] Democracy at war presumes the reinstatement of the human/animal boundary transcended by pet love even as it seems to erase it. People love their dogs. They also love their democracy. These loves prove compatible. If people sacrifice whatever is needed to win a war, including their political principles and the people they love most, why not their dogs, too? The specificity that furnishes dogs (and other pets) with a privileged status renders them ideal for service with the advent of war and democracy's demands for sacrifice, to say nothing of its tendency to crush those who oppose military service, particularly those who oppose a war.

While Ferguson is no doubt right that "even if one strongly believes that humans are more important to protect than are dogs, one may not necessarily act that way," democracy's practices in wartime tend to reverse the reversal.[19] Vast numbers of pets fail to return home conflict after conflict, but owners continue to volunteer them with every repetition of war. Jilly Cooper suspects that if people knew the kind of training their dogs must endure to go to war, they might change their minds. But given that people equate war with death and assume (or at least fear) that their dear pets may not return, the attribution of a protective reaction to pet owners, once fully informed about training, seems unwarranted.[20] Dog owners prepared the ground for their own sacrifices. With the advent of pet cemeteries and ceremonies to bury and memorialize dogs, people were predisposed to mourn the loss of their beloveds.[21] Dying for democracy, the greatest political good, would only double the love they feel for their pets.

BUILD IT AND THEY WILL COME?

In 2004 the Animals in War Memorial was unveiled in London. The monument covers not just the twentieth century and its gruesome conflicts but also warfare throughout history. The use of animals to fight wars did not originate in the modern age, though it may have been pushed to new destructive extremes (thanks to technological prowess) in the 1900s. In World War I, some eight million horses perished. The staggering figure stems largely from the logistical reality that war would have been impossible to wage without them. Given the state of European battlefields, which ultimately rendered trucks useless, horses (and mules and donkeys) became the condition of possibility of war. It did not matter how many died. They enabled war to continue. It would have ground to a halt in their absence, which was unthinkable. Animals in War, then, would seem to have much memorial work to do, especially for a democracy, which values life first of all.

At first glance Animals in War displays a feel for ambiguity. Two inscriptions confront the visitor on one of two large walls. One inscription pays tribute to "all the animals that served and died alongside British and Allied forces in wars and campaigns throughout time." The other inscription states, "They had no choice." Reminiscent of the Vietnam Veterans Memorial wall in Washington, DC, Animals in War seems to understand the dilemmatic character of its memorial undertaking. Nevertheless, the four monumental figures represented – two cargo-bearing mules enacting the burdens of war on the lower side of the walls, a frolicking horse and carefree dog representing "hope for the future" on the higher side of the walls – betray little, if anything, of war's actual experiences. The mules are supposed to be hard at work, depicting sacrifice in action, but the sculptures do not register viscerally. Death has no architectural presence in them. Animals in War is a conservative memorial form. It resembles Frederick Hart's The Three Servicemen at the Vietnam Veterans Memorial complex, a banal representational sculpture designed to convey the youth, innocence, and vulnerability of men at war, ostensibly honoring "sacrifice" while ignoring the war's imperial, arguably genocidal, certainly self-destructive character.[22] Likewise Animals in War seems gestural, corresponding to the supporting role that animals, by definition, play in war. They served, as it were, and died, yes, but their suffering could not compare to what human beings endured. They may have had no choice, but consent is irrelevant regarding animals. The four-word inscription intimates resignation, perhaps a lament, rather than a criticism, rebuke, or condemnation. War deals in necessities, after all. We had no choice either.

Though the memorial seems to suggest otherwise, democracy is also a victim of war, in part because of the manner in which it fights war. An inscription on the far side of the wall to the mules' right informs the visitor that "many and various animals were *employed* ... and as a result *millions died* from the pigeon to the elephant. They all played a vital role in every region of the world *in the cause of human freedom*. Their contribution must never be forgotten."[23] The role they played in the cause they served means mass carnage can be incorporated without a hitch into the traditional (self-serving) narrative that democracies tell – must tell – about themselves. Note the passive, understated formulations. Animals were employed. Millions died. Democracy's self-image and reputation remain intact insofar as things that merely happen cannot alter or affect the ideal on behalf of which civic memorials arise.[24] Animals in War honors creatures who contributed to "the cause of human freedom," which is uniquely associated with democracy. Nevertheless, what do the architectural inscriptions reveal without formally disclosing? What does the mnemonic imperative to memorialize mass death (however sanitized) in perpetuity signify?

America's World War II Memorial also proclaims the duty of eternal remembrance, driven by a notion of debt. Balancing civic accounts helps fund endless sacrifice. Pericles established the official terms of payment twenty-five hundred years ago in his funeral oration, as we saw in Chapter 2. Each generation must surpass the achievements of its forebears and enhance the legacy bequeathed to it (even at great cost). Once this is done, can debts be considered paid? No. New debt has been generated, requiring more sacrifice, leading to new debt. And so on ad infinitum.

Why have I rehearsed this logic again? For animals in war, debt's unpayability works differently. They do not and cannot participate in, let alone benefit from, war's outcome or aftermath. They have no legacy to enhance. Wars to make the world safe for democracy and freedom offer no returns (nor could they) to animals. Debt is not only unpayable to animals. The very notion of debt, implying a reciprocal relationship of some kind, denies what was done to them. Animals did not just die from employment, as the Animals in War Memorial suggests. They were subject to an exterminatory logic to enable, to facilitate, to wage, and to win war. Democracy proves itself more than a match for regimes that, because of their authoritarian or totalitarian character, are thought to enjoy an advantage in war because of their moral and political inferiority. The dog world must do its part.

Again, to appreciate the successful military use of animals, it might be illuminating to compare the treatment of animals in war to the treatment of animals in other domains. It is true, for example, that humans breed animals at industrial scale in order to feed on them at leisure. Here the creation and reproduction of animal life results in countless deaths. Yet it still serves and perpetuates life. The idea is always to create new and more life (if for consumption). Life is thus to be preserved. Death must be controlled, contained. When it comes to war and its celebration, even in democracy, animals fare differently. War, too, produces countless deaths, but if every member of another species were eradicated in the course of a hard-won victory, it would fall within the parameters of democracy's war logic, not run contrary to it. Death may be not just final but also total, suggesting hostility to life in its plurality. What's one fewer species, more or less, if the world is made safe for (our) democracy?

Ultimately, Animals in War not only confirms and solidifies democracy's death logic. It also enhances and extends it. Think memorial art as colonization. The playful horse and adorable dog toward which the mules walk suggest that animal sacrifice enables a better world, including for animals themselves, thus justifying the toll exacted. Death turns out to be good for all creatures, and democracy celebrates it.

The sleight of hand perpetrated by Animals in War is masterful. Compare it, first, to the Cenotaph in Whitehall, London, an "empty tomb" built to salute World War I dead. Deceptively simple in design, the Cenotaph embodies rather than denies the traumas of war, including the doubtful character of victory. Geography forces it into daily city life. Located in the middle of street traffic at the heart of national government, it becomes that which cannot be circumvented. Jenny Edkins argues: "[The Cenotaph] attempts no narrative or interpretation. It marks something that is shared yet inexpressible in more explicit terms. What is shared, we might say, is the inexpressibility."[25] Compare it, next, to the civil rights memorials at Kelly Ingram Park in Birmingham, Alabama. Unlike James Drake's *Police and Dog Attack* or Ronald S. McDowell's *The Salute to the Foot Soldiers*, both of which depict police attack dogs in action to induce in visitors an experience of citizens subjected to state violence, Animals in War effectively erases what it purports to reconstruct. With memorial visitors reduced to mere spectators, they are treated to a scene of mules at work that could be located almost anywhere, anytime, anyplace. Animals in war? What war?

To design a tragic democratic memorial to animals, democracy needs to acknowledge that its commitment to the necessity of its own survival involves sacrificing the lives of creatures utterly indifferent to democracy, not by choice but by nature. This does not mean, however, that they are indifferent to their own lives. To animate war, to materialize its horrors, to render animal "contributions" real, war's destructive impact on the animals themselves needs to be imparted. Since World War I took such a heavy toll on animals, why not convey mules drowning in craters of mud and water? Why not horses dismembered, remnants of body parts strewn about? Why not dog corpses piled on top of dog corpses? Or, more subtly, why not present a mélange of animals on one side of the walls and leave the other side vacant, suggesting that animals enter the war machine but do not exit it? Wouldn't this facilitate remembrance (and perhaps something more)? At this site, however, these kinds of questions are misplaced. Animals in War is a political memorial. If it were actually a memorial to animals in war, it would need to call its very reason for being into question, moving from tribute to counter-monument.[26] Rather, mimicking the Japanese-American Memorial to Patriotism During World War II in Washington, DC, which encapsulates America's apology for incarcerating its own citizens after Pearl Harbor yet largely salutes the country making the apology for in fact making an apology, Animals in War affirms the goodness of a political regime, democracy, that publicly addresses the costs of war – a candor that serves to enhance democratic greatness.

INTERLUDE: *WAR HORSE*

War Horse, according to *The Washington Post*'s Ann Hornaday, constitutes "a meditation on the absurdity of war" and explores "man's inhumanity to man." *Slate*'s Dana Stevens compares Steven Spielberg's recent epic to Stanley Kubrick's *Paths of Glory*, insisting "there's nothing remotely martial about its spirit. Just beneath the movie's folksy sweetness lies a powerful and painful critique of war." Chris Tookey of *The Daily Mail* admits the film made him weep (and insists that we will, too), given its dominant motif: "a sense of the waste of war, its horror as well as its heroism." A. O. Scott in *The New York Times* notes *War Horse*'s "anti-war message," which "registers the loss and horror of a gruesomely irrational episode in history."[27]

These critics understand that Spielberg is a master of sentimentality and emotional manipulation, even and especially when it's heavy-handed. Still, *War Horse* distinguishes itself by making an unusual cinematic contribution to the transcendent power of sacrificial love on behalf of democracy. Here the sacrifice comes at the expense of horses and, by extension, all animals in war. If *Saving Private Ryan* is the official film of Washington's World War II Memorial, then *War Horse* is the official film of London's Animals in War Memorial.

War Horse relates the odyssey of Joey, a thoroughbred colt whose birth at film's opening augurs great things to come. Joey is not like other horses. Not only does he possess the capacity to draw on seemingly unlimited inner resources to survive and overcome any and all circumstances. By virtue of his charismatic example he makes those, human or horse, around him aspire to great things as well. Joey is a virtuoso. Contrary to what Richard Schickel claims, he is not "just a horse."[28]

War Horse revolves around the Narracott family. Ted Narracott, a decorated, quietly disgruntled veteran of the Boer War who rents a farm and tries to scratch out a subsistence living, buys Joey at auction to spite his landlord. We know it is only a matter of time before this reckless decision backfires. Joey is able to delay the day of reckoning by accepting a bridle and learning, with preternatural speed, to become a plough horse. The apparently self-induced transformation saves the family farm (albeit briefly), as Albert (Ted's teenage son) and Joey plough, in a single day, a rock-filled slab of land previously deemed unworkable. Since birth, everyone knew Joey was special. Now there is proof positive. Joey's self-overcoming is matched by Albert's, who exhausts and injures himself alongside Joey to get the job done. Albert is no longer an immature teen. Joey enables the family to be free.

In *War Horse* home may be a beautiful aspiration, always already in the process of realization, but life also seems marred by contingencies. Torrential rains destroy the family's commercial crop, and Ted Narracott is forced to sell Joey to pay the rent and "keep" the farm. The sale happens to coincide with the advent of World War I, and Joey becomes the property of a young cavalry officer who promises, if implausibly, a distraught Albert to bring him home following the war. This being a Spielberg film, war or not, we know it's going to happen. Schickel remarked in *Time*: "Are we more or less convinced that somehow, against all the terrible odds, horse and horseman will be reunited? Yes, I suppose we are. What would be the point of telling this story if it ended tragically?"[29] Schickel's rhetorical question can and must be answered, but the sentimental, nostalgic spirit that leads him to pose it also fuels the film.

Joey is trained to be a cavalry horse and, given his brief but distinguished life to date, there is no doubt that he will make the best of cavalry horses. While charging into battle might seem to fit a thoroughbred, it still requires discipline and fearlessness, a willingness to court danger and to risk not just injury but also life itself. Joey's experience in the fields of Devon has prepared him well to meet the challenge. His nature is also critical. The film projects onto Joey the best human qualities: he is strong, brave, loyal, hardworking, fearless, and even heroic. That Joey doesn't think much also contributes to his virtuous character. He follows orders and does more than what is expected of him, the keys to being a freedom fighter for the ages.

Joey's battle debut starts brilliantly. The British cavalry, assembling in a contiguous wheat field, attack an apparently exposed and unsuspecting German camp. Janusz Kaminski, *War Horse* cinematographer, wanted to depict the unity of soldier and horse, human being and nature, which makes men "feel so powerful." Many enemy soldiers are cut down by the sword, but resounding British victory quickly becomes crushing, embarrassing defeat: the Germans, with machine guns ready, were waiting for them in the woods at the edge of the open plain where they were bivouacked. The horses charge forward at breakneck speed. As the catastrophe unfolds, riders disappear one by one, including Joey's. Still, the horses continue charging, now alone. Spielberg's camera lingers on the horses to signal death through absence. The reversal is jarring. The trap also takes its toll on the horses themselves. Yet, unlike with *Saving Private Ryan*, the audience sees no human or equine carnage as it happens. Combat has been aestheticized and anesthetized.

After the attack grinds to a halt and Joey is captured, a smattering of dead horses can be seen, yet these horses are neatly arranged. The blood that drenched the breaking waves and shoreline of Normandy in *Saving Private Ryan* is missing. Horses die but somehow remain intact, even beautiful. Spielberg's discretion, as it were, suggests that the film has no intention of explicitly disclosing the horrors of war, especially as it pertains to the animals pressed into "service." Does this matter? Might not subtlety work just as effectively by making the audience do the imaginative work? Perhaps, but Spielberg's approach is ethically problematic insofar as it grossly underplays – and thereby obscures, perhaps even erases – the scale of the killing of horses (and other animals) in World War I, where eight million horses alone perished – a number worth repeating. A single cavalry charge, however presented, does not seem adequate to signal the industrial nature of animal slaughter. Aristocratic notions of war and its nobility may have been shredded by German machine guns, but the romance with war continues.

Joey falls into German hands and is put to work as a cog in its military machine. In Spielberg's hands, the Germans subject Joey and other horses to barbaric cruelty supposedly spared them by Allied forces (cavalry horses run, which is their nature, which means they're doing what they were born to do). This led Dana Stevens to comment that the German Army's "treatment of animals alone would be justification for waging war on them."[30] Democracy always maintains its superiority, even in exploitation. Undaunted, Joey again rises to the occasion – and even brings at least one German soldier along with him, who looks out for Joey and his friend, Topthorn, a beautiful black steed sadly lacking Joey's transcendent gifts.

Joey's sojourn in German hands is the occasion for somewhat greater realism on Spielberg's part, though it remains muted. Horses are forced to pull gigantic German artillery pieces along steep, muddy hills. As one horse after another perishes from this brutal labor, more take their places. The exhausted are executed on the spot. There are always more horses to fill the self-perpetuating void the war machine creates. As Topthorn's turn comes, his German caretaker advises against it. Already seriously injured and weakened, he will not survive. Indifferent, the commanding German officer orders Topthorn into the train. Seeing that his companion is about to be placed in harm's lethal way, Joey runs up beside him and effectively protests. A take-me-instead sacrifice, Joey saves Topthorn. Joey's farm experience, however, means that he can meet the demands placed on him, demands that would kill any mere mortal horse.

As Joey makes his grueling way up the hill, nearly buckling several times, Spielberg's camera offers us a glimpse (in the corner of the screen) of a pile of dead horses. As with the overhead shot of the post-charge cavalry scene, the nominal gesture to war's horrors seriously downplays the toll taken on the animal world. Besides, Joey survives Howitzer duty, thus confirming the virtue he possesses as a horse-soldier. Once again, the circumstances in which Joey finds himself realize the best in him. War enables him to achieve new distinction. If virtue names a struggle with and overcoming of limits, Joey is indeed a virtuoso. There is apparently nothing he cannot do or survive. Like John J. Rambo, he was made for war.

Joey's exemplarity ultimately saves his life. Released in the nick of time by his sympathetic German handler, who thereby risks summary execution, Joey makes a mad dash for survival – and freedom. Trapped amid the trenches in no-man's land, Joey runs here, there, back, and around in desperation, getting entangled in more and more barbed wire. Joey's life seems at an end, but English and German lookouts spot a strange sight midway between their respective lines and venture out to see the bizarre spectacle of a horse engulfed in wire. Arriving more or less simultaneously, the enemy soldiers, inspired by Joey's will to live, conspire to free him. Animals make us better. The English soldier dubs Joey "war horse, a strange beast." Joey, of course, is their (our) creation, though the responsibility that attends ownership seems to elude them. It seems that they believe Joey has done this to himself. Once freed, each side wants to take him "home." Awed by Joey, they settle the dispute by flipping a coin. Joey has momentarily brought peace to the front.

Repatriated, Joey is considered and treated like a miracle horse. Ann Hornaday treats Joey's odyssey as a "secular passion play," but Joey does not die. He is a figure that transcends death. Though he performed heroic deeds in the war, his work remains unfinished. Home has been rendered safe from external threat thanks to "soldiers" such as Joey. This military status is bestowed upon him by an Army surgeon who had ordered his death because of a supposedly fatal infection. Enter Albert. Given the war's length, Albert enlisted and, like Joey, acquitted himself admirably. Hearing of the miracle horse nearby, Albert seeks him out. Their reunion signals one last reunion to come, at home, where it all began, where the long-divided family awaits their return – and healing powers. Democracy and life ostensibly triumph in the end, but they do so thanks to the mass death and slaughter of a world war in which democracies eagerly participated. The film's mantra, repeated by friend, ally, and enemy alike, "The war has taken everything from everyone," finds itself repudiated at film's close. Instead Joey joins the animals in the Animals in War Memorial, ready to frolic at last. War? What war?

ANIMAL MEMORIALIZATION: A (BRIEF) GENEALOGY

Animals in War is part of a transnational trend. Equally troubling are the identical war dog memorials built at March Air Field Museum, March Air Force Base, Riverside, California, and at Sacrifice Field, National Infantry Museum, Fort Benning, Georgia. Each showcases a soldier, standing, peering into the distance. A German shepherd, leashed, sits next to him. Both are alert, especially the dog, but not quite tense. They are ready for action, on call for democracy. They ooze power, confidence, security, and strength. At the dedication ceremony in Riverside, California, Associate Supreme Court Justice Ming Chin, a decorated Vietnam War officer, welcomed the war dogs home, repatriated at last – like their human comrades were "returned" through the Vietnam Veterans Memorial wall. Betrayed by the country they served, the Vietnam War dogs were left behind at war's finish, their fate mimicking the POWs and MIAs allegedly abandoned. Chin reminds the audience that dogs have feelings, too. They feel; they hurt; they suffer. But most important of all, they save human lives. Thus dogs are elevated – only to be reduced, put in their place. As the ceremony concludes, hundreds of Vietnam veterans walk by the statue, pause, and pet the dog as if it were real, alive.[31] But only they are alive.

The growing effort to pay tribute to animals in war raises questions that call the enterprise itself into question. How is that millions of animals have died? What were the circumstances of their deaths? What do these circumstances reveal about not just warfare but also the moral and political values of the creature that wages war against itself and implicates other species? Does the democratic scheme of animal memorialization facilitate the cruelties inflicted on animals and make them more likely to be repeated? Do those who document and salute animal service also provide damning substantiation against the very practice they endorse? At the end of the memorial day, does not the use of animals in war constitute another subject for Admission Day (introduced in the last chapter)?

Democracies presume that the onset of war means the animal world becomes available for use as they see fit. Animals are assigned routinely to a number of tasks. Effectiveness is the only criterion, as mentioned above. First among priorities: if animals can be used to save human life, they will be so used. The danger attending the assignment does not matter. Nor does it matter if animals lose their lives in the process. How could it? The point of animal use is to do whatever it takes to protect and save human lives. The number of animals killed likewise makes no difference. As long as war goes on and animals can be used to "good" purpose, they will be so used. If this entails deploying animals without properly caring for them, which in turn can mean working them until expiration – that is, working them literally to death – they will be so worked. The logic is exterminatory. If every member of a species has to be sacrificed to win a war, winning trumps life, including its very plurality. What is the evidence for this?

Even ostensibly humanitarian organizations such as the Royal Society for the Prevention of Cruelty to Animals contribute to the logic of total sacrifice. Starting with the Franco-Prussian War, the Royal Society's advocacy for better care and treatment of animals exacerbated their exploitation. Those wounded could be treated and returned to service – whether they were fully healed or capable.[32] It is better to extract as much labor as is possible from beasts of burden than to let them die and get nothing. For one thing, it was unclear if more animals would (soon) be forthcoming and "there was a war to be won," which meant fueling and refueling the military machine.

This logic takes remarkable turns as it unfolds. In World War I, for example, pigeons were used extensively for communication. Not only did "enlistment" subject them to a life likely to be nasty, brutish, and short. Not only did it subject them to specific countermeasures that escalated their risk (the Germans targeted them with hawks and falcons, thus pitting nature against itself, as well as machine gun fire). Their utter disposability subjected them to eradication, by any means necessary, by the very people exploiting them and recognizing their value. One British commander, rather than let 2,500 pigeons fall under enemy control, set them on fire and burned them to death.[33] In east Africa, 1916–1917, over ten thousand donkeys and horses died from exposure to tsetse flies. Once the first contingent expired, a second shipment was brought in despite the consequences. The temporary cure, arsenic, extended their miserable lives a few weeks before they dropped dead in their tracks.[34] In World War II, the Soviets trained dogs to run beneath tanks with explosives strapped to their backs. Poland was emptied of dogs (it was rumored) for these one-way missions.[35] The British needed mules for transport in Burma, where they were deemed uniquely suited to local conditions. Yet they had a tendency to bray, which could place human lives in danger. The military thus severed the vocal cords of some 5,500 mules before shipping them overseas. Also in Burma, elephants were used extensively to build bridges and roads. But if the British could not use them, no one could. The Royal Air Force targeted elephants employed by the Japanese. When circumstances became dire enough, again in World War I, the British slaughtered transport horses for food and comfort (mattresses).[36] This reduced the subordinate standing from which they already suffered. Not only were horses killed as war exploded at and around them. They were literally deconstructed and converted into so many usable pieces and edible parts.

Once World War I ended, the British War Office insisted on some kind of return on its investment and declared the remaining horses unfit for duty so they could be sold to slaughterhouses.[37] The French required no such rationale, let alone return on investment. They destroyed 15,000 dogs (a policy duplicated by other combatants).[38] Even mascots, animals exempted from combat duty and designed to provide emotional comfort, could find themselves converted to food.[39] Still in World War I, the British, having exhausted their supply of camels, appropriated 3,000 cow camels, most of them pregnant. They were forced to give birth along the way. This doubled the risk to the life of camels as such.[40] At one moment, it makes good logistical sense to slaughter those we claim, at another moment, to be serving alongside us and to be our fellow soldiers.[41] Cooper inadvertently expresses the logic of exploitation: "a dead mule was only a disaster if he floated out to sea with his pack saddle on."[42] By extension, an injured dog was only a disaster if it was deliberately disabled to make it exempt from combat operations, which happened, if infrequently, in Vietnam.[43]

DEMOCRACY AND LIFE ITSELF

How does democracy display hostility to life itself? The answer can be found not only in the logic of sacrifice central to democracy and in democracy's celebration of sacrifice. More than death, more than the potential reduction of plurality, is involved as well. Democracy demands not only the giving and taking of life as *the* test of civic love. It also demands, as a condition of possibility of sacrifice, life's conformity to its political-military projects and dictates.

Life is an elusive notion. It cannot be reduced to one aspect or dimension to provide a definition. Nietzsche, however, posits resistance as a constitutive element of life – as opposed to creation, unity, or harmonization. Nietzsche's projection corresponds to a conception of life as will to power. Insofar as the human animal requires social form to complete it yet is not designed to receive any one form in particular, power performs the work of completion – hence the inescapable element of resistance. Will to power, then, simultaneously engenders opposition to its very exercise.[44]

The Nietzschean projection need not be confined to the human animal.[45] Training animals for war proceeds on the ontological assumption that nature can be mastered and bent to specifications, given human being's creative power and nature's inherent susceptibility to fashioning. Cooper's *Animals in War* records the "heroic" and "sacrificial" deeds of various species of animals conscripted and trained for military service. It also, if inadvertently, documents the active resistance of animals to the military projects of their human overlords and the latter's response to that resistance.

Mules seem particularly predisposed to balk at military work, though Cooper converts resistance into personality quirks, thereby concealing and co-opting their opposition. Mules thus become "mischievous," "tricky customers," "characters" who do not "suffer fools gladly." According to Cooper this means that mules must be handled with particular care, manipulated with the right touch, for "like many husbands, in fact, you cannot coerce the mule, but he will do anything if he thinks it's his idea in the first place."[46] The violence mules direct against their human handlers can thus be redescribed and effectively negated, a sign not of resistance or refusal at the demands that compulsory service entails but of the incompetence of the trainer or driver. The use of mules would be free of incident if only people actually knew – as they should know, since we possess the necessary expertise – what they were doing. Knowledge can preempt, or, if that somehow fails, overcome any infelicity.

Still, Cooper's narrative does not quite convince: "But as [one] General Daunt points out ... it is a case of one bad apple. Of the 200 mules [he] supervised [in World War I], only one was really dangerous; and he was a killer. If you took your eyes off him for a second, he had you in his teeth, shaking you like a terrier with a rat. There always had to be two men in the stable with him, one to groom, one to watch." General Daunt's recollection may be amusing, but examine it more closely. He speaks of "one bad apple." He insists that "only one was really dangerous," but "he was a killer." Insofar as mules do not cooperate as planned, Cooper either

suggests it's just an unfortunate contingency or brings moral approba-
tion to bear on the species, thus indicating where responsibility for failure lies. Either way, bad apples are discarded to prevent contamination
from spreading. Even when complimenting mules, she salutes – in order
to conceal – the violence done to them. One mule named "Jimmy Gray"
becomes a source of ironic amusement: he's a "character" that invariably
performed well under fire but always resented the transportation process
at the start of the work week. At week's close, however, he welcomed it.
Resentment aside, Jimmy always wound up in the truck.[47]

Jimmy and other animals embody Nietzsche's ontological given: resistance. Like humans, animals are not designed to receive nor are they inherently susceptible to the form to be imposed on them. Referring to and
treating animals as if they were fellow soldiers cannot alter this actuality,
though it may deny or obscure it. Violence, therefore, must be deployed
to accomplish the training to which they are subjected. Tellingly, it would
not occur to Cooper that animals might resist the identity selected for
them as an affirmation or expression of life. Such recognition would
differ from Cooper's appreciation of the difficulty of training animals,
which often fails. Failure is attributable not to any constitutive human or
animal characteristic but to this or that contingent aspect of training or
perhaps some temporary human limitation (regarding expert knowledge,
for example).

Cooper's tales of mules shipped to Burma also reveal animal dispositions. They routinely tried to break free of their restraints and would
be shot if they kicked at the plane's interior walls, which might damage them. Difficulties did not end with transport. As mentioned earlier,
mules bray to communicate, and this habit could place soldiers in danger
by advertising their very existence and also their position to the enemy
(which tended not to use mules). Since quiet was the key to the effective
use of mules, they were silenced, their vocal cords cut. The medical arts,
designed to heal, to protect and save life, were deployed to make its sacrifice possible. Rather than heed, let alone respect, animal recalcitrance,
humans effectively disabled one of the principal means through which
anger and annoyance – that is, resistance – manifests itself. If one started
braying, the rest would follow suit (more bad apples). It was not enough
that resistance be overcome by training. The very possibility of resistance
had to be subverted as well, in this case rendered mute. While most mules
apparently "adapted" to mutilation, many did not. They would bite and
kick even more and try to dislodge their cargo. They needed to be handled with additional care.[48] These signs of resistance and resentment were

otherwise ignored. The military's and Cooper's sole concern was that following surgery the mules would return to work as quickly as possible.

Dogs, too, resist human manufacture, resulting in their destruction. To defy human mastery and discipline is to become, by definition, dangerous. Subsequent killing is blamed on the dog, of course – for being defective, that is, untrainable. If a dog cannot be trained, it loses the value it might have acquired through usability. Without value, mere existence cannot justify its life. Recall the strange formulation of Arlene Erlanger, one of America's leading canine trainers, that "the dog world must do its part." The claim at once signals and refuses both the independence and alterity of dogs. The presumption driving the moral imperative reflects and enacts dogs' subordinate status, thereby obscuring their violent appropriation. Morality conceals immorality. War means the lives of dogs cannot be allowed to continue as before, as if nothing has happened – even though nothing has happened as far as they are concerned. They cannot be allowed to be *just* dogs.

Despite domestication, dogs compose a separate and distinct species, contributing to the world's diversity and plurality. Even the best-trained pets resist domestication. Dogs can turn on their owners in an instant. Millions of dogs bite people every year, resulting in euthanasia for thousands. Think also of the beloved pet that sleeps on the forbidden couch, pries open the kitchen trash in search of hidden treasure as soon as it is alone, or jumps onto the stove because it seems like fun. These animals and their worlds have nothing to do with humankind's geopolitical conflicts and crusades. Yet this independence does not shield them from or protect them against human sovereignty, thus human appropriation.

Perhaps Rousseau's characterization of the alleged difference between humans and animals informed Cooper's benign narrative. While humans find themselves endowed, thanks to the Author of Things, with the nearly unlimited faculty of perfectibility, animals find themselves stuck in eternal sameness. Rousseau insists: "an animal is at the end of a few months what it will be all its life; and its species is at the end of a thousand years what it was the first year of that thousand."[49] For Cooper, apparently, it is impossible for an animal to become more than it is. This prejudice, given or nurtured, makes exploitation easier. Cooper again provides critical evidence, though she misses one possible upshot of her own story. In Burma during World War II, elephants built bridges, roads, and ships. They also hauled trees to satisfy England's insatiable demand for lumber. Elephants would lift huge logs ten feet high for transport, an exercise placing their drivers in danger. The risk was not lost on one elephant. After nearly losing control of a log, it "pondered for a minute. Then it searched round for and found a stout stick and wedged it vertically between one of its tusks and his trunk, so the log was checked if it rolled backwards. Thus assured of his driver's safety, it carried on picking up logs and lifting them onto the platform as easily as a mobile crane."[50]

Cooper also recounts a famous Roman battle against the Syrians in 190 B.C.E. in which elephants stampeded the Syrians deploying them. Plutarch describes elephants spearing soldiers with tusks and pitching them in the air. For Cooper this kind of episode indicates nothing more than animal contingency. Yet life does not just allow itself to be converted into standing reserve. Reflexive refusal to appropriation, possession, organization, and use suggests resistance. In war, democracies not only take life; they also crush resistance to their taking it – that is, to life itself.[51] As a result, democracies, the champions of life and freedom, demonstrate lethal hostility to what they could construe as instances or even exercises of independence – and they do so in the name of life itself.

RE-COVERING SACRIFICE

Given the underlying assumption of disposability, animal casualties in war should become not just indefensible but also unthinkable – even for those advocating their use. As the Animals in War Memorial indicates, peoples seek to justify or redeem the slaughter to which they give sanction, an alchemical process at which even democracies excel. One strategy centers on recovering the notion of choice, the hallmark of freedom, the lifeblood of democracy. As mentioned above, animals undergo brutal, oftentimes sadistic training to be able to perform in wartime conditions. Unaccustomed to machine gun, mortar, or artillery fire, they must be exposed, repeatedly, to each of them. Food is the weapon of choice in training. Hunger conquers all, including fear – just wait long enough.[52] Pain is prohibited, scorned – unless other methods prove ineffective, of course. Despite the requirements, goals, and success of training, experts insist that an animal such as a dog cannot be made to do whatever we like.[53] Dogs, the story goes, have a will of their own.[54] In the end, what they are made to do in war, which puts them in harm's way and generates countless casualties, is nothing other than what they (would) want to do for us anyway. Cooper, speaking of the dog in itself, insists: "he acted out of love, not because he was made to."[55]

Armed with this understanding, Cooper writes of one of war's "redeeming" features: the mutual devotion that develops between human and animal. Humans come to experience animals as extensions of themselves. Animals reciprocate the feeling.[56] Hence the story of the dog left behind as his master ships off to France who (somehow) tracks him down overseas. This feat testifies to the unique bond joining humans and animals. The dog could only be at home by his master's side. It might look like we exploit them, but they want to serve us and because they do, service ennobles both them and us and negates the possibility of exploitation.[57] The sense of home and family, which unites human and animal, makes it possible to assert that in war the dog world must do its part. We're in it together. It's a seamless transition for dogs to provide on the battlefield the love and devotion they provide at home. These dispositions must be hardened, sharpened, honed. Then they can be put to the test. Just as a citizen's love of democracy can be truly tested only in war, a dog's love can be enhanced, exalted, and proved through a conflict about which it can know nothing.[58]

Celebrants of animals in war recount, ad nauseam, stories of what animals have done to save human lives for a reason; the exploits so astound that they must point to something deeper, a bond or connection suggesting animals had no choice but to act as *they* did, which would give new meaning to the dominant inscription on the Animals in War Memorial. This is what *they* had to do. Animals cannot just be responding to the training they have received. Training alone would not enable them to endure and overcome the pain and agony they suffer.

Consider in this regard Satan, a half-breed greyhound serving the French in World War I. With one corner of Verdun hanging in the balance and a French position about to crumble, this dog races to deliver news. Shot hundreds of yards from French lines, his master stands up in full view of the enemy and yells, "Courage, Satan, my friend. Come for France." The handler is killed, but Satan rises from the dead and returns to the lines with information that help would be forthcoming. Since Satan also carried pigeons on his back, the beleaguered French were able to communicate the position of German batteries targeting them and target them in return. French lives were saved.[59]

If the explanations of animal advocates seem self-serving, what else accounts for a democracy's extraordinary ability to sacrifice the world's creatures large and small? One possibility: democracy tends to suffer from a foundational ambivalence. Commitment to its own political principles is uneven, unstable, and inconsistent. The people's shaky devotion and dedication to democracy may flow from frustration with its own sovereign power. As Rousseau claims, there is no law the people cannot touch if it suits them – including the best of laws, even the social compact. Democracy, then, tells the people they are sovereign. Constitutions salute their authority. Politicians pay homage to them in elections. Courts interpret statutes on their behalf. Yet the experience of democracy teaches people they are sovereign in name only, and the results democracy routinely produces rarely satisfy them. The people, not surprisingly, often hold democracy itself responsible. Democracy's vaunted strengths look more apparent than real, and people find themselves less than enthusiastic about its inherent value. They do not possess an appreciation for its everyday failures and shortcomings, certainly not as part of its fundamental makeup, let alone as a sign of its success. Democracies do not like to say to themselves, especially in times of crisis: "We're not allowed to do this, even at the risk of our polity." In war they can "safely" allocate to themselves power they can only dream of in peacetime. And when the opportunity comes, it extends to things great and small.

Democracies also wrestle with their own sense of exceptionalism, the conviction that they represent a superior political form. Democracies can invoke or rely on their political status as they pursue problematic courses of action, especially in times of emergency. Because they believe they enjoy lofty credentials and have built solid records of achievement, they also believe they can afford a few debits on their otherwise sound moral and political ledgers. Democracies may also presume their superior political identity transforms the character of objectionable acts into acceptable deeds (when rooted in necessity, of course). Democracies can even consolidate their pedigree by citing the damage they do to themselves when knowingly transgressing their own norms. This very willingness and ability confirm their good intentions. Thus violating norms can perversely prove commitment to them, not despite but precisely because of bad acts.

If, then, a democracy resorts, on occasion, to evil, it retains its privileged moral and political identity. This might be especially true in times of war when a democracy, feeling the pressure of events, converts strengths to be celebrated into impediments to be removed – if temporarily. Thus a democracy can find itself compromising its fundamental values – whether sacrificing liberty for security or exploiting resources available to it, human and animal, that should remain untouched. A curious kind of existential bitterness may also be operative, as democracies recoil at the limits (expectations, standards, demands, constraints, etc.) placed on them that other regimes do not experience and would have no qualms about breaking if they were subject to them. Democracies, then, resent the "handicaps" they place on themselves – and the world insists they obey – and make others pay the price – in this case, animals. When democracy feels weakness manifesting itself, it can reassure itself by dominating the weakest among it. The dog world must do its part.

These dynamics reveal antidemocratic tendencies and temptations in democracy. A democracy, then, must be alert to its self-destructive propensities and redouble efforts to adhere to its basic principles. It must understand itself as a tragic form of life that entails inherent risks. Democracy has to be willing to accept and affirm exposure to potential calamity rather than readily violate fundamental values in the name of safety. Democracy means taking chances in a world always inhospitable to it. And it needs to make this stance public, as if to put itself on notice.

The model here, as we saw in the Introduction, is Oedipus. He left home in Corinth to protect his family, thereby surrendering the security of his royal station and placing himself at risk in a violence-ridden world. Still, he presumed that he might do great harm in life without intending to do so. He thus took action to put his do-no-harm ethos into practice at his own expense – not someone else's. He succeeded better than most realize, for his family in Corinth, with the only mother and father he ever knew, survived. Ransom Stoddard also took a great risk when he took to the main street of Shinbone to bring a democratic order into being. He did not impose his risk on others – not knowingly anyway, since he had every reason to believe Tom Doniphon had abandoned him. He insisted on fighting his own battles and living with the consequences.

WE ARE THE WORLD

Insofar as a memorial to war animals fails as a tribute because it refuses to present itself as an admission of wrongdoing and a warning about exploitation, the recent surge in memorialization enhances democracy's narcissistic exceptionalism. Peoples effectively salute themselves – for saluting – as they salute those who have no choice. The "loss" of animal life may be officially regretted at various animal memorial sites, but animal death primarily testifies to the value of the democratic cause served. The suffering inflicted – deliberately, not incidentally – on animals must have – must be given – meaning. As democracies recognize and acknowledge the horrors of war, they become worthy of the sacrifices they impose on animals in furtherance of their great pursuits. Through remembrance they redeem themselves. Animals are forgotten.

In democracies, especially the United States, the will to memorialize runs rampant, threatening to trivialize itself. The animal world has provided it with much-needed sustenance. Through memorialization democracies would transform victims into heroes, abomination into virtue, gratuity into necessity, cruelty into camaraderie, exploitation into love, death into life, transformations that deflect questions of responsibility for wars waged not against enemies but against the very animal world they would ostensibly honor. Cooper pays homage to animals with words that actually indict her eulogy and signal its emptiness: "Most animals who died have no memorial. Sick, wounded, starved, slaughtered, they have perished as though they had never been. The only way we can repay them is to treat them with more kindness in peace, and hope that in the future they are drawn as little as possible into our wars."[60] Contrary to Cooper's absolute claim, there are many ways "we can repay" animals. Contrary to Cooper's passive formulation, animals should be banned from wars, not hopefully "drawn as little as possible" into them. The problem with Cooper's well-meaning gesture is that she presumes and reaffirms the ethic toward animals – disposability – that not only defeats the very notion of repayment but also subverts the lament and hope expressed in her weak appeal on their behalf. If anything, the debt owed them is likely to be exacerbated.

Democracy, of course, lives on the perpetual issuance of debt and the enforcement of sacrifice. The use of animals in war, especially pets, thus captures the violence inherent in democracy. Pets enjoy a distinct moral status – precious because vulnerable, vulnerable because dependent. They resemble small children, even infants. Yet democracies sacrifice them without question, without hesitation. Democratic exceptionalism makes it not only possible but also mandatory. There is no apparent limit to what a democracy can prescribe for animals. Magically, democracy discloses its goodness through mass animal death and killing. Willing to make this sacrifice, despite its own values, democracy must not only be doing good, but it must also be good itself. The greater the loss, then, the greater democracy makes itself. This is democracy's exceptionalist logic, newly and neatly exemplified by its use of animals in war.

Perhaps this is too harsh. In the ever-present aftermath of war, American, British, and Australian democracies (to name three) insist that animal contributions "never be forgotten." What kind of memory, though, is to be cultivated at animal memorial sites dedicated to their contributions? Is it political, rooted in appreciation of the key roles animals played in the last century's freedom wars? Is it military, rooted in the esoteric knowledge that animals possess unique talents that, unused, could mean defeat in future wars? Is it civic, rooted in an ethic that democratic societies must be prepared to mobilize from top to bottom to defend themselves, which includes placing everyone and everything on call, including animals? If the memory in question is political, military, or civic, it is a memory of entitlement. It presumes that "we the democratic people" enjoy the right to take life or let live, and it means we deny the "good" that war achieves can only be secured by also doing great and gross wrong. Animals in war suggest that no scale of death is too great if it means the life of democracy. Animals in war suggest that no manner of death is too horrific if it means the life of democracy. Animals, including humans, are disposable. As is the world that houses them. Democracy's perfection, then, might comprise the domestication of extinction. What greater proof of love of democracy could there be than sacrificing everything for it?

4

Forcing Democracy to Be Free

Rousseau to Springsteen

After a great victory. – What is best about a great victory is that it liberates the victor from the fear of defeat. "Why not be defeated some time, too?" he says to himself; "Now I am rich enough for that."

Friedrich Nietzsche, *The Gay Science*

Not to perpetuate cowardice against one's own acts! Not to leave them in the lurch afterward. The bite of conscience is indecent.

Friedrich Nietzsche, *Twilight of the Idols*

Thanks to democracy, sacrifice enjoys an esteemed place in the history of democratic political thought. The same cannot be said of violence, however, despite its connection to sacrifice and indispensability to democracy. Richard Rorty, John Schaar, Charles Taylor, Benjamin Barber, and other contemporary political theorists insist that patriotism (and thus sacrifice) is crucial to a democratic community, but they make no claims on behalf of violence.[1] Laden with much-needed affect, patriotism furnishes citizens with the loyalty, commitment, devotion, and sense of common enterprise on which democracy depends. It enables them, in short, to sacrifice – themselves, others, fundamental principles, whatever democracy requires. To maintain that patriotism (and thus sacrifice) is essential to democracy, then, is effectively to admit that violence is essential to democracy.

Democracies, as a rule, do not embrace or advocate violence. Opposition, dissent, disobedience, and resistance find their celebrants, but nonviolence is the norm that governs these practices. Many thinkers on the democratic left consider these elemental forms of political participation patriotic, rejecting violence in the process. The latter is deemed gratuitous and indefensible – except under rare circumstances. Democracy, all things considered, represents a better way of political life. From a tragic perspective, this impeccable political vision seems, well, a little too pristine. Put differently, democracy cannot think of itself in terms of violence, more specifically, the violence it enacts every day. To do so would be to welcome, so to speak, the fundamental forbidden into the social and political order. Nevertheless, democracy has a violence problem that can be traced to its beginnings. Democracy's founding is troubled, flawed, in short, tragically violent, a harbinger of things to come that must be denied, disavowed, deflected, and refused for democracy to fulfill its promise. The tragic is assumed to be antithetical to political life, not constitutive of it.

Rousseau, well-known champion of patriotism but scourge of violence, approaches the question of democracy with a great sense of urgency. He writes in a world in which it has yet to gain a foothold and fights for its very life. For Rousseau, more importantly, democracy will always be fighting for its life. Not only does the founding of a self-governing polity mark a precarious experiment rather than a secure achievement. Democracy also finds itself under siege from its moment of birth until it expires – especially from immanent threats.[2] Rousseau warns those who clamor for freedom that if its responsibilities were understood, they would fear it more than slavery and run from it in terror.[3] The unorthodox warning seems to flow, in part, from the self-sacrificing demands of citizenship. It could just as easily have flowed, however, from an appreciation of the tragic character of democratic politics, which includes the exercise and production of violence, as I argue below.

This is the fraught context within which Rousseau theorizes democracy, citizenship, and politics. It is characterized by tragedy, yet Rousseau insists the social compact can be introduced without loss or remainder ("it is so false that the social contract involves any true renunciation").[4] The circumstances surrounding a republic's birth coupled with the contradictory nature of its institutional design (which both enables and endangers its life) signal its perpetually problematic condition. For Rousseau the art of politics is to prolong the life of the republic as long as possible, but violence and death inevitably await it. If Hobbes incites and then capitalizes on a subject's fear of violent death as a necessary tool of sovereign rule, Rousseau incites and deploys a community's fear of a cancerous death to mobilize and energize the republic. Rousseau will not hesitate to use the coercive powers of the state to defend the rule of law, including through the death penalty, but in any well-ordered society the need should be minimal.[5] Violence is not supposed to play an undue role in the polity. The more important point, however, is that Rousseau's theorizations work to deflect attention from the tragedies democratic politics engender as well as the productive possibilities that accompany them. The everyday violence that is a part of any democratic political order becomes invisible.

Contemporary democracies do not embrace Rousseau, but a Rousseauean spirit informs their attitudes and orientations to the question of violence. It's timely, then, to affirm a tragic perspective and assist democracy as it enacts and disrupts its own unfolding. Rousseau, ironically, can be of assistance. His idealized conception of politics in *On the Social Contract*, for example, requires institutional schemes and organizational directives that can be pushed in new directions to contend with the ambiguous results they generate. What's more, Rousseau's virtuous republic fosters the kind of troublemaking citizens (Rousseau calls them malefactors) critical for a democratic polity to address the tragedies it encounters and begets.

Later in the chapter, I turn to contemporary Rousseauean Bruce Springsteen and would-be tragedian Danielle Allen to illuminate further democracy's tragic character and the possibilities for political reinvention it offers. Both Springsteen's and Allen's work suffer, explicitly or implicitly, from patriotic obsessions, but it is precisely the darkest, most desperate moments of Springsteen's songs that suggest a way forward, a way that Rousseau could envision but, given the violence involved, did not dare recommend, let alone pursue.[6]

A REPUBLIC'S FRAUGHT BIRTH

Banned in France and Geneva, Rousseau's *On the Social Contract* inspired, even thrilled, readers, suggesting the distinct possibility of a new and radically different order of things.[7] No actually existing state could withstand, let alone welcome, Rousseau's reflections on a legitimate political community, a combination of critique and possibility. At the same time, *On the Social Contract* conveys an air of foreboding, perhaps menace. The republic-to-be does not promise all things to all people. If anything, Rousseau's candor about life in democracy resembles Hobbes's caveats in *Leviathan* about life in his commonwealth.[8] Given the conditions informing the republic's emergence, this should come as no surprise. Rousseau seems to be channeling Hobbes in the often-neglected opening to book I, chapter six, where he writes: "I assume that men have reached the point where obstacles to their self-preservation in the state of nature prevail by their resistance over the forces each individual can use to maintain himself in that state. Then that primitive state can no longer subsist and the human race would perish if it did not change its way of life."⁹ Far removed from the naturally peaceful world depicted in *Discourse on the Origin and Foundations of Inequality among Men,* here Rousseau imagines a hypothetical state of nature characterized by conflicts threatening human being with extinction.¹⁰ The condition he describes with antiseptic care reads very much like an unrelenting state of war, each against all. The origins of democracy, accordingly, cannot be separated from existential crisis. Still, Rousseau has no doubts about the superiority of society to nature, though the transition from one to the other apparently comes with considerable costs accompanying it.¹¹

Rousseau's candor on the question of founding, however, is qualified: the violence inescapably accompanying it must be deflected or obscured. Political birth has all the makings of a tragic narrative, but it does not emerge. Instead, in book II, chapter seven of *On the Social Contract,* founding, now a surprisingly peaceful affair, relies on a mysterious Legislator who appears out of nowhere to deliver the gift of laws uniquely appropriate to a people. This deus ex machina complicates the political pedigree of the community, but on Rousseau's account the enigmatic figure circumvents democratic self-determination in order to inaugurate it. In the beginning, people do not possess the civic skills or temperament necessary to assume their duties as citizens, which require the introduction of the community they seek. The community they seek, however, is beyond their reach. But if they can only acquire the necessary character and talents in the very society they cannot themselves realize, what are they to do? This is a vicious circle to which they seem forever consigned.

Hence Rousseau's introduction of the Legislator, who breaks the impasse by giving the gift of law to the people. With reason ineffective and force unavailable – the people understand self-interest alone and the Legislator possesses no army – he appeals to a higher "order of authority" to perform his mission. Rousseau claims that "the fathers of nations," lacking options, have historically resorted to this oratorical move.¹² It is not a question of deceit or deception but necessity. The paradoxes of the founding situation dictate it. Founding could not proceed otherwise. If successful, the Legislator renders himself a transcendent figure who invokes the gods to channel authority and establish law. A people can always affirm, change, or reject what it acquires at the founding, but the need for action is immediate in the closing stages of the state of nature. To wait for the people to acquire the discipline, cultivate the judgment, and forge the general will required for self-rule would prove suicidal. If the people proceeded on their own without the capacities necessary for self-government, the polity would die stillborn. The people stand in need of assistance, guidance, action. There are no patriotic heroes at the founding. Nor is there any tragedy. As Bonnie Honig notes, Rousseau's Legislator serves but does not unsettle the regime.[13] He is productive but not a problem. She concludes: "there is surely something too neat about this script." It is too neat in that it denies the violence, thus the tragedy, it enacts.[14]

Remarkable abilities notwithstanding, the Legislator only shows the people what to will. He cannot furnish the will itself. The Legislator executes his founding task and departs to guarantee its integrity. No one can accuse him of playing politics. Still, the formation of wills takes time. Whenever the Legislator leaves – the timing is not specified – it is too soon. The very idea of generality outstrips the narrow calculations of interest that tend to preoccupy people. Passion for the common good is foreign to creatures who think principally of themselves. Citizens must learn how to reason properly. They must also learn what and how to feel, that is, to love something new, the newborn republic. If good laws require good citizens and good citizens require good laws, can the Legislator successfully install the laws he provides or are they effectively discarded as soon as he leaves? There is something, however, at which would-be citizens can excel from the get-go: violence.

THE LEGISLATOR AND THE TRAGIC

Given Rousseau's dread of civic indifference, the founding would seem to offer an unparalleled occasion to tell a mythic tale on which a republic can rely for political nourishment for generations to come. Founding stories ordinarily face no competition when it comes to achievement insofar as mere dream becomes reality for the first time. They represent the culmination of heroic struggle, noble sacrifice, and daring deed. Founding, as the original creative act, is the condition of possibility of political life. It requires marking as such. The transition from nothing to everything is narratively second to none. In Rousseau's hands, founding amounts to an impossible undertaking nevertheless achieved. It seems to be something of a miracle. Ambiguity, let alone tragedy, does not spoil it.

Nevertheless, Rousseau offers a troubling account of the origins of the legitimate republic. Not only do the people not give themselves laws. The idea of a social contract seems to be a fiction. How can people be free if they do not give themselves laws but must rely on the good fortune of a godlike Legislator arriving on the scene in timely fashion to do the work instead? What is really going on here?

Honig argues that Rousseau's Legislator can be read as a foreigner who also serves as a scapegoat to absorb and deflect the violence that necessarily accompanies founding.[15] Rousseau's invocation of the Legislator, then, signals not the general will's failure but its success.[16] Once the Legislator departs, the taint of violence departs with him. How does violence necessarily accompany the founding? Rousseau argues that in order to guarantee the freedom of the founding moment, unanimity is required at least once. This would be difficult under the best of circumstances, to say nothing of the extinction Rousseau assumes threatens the human race. Those opposed to the contract, then, must be excluded from it. Otherwise they are slaves. Given the impossibility of complete agreement on an undertaking as complicated as a founding, segregation is inevitable. And given the stakes involved, those denied membership, whose own political vision was defeated and denied, cannot be expected to quietly disappear into political disenfranchisement. Those at the brink of acquiring power are unlikely to accept imposed powerlessness. This is the space of and for democratic violence, which can also energize and unify the republic. Though founding embodies creative destruction, destruction and the thrill it entails are drained from Rousseau's narrative, presumably to avoid soiling the legitimacy of birth. The irony is that violence assumes a disconcerting presence in Rousseau's founding narrative by virtue of its fabulous absence.[17]

What would happen if Rousseau's Legislator were replaced in the founding narrative? People would perform founding assignments themselves, but lacking a transcendent political vision that can preempt or overcome disagreement and provide unity, violence seems not just inevitable but implacable. There are no settled institutions in place to resolve disputes, to sooth enmities. This is what founding achieves. Thus force decides where talk fails. As Honig notes, however, this is still a success. I would add that it is a tragic success, a violent success. Thus, success must be newly understood to mean an ambiguous achievement – which occurs not only at the moment of founding but also in the life of the republic subsequently.

The war threatening to consume the human race that Rousseau initially posits miraculously never materializes. The myth of the Legislator is the kind of story people must tell themselves, something to be believed but not closely examined. They know all about the founding violence to which they cannot admit. The logic of the story presumes a distinction between the arbitrary violence deployed to introduce a republic and the ostensibly legitimate violence employed to protect a republic already in existence. The casualties generated in founding cannot be sanctioned by any legal right of self-defense and its inevitable consequences – hence the tragedy of it.

No one, of course, would be opposed to a social contract. It would amount to a death wish. Those in opposition object to one particular version of a contract – hence their exclusion, a euphemism for the violence necessarily leveled against them to secure *a* founding – later *the* founding. To conceive life thus requires taking it. Founding, the fount of life, traffics in death. Those excluded from it, however, were not morally, let alone politically, culpable. Founding reveals the blood on the hands of citizens as much as the wounds to be worn proudly in public after their glorious triumph.[18] Democracy relies on sacrifice, including violence, but it must be righteous, which founding denies it – because it's impossible. The conditions for it do not exist. Honig argues that the turn to the Legislator comes at the price of democratic agency. It also separates that agency from the stain of arbitrary violence.

Rousseau insists that those excluded (they did not exclude themselves) from the contract submit themselves to sovereignty if they remain in the polity. This, it could be argued, constitutes a second act of violence, for those excluded would still be opposed to this version of the social contract. It seems as if they are supposed to do to themselves what their opponents at the founding could not fully accomplish. Exclusion is the first injury the suffer; the second is subordination. Rousseau does not acknowledge the debt that is owed to these "foreigners" among the people insofar as their sacrifice (their being excluded) made the success of the founding possible.

Rousseau's omission speaks to the great failure of his Legislator narrative. Given the account of the volatile circumstances preceding founding and the demands attending it, violence necessarily abounds. The Legislator, with the assistance of (at least some of) the people themselves, must capture, harness, and direct it to productive ends, precisely the dynamic Max Weber affirms a century later. Problematic means must be deployed for good ends, which is why politics is a vocation only for those with strong constitutions. The nonpareil political challenge is to affirm the exercise of violence and find a way to become worthy of it, which means that the last, worst thing for a Legislator to do is exit the scene. His work is not complete, something Ransom Stoddard figured out quickly (with help, of course). Success cannot rest content with a single act. But Rousseau's Legislator does depart and takes his violence with him, thereby setting a dubious, destructive precedent.

The greatness of the Legislator, pace Rousseau, is that he did deploy violence without triggering a Hobbesian war of each against all. Blood did not preclude beauty. Nor did it eliminate the need for violence in the future. The Legislator needs to stand as an exemplar of how violence is done well. After all, it is not confined to the founding period. *The Man Who Shot Liberty Valance*, as we have seen, offers a model. The legend of Ransom Stoddard contends that he went west bearing law books rather than a gun. He became the awe-inspiring champion of law and order, but violence is drained from the official story, beginning with Mr. Peabody's convention hall speech. While it's true that Stoddard did secure a gun to confront Liberty Valance, his incompetence with a firearm effectively disarmed him. It was his example, however, his willingness to employ violence, which spurred another (Tom Doniphon) to deploy it alongside him with the expertise needed. Ironically, the speech that Cassius Starbuckle delivered on behalf of the long-dominant cattle interests denouncing Stoddard for his extralegal exploits more than likely backfired, catapulting – rather than sabotaging – Ransom's political career. What Starbuckle inadvertently revealed is that Stoddard recognized the exceptional circumstances when the law is necessarily put aside – in favor of violence, in the name of law.

A GENEALOGY OF DEMOCRATIC LIFE

What kind of democratic life is delivered to the people, whether by the Legislator or by the people themselves? Rousseau scatters his reflections on the institutional conduct of politics throughout *On the Social Contract*. After the founding and (un)timely departure of the Legislator, the people are supposedly well-positioned to realize their common principles and interests, but this does not mean they can rest content with his handiwork. Since a republic, on Rousseau's account, starts to decline at inception, citizens face serious responsibilities and formidable challenges from the moment they assume control of their sovereign prerogatives. Rousseau's republic thus works hard to enable citizens to meet their solemn civic duties. It provides an institutional framework for legislation that furnishes it with a completed, finished quality attesting to the harmony, unity, and accord of the political community. The legislative enterprise concentrates on producing agreement among citizens, which means success is understood narrowly. For Rousseau there is no sense of responsibility attending the formal public expression of the general will.[19] Those who find themselves on the wrong side of a question are owed nothing. Rather, they must do what it takes to bring themselves into alignment with the community's will. The order's obligations, however, have been met.

What Rousseau does not entertain is the idea that a democracy should confront the tragedies issuing from the self-legislating activities of citizens, including the realities of political violence. Nevertheless, the very exercise of sovereignty will make manifest these realities from the start – despite any pretenses, denials, or disavowals to the contrary. That is, the violence necessarily present at the founding does not magically disappear once the order comes into being. Rousseau's argument that remedies to political problems are to be drawn from the ills themselves can be applied to legitimate democracies as well.[20] Thus, Rousseau's institutional arrangements can be supplemented and employed in newfound, productive ways, even if Rousseau would have counseled against it, fearing political destabilization. Modern democracies, unfortunately, tend to possess a Rousseauean spirit that, first, legitimizes political outcomes however problematic, even objectionable they might be; and, second, compromises their ability to recognize and address the self-made troubles that plague them.

Rousseau's account of citizen voting in the assembly, to cite one example, simultaneously reveals the logic of the general will and conceals the harm it necessarily inflicts on (the) people. Everyday politics thus repeats the disconcerting combination of success and violence necessarily present at the founding. In book IV of *On the Social Contract* Rousseau instructs would-be citizens on their legislative duties. When voting, they are not being asked to render judgment on a specific matter. Rather, they are being asked whether the proposal in front of them "does or does not conform to the general will that is theirs."[21] If citizens finds themselves on the losing side of a vote, this means that they misidentified the general will, which can always be found, thanks to Rousseau's leap of faith – in other words, to the need for a governing political fiction to confer legitimacy on legislative results – in the majority. And since the general will benefits or burdens (the) people identically, it does not harm any one of them alone. The articulation of Rousseau's political ideal, however, accentuates its impossibility. Not even the most homogeneous community enjoys (or engenders) the myriad conditions requisite to unanimity – and thus a lack of violence.[22] Laws always benefit or burden citizens differently.

Rousseau insists that specific principles regulate voting in the assembly. The more serious the issue is under discussion, the greater the need for unanimity. For matters that require immediate decisions, the smaller the difference of opinion should be. Still, nothing more than a single vote is required for a resolution.[23] The advice seems like common political sense more than an aspiration for any well-ordered society. Indeed, crisis or emergency may produce the commonality of sentiment that Rousseau desires as citizens rally around a single cause or purpose. It is a noble, even thrilling vision to imagine citizens coming together, but extraordinary times or circumstances can also elicit profound differences and bitter divisions. It is on such occasions that fundamental principles are likely to be at stake, and this rarely fosters harmony or consensus. According to Rousseauean logic, however, those on the "wrong" side of a question, that is, those who supposedly cannot distinguish their private will from their general will, have made a grave mistake. Unanimity still prevails despite the appearance of vehement opposition. The conclusion neatly allows the republic to sidestep the thorny question of (the) people harming some part of their own as they reach and implement a decision. This is the silent space of violence and tragedy in democratic politics. Rousseau's formula entails success, but that very success cannot escape simultaneous failure (harm, injury, sacrifice, etc.). The very formation of a general will produces responsibility for the particularity it decries.

Rousseau's procedural axioms for the assembly find expression in *The Man Who Shot Liberty Valance*. For much of the film, residents of Shinbone exhibit ambivalence about the desirability of statehood. Declarations of support are combined with passivity, inaction. What kind of community elects Link Appleyard year after year as town marshal? Not only does he refuse to carry a gun; he possessed neither the ability nor the inclination to do the job. Everyone knew about Liberty Valance but no one acted against him, including Tom Doniphon. Shinbone was a community uncertain it wanted to be one. Yet at the crucial moment, election day, Shinbone voted unanimously for two candidates for the territorial convention who unequivocally supported statehood. Liberty Valance tried to steal the election, but he was overwhelmingly defeated. Valance did not contest the election's legitimacy, but he did dismiss the results given the violence at his disposal, a violence that could effectively overturn the outcome.

Valance's resort to violence to derail the democratic process tends to obscure the violence of the democratic process itself, as seen in Chapter 1. Shinbone was self-consciously voting to bring into being a new form of life. It was also voting to hasten and formalize the destruction of an alternative way of life locked in mortal struggle for its existence. Blinded by enthusiasm, the people could not see or feel anything but their own rightness. The opposition within was always already discredited. The territory, to say nothing of Valance and his Myrmidons, had to be forced to be free.

While the film's dominant narrative insists there is no real loss incurred by the triumph of statehood, the figure of Tom Doniphon suggests otherwise, also seen in Chapter 1. Doniphon's demise is problematic in itself. It also serves as a reminder that the once-ascendant and life-giving pioneers who settled the land suffered erasure in the wake of history's inevitable forward march. Nevertheless, each represented a creative-destructive force necessary for Ransom Stoddard to emerge to imagine and introduce a new form of life. Democracy prevailed, but victory entailed great cost – the elimination of those who helped make it possible at great cost to themselves. Forgetting the costs means that democracy's relationship to violence can be minimized and ignored. Still, Stoddard's ascension was made possible by virtue of an independent, self-sufficient, individualistic form of life that relied on and respected the role of violence, which Stoddard partly embraced. As he himself remarked, "when force threatens, talk's no good." He wanted desperately to believe that "education is the basis of law and order," but events proved such faith insufficient. Stoddard may have retired *his* weapon after confronting Valance, thanks to Doniphon's rifle, but this signals the public monopolization and intensification of the means of violence. Founding results in a new beginning, yes, but it also guarantees new rounds of political violence when the art of politics assumes its responsibilities and meets opposition and resistance. Legitimate sovereign power cannot erase the violence (injury, harm, damage, brutality, cruelty) to which it is inherently prone.

A ROUSSEAUEAN REVERSAL

At the close of book II of *On the Social Contract*, Rousseau addresses the role of fundamental laws in the republic. The idea of politics is to "give the commonwealth the best possible form." There is no nobler aspiration, no greater achievement in democracy. Assuming that "there is only one correct way to organize each State," once the sovereign people have identified the right laws for themselves, they should install and preserve them. On the other hand, if something goes wrong, if the laws are bad, the people should change the laws by which they live. Rousseau recognizes that even when the people perform superbly, they may, without a moment's notice or hesitation, abandon their own well-crafted institutional creations. The most likely culprit is corruption, which can manifest itself in any number of ways (self-interest, venality, laziness, indifference), but the result is always the same: freedom lost, the dissolution of the republic. Rousseau seems philosophical about the possibility, even likelihood, of such a development when he writes, rhetorically: "if [a people] wishes to do itself harm, who has the right to prevent it from doing so?"[24] Rousseau takes it for granted that the people may act irrationality, impulsively, mistakenly, or stupidly and thus injure themselves through the very process that gives them life: legislation. Since they are sovereign, there is nothing, in the end, that can be done to avert such an occurrence. Politics has failed.

Rousseau, however, conceives of the possibilities of harm in the republic too narrowly. We have already seen that he considers it impossible for the people to harm themselves, even some part of themselves, when they authentically express the general will through sovereign lawmaking, even though this is always one of the consequences attending politics. Because he cannot see that the people necessarily harm themselves, he also cannot imagine that the people, as a fundamental aspect of their political life, might find themselves in situations where, as a matter of principle, they ought to harm themselves, as it were. He presumes that the republic at its best lives without remainder – namely, that its basic legislative undertakings do not affect different citizens differently, benefitting some and therefore harming others – that they do not routinely produce injustice. Yet once this political fiction is exposed and abandoned, it becomes necessary for the people to revisit its own ethos of political action and responsibility. What it means for the people to hurt itself can be recovered to include something other than self-destruction. The people might choose to "hurt" itself for good reason – that is, to follow Nietzsche's advice and accept the burdens of success, to allow for its own defeat, to surrender or give back (some of) what it has achieved in order to make amends or atone for the price of its own legitimate accomplishments. The sovereignty of the people is perfected, so to speak, not only in the full exercise of its power for the common good but also in response to the exercise of that power on behalf of those the common good injures. In politics there is always more work to be done – even when things go well.

In "On the Legislator," Rousseau claims the people, especially in its relative infancy, cannot "appreciate the healthy maxims of politics" or "follow the fundamental rules of statecraft."[25] Social and political education has yet to convert men fully into citizens, which is why a Legislator must intervene, at least in the beginning. Yet the very idea of a Legislator obscures an important point. Regardless of the experience and skill of citizens or the intent and sophistication of the legislation, the tragic dynamic of politics cannot be avoided. The people *cannot not* hurt themselves. Not even the Legislator, for all his godlike qualities, can avoid or overcome this actuality. Rousseau notes that "a people is always the master to change its laws – even the best laws," but it may be more important to understand that even the best laws are suspect. This may sound counterintuitive, but the best laws are not as good as commonly presumed. They, too, are intrinsically flawed, even profoundly so. Rousseau insists that politics affords opportunities we tend to overlook. Still, even if "the limits of the possible in moral matters are less narrow than we think," serious limits remain.[26] When the sovereign people swing into political action, they simultaneously (sometimes? often? usually? always?) do good and ill. Rousseau argues in *Considerations on the Government of Poland* that liberty and repose are incompatible. Citizens must not be content to pass (a system of) laws and retire from a life of active citizenship. The legislative enterprise, the embodiment of sovereign power, always already calls for remedial work. Action inherently creates the need for a response to its unfolding. Action thus tends to find itself trapped in an infinite regress it initiated. This reflects the tragedy inherent in politics. Rousseau may not pursue this specific line of thought, but the institutional design of his republic suggests it nonetheless.

Admittedly, Rousseau imagines politics unfolding smoothly. In the assembly, the first citizen to propose a law states a need everyone already recognizes and understands.[27] The ritual of politics operates to confirm publicly political truths already known to the polity. Once citizens assure themselves they are in formal agreement, legislation can proceed given the mutual trust affirmed. This is not to say that political opposition, resistance, or refusal might not materialize, but these reactions can be attributed to individual moral failing, a lack of virtue in citizens. Legislative success, in other words, cannot be responsible for it. It remains pure, untouched. The romanticism of this idealized account of politics is pernicious. It assumes an impossible uniformity of will and effect, that when it comes to legislation citizens share obligations or burdens alike. At its greatest moment of life-affirming creation, democracy denies the damage it also inflicts.

As I indicated, the logic of Rousseau's institutional design suggests a remedy to be drawn from the ill. He assumes the death of the body politic begins at the moment of birth. The republic – and it alone – is responsible. Nothing can eliminate "this natural and inevitable tendency," not even in the "best constituted governments."[28] But it can be delayed. Thus Rousseau insists that in addition to the extraordinary assemblies that must be called in response to unforeseen circumstances (crisis, emergency, etc.), regular assemblies must be convened on a given date set by law. Nothing can alter or abolish these mandatory legislative sessions. No hard and fast rule can set a fixed number of these assemblies, but the stronger the government, the more often the sovereign people should show themselves to exercise their freedom. Rousseau presumes that government poses an inherent threat to the sovereign and any good institutional scheme must take account of it.[29]

Government, however, is not the only threat the sovereign faces. As Bonnie Honig argues, it may not be possible to distinguish the general will from the will of all.[30] For law to be legitimate it must express the general will. This requirement does not guarantee that it will express it, however. The people must convene to ensure their freedom, but they can also undermine that freedom in its very exercise. How does the sovereign threaten itself in the very exercise of its powers? By benefitting some citizens and harming others, the formal dominance of the general will notwithstanding, the sovereign delegitimizes itself. As a result, Rousseau's institutional scheme requires supplementation. More specifically, an annual reparations assembly must also be mandated by law, an assembly of redress, which listens and responds to the grievances of citizens who have been harmed and injured by politics. This does not mean that the republic cannot take the initiative, unprompted. Either way, the American Serviceman's Readjustment Act of 1944, more commonly known as the G.I. Bill, is exemplary. A democratic society that sends its citizens into war, however necessary, good, or unavoidable, and cannot undo the damage it thereby inflicted on them – taking lives, bodies, and psyches – responds with a civic gift. Though not equivalent, the democracy that took so much gives something that is more than symbolic in return: the opportunity, through financial support, to build a new life in the aftermath of war. While American democracy thinks of military service as the exception not just for this kind of state benefit but also for this kind of comportment, it must become the democratic norm. The harm military service generates is not to be privileged – not in democracy.

If, for the regular assembly, citizens rush to the chamber to express their general will anticipating its ascendancy, for the reparations session their demeanor would be decidedly different – modest, chastened, perhaps a bit somber. If, in the regular assembly, the first citizen to speak articulates a need commonly experienced and states the course of action people already believe to be necessary, a course that merely awaits public voice to be implemented, the reparations assembly would begin by following Athenian custom and asking, "Who wishes to be heard?" The discursive ritual is rooted in necessity, the necessity to address and redress, in some way, the inevitable shortcomings and wrongdoings of law that emerge regardless of sovereign intent, expertise, or success. Unlike the results of the original legislation, shortcomings tend not to be "universally seen," let alone experienced. Eloquence may be needed to make them real for those unaware of them or those unaffected or unconcerned by them. Until the moment arrives when proposals for redress need to be offered, only those citizens who have been harmed by the law may speak at the reparations assembly.

Once grievances have been documented and catalogued, a citizen would rise to offer a sequel to the first speech in the regular assembly. In this second speech of tragic responsibility, citizens are not to be flattered or humored but told precisely what they do not want to hear, namely, that they have done well and in the process have harmed others – their fellow citizens, their political equals who are entitled to the dignity they claim for themselves. The point is not to lay blame but to publicize, render accountable, and repair.

Rousseau argues that ancient laws enjoy great respect because the sovereign tacitly affirms them by not revoking them when it is always free to do so.[31] Things are more complicated. Respect may be accorded laws by some citizens but not others, not those harmed by them. Laws may remain in place because citizens have an investment in them and thus incentive to deny, evade, ignore, or even cover up their deficiencies. Laws may also stay on the books because, on balance, they are good laws. This does not mean they are free of problematic consequences that need correction or augmentation. Accordingly, the reparations assembly reflects sovereign modesty and generosity more than it channels sovereign power and pride. Politics cannot be concluded at a single stroke. Think of legislation as a musical process that entails overdubbing. Pieces must be added to round out the original composition, which ought to be considered a layered whole – always imperfect and in need of fine-tuning. The mere existence of a reparations assembly signals a confident, principled democracy that is not afraid – but makes it a point of pride – to reflect on itself and its achievements and admit its imperfections. An institutionalized will to repair reflects the internalization of a tragic democratic sensibility – the opportunity failure provides to do something new, something creative. It would be an ideal complement to Admission Day, introduced in Chapter 1. A reparations assembly, ideally, punctures the illusions of mastery accompanying (the exercise of) sovereignty. At the same time, it might inadvertently contribute to them, suggesting that the past can be mastered and wrongs righted. The past and its effects, however, cannot be undone, even if they can on occasion be mitigated. Any reparations session, moreover, that addresses and responds to the past would of necessity create new problems for future sessions to consider. Reparations do not entail resolution; rather, they imply displacement and redistribution. Yet a politics of displacement, perpetual displacement, provides hope in a world of tragic realities.

LONG LIVE MALEFACTORS

Rousseau's institutional arrangements place heavy burdens on citizens, some more than others. The order needs loyalists, but it also needs those who, like Socrates but minus the unthinking patriotism, can put themselves at risk in the name of right and on behalf of the common good when the order suffers from blindness or density. From where will such citizens come? Once again, Rousseau's republic produces them itself. It just doesn't know it yet.

Rousseau's theoretical reflections on citizenship reach a point of perfection with the introduction of malefactors, the notorious figures that "prevent the citizen from being free."[32] Rousseau articulates the political logic that produces the malefactor in book IV, chapter two of *On the Social Contract*. It follows his vision of a seamless politics in the assembly. Rousseau fears that citizens might wonder how they can be subjected to a law passed explicitly against their will and remain free. He famously responds that "the question is badly put." It is badly put because it misunderstands the conduct of politics in the assembly. When voting on a piece of legislation citizens are asked not whether they favor or oppose it but whether the law under consideration "conform[s] to the general will that is theirs."[33] If any one citizen finds himself on the losing side of the vote, this means he has misidentified the general will. Nevertheless, the law passed. And it passed because "all the characteristics of the general will are still in the majority."[34]

Rousseau makes another assumption here worth exploring. He assumes, as mentioned, that those in the minority misidentified the general will. When citizens voted no, they were wrong. What if, however, they voted no for another reason altogether? What if they identified the general will correctly and voted no regardless? What if, that is, they voted no because they were concerned about the consequences of the law passing despite or even because it reflected the general will, concerned, that is, about the damage it might do? Rousseau, recall, insists that "every act of sovereignty, which is to say every authentic act of the general will, obligates *or* favors all citizens equally."[35] Yet no society is homogeneous to the point where such effects can be controlled, let alone produced on demand, as previously indicated. What's more, Rousseau does not say obligates *and* favors all citizens equally. This means that only one side of the political equation needs to be equal. Equal obligation might not produce equal benefit. Equal benefit might arise from unequal obligation. In such circumstances, a citizen might be opposed to the sovereign people undertaking a legislative initiative. Sensitive to the harm that a democratic polity can inflict even when it genuinely seeks to do right by and well for its citizens, he might think it best if the polity did not pass the law under consideration. He might think it best if the polity did nothing, at least for the time being, or that it did something else. Since Rousseau admits that faith is required to locate the general will in the majority, might not a razor-thin vote (decided by a single citizen, for example) lead one to question or even doubt the common faith?

The malefactor, here a democratic citizen in opposition, is a tragic figure of patience and restraint who lands in jail for his principled stand.[36] Rousseau, of course, would automatically convert even a principled political act into an instance of rebellion and thus treason. Imprisonment, subsequently, crystallizes the republic's effort not just to eliminate opposition but also to kill it outright – through prison and galley chains.[37] Resistance, though, can be reinterpreted as a sign of a vibrant political life. From the bowels of consensual citizenship, democratic possibilities emerge. What enables the malefactor to take a principled stand? Perhaps he is able to dissent in front of a disapproving community, no mean feat, thanks to a certain distance that prevails between himself and the republic, to the failure of identification between the self and the order Rousseau's republic seeks. This failure, inevitable in all polities, which must make the citizens appropriate to them, puts him in a position to understand the tragic responsibilities that democratic citizenship entails. The malefactor's civic gift is to reveal to the polity what it owes those it harms through its very success.

Rousseau's malefactors, after all, emerge coeval with the founding of the republic, though he prefers to call them foreigners. In the beginning, those who possess the force to bring it about exclude those opposed to the formation of the polity as conceived.[38] Yet Rousseau's republic does not feel any sense of responsibility to them, perhaps because the founding achievement is nothing short of miraculous given the terrifying circumstances overcome. Thus Rousseau insists that in the post-founding situation, residency implies consent: "To inhabit the territory means to submit oneself to sovereignty."[39] Rousseau focuses attention not on what the order can do for the defeated but on what the defeated must do vis-à-vis the order. They must pay the price of a defeat for which they are not responsible. This amounts to a double victimization. It also denies the tragic dynamic operative at the founding and prevents the order from seeing its continuation throughout the life of the republic.

Rousseau's imperative regarding submission to sovereignty is not absolute. A number of factors can compromise the freedom of the citizen. "Family, goods, the lack of a place of refuge, necessity, or violence" can keep an individual "in the country against his will."[40] These kinds of circumstances are not unique to the founding moment. They apply equally to each new generation of citizens whose consent cannot necessarily be obtained in any politically meaningful fashion. People may effectively consent to the terms of membership and be content (or not). Others may submit to sovereignty and take up opposition against the general will in the belief that the faith projected onto the majority as its agent is misplaced. The conditions of birth and the subsequent life of Rousseau's republic thus allow for, even encourage, the articulation and cultivation of a tragic sensibility, but Rousseau does not want the strife he pretends to skirt at the founding to define the republic. But it does define it. Rousseau's democratic legacy can be enhanced thanks to and despite himself. The excluded, after all, made the inauguration of the republic possible. Not only is a debt owed to them; the moral character of the polity depends on how it treats those it harms, even and especially if that harm came about as the result of doing genuine good. By trying to consolidate and solidify the founding achievement as is, Rousseau's republic puts itself in danger in the long term. The malefactor is a figure of resistance, of democracy, of life in Rousseau's republic. Reaching out to so-called malefactors entails risk, but a democracy lays claim to nobility when it puts itself in harm's way. The political logic that governs Rousseau's republic demands the sacrifice of malefactors ("in a country where all such men were in galleys, the most perfect freedom would be enjoyed"), but this self-same logic imposes a tragic responsibility the staying power of which is ensured by the political effort to ignore, deny, or erase it.[41]

SPRINGSTEEN'S DEMOCRATIC MALEFACTORS

If anyone knows malefactors, it's Bruce Springsteen. These antiheroes don't prevent the citizen from being free. They provide democracies with an opportunity to prove their commitment to equality and justice. In 2012 Springsteen released *Wrecking Ball*, which may constitute his angriest recording, a provocative possibility considering the visceral charge of *Darkness on the Edge of Town* or *Nebraska*, works of not just his angry youth but also his creative peak. *Wrecking Ball* is Springsteen's civic retort to America's neoliberal neo-depression. Among other things, it recounts the damage done to countless American lives while the country, unduly captive to Republican free market ideology, rhetoric, and obstructionism, dithers. At a Paris press conference, Springsteen remarked, "What was done to our country was wrong and unpatriotic and un-American and nobody has been held to account."[42] *Wrecking Ball* indulges fantasies of violent reprisal, holding responsible those parties (fat cats, robber barons, etc.) who committed economic crimes with impunity. It not only names some names. It also targets some of those who benefitted handsomely from their depredations.[43] Springsteen's reconstruction of political agency to incorporate violence constitutes a tragic moment. Democracy's inner workings, combined with the inherent instabilities of a capitalist economy, produce actors contributive to and destructive of the polity.[44]

Springsteen's *Wrecking Ball* tour was governed by an abiding faith in America. Consider the April 1, 2012, show at the Verizon Center in Washington, DC. It began in deadly seriousness with "We Take Care of Our Own," an ironic account of America's pat response to the fallout from its political and military failures. Despite citizens stomaching economic loss, privation, and devastation at home; despite soldiers fighting and dying in war zones abroad from which they return mangled, maimed, broken, and scarred; the United States caters to the rich, the powerful, and the well-connected, leaving the rest to suffer the insufferable calamities imposed on them.[45] As with several other songs on the record, Springsteen chides the country he loves for its indifference and inaction. He presents himself as an angry patriot appalled by the callousness and cruelty the country displays toward so many of its citizens, on so many occasions, in such varied circumstances. "There is a real patriotism underneath the best of my music, but it is a critical, questioning, and often angry patriotism."[46] America is the country that he loves – that he *cannot not love*. In Washington, Springsteen seemingly pushed critique of country to the edge. In one sequence he performed "Jack of All Trades," "Trapped," "Adam Raised a Cain," and "Easy Money," the first about a man desperate for any work he can find who also fantasizes about the violence he would do if he had a gun, the last a song about a justifiably enraged man who, one night, targets the better part of town armed with his .38 for whatever cash he can get, however he can get it, thus mimicking, with a twist, the criminals on Wall Street.[47] Turnabout is fair play.[48]

Springsteen, however, balances critique with earnest pleasure and celebration: "Waitin' on a Sunny Day," "Out in the Street," and "Dancing in the Dark" found their way onto the night's play list.[49] Springsteen insisted the audience rise, sing, dance, and throw their bodies around with abandon. Experience the joy of it all. Let the resignation, impotent aggression, and desire for connection expressed in these songs find release. Springsteen assumes that unrelenting critique cannot be sustained on any register for long and that some diversion and distraction are essential to life. More importantly, the American Dream remains an article of faith. People must not give up on it, no matter the dream's provenance (what kind of country concocts such a fantasy?) or the contemporary evidence suggesting its cruel absurdity. In short, critique is combined with frivolity and recommitment to the Dream. Thus, Springsteen's song sequence (to which he gives a great deal of thought) started with "We Take Care of Our Own," and was followed by "Wrecking Ball," a whimsical ode to Giants Stadium in New Jersey whose appeal would be mostly regional and lifespan rather limited. Even upon release, the song felt dated. Whatever energy "We Take Care of Our Own" might have generated fizzled with "Wrecking Ball" as its follow-up. Impersonating a sports stadium on the verge of demolition might strike football fans as amusing or clever, but it is hardly political – the "hard times come, hard times go" incantation notwithstanding. Not even neo-depression can transform and save it.

By the time the concert concluded with a posthumous tribute to Clarence Clemons, former E Street saxophonist and beloved friend, no one seemed to remember Springsteen's political interventions. "Tenth Avenue Freeze-Out" made for a brilliant mourning song for Clemons, and Springsteen led 18,000 people in paying proper tribute to a lost member of the musical family. The minute-long roar for Clemons capped the night, as the sense of personal loss overwhelmed and supplanted feelings of political outrage.

America's democracy lives on, of course – regardless of the ruination it unleashes, generation after generation, on its own people. The destruction it brings also entails (some) creation, but the casualties accumulate on such a scale that degradation and death become central to life. Ironically, loving, even celebrating the country precisely for this reason becomes mandatory. Destruction this impressive must be given meaning and purpose. It must, moreover, confirm the country's self-understanding. Springsteen's songs on *Wrecking Ball*, therefore, cannot be the occasion to revisit the sensibility of patriotic democracy, not ultimately anyway. As a good patriotic democrat, therefore, Springsteen doubles down on America and locates a set of domestic enemies (bankers, financiers, etc.) to whom responsibility is assigned for the country's failure to live up to its promise.

American democracy's failures energize Springsteen. The so-called gap between ideal and reality allows him to breathe life into the American Dream – the ideal proves indestructible, of course, thanks largely to the gap's persistent reiterations rather than the Dream's actual realization: "I have spent my life judging the distance between American reality and the American dream ... Pessimism and optimism are slammed up against each other in my records, the tension between them is where it's all at, it's what lights the fire."[50] Springsteen, like many political activists before him, projects the very idea of an American Dream onto a recalcitrant social, political, and economic world: necessary political fiction indeed. The fire of which Springsteen speaks is love of country, a love that feeds on the refusal to admit the impossibility of its consummation. Don't we love what we cannot have all the more?

Wrecking Ball, then, is no revolutionary recording. On it "Land of Hope and Dreams," a 1999 song released on multiple live recordings that professes faith in the possibility of individual reinvention despite life's vicissitudes, makes what appears to be a strange appearance. It reminds us that the past does not define the present. The present need not repeat the past. And the future is open-ended – the intransigence of current circumstances notwithstanding. We just need to believe in America. If we do, we will be rewarded. Dreams can and do come true. Springsteen made the song part of the night's program, too, as if he did not want anyone to walk away from his concert angry let alone bent on exacting personal justice – not really, anyway. *Wrecking Ball*, both tour and record, develops and then defuses its own critique.[51]

REDEEMING SACRIFICE?

Danielle Allen, like Springsteen, theorizes the distance between America's democratic promise and its reality. She attends to a democracy's inability to consummate its identity, offering a trenchant critique of its (often) hidden costs. She argues that while a democracy claims to seek the good and well-being of all its citizens, some members of the polity invariably benefit at the direct expense of others. This deplorable aspect of democracy may or may not be the intended result of a political program or policy, but some invariably sacrifice (or are sacrificed) for others. What's more, those who accept or absorb the damage (or fallout) that accompanies politics thereby do democracy a great service, for their acceptance not only provides the polity with stability. It also enables political action in the first place. Democracy could not be if not for sacrifice. The most highly prized political order thus comes with a terrible price, which includes violence.[52]

Yet Allen foregoes the language of tragedy – even though the dynamic to which she draws attention seems essentially tragic. As a democracy pursues courses of action that benefit the country as a whole and actually succeeds in doing so, it also harms many of its citizens in the process. Doing right, in short, entails doing wrong. A democracy, then, not only routinely harms the critical material interests of its citizens. It also subverts the sovereignty it promises them. Citizens are empowered in theory only to find themselves disempowered in fact. Democracy raises hopes and then dashes them.[53]

To illustrate the kind of dilemmas facing democracy, Allen turns to economics, which also brings her thinking into contact with Springsteen's political-musical art. As the country promotes growth and prosperity, the Federal Reserve, official steward of the economy, routinely runs into a conflict between employment goals and price stability. If unemployment drops too low, it can trigger inflationary pressures. To maintain what is believed to be a proper balance, if and when the economy succeeds too well in the quest for full employment, the Federal Reserve, true to its statutory mission, raises interest rates and looks for a rise in unemployment to cool down a supposedly overheated economy. Such an approach is designed to advantage the country as a whole, but it can also lead to millions thrown out of work.[54]

Allen recognizes the reality of the sacrifice made and the debt thereby incurred, but when it comes to addressing actual damage inflicted, she writes that "the effects of unemployment on those who lose jobs cannot easily be undone."[55] Unlike the stories told in Springsteen's songs, this kind of description tends to slight the suffering that accompanies unemployment, which leads not only to various temporary setbacks but also to lives ruined, even lost: careers ended and eliminated; savings and retirement accounts depleted; homes foreclosed; families split; health compromised; and worse. Suicides increase thanks to unemployment. If Allen seeks not only to make people aware of democracy's sacrificial logic but also to mobilize a counter-response, the apparently deliberate understatement seems odd. It's not that Allen is unaware of unemployment's brutal impact, but the narrative omission of its deadly effects may be politically calculated. Allen not only exposes the workings of democracy. She also seeks to redeem them. Sacrifice cannot be eliminated. It must, therefore, be reinvented.

Allen calls for democracy to be practiced and experienced afresh. She thus invokes a notion of political friendship to address its quotidian failures. We must act as if our fellow citizens are our friends.[56] There is no emotional intimacy to this conception of friendship, but it does require rethinking the Hobbesian conception of self-interest common to American citizenship and replacing it with an equitable version in which we fold the interest of others into our considerations.[57] Allen appreciates that many citizens already effectively practice citizenship in this way and have been doing so for generations, especially along racial lines. People on the lower rungs of the social and political ladder have been the dominant practitioners of this kind of civic "giving." She would like to see the practice spread, preferably far and wide. Those who have benefitted from the sacrifice of others need to recognize it, acknowledge it, and eventually reciprocate. Allen's ethos: the democratization of sacrifice. Share it. Once people understand the debts they incur, they find themselves in position, under pressure even, to return the gift that has been given to them. This can work with a new conception of citizenship as friendship.[58]

According to Allen's democratic vision, for the practice of sacrifice to be legitimate, it must be done knowingly and willingly. It must be honored. And it must be reciprocated.[59] If this ideal can be converted into reality, America, so the hope goes, would more closely embody its democratic principles, thus closing Springsteen's troubling gap. Paradoxically, Allen may well presume, in order to resurrect, America's exceptionalism. The nation must and can better itself. The goal is to distinguish legitimate from illegitimate sacrifice and minimize the latter, which turns citizens into victims, often to the point of "insignificance."[60] If some people, groups, classes, minorities, or constituencies are always making illegitimate sacrifices, they become victims of their own democracy. This cannot be tolerated. Still, those who already sacrifice, without being either asked or rewarded, testify to the worthiness of the country nonetheless in need of transfiguration.

Each of democracy's sacrificial requirements, however, possesses a problematic dimension. Many, perhaps most, of the daily sacrifices democracy demands or exacts fall outside the scope of choice or consent. Allen would convert impotence into volunteerism, a rather romanticized reinvention of democratic life. The kind of economic sacrifice Allen cites as an example of democracy's cost is by definition imposed. No one would knowingly and willingly accept it given the horrific consequences, more often than not permanent, it entails (think here of unemployment). It is precisely the irrecuperable dimension of sacrifice that renders it tragic.[61] Allen wants citizens to stop thinking of politics as a zero-sum undertaking and focus on reciprocity, but thinking won't make it otherwise, despite Allen's astute remark that since we are talked into our feelings of anger and resentment regarding democratic decision-making, we can also be talked out of them. For Allen such negative emotions, by virtue of a conversion program, must be translated into generous dispositions, including goodwill and confidence.[62] If we know that others make sacrifices on our behalf or that benefit us, we can rework our experience of sacrifice and convert it into something that can be affirmed. Reciprocal sacrifice, to the degree that it is possible, sounds not only fair but also indispensable. Yet Allen's "knowing and willing" proposal seems to require citizens to exercise a kind of rational detachment that seems unlikely or draw on a reserve of emotions, like patriotism, from a register of political being unavailable to them given the circumstances. Love of country, however, might enable people to treat strangers, their fellow citizens, as if they were friends.

Following Ralph Ellison, Allen's democracy would honor the everyday sacrifices made by citizens no differently than it honors the purportedly more heroic, certainly more esteemed, sacrifices made by soldiers.[63] Each incarnation of sacrifice falls on a continuum and each, intrinsically related to suffering or death, is necessary for democracy to flourish. The practice of honoring sacrifice as an eminent civic virtue, however, feels too much like a militarization of citizenship. To develop solemn rituals to salute the fallen amongst us is to convert the citizen into a national hero whose life becomes disposable for the greater good of the country. The military example also indicates the difficulties of reciprocal sacrifice. The young and able-bodied fight a country's wars. So do certain classes of citizens from specific cultures and regions (those comprising the warrior class in America). These realities do not lend themselves to turnabout, which may partly explain why Allen's invocation of a politics of friendship feels like the pursuit of patriotic democracy by other means. That is, Allen's democratic project may presuppose a patriotic culture that can predispose citizens to formal political conversion to her new democratic identity. If so, it needs to consider that other citizens can be more than just strangers. Some are considered enemies whose visions of a good polity and a good life are incommensurable with our own. How is that kind of political experience to be reworked in Allen's refashioned democracy? A polity consisting of citizens-strangers-friends dealing with troubles that can be shared and resolved through politics presupposes a different kind of world than a polity consisting of citizens-strangers-enemies confronting antagonisms that lead to repeated injury, loss, and defeat – not despite but because of politics. The one world is difficult, hard. The other is tragic.

Allen notes the unequal historical distribution of sacrifice in the United States, which tracks and exceeds racial lines, but imagines it can be overcome. Perhaps this reverie accounts for the lack of a tragic perspective, depictions of democracy's self-subversions notwithstanding. Allen's re-presentation of the difficulties a democracy faces allows them to be tolerated, for a time, never fully detailed, and then negotiated. The narrative reduction of sacrifice may allow it to be managed, but manageability requires effectively masking the complete range of effects involved. Allen, then, may ultimately erase the very victims she champions. They move from invisibility to visibility and back again. The new, improved democratic political order to which she aspires reproduces, with a veneer of acknowledgment, the injuries and exclusions that animated the need for democracy's rebirth. She thereby mimics Springsteen, excavating discrepant experiences of loss, anger, and fury in the polity only to defuse and make them safe for democracy. She and Springsteen both have their dreams. We wouldn't want citizens not to love their country. For Springsteen this would make life in democracy unduly violent, risky, and unpredictable. For Allen this would make political friendship unthinkable and place the polity on the brink of a Hobbesian war of each against all. Despite these shortcomings,

Springsteen and Allen pinpoint democracy's violence against its own citizens and point to possible tragic resolutions.

ROUSSEAU AND SPRINGSTEEN: A DUET

Let's return to *Wrecking Ball*. Like previous Springsteen recordings, it purportedly documents the destruction of the American way of life. The institutions, practices, and ambitions that govern the country produce tremendous prosperity, making it the envy of much of the world. People flock to American shores seduced by its self-advertising and image. But the country also tends to concentrate the wealth it produces rather narrowly. The few necessarily thrive to the detriment of the many. The many, in turn, pay a prohibitive price for the well-being of the privileged few. Americans by and large accept this situation, even as they resent it, hoping perhaps to one day join the select.

To add plutocratic insult to democratic injury, when things disintegrate, as invariably they do, the rich few survive just fine while the many suffer even more. Worse still, these few are rarely, if ever, held accountable for their predations. Democracy's liberties routinely subvert themselves. On occasion, however, the people retake what was appropriated from them. Taking, with or without legal standing, is part and parcel of the democratic tradition, as Bonnie Honig argues in *Democracy and the Foreigner*.[64] The taking might transpire in a traditional political arena, or it might unfold in a more unconventional manner.

In Springsteen's "Easy Money," discussed briefly above, a husband and wife go out on the town. He has targeted a well-to-do enclave for a night of robbery and violence to be concealed beneath their date. The titans of finance and industry may laugh at the chaos they unleash, but tonight, confronted by an armed revolver, the roles will be reversed. The default distribution of power and affluence will be turned upside down – if only briefly. Here Springsteen's character may be superior to its creator. Springsteen deploys him for critical patriotic purposes, but the character eludes him. The nameless protagonist of "Easy Money" knows intuitively that the order of things cannot be justified, let alone tolerated. He feels no guilt, no remorse, thus no hesitation. No one can be said to deserve his or her position in society. Slots are random at one level, the product of power and influence at another. He proceeds as if it's high time to redistribute the benefits and burdens shared unequally in the country (this is probably not what Danielle Allen had in mind). Those who have suffered thanks to the success of others need to be compensated, even rewarded, for "accepting" their bad fortune. Inequality can be remedied, at least to some extent. Springsteen's antihero thus takes to the streets, forcing an encounter with his unequal, antidemocratic other. He will take from him what he can get. He will make him experience, briefly but memorably, not just anger and outrage at criminal injustice but also a more fundamental existential anxiety, namely, the contingency, vulnerability, and finitude that so many people live every day.

Writing, recording, and releasing "Easy Money" poses no political issues for Springsteen. He is an institution, for both good and ill. Performing the song in concert, on the other hand, involves some risk. Given Springsteen's relationship to his audience, to whom he sings, reminisces, and preaches, the song becomes a political object placed in public circulation over which he has little or no control. Given the passion, energy, and conviction with which he invests every song, it would be unsurprising if the narrative was experienced and interpreted as a call to arms. Springsteen tends to segregate his left democratic political activities and commitments from his concert tours, but the separation is imperfect. The fact that the protagonist of "Easy Money" is a Springsteen character ironically gives him popular credibility. Springsteen does not just present him to the audience. He depicts him with sympathy. This social bandit does what he has to do under the circumstances. As a political figure he is as inspiring as Ransom Stoddard, who effectively took over the role of town marshal, turned to violence, and, with a killing to his credit, became a legend.

The appeal of Springsteen's character aside, those targeted in this democratic crime might find themselves chastened by the encounter, a welcome outcome engendered through dreadful, if also explicable, methods. It shatters the illusion of the rich, the well-connected, the privileged – the so-called masters of the universe – that they have the rightful power to control the circumstances of life – not just their lives, or the lives of others, but life per se. The subject of the armed robbery discovers that the world makes its own demands and exacts its own payments. In this scenario, Springsteen's antihero has performed a valuable public democratic service, however violent the means. Still, the individual violence perpetrated cannot compare to the social and economic violence that devours him (and tens of millions of others like him at the lower and lowest ranks of the social, political, and economic orders). Nevertheless, he refuses to surrender to resignation, or assume that nothing can be done, or wallow in resentment. A tragic democratic perspective entails recognizing the impossibility of a situation and resisting it, knowing that things may go terribly wrong – or something new and unexpected might happen. There is no way to know in advance, which Oedipus intuitively understood. The uncertainty surrounding Springsteen's antihero, as we imagine him beyond the narrative details of the song, produces not pity or fear, the supposed stuff of tragic legend, but a sense of exhilaration. The tragic inspires.

A tragic perspective, then, appreciates reversals of fortune. They are part and parcel of life. Springsteen's troubled and troubling character in "Easy Money" enacts, however problematically, tragic responsibility on his own terms. After all, good fortune is largely the product of contingency or luck subsequently frozen into place by structures of law, themselves the product of entrenched power relations. In a democracy that values justice, fairness, and equality, why should anyone enjoy his or her success unfettered, indefinitely?

What might it mean to codify a tragic democratic sense of responsibility? In *On the Social Contract* Rousseau experimented with institutional mechanisms to protect and promote democracy. He, like Machiavelli, assumed that the people cannot necessarily be trusted to meet their political obligations. A politics of virtue is necessary but also insufficient. Thus the coercive power of law can do (some of) the work on their behalf. For example, as seen earlier, the sovereign people meet on a regular basis to discharge the official duties of citizenship. Their power is both absolute and limited. Once assembled, the people can reinvent the terms of their association as they see fit. They are well-advised, however, to attend to the conditions of their own sovereignty. They always need to keep the government in check because it is always encroaching on their rightful power. There are no guarantees, of course, but Rousseau's republic refuses to leave politics to the vagaries of will alone or to good luck.

A tragic democratic perspective concerns itself with more than political process. Alert to the suffering and hardship that flow directly from political life, it also attends to democracy's conditions of possibility. Here the spirit of Springsteen's protagonist in "Easy Money" can be institutionalized. Rousseau insists that freedom is impossible absent equality. Insofar as economic power translates to political power, which in turn entrenches and accelerates inequality, which then leads to greater disparities in political power, economic resources must be regularly redistributed as a matter of law. In the United States, for example, once the top 1 to 10 percent amasses more than its (roughly) proportional share of the nation's wealth, it should get recirculated to bolster the common freedom. American democracy can reintroduce the confiscatory tax rates of the Eisenhower years and impose a top marginal rate of 91 percent.[65] It can prohibit CEOs from making more than five times the average worker's salary. It can strip corporations of the legal fiction of personhood and remove them from politics altogether. It can ban individuals worth more than one million dollars from holding any government position. It can prevent individuals from spending their own money to win elective office.

Stringent estate taxes would perform a similar function. No one should enjoy an undue head start in life with a privileged position of any kind. These schemes, executed on behalf of democracy, might seem arbitrary. If they are, they are no more arbitrary, from a moral point of view, than the initial conditions to which they respond. Insofar as standard electoral mechanisms and legislative devices cannot be trusted to democratize economic power and make it compatible with social and political freedom, these adjustments must be folded into any basic constitutional framework.

Democracy, we should remember, routinely curtails itself in the name of self-realization. First Amendment rights are not absolute in the United States. Speech is limited in various respects so it can be meaningfully exercised. Both procedural and substantive measures are implicated. Not everyone can speak at once. Speech may be limited to certain times and places. Hate speech might render participation impossible for some citizens. Here ancient Athens can be invoked. The city practiced the political art of ostracism, sending into exile successful political figures possessing undue influence in order to protect democracy, as seen in Chapter 1. They had not necessarily done anything wrong and were not being punished. Democracy itself was being protected in order to guarantee its continuation. If Rousseau is right that freedom presupposes equality, including a rough equality of economic resources, then economic restructuring becomes indispensable for a democracy whose well-being can be privileged over mere economic accumulation, consumption, and display.

The protagonist in "Easy Money" embodies the tragic ethos a democracy requires. If most listeners find the contingent justice he performs unacceptable, what exactly makes the current antidemocratic system of rewards and allocations – and the violence they entail – more acceptable? Springsteen's songs alert us to the need to push Rousseauean protective measures beyond the political realm to the economic, which constitutes a dire threat to the sovereignty of the people. If a democracy were to acquire such a perspective, it might help disable the very conditions that produce Springsteen's supposedly wanton criminal in the first place. Springsteen's protagonist does not act out of a transcendent love of country and mutual affection for his fellow citizens. His passions do stem, though, from a sense of justice (and injustice) the democracy induces in him. We may or may not like him, but we know him. And he may not think of himself as such, but he is a political phenomenon, even a political agent.[66] He points the way to a tragic democratic ethos and politics that would obviate the brutal, terrifying violence to which he resorts. This is not to say Springsteen advocates violence. Springsteen concerts, as mentioned, point in many directions and even seem designed to defuse themselves so citizen-fans will not leave the concert hall brimming with problematic ideas or affects. Either way, Springsteen's concerts do not induce sprees of street violence. Democracy thus needs more than brief musical provocation followed by pacification. It needs tragic democratic activism, which Springsteen's stories express and inspire even if Springsteen retreats behind patriotic proclamations that sustain a love of country not only unwarranted but also counterproductive to democracy.

What might Rousseau say in response to this new Springsteen? After all, Rousseau famously delineated the preconditions for the exercise of the general will, which a people had to be fortunate enough to enjoy but could not bring about themselves – not without disastrous results anyway. Hence Rousseau's comment that "what makes the work of legislation difficult is not so much what must be established as what must be destroyed."[67] Rousseau warns the sovereign people that they cannot rest content with the establishment of a basic framework of laws. Too many forces threaten sovereignty. Rousseau issues warnings precisely because, following Machiavelli, he knows that the people sooner or later tend to withdraw from, even spurn, political life. They may assume that freedom is something to be enjoyed rather than regularly exercised, defended, and retaken. They may believe they have done enough already and prefer to focus life's energies elsewhere and let others take care of politics. Whatever the reason, Rousseau folds a preemptive strike, as we have seen, into democracy's constitutional structure. He knows that freedom's fate cannot be left to hang in a precarious balance. He does what he can institutionally, but he also displays restraint, noting if that the people are determined to hurt themselves, no one has a right to stop them.

But the people themselves might design prophylactic measures to protect democracy from what makes it impossible, thus from itself. Democracy's freedom entails the possibility of developments, in the economic sphere, for example, that threaten and endanger it. While Rousseau notes that a democracy cannot foresee and plan for every contingency, democracy must plan for what it can foresee. The damage inequality can be expected to inflict on democracy is predictable and known. This damage can be seen and felt in Springsteen songs across his career. Democracy needs to restore, periodically, economic balance in order to preserve and protect itself. Some citizens may balk at such an arrangement, but in democracy's table of values political freedom trumps mere economic accumulation, especially undue accumulation. The loss of resources, while perhaps regrettable to some, serves a great public service from which all, rather than just a few, benefit. If it is necessary to exercise freedom in order to maintain it, it is also necessary to promote and preserve the conditions that make its exercise possible. Democracy must be forced to be free. We could leave this task to the uncertainties of the political sphere rather than structure it into basic constitutional arrangements, but, as William E. Connolly argues, to cultivate a tragic vision of politics is to proceed knowing that political success is both possible and contingent upon a number of circumstances and forces aligning at just the right moment.[68] This unpredictability poses one of the challenges that democratic politics faces in a tragic cosmos. It can inspire citizens to be at their best. It is also possible for democracy to lessen the roles contingency and luck play in politics (they can never be eliminated, of course), even if such efforts also generate new dilemmas to be addressed. Either way, let the tragic experiments of democratic politics begin.

5

Two Cheers for Democratic Violence

> I do not say that democracy has been more pernicious on the whole, and in the long run, than monarchy or aristocracy. Democracy has never been and can never be so durable as aristocracy; but while it lasts, it is more bloody than either.
>
> John Adams, *The Letters of John and Abigail Adams*

> Constitutional patriotism – again, understood as a post-national, universalist form of democratic political allegiance – is rejected on account of its abstract or, as an especially inappropriate metaphor goes, "bloodless" quality.
>
> Jan-Werner Müller, *Constitutional Patriotism*

Does it take Bruce Springsteen and his outlaw couple to raise and force the issue of democracy's everyday dissemination of violence as well as its blindness, indifference, and willful helplessness in the face of it? Democracy legitimizes violence by the state, but this violence is performed for democratic ends infrequently. The state, though democracy's official representative, routinely acts against democracy, including when the people themselves try to act on its behalf. If democratic societies need to install constitutional mechanisms that precommit them to minister to democracy's conditions of possibility, what else needs to be done? Do democratic citizens need to break the state's monopoly on the legitimate use of violence when the state fails to protect or itself violates their basic social and political rights, including the right to a life free from assorted violence? Do democratic citizens need to cultivate a tragic ethos that presumes democracy has enemies, including at times the state, and that credibility is not just an inherent political anxiety in its foreign affairs but also a critical political concern in its domestic affairs to which they must attend with vigilance and zeal? Constitutional patriotism seems a well-suited vehicle to address these questions – at least initially.

DEMOCRACY'S DRAMATIC TURN

Constitutional patriotism enjoys a distinct theoretical presence in contemporary democratic thought (more so perhaps in Europe than in the United States) by issuing a tantalizing political promise. Situating itself between liberal nationalism and cosmopolitanism, the first plagued by the ineliminable dangers of its ethnic cousin, the second by the amorphous quality of the community it signifies, constitutional patriotism proposes a form of civic identity rooted in commitment to democratic principles and procedures and replete with the kind of affective attachments on which democracies depend for their prosperity.[1] Constitutional patriotism endeavors to reinvent democratic citizenship and revive democratic politics.[2]

Still, for all its confidence, constitutional patriotism suffers from a kind of existential insecurity. On the one hand, it bristles at the charge of liberal nationalists that it is too abstract to provide the loyalty and devotion patriotism necessarily implies and democracy requires. The shorthand for this criticism is that constitutional patriotism is "bloodless."[3] Constitutional patriotism, however, thinks of itself as a political force to be taken seriously. On the other hand, constitutional patriotism rejects the notion that it amounts to a new form of identity politics that can establish itself only by resorting to the illiberal practices of traditional versions of patriotism and nationalism, more specifically by presupposing and engendering an enemy (or other).[4]

Constitutional patriotism, then, presents itself as patriotism with a difference – with an edge. It foregrounds commitment to democratic values and practices even as it relies on more traditional patriotic forms to succeed. Thus, it does not deny that it faces serious obstacles and objections. It even refuses the compliment that it amounts to a healthy form of patriotism by focusing passion on a different (read: safe) object of attachment, something other than the ethnic nation. Instead, constitutional patriotism insists that it possesses the resources needed to address the very problems it will (also) generate.[5] Constitutional patriotism, that is, believes it can contain the lethal compounds that, in part, compose it. It would seem

to be a political ethos that a radical democrat such as Bruce Springsteen
could affirm.

What kind of promise, ultimately, does constitutional patriotism hold for a democratic polity? What accounts for its sensitivity to the allegation that it is bloodless? If constitutional patriotism
calls for ambivalence on the part of citizens (attachment, yes, but not
too much), does such a complex emotional disposition suggest that it
amounts to a tragic political ethos, one both indispensable and inimical to the democracy it would serve? If constitutional patriotism must
draw on traditional patriotic resources to succeed, does this dependence threaten to render it indistinguishable from its problematic rela-
tives? If it must resort to supplements, in other words, can it do so
without defeating itself? What if, alternatively, constitutional patriotism represents a political project that simultaneously draws on, but
finally disavows, the violence that is a constitutive part of democratic
politics? In that case, perhaps it is better to confront, even cultivate, the
violence head-on and make it democratically responsible and productive rather than relegate it to the shadows where, ironically, a paler version might prove less effective and more susceptible to antidemocratic
reaction? In short, might not democracies be well advised to acknowledge, affirm, and then address the violence and tragedy to which they
routinely give rise – a politics that constitutional patriotism seems to
promise but not deliver?

A GENEALOGY OF CONSTITUTIONAL PATRIOTISM

With the resurgence of nationalist sentiments following the collapse of
the Soviet Union and its Eastern European satellite states, patriotism
experienced a distinct theoretical revival. Maurizio Viroli, for one, insists
that patriotism alone possesses the affective ability to contest nationalism
on its own political terrain. This is a challenge that must be met. To abandon the political field to nationalism portends trouble, perhaps calamity,
for liberal democratic states new and old.[6]

Patriotism, of course, enjoyed its champions prior to revolutionary
events in Europe. In the United States John Schaar issued an elegant,
enticing plea for a critical patriotism, thus a renewed citizenship, in
the immediate aftermath of Vietnam and Watergate.[7] While doubting
his chances of success, Schaar deemed patriotism a more or less natural phenomenon indispensable to the well-being of a democratic political community. Margaret Canovan posited an additional factor in the

revitalization of patriotism: the communitarian critique of liberalism in the 1980s.[8] The abstract (rootless, unencumbered) individual did not speak to the complex moral and emotional lives of ordinary people for whom attachment, significance, and meaning are to be found in the wider political community. George Kateb, similarly, claims that patriotism in one form or another, to one degree or another, is nearly irresistible, for most people cannot bear the burdens of individual selfhood, the terror of living life on their own, suggesting that patriotism is always on the political agenda even if it is periodically dormant or ostensibly discredited.[9] In short, the "renewed" interest in patriotism does not lack determinants. In addition, the circumstances attending patriotism's reawakening are riven by pressure and peril. Citizenship is more than a scholarly question, leading Jan-Werner Müller to think of constitutional patriotism as a wager – indeed a high-stakes wager.[10] Müller, however, does not hesitate to make it. Or so it might seem.

Constitutional patriotism's origins can be effectively located in West German politics, claims it has been more or less coeval with democracy notwithstanding.[11] Delivering a "brief history," Müller highlights the ghost of Weimar haunting constitutional patriotism. Given the Republic's manifest failures and their horrid consequences, a democracy must consider how it can successfully defend itself against its enemies. How can the constitutional order survive those determined to defeat and destroy it and use their own strengths against it to do so? Constitutional patriotism, accordingly, combines what Müller calls memory and militancy. It must recall crimes of the past – not just to avoid repeating them but also as a reminder to stay vigilant for new dangers. It must resist transgressions in the present – not just to defend democracy against efforts to use its own principles, institutions, and practices to subvert it but also to honor and redress the past.[12]

Rather than bury the horrors of the Nazi regime, particularly the Holocaust, West Germany's incipient democracy foregrounded memory of the recent past (a negative model) as it struggled to articulate an identity for itself and define its place in the world. The cultivation of memory featured an obligation to assume responsibility, insofar as this was even possible, for the crimes of the Nazi state and to make (some kind of) amends. The assumption of militancy entailed protecting the new democracy from self-declared enemies who would return to or reinvigorate the Nazi past or who looked to the morally and politically compromised communist East for political inspiration. Threats emanated equally from the right and left wings of the political spectrum. In the name of democratic freedom and plurality, West Germany did not hesitate to suppress certain forms of political action and speech.[13]

Dolf Sternberger publicized the term *constitutional patriotism* on West Germany's thirtieth anniversary in 1979, though he had been pondering appropriate patriotic affects in a democratic state for some twenty years, determined to develop a notion of citizenship involving active, even aggressive defense of the constitutional order against its enemies. During the heyday of the Red Army Faction, Sternberger's ethos materialized in restrictions on civil liberties and civil service employment as West Germany defended itself against left-wing political terrorism.[14] Not surprisingly, these restrictions did not disappear with the demise of the threat to which they were a response. Enemies of the liberal democratic constitution come and go. Enmity toward it, however, is permanent – whether real or potential. Sternberger's politics resembled Karl Loewenstein's 1938 notion of "militant democracy," according to which democracies cannot be concerned with constitutional formalities or legal niceties (the mistakes that led to Weimar's destruction and facilitated the rise of fascism across Europe) as they defend themselves against fundamental threats.[15] Sternberger posited a form of citizen identification with the state rooted in both rationality and passion. "Friends of the constitution" must be prepared to act in its defense with the pride they feel for it – in creating, sustaining, and owning it – informing their affective dispositions.[16]

Still, Müller's account of the necessary connection of memory and militancy to constitutional patriotism, offered as he distinguishes initial from recent versions of it, reveals more than he may realize or want. Constitutional patriotism's context of creation furnishes it with self-conscious *street credibility*. Forged in the aftermath of Nazi Germany and confronted with the terrorist threat of the 1970s, constitutional patriotism is not a theoretical exercise detached from worldly affairs but a material practice animated by first-hand familiarity with unbridled passion and unspeakable violence. Addressing the concern that constitutional patriotism might take problematic form (on its own terms), Müller issues a cautionary note:

[T]his is not to say that *all* forms of constitutional patriotism would have to come with a *strong* emphasis on memory and militancy. In other words, and contrary to one of the most widespread clichés of our time, not every "identity" needs *primarily* to be "constructed" through an "Other" … There *might* be good reasons, however, not to put *too much* stress on memory and militancy as aspects of constitutional patriotism, as both have an illiberal side.[17]

Ostensibly counseling moderation and restraint, Müller's version of constitutional patriotism nevertheless *emphasizes* and *stresses* memory and militancy and constructs its political identity through *enmity*. It thus seems to mimic traditional patriotic conceptions in ways it aspires to minimize or avoid.

Either way, constitutional patriotism gestures toward a tragic conception of politics. Müller concedes that it is Janus-faced. A finely tuned memory might foster a deep and troubled militancy (Müller seems to trade on the multiple meanings of militancy). The concession, however, feels somewhat matter-of-fact, as if admitting to constitutional patriotism's possible (nominal) dangers legitimizes its place in the political scheme of things.[18] This feels not so much the beginning of politics, as in a tragic conception, but its end. In West Germany, for example, Nazi wannabes and domestic terrorists name two concrete enemies, but they do not – they cannot – exhaust any constitutional patriotism enemies list. Each merely provides specificity to a general concern. Nazism may be historically unique, but fascism is not, nor is the communist Red Army Faction's violent reaction to its liberal variant. What's more, constitutional patriotism concerns itself with political agents (activists, lawyers, etc.) that might assist those opposed to the constitutional order by defending their individual rights and liberties or by opposing possible restrictions on rights and liberties per se. These third parties may also be labeled enemies (however unwitting) of the constitution. Once that happens, fourth and fifth parties may get involved, coming to the defense of the newly criminalized, thus making themselves enemies, too. Constitutional patriotism, in short, seems poised to create a potentially endless number of enemies as it articulates and refines its protective constitutional posture. It is serious, committed, and passionate in its defense of the democratic state, especially when it is under (perceived) threat. Yet it's not clear if Müller recognizes the tragic character of this political dynamic, let alone the responsibilities it engenders, which might provide new opportunities for democracy to reinvent itself.

In the end, Müller's short history of constitutional patriotism vindicates rather than destabilizes it. The search for origins honors its object of inquiry. Constitutional patriotism's survival of "genealogical" scrutiny is a "failure" Müller celebrates. Nevertheless, a more Nietzschean genealogy of constitutional patriotism reveals potentially fatal shortcomings in its basic architecture otherwise concealed. Genealogical investigation suggests, in other words, that while constitutional patriotism rightly insists that democracy attend to difficult questions regarding its political character in a dangerous world filled with enemies, it cannot succeed (not fully anyway) in its self-assigned task. Though constitutional patriotism strives to demarcate a new, improved, and purified form of patriotism with solid credentials, it ultimately flinches when faced with the kind of tragic results democracy necessarily produces – such as nativist or neoliberal violence that kills citizens as the state looks on. To be a compelling option, constitutional patriotism would need the ability, when necessary, to eschew what it affirms (constitutionalism) and affirm what it disavows (violence). Moreover, the people must give the state – and, in the current context, its neoliberal masters – genuine reason to respect, even fear, its sovereign democratic power. Constitutional patriotism excels at identifying democracy's predicaments, but it cannot, appearances notwithstanding, adequately finesse them. The courage of liberal democratic convictions, including a militancy more apparent than real, cannot suffice. While constitutional patriotism proffers a one-dimensional militancy, contemporary democratic states in America and Europe give themselves license to cordon and domesticate oppositional democratic politics (think Occupy Wall Street or, more recently, Ferguson, Missouri). They act as if they are free to deploy overwhelming preemptive force or reactive violence against citizens who take to the streets in protest and dissent, without giving their legitimacy or repercussions a second moral thought.

DANGEROUS LIAISONS

Clarissa Rile Hayward provides a valuable survey of constitutional patriotism, including a reconstruction of Jürgen Habermas's (initial) reflections on it that reveals the difficulties constitutional patriotism faces as it searches for a place in democratic life. [19] It oscillates between a potentially tragic approach to politics that appreciates limits and ambiguities and a kind of Platonic confidence that assumes it can successfully fashion political outcomes without (serious) remainder.[20] Spinning a web of contradictory and combustible commitments, passions, and principles, constitutional patriotism finally adopts an unduly cautious or prudent ethos too easily satisfied with success on its own stripped-down terms. Let me explain.

Habermas's work on constitutional patriotism stems, in part, from the difficulties that liberal democratic citizens experience in identifying with their polity following a horrific event or deed. While this is often thought to be a distinctly German problem, it is shared by other democracies. Citizens of the United States could well wrestle with their own national commitments and identifications given the country's genocidal policies and practices vis-à-vis African slavery, the removal and eradication of Native Peoples from their ancestral lands, and, more recently, the Vietnam War. Richard Rorty's example notwithstanding, how do democratic citizens negotiate a legacy they find, at least partly, despicable?[21]

For Habermas, identity is not fixed or static. It is subject to reinterpretation. Citizens reimagine and reinvent themselves through public conversations, debates, deliberations, and disagreements, a perpetual (learning) process in democratic society.[22] Ideals such as equality and participation can be extended to incorporate previously silenced, marginalized, or excluded groups and constituencies. Call it the democratization of democracy. Citizen identity cannot be fabricated willy-nilly, of course. It is always (to some extent) encumbered by the past, but the past, too, can be reopened and reassessed.[23] Citizens might affirm certain aspects of their history and reject others based on a new set of liberal democratic constitutional principles adopted by the community. The past can be overcome but also preserved, negatively, in this way. Germans now reject racism and violence as anti-democratic, for example, and fold these principles and commitments into their normative self-conceptions.[24]

Not all commitments, however, are created equal. Rejection of racism may be absolute, but violence can be legitimately deployed by the state in a variety of circumstances. Individual instances of violence (repressions, wars, etc.) might be opposed while the general need for it remains fixed. The resort to arms that proved problematic in one context might play out differently in another historical setting. A political culture or sensibility, then, might encompass an abstract willingness to utilize violence for selected purposes and draw sustenance from the specific, even perverse occasions when it was previously (if regrettably) deployed. Any resort to arms contributes to a culture of sacrifice that can be put to creative (and problematic) use. As long as citizens are willing to sacrifice, it does not necessarily matter from what sources they take inspiration. For constitutional patriotism, what polity's history does not potentially lend itself to innovative and productive reinterpretation? Alternatively, while democracies supposedly want citizens who can and will hold the state accountable, they do not want citizens to make their own choices regarding national security, war, or violence. Constitutional patriotism lives comfortably in close relation to a political culture that approves of violence in general, a willingness to sacrifice (kill and die) in particular, even though it goes wrong again and again.

Constitutional patriotism, it can be seen, does not refer to a set of universal political principles to be introduced "as is" regardless of time and place. Rather, it must unfold within a specific political and cultural context, drawing on what Patchen Markell calls "supplements of particularity" for successful installation.[25] Consider two possible but problematic examples of supplements. In the United States soldiers who fought for the Confederate States of America, a regime determined to enshrine a slave society in the south and expand it westward, are buried in Arlington National Cemetery. Close to 400 southern soldiers enjoy the patriotic environs of Arlington thanks to a 1900 act of Congress. Arlington also serves as a home to the Confederate Monument dedicated to "*our* dead heroes." United Daughters of the Confederacy lobbied to have the monument built, but the United States government consented to and even embraced the idea. Beneath the salute to "our dead heroes" is a Latin inscription that reads: "The Victorious Cause was Pleasing to the Gods, but the Lost Cause to Cato." The United Daughters thus continue to wage – in memorial form – the civil war the South lost. It associates the Confederacy with Cato, the Roman citizen of exemplary republican virtue who opposed tyranny. The North may have been victorious thanks to military supremacy, but that does not mean it was in the right. The Lost Cause lives on, thanks here to democracy's assistance in the name of a unifying patriotism.[26] The monument's central inscription reads: "Not for fame or reward; not for place or for rank; not lured by ambition or goaded by necessity; but in simple obedience to duty as they understood it; these men suffered all; sacrificed all; dared all – and died." The repugnant inscription (imagine an African American reading it) cannot withstand minimal scrutiny: their suffering did not approach the evils of slavery; the vast majority returned home after the war to a life of freedom; and duty as they understood it entailed fealty to a racial dictatorship defined by rank. By placing the memorial in Arlington National Cemetery, however, the country converts criminal traitors into noble warriors, respecting, honoring, and valuing the willingness of ex-citizens to die for their slave state even though it was hell-bent on destroying the democracy that now salutes them.[27]

Since the memorial's dedication in 1914 (Woodrow Wilson presiding), American presidents have sent flowers to it each Memorial Day. This presented a problem for Barack Obama his first year in office. Kirk Savage argued that Obama should continue the tradition, though not without alteration: he recommended that Obama also send a wreath to the African American Civil War Memorial in Washington, DC. Apparently taken by the transcendent power of mortal service to country, Savage wrote: "the men buried around the Confederate Memorial sacrificed, suffered and died just as the black and white soldiers of the Union did."[28] A strange claim: black soldiers were not considered soldiers by the South; they were subjected to special treatment on and off the battlefield according to their race – the men buried at Arlington would have executed them on sight, even if wounded or surrendering. In addition, Northern soldiers suffered and died in an illegitimate, unconscionable war responsibility for which lies solely with the South. Curiously, Savage compares the Confederacy with Nazi Germany but insists that "the Confederacy and the Third Reich are not, *in the end*, comparable." He may be right, in the end, but what about in the meantime? Given the partial validity of the comparison, how is it that Savage does not draw the conclusion opposite the one he reaches? How do Confederate soldiers and African-American soldiers become memorial equals? Patriotism, it seems, can justify anything, thereby escaping responsibility for what is done in its name. In short, there seems to be little of potential value for an ethos of memory and militancy at work here but much on behalf of obedience to an anti-democratic regime. What kind of constitutional patriots would devotees of the American Confederacy make? This kind of supplement values active forgetting, nostalgia, and the worship of false idols.

This patriotic dynamic might also illuminate the controversy surrounding Ronald Reagan's notorious 1985 visit to Bitburg Military Cemetery, part of the fortieth anniversary celebrations of VE Day. Reagan's trip constituted payment of a political debt to Helmut Kohl for his steadfast support of Reagan's nuclear missile program in Western Europe. It was also the occasion to champion the reconciliation of former enemies as they battled a new common foe, communist totalitarianism. Bitburg, it so happened, contained members of Hitler's Waffen-SS alongside thousands of ordinary German soldiers, a not uncommon occurrence in German cemeteries. Reagan tried to deflect the fallout from the ill-conceived visit by noting that the regular soldiers buried in the cemetery were very young men serving their country in a terrible war, making them victims in their own right. It was impossible to know which of the buried supported Nazi war aims and which served solely because they were drafted. Countries can and should be criticized, even condemned, for the use they make of their youth in war, but those who serve do not necessarily deserve reproach even if the war is immoral. Their country calls. They answer that call. They answer it with their lives. Patriotism's connection to death can transcend any moral qualm, political division, or national border.

The passion that killing and dying engenders is apparently too valuable a resource to squander. Again, what kind of constitutional patriot would a devotee of the German nation across its entire history, regardless of the record of any one regime, including the Third Reich, make?

Müller acknowledges that constitutional patriotism relies on problematic supplements to sustain itself. It is "thicker" than many of its critics – who reduce it to attachment to political principles and procedures, which, in turn, does not have the affective stuff it takes to promote civic identification – mistakenly contend. Müller thus addresses a problem typically associated with thickness: it courts the very dangers it prefers to avoid.[29] Not surprisingly, then, Müller spurns the idea of awe-inspiring heroes and thrill-inducing triumphs that involve "unquestioned pride" and unswerving loyalty. Democracy must have its inspirational stories, singular deeds, and memorable figures, but democracy must also be attentive to the complexities that invariably accompany achievements worth commemorating: "it is adding this ambivalence that makes the difference for constitutional patriotism."[30]

What ambivalence can be added to America's reconciliation with Southern slavocracy and Reagan's reconciliation with (Nazi) Germany? Are constitutional patriotism's resources too thick for its own good? What kind of defense of democracy can be mounted when a political culture includes in its archives a history of violent, obedient service to racist antidemocratic regimes? What kind of sustenance does the loyalty and service of Confederate soldiers and Hitler's Wehrmacht effectively force-feed democracies? Alas, each might be a resource for National Guard soldiers who fired indiscriminately at Kent State students in 1970 protesting the Vietnam War (a subject treated in Chapter 6). Their example might encourage American patriots to disrupt the ritual of Admission Day (articulated in Chapter 2). Constitutional patriotism's supplements problem is that many of them may lack essential democratic components, which means they cannot contribute to a sensibility that valorizes democracy as a tragic enterprise. Yet how can constitutional patriotism filter unwanted or counterproductive political cultural elements likely to undermine democratic prospects? After all, doesn't constitutional patriotism need to appeal to multiple constituencies to be an ethos of citizenship that speaks to more than a narrow band of true believers?

This is not to suggest that ambivalence cannot temper tendencies to veneration, but the reconstructed pride that Müller counsels for citizens not only allows much room for abuse. It also fosters it. Müller would not necessarily disagree. If anything, he seems resigned to patriotism's, including constitutional patriotism's, capacity for ugliness and its inevitable expression. He advises us to "remember Benjamin's dictum ... that there is no object of culture which is not at the same time an object of barbarism."[31] Given patriotism's propensity to hatred, violence, and chauvinism, why pursue a new political ethos that must rely on a political passion that lends itself to barbarism? After all, insofar as constitutional patriotism nourishes itself, like other forms of patriotism, on enmity, it tends to find or fabricate threats ad nauseam and depict them to suit its needs. The ambivalence Müller cites as a critical component of constitutional patriotism is not easily added – or if added, sustained. What's more, patriotic cultures tend to be allergic to ambivalence, perhaps especially if it's perceived to be an additive and thus artificial, forced. Ambivalence, when it comes to patriotic politics is likely to be little more than a precursory stance that inevitably gives way to a definitive posture that leaves doubt behind, as seen in Chapter 2.

Müller concedes these dangers and knows they can lead to serious harm. He contends that constitutional patriotism, unlike, say, liberal nationalism, possesses the internal resources to respond to and correct the dangers it poses. In Rousseauean terms, it is the cure to its own ill. Müller's anodyne assessment of what can happen in the interim – that is, what can happen while constitutional patriotism looks for remedies – may not provide much solace to critics, let alone its casualties, however. "Clearly, such corrections in particular might take time to have an effect – in which case it might be too late for some who have suffered from the 'identitarian' illiberal dangers that might be associated with constitutional patriotism."[32] Müller's self-critique does not go far enough. Not only might constitutional patriotism not actually produce the necessary corrections. It might also find itself issuing undue corrections since it is the source of trouble, which does not seem to concern Müller overmuch.

Müller's casual stance is reminiscent of Richard Rorty's nonchalance regarding the damage that results from patriotic democracy's initiatives.[33] Müller's position seems immunized from responsibility – to some extent – by the affirmation that politics entails risks, which means that if and when things go wrong, even terribly wrong, no one should be surprised. It is the price of any politics. Perhaps democracies should even be resigned to the necessity of collateral damage in a world lacking guarantees.[34] Either way, damage discloses nothing dispositive about constitutional patriotism. This seems to be Müller's stance on one particularly notorious instance of patriotic democracy gone wrong: McCarthyism. Loyalty can breed fanaticism leading to outsized fears and crazed persecutions. Given

constitutional patriotism is a matter of choice rather than birth or inheritance, it feels natural to be concerned about the sincerity and reliability of
other citizens (most of whom are strangers). How can it be known who is
trustworthy and who is traitorous? A loyalty oath provides the occasion
for citizens to make formal decisions and public declarations (one way or
the other). This means there is, potentially, a dark side, since "belonging
will be dependent on potentially changing standards of political behavior
... the possibility of political choice makes for exclusion." In addition, it
cannot be known whether a citizen is truly loyal absent an "attractive
alternative."[35] The existence of such an alternative, however, fosters existential anxiety and often incites the creation of (endless) enemies.[36]

     Again, Müller does not seem unduly concerned insofar as McCarthyism
represents an aberration in democracy's history. There is no justification for or defense of it. The constitutional system misfired, and it had
to be repaired with all deliberate speed.[37] But McCarthyism poses no
great moral or philosophical questions, which seems too easy. What if
McCarthy had been sincere and right? Does the possibility suggest that
the state's monopoly on violence must, if and when necessity arises, be
exercised against domestic enemies in the name of democracy – because
too much is at stake to hesitate or flinch? Even if militancy as violence is
not the first response of a democratic regime or its citizens, does it need
to be in their repertoires? If so, what understanding accompanies the
deployment of democratic violence? Is it a kind of tough-but-necessary
love? Does its good faith speak for itself – with no need to apologize,
let alone make amends for, its expression? Or, unlike with McCarthyism,
what happens in a situation where the democratic political order, to protect its way of life, knowingly does wrong, thus where the harm it inflicts
is deliberate? Is constitutional patriotism prepared to take such (tragic)
action, particularly if it entails violence, even against enemies? Does it
possess the sensibility of Ransom Stoddard and Tom Doniphon or of
Link Appleyard?

WHY NOT MOB RULE?

To address these questions and chart in more detail the promising but
ultimately problematic bent of constitutional patriotism in the life and
times of democracy, there is no better guide than Patchen Markell. In
"Making Affect Safe for Democracy? On 'Constitutional Patriotism,'"
Markell's sober reconstruction of constitutional patriotism includes a
reluctance to embrace its more protean but also risky and dangerous

possibilities, especially insofar as they might parallel the morbid trajectories characteristic of traditional patriotic forms or the volatile uncertainties of a more radical or militant democratic politics.[38]

For Markell the story of constitutional patriotism begins with a problem in liberal thought: the role of passion in politics. Liberals prefer the cool, confident tones of reason to the fevered, flushed pitch of passion, but this leaves liberalism open to the charge that it cannot adequately account for citizen motivation and participation. In short, liberalism suffers from an affect deficit. To remedy the perceived shortcoming, liberals have capitalized on the renaissance of the distinction between civic and ethnic nationalism. Liberals insist they can generate the loyalty, commitment, and devotion the political community needs not only to survive but flourish. They rely on what they take to be a safe form of political passion rooted in liberal principles and procedures rather than the more problematic identifications with birth, blood, and descent typical of nationalism. This move relies on a distinction between civic and ethnic nationalism. Markell calls this "the *strategy of redirection*. This strategy claims to render affect safe for liberal democracies by redirecting our attachment and sentiment from one subset of objects (the 'ethnic') to another subset of objects (the 'civic'). Since the ethnic conveniently turns out to be the source of all of affect's pathologies, the civic can offer all the benefits of affect while" avoiding its pitfalls.[39]

Constitutional patriotism, Habermas's version in particular, seems well-suited to fill liberalism's affective hole. Some of Habermas's *early* reflections on constitutional patriotism can be read in this way, as Markell notes. The strategy of redirection holds many attractions. In a pluralized and pluralizing world rife with conflicting passions reflecting a multitude of deep-seated ambitions, sacred causes, and fundamentalist agendas, and portending destructive social divisions, constitutional patriotism appears on the scene as a constructive way to bring a political community together. The usual suspects (blood, religion, culture, language, history, etc.) no longer work (assuming they ever did). The creation of a homogeneous political community ineluctably exacts considerable, unacceptable cost. Nationalist political programs that cultivate intolerance and sanction a cleansing violence in the name of a pure unified order have been repeatedly discredited and defeated. In modernity people are called on to leave behind unthinking attachments to fixed, given identities and traditional customs and commands rooted in pre-political connections to family, ethnos, and nation, and adopt a post-conventional stance in which the autonomous individual armed with reason forges new attachments characterized by universal principles and norms.[40] The nation is no longer to be conceived as a community of descent, but as a "self-determining political community."[41]

Still, citizens in a diverse community require something to share, which, given their many differences, must be conceived in minimal terms.[42] Making commonality as thin as possible enhances its chances of success – hence the invocation of universal liberal political principles, both substantive and procedural. These principles can transcend and subordinate the faults and rifts that otherwise distinguish peoples. They stand alone, self-sufficient, capable of uniting people around them. The specific histories or concrete cultures of people fade to the background. Universal political ideals – the more abstract the better – now draw people's affection, loyalty, and commitment.

Yet, as attractive and reasonable as this approach might sound, it turns out that constitutional patriotism not only involves but also requires more than commitment to a set of abstract universal principles and values. Constitutional patriotism is thus misdescribed or misconceived as a strategy of redirection. Proffering a safe form of affect cannot succeed politically. Markell argues that constitutional patriotism's ambition does not entail making affect safe for democracy at all. Initially this may have been a plausible way to approach it (again, Habermas's early efforts on the subject lend credibility to such a reading), but constitutional patriotism knowingly depends on what Markell calls "supplements of particularity" to articulate and sustain itself. Thus, the generation of civic affect to which constitutional patriotism aspires thus relies on mediation through lived histories and cultures that do not exactly match the universal norms they allegedly manifest.[43] There is a fraught relationship between the universal and the particular. The universal needs but is also endangered by the particular. The discrepancy between the two is critical – productively so. Markell writes:

If universal normative principles always depend on supplements of particularity that enable them to become objects of attachment and identification but that are also never quite equivalent to the principles they purport to embody, then constitutional patriotism can best be understood not as a safe and reliable identification with some pure set of already available universals, but rather as a political practice of refusing or resisting particular identifications – of insisting on and making manifest this failure of equivalence – for the sake of the ongoing, always incomplete, and often unpredictable project of universalization.[44]

Refusal and resistance, nevertheless, need a base of operations. They presuppose prior identifications and affirmations, which need not be complete or total (just the opposite), but they do need to carry weight. Otherwise constitutional patriotism cannot be a meaningful patriotism. Refusal and resistance are thus always partial. As a universal project constitutional patriotism draws on the particular (patriotic) history of a given political culture to sustain itself. This involves, generally speaking, memory, ritual, ceremony, commemoration, recognition, tribute, celebration, and so on. More specifically, the patriotic particular involves holidays, dates, songs, wars, battles, heroes, deeds, sacrifices, statues, monuments, memorials, examples, and events. The more specific and detailed it becomes, the more it explicitly and implicitly draws on the ambiguous, problematic, even objectionable aspects of the larger patriotic culture. Markell, accordingly, theorizes an ambivalent posture toward the political community (and one's fellow citizens) that combines emotions such as love, pride, and loyalty on the one hand but includes emotions such as shame, anger, and indignation on the other.

Here Markell's analysis of Habermas's interventions in contemporary German politics to illuminate constitutional patriotism as "a habit or practice" calls for special attention since the need for supplements emerges most clearly in the conduct of politics itself. According to Habermas, one deficit from which the supposedly safe version of constitutional patriotism suffers is that no one fights for an abstraction.[45] This worry is no mere figure of speech, nor is it a concern about war. While Markell acknowledges that constitutional patriotism "carries … risks analogous to those borne by other nationalisms," he does not offer a risk assessment.[46] Is the idea here that constitutional patriotism's hazards should be minimized and contained, or that they should be taken advantage of and put to good political effect?

Markell discusses one event in detail, a neo-Nazi bombing of Turkish immigrants. Habermas condemned the violence on behalf of the "standards of civic intercourse." Criticism was also directed toward the government. State officials failed to act decisively, and people took to the streets to express their outrage and disgust at both the violence and the paltry official response from political elites. Not all forms of protest were identical in style, tone, or substance. Some were quite vocal, while others were silent. These differences themselves became the subject of political dispute. Some dismissed candlelight vigils as insufficient. Apparently apolitical in character, they were deemed narcissistic exercises that might appease the consciences of attendees but were otherwise without impact. Something more pronounced was called for. Demonstrations – loud, noisy – against violence drew hundreds of thousands into the streets of German cities (not just the site of the attack). This was constitutional patriotism at its finest. Habermas applauded the angry, supportive sentiments these rallies brought together and released. Organizers in Munich issued a revealing statement: "By participating people will show that we do not accept attacks on hostels for asylum-seekers, vandalism of Jewish cemeteries and assaults on foreigners; *that we are ashamed by the helplessness and slowness of our government*, and that we are increasingly ready to defend democracy."[47]

For Habermas the protests expressed both empathy and democratic indignation – hence the phrase that Markell italicizes. Markell also makes a point of stating, as if for the record, that he is not "endors[ing] mob rule over the rule of law." Let's pause here. Why deny an accusation no one is likely to make or a conclusion no one is likely to reach? What is the source of Markell's anxiety? Is something more than anxiety at work here? Fear of democratic violence perhaps? If Markell answers an unmade accusation, let it be made. In the Munich organizers' statement, the declaration that concludes it is the most revealing and provocative. What does it mean to swear publicly that "we are increasingly ready to defend democracy"? Assuming the proclamation refers to accountability, is it directed to the state? Is it addressed to neo-Nazi skinheads? Has democracy itself been put on notice? Is the declaration a statement of fact? Is it an invitation? Is it a warning? Is it a threat? Who is the "we" invoked? Do the organizers represent the people on the streets of Munich? Do they represent the people on the streets across all of Germany? Is it a claim to represent the people themselves, however imperfectly, whether or not they are on the streets? Against whom or what will democracy be defended? Its enemies? What enemies? Are they limited to fascists and their sympathizers? Is the state implicated? Elected officials? Appointed officials? What does defense entail? A general strike? Is violence a possibility? If so, what kind of violence and directed where? What might an ashamed, indignant people do? What if they were to attack government facilities as a show of democratic power and a demand for action? Violence enjoys a long historical tradition in democratic politics. In the United States, for example, violence against property ranges from the Boston Tea Party in the eighteenth century to the Catonsville Nine in the late twentieth.[48] What does "increasingly ready" to defend democracy imply? Does it mean people are considering the use of, or are even preparing to deploy, legally problematic measures in a climate of violence against a backdrop of official indifference? The lack of specificity feels somewhat ominous. Perhaps it's deliberate.

Whether the Munich organizers' declaration is a statement of fact, an invitation, a warning, or a threat, it needs to be credible – no small feat. At a minimum, the addressees are neo-Nazis and the state: neo-Nazis arrogate to themselves the right to exercise violence at will; the state presumes a monopoly on violence, including against citizens in the street protesting it should the necessity arise. What might provide the statement with credibility? Isn't this where constitutional patriotism's supplements of particularity perform background work, lending the people-in-protest some of the resources at their disposal? Insofar as patriotic particulars include heroic self-sacrificing deeds; sudden, unpredictable action in concert; shows of popular force through number and voice; and the possibility, even reality, of spontaneous violence, it would seem that constitutional patriotism commands serious respect. Is this why the candlelight vigil generated scorn? Do silent protests make the state tremble? Don't they lack the protean possibilities constitutional patriotism folds into its identity? Perhaps now it can be understood more fully why constitutional patriotism abjures the project of making affect safe for democracy. Democracy itself cannot be "safe" if affect is tamed, domesticated, rendered predictable and secure. What if democratic politics in contemporary conditions requires something to which Markell's constitutional recommendations point or allude but do not explicitly specify or sanction? What if constitutional patriotism must live on the edge, courting ambiguity about its character, intentions, and possibilities? What if it needs a dose of menacing uncertainty in its political DNA? Markell argues none of this, of course. No advocate of constitutional patriotism recommends the strategic use of violence. It is antithetical to its creed. This is one thing that separates constitutional patriotism from a tragic democratic perspective and circumscribes its relevance in contemporary politics. Or so it seems. My wager is not exactly Müller's wager.

THE RETURN OF THE GOTHIC

Margaret Canovan can also be of assistance in fleshing out constitutional patriotism's predicament. She writes:

[In] the new discourse of patriotism ... the military concerns that loomed so large in the past have almost dropped out of view. The first duty of a patriot is no longer to lay down his life for his country; in the eyes of new patriots it may instead be to campaign actively to make that country live up to its pretensions by respecting human rights.[49]

Canovan's assessment of patriotism's (apparently) progressive evolution contains an irony. Even if patriotism has become less militarized, less focused on death and dying, the responsibilities of democratic citizens (my term) might be more complex and equally arduous. The claim she floats about the first duty of new patriots suggests that democratic citizens must be able to risk comfort, security, limb, and perhaps life to ensure that democracy adheres to its commitments and ideals, including respect for human rights. She notably couples "campaign actively" with another action verb, "make." The key is to put pressure on, even coerce, a democracy – *make* it match practice to ideal. The deployment of force or violence, either through the medium of the state or against it, cannot be ruled out in advance. For a democratic citizen, then, campaigning might entail military service abroad in a humanitarian military intervention. Constitutional patriotism can easily accommodate such activism. Campaigning might mean taking to the streets in one's hometown to oppose state violence against minorities despite police efforts to prevent, disrupt, or silence it. How does constitutional patriotism respond to the democratic state's own violence against democracy?

Canovan catalogues the problematic history of patriotism's connection to universal principles, one that its proponents may ignore or miss altogether: "the fusion of ancestral with ideological passions can also be damaging, making it hard for patriots to see any difference between the interests of their country and the interests of humanity."[50] The combination of the universal and the particular can produce highly "effective political mobilization," but there is also the risk that the universal will become the prisoner of the particular, which Habermas, Müller, and Markell willingly chance. Still, high levels of political participation embody both virtues and vices, and the latter haunt Habermas who, Canovan writes, "is understandably worried about *what may come crawling out of the grassroots*: German nationalism, in fact."[51]

The Gothic horror allusion feels apt. In Chapter 2, we encountered a political creature that came walking out of the woods, John J. Rambo, one of democracy's monstrous creations. The destruction he unleashed against democratic society for its betrayal cannot be justified. That said, might the figure of Rambo still be recovered and deployed for democratic purposes? People besides disaffected veterans filled with romantic revenge fantasies that cannot be fulfilled question, challenge, and stand up to the state. Perhaps Canovan's imagery can serve a tragic democratic politics, in part because it suggests that a politics committed to abstract principles does not have to suffer from fatal affective weakness.[52] If so, though

Canovan seems inclined to give advocates of constitutional patriotism the benefit of the Gothic doubt (nothing is likely to come crawling out of the grassroots), why not let a certain Gothic fear circulate? The specter of the democratic people themselves in the streets of Germany as some kind of political force (monster) whose capabilities are unknown could prove productive, especially if there is a tragic democratic theory of resistance to inform it rather than a nationalist history of intolerance. Thus, when German citizens acting in concert to oppose racist violence declare they are increasingly ready to defend democracy, democracy needs the declaration to be taken seriously, which means the state should experience a moment of trepidation. How do the people make the polity live up to its ideals? This is not necessarily an endorsement of mob rule, but invoking the democratic power, including violence, of the sovereign people, even if it also seems to rely on the specter haunting German politics, could be a sound move in the political arena. The people's monster starts out crawling, but it soon learns to stand, walk, run, speak, resist, fight, and so on. Can it develop democratic political capacities through democratic politics itself, forging a legacy of democratic supplements as it proceeds?

DEMOCRACY AND VIOLENCE

If constitutional patriotism flirts with but ultimately rejects the principle of democratic violence, is it right to do so? John Keane is one of the few contemporary political theorists to tackle the relationship between democracy and violence.[53] At first, there doesn't seem to be much of a relationship. Keane declares violence "anathema" to democracy – not just to its "substance" but also to its "spirit." Violence, then, is democracy's "greatest enemy." For Keane, this characterization nearly goes without saying when considering democracy as "a way of life" and a "set of institutions," an assessment that puts him in good company with constitutional patriots.[54] Nevertheless, Keane recognizes that the relationship between democracy and violence is complicated. Not only does democracy confront political forces and agents hostile to it that make violence inescapable (World War II is an example). Democracy also finds itself implicated in violent conflicts to preserve and protect its way of life that can take a wrong turn and spiral out of control (the Vietnam War is a possible example). Historically speaking, of course, democracy has been established through violent means – the American Revolution is the classic case Keane cites. While democracy rejects violence as a matter of principle, it cannot always refuse it. Exceptions are permitted – moments and occasions when violence is warranted, that is, legitimate. This leads Keane to call for a democratization of violence – an altogether necessary undertaking if democracy is to keep faith with its ideals. It is the meaning of this call, which distances Keane from advocates of constitutional patriotism, that must be explored. The point is not to oppose Keane's approach or recommendations but to question whether his analysis covers as much ground as democracy requires given the nature of its violence problem.

Keane challenges the Hobbesian commonplace that violence is natural, an ineliminable feature of the human condition. For Keane violence is both contingent and removable. He insists that a democratic community free of violence can be imagined and, at least in theory, achieved. Keane, then, is determined to name, contain, and root out problematic instances of violence.[55] He seems to be on the right track when he writes,

It might even be said that a distinctive quality of democratic institutions is their subtle efforts to draw a veil over their own use of violence. There are also plenty of recorded cases when democratic governments hurl violence against some of their own populations. Such violence is called law and order, the protection of the public interest, or the defence of decency against "thugs" and "criminals," or "counter-terrorism."[56]

Nevertheless, Keane proceeds on the assumption that violence, by and large, is a problem alien or external to democracy. When democracy does turn to violence on its own initiative, it is a political practice or tactic mistakenly or unnecessarily employed. The problem for democracy is that violence is brazenly utilized by others: "faced with the violence of their opponents, democracies find themselves trapped within a conundrum: whether or when or how to develop and deploy their own means of violence in order to repel or eradicate that of others."[57] Keane does not deny that democracy, when faced with necessity, can rightfully employ violence. It can stop the killing of others, which means the failure to exercise violence could result in death, potentially including its own.[58] He concedes that resistance to domination and injustice can authorize violence, even render it rather uplifting and transformative. The American Revolution provides "counter-evidence" that violence works.[59] "There are times and circumstances – the caveat is crucial – when violence functions as a basic, if highly paradoxical, precondition of the pursuit or preservation of a civil democracy."[60]

Keane's crucial caveat does some unacknowledged work. The exception of the world-historical American founding aside, violence must still be understood as not just anathema to democracy but also inherently foreign to it. In other words, violence is in no way constitutive of democracy or integral to its mode of being in the world. Violence is always incidental to democracy. Founding violence, for example, expires with success and thereby contains itself. As mentioned, though a democracy may have to resort to violence, democracy always "points ultimately to a world without [it]."[61] Thus Keane's first example of creative political violence is not the American colonies but Jan Palach, a Czechoslovakian citizen who burned himself to death in early 1969 in symbolic protest of the 1968 Soviet invasion and to inspire others to peaceful resistance. Palach's act was both protest and wish, the latter for "a future world freed from the scourge of violence."[62] Keane knows that Palach does not represent a generalizable model of politics. More importantly, self-violence does not present the same moral and political difficulties that violence against others poses. What if Palach had turned his incendiary imagination outward? What if he had immolated a Soviet official? What would Keane conclude?

Keane's theoretical edifice turns on what he calls the "triangle of violence," a term designed to capture the threats and dangers confronting democracies today.[63] There are three sides to the triangle: the threat of nuclear war and one of its byproducts, nuclear terror; the emergence and spread of uncivil wars engulfing and destroying societies; and a new species of terrorism, global apocalyptic, which al-Qaeda instantiates. Democracies such as the United States make their own contributions, directly and indirectly, to one side of the triangle (the nuclear side). They tend to find themselves drawn into or targeted by the other two sides.

Keane's discussion of violence encompasses many troubling political phenomena, but it tends to remove from consideration the everyday operations of democracy that stage violence, as discussed in Chapter 4. This refers, in part, to what Slavoj Žižek calls systemic violence.[64] Not that Keane doesn't recognize the violence generated by democracies within their own territorial confines. He writes:

Violence seems increasingly to be mediated by large-scale institutions, like armies equipped with state-of-the-art surveillance and monitoring and killing equipment. These institutions of violence have the effect of blurring the intentions and camouflaging the culpable negligence and responsibility of the violent. Those who inflict physical pain and suffering upon others do so not because they are thugs and sadists (although they may be this), but because they are trained in the habits and skills of behaving in accordance with the logic and imperatives of the institutional system in which they are operating. Violence tends to become "anonymous." Harm earns the status of a profession.[65]

Keane has military establishments in mind here, though he also includes the disciplinary institutions patiently documented by Michel Foucault: hospitals, schools, prisons, factories, and so on. Later Keane turns his attention, albeit briefly, to capitalism and civil society as purveyors of violence. He does not devote much attention to them insofar as his definition of violence focuses on the "unwanted physical interference" of bodies in motion. He recognizes that harm can take mental forms as well, but violence tends to be material in its point of origin and final destination. Here the problem, meaning limitation, with Keane's definition of violence involves an undue emphasis on immediacy. For example, the effects that neoliberal capitalism produces take time to unfold and enjoy a certain effective invisibility. Not that neoliberalism doesn't kill. It kills slowly, often imperceptibly – and legally. Impoverishment, including forced homelessness, lack of nutrition, and limited access to medical care, shortens individual life spans and increases infant mortality rates. In times of economic crisis, suicide rates surge.

These are structural forms of violence that Keane does not theorize. He recognizes that civil society entails "the creation and *humiliation* of losers," who in turn may respond to its flagrant failure to live up to the promises it makes for "openness, freedom and justice for all" by exposing its brutal hypocrisy. Yet Keane seems to think this is a relatively isolated and contained phenomenon. Moreover, he seems to resent the response of so-called losers, which renders democracy "vulnerable to those ... hell-bent" on disclosing society's impostures through violence, which only casts due suspicion on their actions, however understandable they may be.[66] Keane's formulations appear candid, but they also obscure the violence endemic to democracies. They not only produce losers, a characterization that possesses an air of inevitability about it, suggesting no one is responsible and there is nothing terribly regrettable about it either. They also produce what Danielle Allen calls sacrificial victims, which is altogether different. While Keane admits that violence exercised by people on the short end of things in the contemporary world might not be "irrational," he resists entertaining the idea that violence from democracy's so-called losers, under certain conditions, can also be legitimate if it is democratically inspired, executed, and productive.[67] Keane does not listen to Bruce Springsteen.

Rather, Keane is haunted by the specter of Weber, who presumed that politics would routinely dictate the turn to problematic methods to achieve desired ends, thus qualifying, even changing – though not necessarily compromising – the good secured. Weber also presumed the resort to dubious means would likely have (at least some) morally and politically objectionable consequences. In the face of Weber's conviction, Keane maintains faith in a world where violence has been (can be) eliminated.[68] He thus cultivates a fear of violence, presumably to discourage it, by suggesting that any use whatsoever always already threatens to spiral out of control, with the means devouring the ends and violence becoming nothing but a fetish. Yet this project of fear, if anything, discloses an inability to see fully the violence that necessarily constitutes daily democratic life. Thus, insofar as Keane thinks of violence as exceptional, in terms both of its occurrence and justification, he does not have to discuss what is to be done in a democracy in its ever-present aftermath, that it might be the task of a democratic political order characterized by violence to become worthy of it. He does cite the need to "[hold] those who use violence or control the means of violence publicly accountable," but seems concerned only about individual deterrence or punishment. The focus is too narrow. What about the violence that is endemic to democracy? Legitimacy does not obviate responsibility. More importantly, what happens when official institutions of accountability fail to perform, when they fail to hold those responsible to account? Does democracy rely on its citizens to take matters into their own hands, including using violence, when the state disappears?[69] If so, what happens then?

Keane insists that democracy must be committed to the rule that violence is legitimate only if it "serves to reduce or eradicate violence."[70] The seemingly laudable ambition not only presumes a world in which the goal is possible but also apparently ignores the myriad ways in which democracy contributes to a (more) violent world itself. Even so, when violence is employed, one intention may well be its reduction, but the effect of any action cannot be known, let alone guaranteed, prior to its initiation. What if the best that can be achieved is equilibrium? Is that a failure, despite its other good effects? Or does it call for an ethos of experimentation with violence, something to which Keane seems ill-disposed? His decidedly anti-tragic sensibility rules out the redistribution of violence, which may or may not entail its reduction, let alone eradication, but might well serve a number of democratic ends.

Either way, Keane emphatically rejects even the consideration of what he calls a "General Theory of Violence." Rooted in "formal ethical principles and abstract-general reasoning," it poses a menace to democratic society. Approaching the subject of violence in such fashion may "succor the violent and so increase the probability of violence in human affairs."[71] Ironically, the text in which Keane issues this dire warning could be read as a general theory of violence, addressing the circumstances in which it is legitimate, the limitations that must be applied to it, and questions of accountability relating to its exercise. Keane may not develop what he decries (*absolute* normative principles), but he does develop *decisive* normative principles – hence the project he champions, the democratization of violence. While rigid or formulaic thinking may not have much to offer politics, apparently the articulation of a General Theory of Violence, understood as such, would acknowledge what Keane takes great pains to elude and elide: the constitutive presence of violence in democracy. What he calls a General Theory of Violence could well assist or benefit activists, dissenters, opposition or resistance movements, and others working in concert to further democracy, much as international relations theorists develop criteria for the conditions to be met for humanitarian war. Keane's advice feels state-centric, inadvertently suggesting that democracy has every reason to be defensive about violence, that violence is anything but exceptional, which is precisely why the presence of violence in democracy cannot be (fully) admitted, at least not publicly. Violence in response to democracy's unfolding is not the problem to be feared. Violence in democracy's unfolding is the problem to be addressed. For example, when Keane offers recommendations in his concluding chapter, he writes, provocatively, "Democracies continue to harbor many forms of violence that are suffered in silence."[72] He cites rape as an example. Rape is a serious problem, but does its persistence flow from democracy's everyday operations as a democracy?

Again, Keane's account of violence presents a veneer of candor, ostensibly confronting an intractable problem otherwise obscured, but his concrete discussions too often conceal the structural problems democracy generates. For Keane, then, a democracy defending itself in war, when necessary, poses no serious ethical challenge for it. His theoretical edifice, however, does not have room for the kind of war that democracy wages against its own citizens or against animals, discussed in Chapters 2 and 3, which possess their own brand of necessity. Perhaps they would be treated as mere losers, too, or Rousseau's malefactors.

Keane, as noted, privileges the American Revolution for its creative turn to and use of violence, citing the critical military engagement at Trenton early in the war – when all seemed lost – as exemplary. Keane's appreciation for America, however, feels safely historical, rooted in a distant past that only proves the exceptional character of violence. Keane recounts a mythic military engagement, but what about everyday life in the recalcitrant colony of the British realm? Military desperation in soldiers is one thing. What about the ordinary political dispositions of these same citizens before the war? What was their understanding of violence and its relationship to politics? What might contemporary democratic citizens learn from them? And what does Keane's post-founding America, where violence presumably disappeared, have to teach democracy about the conduct of violence? Perhaps the democratization of violence, pace Keane, requires a new and improved distribution.

A GENEALOGY OF DEMOCRATIC VIOLENCE

Pauline Maier catalogs the resort to violence against property and person as the incipient United States seeks redress and ultimately independence from Great Britain.[73] From Europe to North America, Maier describes a world in which "riots and tumults" were considered unremarkable, even to be expected, given the nature and conduct of government. They signaled that politics was alive and well. If anything, the absence of riots and tumults would be cause for concern. When and where normal channels failed, uprisings constituted an effective social and political force, contributing to the common good.[74] This was not violence for the sake of violence. Death, though not unheard of, and despite some military-style actions, rarely resulted from resistance in the colonies.[75] But it was also presumed to be a real possibility.

Maier cites the impressive discipline of American radicals, who, by and large, endorsed violence against property (tea) but deplored violence against people (tax collectors). Even so, when faced with the reality of riots, the dominant political presumption was not to increase the power of the state to suppress them but to make riots unnecessary.[76] Citizens enjoyed the benefit of the doubt – not government. This sensibility, in part, corresponded to the criteria that governed the turn to violence.[77] It could not be the first option. It could not be for trivial causes. And it had to involve the greater public good. Colonists both affirmed the necessity of uprisings and feared, Hobbes-like, the possibility of anarchy.[78]

Maier's story of resistance nicely delineates the requirements of civic membership. Citizens must not only be vigilant for possible state encroachment on their liberties. They must also be ever-ready to pick up arms should the need arise, which means they must be prepared to respond with force at the first sign of the abuse of state power.[79] It is the latter disposition in particular that proves to be protective, in preemptive fashion, of basic rights and liberties. Governments need something serious and substantial to fear from citizens should they violate constitutional principles and their basic duties to uphold them. What Maier's narrative reveals but does not admit is the productivity of what ultimately comes to be seen as objectionable, namely, "excessive" violence.

American opposition to unpopular British measures was nonexistent in the beginning. Passivity and despondency, fueled by a sense of inevitability, tended to rule the day in colonial America.[80] (The same could also be said of John Ford's Shinbone, as seen in Chapter 1.) Not until violence was deployed by a few did meaningful resistance commence, which, ironically, included condemnation of certain forms of violent action. Still, it appears that nothing would have happened at all if not for an initial, if also problematic, violence. Threatening the life and home of Andrew Oliver so he refused a position as stamp collector was to be applauded. Widespread targeting of British officials' homes and marauding through the streets of Boston for days on end was to be repudiated. Controlled violence, yes. Anarchy, no. In short, the birth of democracy required a potential for violence it would subsequently disavow.[81] What reason is there to think that contemporary conditions of democracy are different?

The productive relationship between democracy and violence is not confined to the founding period. Democratic activism took violent form during the Jacksonian Era in "labor strikes" and "economic protest."[82] Residents of the Kensington section of Philadelphia were particularly effective in the use of intimidation and violence to stop the Philadelphia and Trenton Railroad from building a stretch of track in their neighborhood to connect two terminals designed for the convenience of customers. They feared for the safety of their homes and children, the value of their property, and the character and viability of their local economy. Though the Philadelphia and Trenton Railroad, given its economic power and political influence, obtained state approval for its project, the people of Kensington did not hesitate to pursue extralegal action to stop construction. They bullied, threatened, and injured workers to prevent them from doing their jobs. When the police were called in and work began, residents changed tactics. At night they would remove the track laid on their main street and restore it to its original condition. When this did not suffice, they burned the tracks laid and staged an impromptu bonfire celebration. When more police were deployed to protect workers, people attacked and burned the tavern at which they gathered, forcibly preventing the fire department from dousing the inferno. Despite persistent legal setbacks and increasing numbers of police to enforce corporate interests, the people of Kensington persisted in their campaign of sabotage, which gave them the time to pressure the state legislature to repeal the grant given the railroad. Eventually they succeeded. The violent opposition that energized them also made their political triumph possible.[83]

Moving into the twentieth century, the Civil Rights Movement, hailed for its nonviolence, relied on armed militancy for (at least some of) its success. The possession of guns and the willingness to use them afforded civil rights activists critical security. In order to conceive public actions in the Deep South, the movement needed secure private space where they could meet safely. They did this in their own homes in their own neighborhoods. The forces of white supremacy, vigilante violence, and racial segregation, both public and private, knew of this maneuver. In fact, the police, the Klan, and other racist elements knew very well that blacks were gathering and planning their resistance activities. Despite the tools of terror at their disposal, they also knew that in many instances they were powerless to do anything about it. They were not prepared to enter certain black neighborhoods filled with armed democratic citizens ready to use deadly force to protect themselves and their ability to conspire.[84] This militancy does not deny the physical bravery of civil rights demonstrators or their commitment to nonviolence, but it does indicate the necessary and creative use to which violence can be put in politics. Violence enables democratic life. In the South, the law and the police were official representatives of racial oppression, and democratic citizens were prepared to violate the law and kill police if they interfered with their rights to assemble, to oppose, to resist. Ironically, it was the very ability and willingness to use violence that also meant it might not be deployed. When contemporary American politicians automatically denounce the use of violence and declare there is no excuse for it (Barack Obama made such a pronouncement in response to the uprising in Ferguson, Missouri, in August 2014, following a dubious police killing in which race was involved), they display their ignorance of their democracy's violent political history. What, then, might be made of a recommendation for a Machiavellian democracy, the very conception of which suggests a tragic sensibility regarding the question of violence?

MACHIAVELLIAN DEMOCRACY

Contemporary American democracy is in deplorable condition. Among other things, political and economic elites operate more or less free from meaningful public accountability thanks to a mutual exploitation arrangement. With ordinary citizens effectively disempowered (regular elections notwithstanding), the wealthy and their designated servants in office exercise control of the legislative and policy-making processes, thereby enriching themselves in utter disregard and at the expense of the common good. Money buys elections and offices that, in turn, indulge moneyed interests. John McCormick addresses this dire situation with an astute class-based analysis and corresponding recommendations for institutional reform. Drawing on Machiavelli, McCormick turns to Renaissance republicanism to reinvigorate the American polity with several provocative Constitutional remedies designed to democratize it. The remedies are extra-electoral, an admission-cum-accusation that periodic elections do not constitute anything close to an effective regulatory mechanism to check the ambitions of the economically powerful and politically well-positioned.[85] This sounds rather distanced from questions of violence, but is it?

What attracts McCormick to Machiavelli's thought? Focusing on *The Discourses* rather than *The Prince*, McCormick recovers Machiavelli's claim that the wealthy pose the greatest threat to freedom in a self-governing republic.[86] More than the accumulation of material wealth and earthly possessions, the rich want to dominate and oppress the lower (and what they see as the lesser) orders of society. This is not just a question of control, of imposing their will and making others bend to it. It also involves an ugly politics of harm. The wealthy are meant to prosper and the rest to experience deprivation, loss, and injury. The wealthy will not hesitate to employ violence to protect what they deem rightfully theirs, particularly if they suspect any redistribution project afoot. McCormick notes that Roman reformers were killed on the streets rather than allowed to alter basic property arrangements.[87] Contemporary titans may not (yet) resort to brazen acts of violence, but they are more than willing to impose and allow untold suffering, including death, if it means they can retain their vast holdings and maintain their preeminent position in society. They also have the police at their disposal should dissent mount any notable challenge to their interests, as the military-style assaults on Occupy Wall Street proved.

Machiavelli operates on the assumption that society is divided into relatively distinct classes, the nobles and the plebs. The former is a socio-economic rather than hereditary category. For freedom to prosper, the conflict between classes must be made productive. Here Machiavelli admires Roman political institutions for their ingenuity.[88] According to Machiavelli, students of politics should not focus on the tumults that tended to characterize Roman politics. Rather they should note the salutary political effects produced by class conflict. The antagonism between the upper class and the people generated fear that Roman politics might spill out into the streets in spasms of violence, which, in turn, might degenerate into civil war and self-destruction. Yet this did not happen. The actual violence was minimal, as seen in Chapter 1. Machiavelli writes:

for ... more than three hundred years, tumults in Rome seldom led to banishment, and very seldom to executions. One cannot, therefore, regard such tumults as harmful, nor such a republic as divided, seeing that during so long a period it did not on account of its discords send into exile more than eight or ten citizens, put to death very few, and did not on many impose fines.[89]

These clashes did lead to "the creation of the tribunes," however, converting an always precarious class antagonism, via institutional channeling, into a class-based agonism, which serves the republic's liberty.

McCormick also notes Machiavelli's respect for the institution of public indictment.[90] Citizens could bring charges against any fellow citizen (holding office or not) deemed corrupt or politically dangerous. This judicial mechanism would both deter and punish transgressions by political officials and potent social and economic actors and, perhaps more importantly, provide a safe institutional outlet for the release of the social frustration, rage, and anger that accrues and concentrates in any polity, but especially one marked by profound class divisions and corresponding inequalities and injustices. Through this institution powerful officials who committed crimes against the people could be brought to trial and, if found guilty, punished. If the offense were severe enough, the penalty of death would result. The privatization of violence, on the other hand, with suspect citizens killed on the streets or in their homes by angry mobs of citizens might trigger a chain of events leading to the formation of factions and, ultimately, civil war.

In the institution of public indictment formal judicial procedures (evidence, corroboration, witnesses, etc.) gave the outcome legitimacy, which meant families, friends, and allies of the accused were much less, if at all, likely to seek revenge for guilty verdicts – a reaction that could also trigger civil war or lead to an invitation to a foreign power to intercede on their behalf.[91] Either way, it could spell the end of the republic.[92] McCormick notes that for Machiavelli there is a great difference between justice delivered by a deliberative people and justice inflicted by an angry mob. One protects liberty and stability; the other subverts them. Ironically, those who insist that the people cannot be trusted in matters of politics and law would bring about the very disorder they fear if they do not trust them.[93]

Given the trajectory of American political life, Machiavelli's public indictment could be a welcome and useful device. Republicans in the legislative branches and conservative justices in the courts who have been making repeated efforts to disenfranchise selected groups of American citizens (targeted by race, age, and class) make prime targets for accusation, formal charges, and prosecution.[94] They cloak their electoral initiatives and legal rationalizations in claims of voter fraud and electoral integrity, but the evidence is (virtually) nonexistent. Moreover, some of those pressing for contraction occasionally slip and confess the partisan reasons behind them.[95] Such schemes, expressing a blatant drive for permanent political domination by a minority of citizens unwilling and unable to accept their newfound minority status, constitutes a crime against democracy and, according to Machiavelli's political logic, should be met with the severest of penalties. It amounts to a capital political crime. What greater offense against freedom could be imagined?

If not indictment, the American revolutionary tradition suggests other methods for addressing public officials implicated in political corruption and domination. The people themselves once enjoyed a role in the conduct of politics that has largely disappeared. What is an appropriate popular political response to legislative and judicial officials responsible for denying the franchise to others, including those suffering from a history of racial oppression and violence, thereby depriving them of basic rights and rendering their already precarious place in society more vulnerable? Narrowing the focus, what is an appropriate popular political response to judicial officials who, in addition to disenfranchisement, are responsible for privileging a licentious understanding of the First Amendment at the expense of women's reproductive freedoms, thus subjecting them to the physical and rhetorical terrors of speech as they try to secure basic health care? John Roberts's activist court grants itself political license to ignore precedent and issue one regressive or repressive ruling after another, many favoring the powerful and wealthy that serve to enhance and solidify their power and wealth at the expense of the rest, making the people increasingly susceptible to the vicissitudes of reactionary passions and interests.[96]

Modern conservatism, Corey Robin persuasively argues, is determined to keep certain classes and categories of people not just in line but also in what is believed to be their proper place.[97] The damage to lives that justices with lifetime appointments to the nation's most powerful court can inflict, given their immunity from democratic politics, knows few limits. Short of dispensing with judicial review, the court's sublime institutional usurpation of power, what might keep an activist, anti-democratic court itself in line? How can it be taught to know its rightful place in a democracy? One option: foreclose on its implicit grant of immunity from politics and subject it to regular democratic assessment, however informal. What might this look like? No doubt John Roberts drives (or is driven) home each night to his comfortable, spacious, million-dollar property in the Washington, DC, suburbs secure in the knowledge that he can enjoy his domestic life in peace and quiet. Is this a good thing, always, democratically speaking? Or should Justice Roberts possess a healthy fear of democratic citizens acting in concert to defend their freedoms in a system the few are bound and determined to rig to their advantage? Should these citizens know that he lives at 6805 Meadow Lane in Chevy Chase, Maryland, which is just northwest of the intersection of Connecticut Avenue and Rosemary Street across the District line?[98] Why should Roberts (or Scalia, Thomas, Alito, or Kennedy) be immune to the political treatment accorded royal tax collectors in the eighteenth century? This is not to suggest that Roberts should be subjected to a continual fear and danger of violent death (to borrow from Hobbes). Rather, insofar as the court's decisions routinely entail consequences that put the lives of others at grave risk, public officials in his position should not be able to unthinkingly rely on a public/private distinction (mutilate democracy at work, relish safety at home) that derails public accountability. Why shouldn't all manner of public officials experience the contingencies and vulnerabilities of life they impose on their fellow democratic citizens?[99]

It might be argued that even blatant legislative and judicial initiatives against democracy characterize, at least in part, robust civic contestation, and, if they are successful, they should be accorded the respect due any triumphant political endeavor publicly pursued. Yet, as Stephen White argues, democratic agonism entails a number of possible dispositions. One might initially engage an enemy critically but with a presumption of generosity rooted in the recognition that we all possess metaphysical beliefs that lend support to a particular way of life others find contestable. This approach embodies Nietzsche's call for a spiritualization of enmity. It could privilege an engagement in which the institutions used to damage democracy were also used to repair it. The approach of choice would depend on context and circumstances – which means that self-defense might be warranted. Thus, as White reluctantly concedes, if a political "movement really threatened … the fundamental values of democracy," violent conflict could be justifiable.[100] The resort to violence would mark the shift from agonism to antagonism. Fifth-century

Athenians negotiated this relationship with great skill. The Greeks cultivated an institutionalized form of competition rooted in passion and ambition to prevent declension into open combat and warfare.[101] Cultivation of agonistic encounters preempts more deadly antagonistic engagements. Displacement may not always prove possible, however. Thus Romans, on Machiavelli's reading, were ready to act when threatened with domination.

What would McCormick do? He conducts a thought experiment that involves amending the American Constitution to include a tribunate. McCormick cites a wrong turn that American republicanism took in the eighteenth century, embodied in the (early) thought of James Madison.[102] Veering sharply away from Machiavelli's identification of the rich as the principal threat to republican freedom, Madison and company insisted that government officials and the people themselves were the primary dangers confronting a republic – hence the brazenly anti-democratic features of the Constitution, which set the stage for its subsequent corruption and collapse. In short, the document designed to guarantee freedom enabled and enacted its own demise. Recognizing that American elections have been captured by corporate and financial interests serving the will of the top one-tenth to the top 10 percent of society, McCormick proposes the creation of a class-exclusive institution, the Tribunate mentioned above, that can ameliorate some of the more egregious, that is, inegalitarian, features of American life. It would have the ability to repeal legislation, propose national referendums, and impeach either elected or appointed federal officials.

McCormick lauds Machiavelli's neo-Roman political creativity, especially the elimination of violence from the normal exercise of politics. This feature recommends itself to American translation, where democracy prides itself on nonviolence. What McCormick seems to overlook, however, is that in Machiavelli's institutional hands, violence plays a critical role as institutional precondition and guarantee. Yes, Machiavelli argues that a republic needs a formal institutional outlet for the understandable anger felt by citizens so they do not turn to "abnormal methods," but this kind of mechanism still presumes a citizenry poised on the edge of violence. That is, the very real threat and possibility of violence acts – and must act – as incentive and collateral. This is the paradox: Machiavelli's institutional mechanisms designed to remove violence from politics rely on its presence just beneath the surface of things. If the people were passive and quiet, there would be no need for the institutional cures he proposes. Thus, Machiavelli, as noted above, does not praise his reforms for the complete elimination of violence, let alone the domestication of the citizenry, but for its minimization and their discipline.

McCormick considers his Constitutional proposals a thought experiment. He has no illusions about their implementation. Yet one reason they will not be implemented is that the United States possesses a relatively passive citizenry that, for example, thinks of the second amendment, ultimately, as an individual consumer right. McCormick's recommendations suggest a larger tragic dynamic, namely, that democracy as a nonviolent way of life rests on a background of violence that must not be allowed to move to the foreground. Yet democracy must experience a kind of fear that violence might well erupt and explode in the face of systemic injustice and domination. Violence, then, would be needed to bring McCormick's proposal to life, a proposal designed, ironically, to preempt it.

Perhaps McCormick recognizes the tragic aspect of republican political life, no matter how much he might also like to skirt and evade it.

In fact, to Machiavelli's mind, popular indignation is an almost unequivocal good: republics best realize liberty precisely when the people respond spiritedly to domination by grandi – *especially*, he suggests, when such responses become instantiated in new laws or result in the public execution of prominent but dangerous citizens. Republics are doomed, Machiavelli insists, unless the people, in addition to participating substantively and directly in lawmaking, also vigorously check the insolence of the grandi through accountability institutions such as Rome's tribunes of the plebs and popularly decided political trials.[103]

Notice McCormick's insertion of "especially" in the first sentence quoted above. Liberty might be best realized if popular indignation finds institutional expression, but it may not – perhaps should not – restrict itself exclusively to formal channels insofar as the resort to new laws and public trials depends on the possibility that a spirited people might turn to extralegal (not just extraelectoral) modes, the ultimate check on the grandi. One may not be for violence exactly, but one may not necessarily be against it either.

Tellingly, McCormick cites two instances where the people and the grandi clashed over the tribunes, which the people demanded as a safeguard of liberty (not just their liberty). When the tribunes were abolished, the plebs abandoned the city. These secessions forced the Senate to restore them in 494 and 449 B.C.E. McCormick notes a difference in opinion between Machiavelli and Livy regarding the linchpin of relations between the nobles and the plebs. According to Livy, Roman officials feared actual attack by armed citizens in these domestic struggles, whereas Machiavelli underlines the potential inability of the nobles to survive foreign attack without plebian support. McCormick concludes: "Either way, the fact that the people are armed enables them to compel the patricians to grant them their own exclusive magistracy."[104] McCormick emphasizes the restraint and discipline of the people (they "did not automatically lash out with widespread and arbitrary violence against their oppressors"), but the very real possibility of violence from an armed populace remains the key to plebian political maneuvering. They may not have partaken of "egregious looting or excessive violence," but it seems they did indulge them to some degree. McCormick sums up Machiavelli's logic of popular government: "arm the people militarily with weapons and collective discipline and politically with tribunes and assemblies."[105] McCormick's proposals for the United States, however, divest Machiavelli's logic of its military component while pursuing the political dimension. If it wouldn't work in Machiavelli's day, why would it work here, now? As Machiavelli remarks (and McCormick repeats): "The few always behave in the mode of the few."

McCormick's Constitutional scheme appears radical, but its appearance stems from the radically antidemocratic character of the document it seeks to alter. To read his Constitutional proposal is not just to magnify the flaws of the original. It is also to experience their unacceptability, their objectionability. McCormick describes his political project as meliorist. Its modesty can be seen not just in the limited interventions in American politics it enables but also in the provision it makes for further democratization, that is, for expanding and enhancing the powers of the tribunate he recommends.[106] As with the original Constitution, change would not be easy (though not nearly as cumbersome either). Regardless, it is necessary to start small. If Roman citizens balked at the elimination of the tribunate and placed the order in jeopardy, in the American democracy no one knows of its "absence." No doubt this newfound exercise of power would strike American political minds as spectacular, which is a symptom of how badly it is needed and how unlikely it is to come to pass. The tragic paradox is that the institution that only the people can bring about presupposes a people that it must create through its very success. What might jumpstart the Constitutional amendment process? Perhaps the answer is precisely the kind of violence democratic republican thinkers such as McCormick would like to disable. If so, McCormick's project for "constitutionally enabling citizen participation and control of economic and political elites today" lacks Machiavelli's tragic dimension.[107]

American Dionysia

VIOLENCE AND POLITICS

Müller's constitutional patriotism and McCormick's Machiavellian democracy devote serious attention to militancy, class-conflict, enmity, and the risks inherent in politics. Still, they seem too civilized by half. They assume that violence is a rare phenomenon in democracy rather than common, widespread, and daily. If one starts with the latter presumption, however, the key questions democracy faces regarding its violence revolve around distribution more than reduction or elimination. To illuminate the limitations of Müller's and McCormick's political initiatives – and pinpoint their differences from a tragic democratic ethos – let's consider the question of democratic violence and its creative, productive possibilities in a neoliberal context.

In Zal Batmanglij's 2013 film *The East*, determined anti-corporate activists execute several deeply contestable stratagems (in the film they are called jams) to call attention to lethal corporate malfeasance and achieve some modicum of justice for its victims. These guerrilla agents contest traditional understandings of political action, nonviolence, and responsibility.[108] There is no doubt about the immorality or criminality of the wrongdoing, and the corporate actors in question are effectively beyond the law's reach. In the neoliberal age, political parties and politicians can be bought by economic interests, resulting in statutory and regulatory climates tailor-made for their particular needs and misdeeds. National and local police are ready to lend their aid and comfort as needed. The exorbitant profits secured in the business-friendly world skew the political process. Corporate entities get what they pay for, and what they pay for gets them more and more of what they want: license. It is a vicious, self-perpetuating circle that, apparently, cannot be broken through established channels or procedures, whether legal or political. These have been colonized. The problem for a democracy is that it's all perfectly legal and reflects a free way of life. What, then, is to be done? What kind of recourse, if any, is available? What kind of accountability, if any, is possible? For citizens in a democracy, how do we resist an apparently irresistible force, especially one that is literally killing us?

Democracy sanctions civil disobedience and other forms of nonviolent action that involve law-breaking to protest wrongdoing and injustice. These may provoke a violent response from the state (and private security forces), but the resistance offered by peaceful activists does not involve violence – hence the exalted status it enjoys in democratic

political circles. Democracy rejects deadly violence directed against
public officials, including assassination, and violence against state
structures, including attacks on military and military-related facilities.
When action takes these forms it is generally met with universal and
unqualified condemnation. Democracy also rejects, at least in the contemporary age, violence against property. Nevertheless, this kind of
political action is all too familiar to it. In the United States, the Boston
Tea Party (1773) is undoubtedly the most famous and celebrated
instance of democratic violence against property – though it is not
ordinarily remembered in terms of violence. The Sons of Liberty who
conceived and executed the anti-tax protest are considered national
heroes, quintessential patriots. The Catonsville Nine (Catholic priests
and activists) who burned military draft files with homemade napalm
in 1968 to protest the American War in Vietnam are less widely known
and not generally considered heroes or patriots. ROTC buildings were
burned down on college and university campuses in at least twelve
states to protest the American War. This violence against property was
not tolerated, let alone celebrated. Students implicated were subject to
arrest, expulsion from school, prosecution, and imprisonment. Finally,
violence against "private" individuals is considered especially problematic. The killing of doctors who perform abortions would be one
example.

The East thus raises troubling political dilemmas and moral issues.
A super-secretive environmental group known as The East polices
American capitalism and assigns responsibility for known corporate
criminality to specific high-level officials in the companies involved – for
decisions taken, policies implemented, and consequences generated. This
is no arbitrary undertaking. The East operates according to an ethos. The
punishment they deliver directly corresponds to the crime committed.
One act of violence begets its twin. If a pharmaceutical firm puts a wonder drug on the market and touts its safety despite knowing its crippling,
lethal dangers, the CEO may find himself drinking (unknowingly, at least
initially) that same drug in a glass of champagne at a party celebrating
his success. He is forced to become one of his own victims – and it may
cost him his life. If a coal mining company manufactures a product, boil-
erplate denials notwithstanding, that results in pollution that, in turn,
kills people, including children, the CEO might find herself kidnapped
and forced to take a swim in some of the very same waters she has poi-
soned.[109] She is forced to become one of her own victims, perhaps at the
cost of her life. The violence is not exactly identical, as the activists claim.

The scale and scope of harm inflicted by corporate wrongdoers greatly exceeds the violence permitted to answer it.

For the ecological activists, the turn to violence is a matter of justice, politics, and necessity. Institutions work to insulate and protect corporations, which are free to do as they please without fear of effective public response, let alone reprisal. Those harmed or endangered by their activities enjoy no official recourse for redress, which means the political must be made personal. The retributive violence deployed is individualized, based on a pinpoint determination of responsibility. Corporate officials become targets. Unless and until they are made to experience – and suffer – the consequences of their decisions, they will continue to inflict disabling and deadly injury on others.

Earlier I made the claim, pace Keane, that democratic violence can attain legitimacy to the extent that it is democratically inspired, executed, and productive. Thanks to The East the details can be spelled out. Informed by the nonviolent ways of life they practice and indignant at the violence they see perpetrated daily against others, they deploy their own precision violence to stop its current (and possibly reduce its future) exercise; they weaken dangerous and potent anti-democratic elements in the polity responsible for violence; they obtain a modicum of redress for people harmed by violence not otherwise available to them; they see that citizens are treated with the dignity and respect due them; they restore some of the state's regulatory capacities to check violent antidemocratic entities in the polity; they set an example for a militant democratic citizenship capable of inspiring others – that is, democratic citizens have empowered themselves in a context designed to deny them agency. None of these effects can be guaranteed in advance. Thus a tragic democratic politics calls for experiments in the exercise of violence, knowing full well that it all might go wrong and might also (uncomfortably) resemble the state and the violence it unleashes on citizens and society.

This is not to deny that The East's ecological militancy comes at a steep, potentially damning ethical price. The actions taken are disturbing, shocking. Condemnation is indeed tempting but may close down thought prematurely. What if, for example, democracy not only benefits from, but relies upon, the periodic (or routine) exercise of democratic violence to realize its promise and potential? We have already discussed a small sample of democratic violence from America's founding to the Civil Rights era. Does American democracy need violence to push it to the brink of moral or political crisis if it is to have serious hope of addressing its structural flaws and failings? One may not want to recommend or applaud violence while nonetheless recognizing, even appreciating, its salutary effects.[110] If this ambivalence is possible and productive, can violence be the automatic subject of disapprobation? What if democracy benefits from the "criminal" actions of those it will punish severely for committing them?

The East ends on an upbeat note. After several successful jams, the group plans to secure a confidential list of corporate undercover operatives inserted across the globe whose job is to protect multinationals and make it possible for them to do their profitable dirty work. The member who actually steals the document is herself an undercover corporate agent who has turned against her employer. Still, she will not hand over the list to the leader of the militants, fearing that it could cost these agents their lives, apparently not recognizing what a damning admission of guilt she has just made about the corporate world she has served so well. As the credits roll, in a series of still shots, she travels far and wide appealing directly to her fellow operatives to switch sides and work with her to expose corporate wrongdoing. She enjoys some success. What the film does not mention is that she would not have broken with her corporate masters and turned activist herself if not for the violence of The East. When she first infiltrated the group, she felt like an alien. The longer she stayed undercover, however, the more she came to identify with them and their cause, if not necessarily their methods. Yet it was the double violence, the quotidian violence of corporations and the exceptional violence of activists, which spurred her transformation. Violence recreated her. And democracy benefitted.

LIVING WITH VIOLENCE

John Keane, following Hannah Arendt, worries that violence as a response to violence only makes for a more violent world, especially insofar as the state enjoys an effective monopoly on the means of violence (which it is happy to dispense on behalf of and share with its corporate overlords).[111] In the film, noticeably, The East practices a communal, fraternal, sororal, nonviolent way of life between and among its members and also in relation to the earth and its creatures. They live in a burned-out house with minimal electricity for their political work. They survive on discarded food (trash) that is nonetheless fit for human consumption. They develop bonds of intimacy and trust in everything from cooking to bathing to sleeping to working. The lives they lead with each other, which reflect and enact a pacific ideal on a small-scale, question whether those who turn to violence necessarily make the world more violent. If they exacerbate violence on one register, they ameliorate it on at least two others.

Keane, as noted, thinks of his task as a democratization of violence. The East enacts a democratization project of its own. In their public statements drawing attention to their jams, they declare themselves to be the equal of their corporate enemies: what you do to us, we will do to you, they intone. In taking decisive action couched in the language of responsibility, they also declare themselves to be the equal of the government and the state. In risking their lives for the greater good (one of them is killed in one of the jams), they prove that their commitment to life, justice, and democracy is as great as their attachment to this-worldly existence.[112] This is not to say that they champion an ethos of sacrifice, in which killing and dying for cause or common good are prized. They act out of gratitude for and from a sense of abundance in life.[113] In planning their jams, they discuss and debate, sometimes angrily, the ethical character of the violence they plan to unleash. They worry they may come to resemble the enemy they fight. As democratic agents working for the common good, contra Arendt, they are anything but thoughtless.[114] They aspire to consensus but operate according to majority rule. In publicizing their actions, they submit themselves to the judgment of the very people on whose behalf they act. A popular verdict may be difficult given corporate control of the media, but they do not seek to satisfy only themselves. As practitioners of violence, they can at the very least make the claim that they use it as a precision instrument for immediate results and productive purposes. In other words, they are good at what they do, and it leads to reduced corporate violence and killing (which is not to say that it might not be short-lived or overwhelmed by additional corporate violence). Either way, they recognize that what they are doing is ethically problematic and unpredictable, and that they mimic the enemy they fight, perhaps because this is the only method the enemy will respect. But politics always involves risks (Müller's assessment), and they are willing to take some.

The East, as mentioned, is nothing if not meticulous in its use of violence. They seek to shake people out of their resignation and passivity, demonstrating that resistance is possible – even to something as nebulous as neoliberal capitalism. They disconcert because they call attention to and challenge what Žižek refers to as the normal nonviolent condition, control of which is the true act of violence, and against which they and their alleged terrorism are assessed.[115] In the film, the background violence enabling the neoliberal order of things to function is exemplified by the lawful and secure global distribution of the dangerous wonder drug exposed by The East. When the corporate operative first infiltrates the cell, she wonders, "If the side effects are so deadly, how can it be allowed on the market?" They're listed on the warning label, one of its victims observes. "That's how they rape you in broad daylight."

VIOLENCE IN PLAIN SIGHT

The East was released in 2013 and cost nearly three times as much to make as it generated in box office receipts. Apparently capitalism's depredations do not draw audiences. This does not mean that democracy's routine violence does not find some presence in American political discourse. *The New York Times* columnist Paul Krugman periodically delineates, if inadvertently, the violence that characterizes everyday life in America. In September 2013, Krugman noted that the recovery from the Great Recession that started in late 2007 and early 2008 had been limited to the upper echelons of American life. He argued that the country desperately needed "the kind of transformation that took place under the New Deal." With a gift for understatement he admitted that such transformation "seems politically out of reach." To compensate, as it were, Krugman seized on New York Mayor-to-be Bill de Blasio's proposal for universal prekindergarten funded by a tax on the superrich. This would amount to a small step, but Krugman had nothing else to offer – the current context, we were told, would not allow serious initiatives to address gross inequality and injustice. The proposal was admittedly modest. The only reason it did not meet with accusations of obscenity is that Krugman preceded it with a relatively mild account of contemporary social conditions – his recitation of the redistribution of wealth to the upper echelons notwithstanding. Krugman's habit in his columns is to drain and domesticate the violence that characterizes American life in the neoliberal era, even after the Great Recession and the austerity measures imposed in its wake.[116]

What Krugman cannot bring himself to say, though Pope Francis can, is that neoliberalism kills.[117] Some would make a distinction between effects attributable to recession and those linked with austerity, but here I treat recession (or worse) as a constitutive dimension of neoliberalism and austerity as the pursuit of its perfection. Recession, that is, allows for the pursuit of policies and programs (budget cuts, downsizing and degrading the social safety net, deregulation, etc.) that might otherwise prove impossible to implement.[118] How does neoliberalism kill? Capitalism's everyday destructive operations are well known and documented from Marx and Engels to Bruce Springsteen. When in crisis, its ruinous dynamics accelerate. According to public health experts, "In the U.S., Greece, Italy, Spain, the U.K. and elsewhere in Europe there were more than 10,000 additional suicides from 2007–2010." In addition, the decimation of national health budgets has resulted in profound suffering and misery: HIV infections have exploded; malaria and tuberculosis epidemics have erupted; infant mortality rates have surged. In a trend that goes beyond the current neo-depression, life expectancy in the United States "for the country's least educated whites" has been reversed. Parental lifespans no longer automatically exceed their children's.[119]

These developments, as Krugman argues, warrant massive public response, and while some governments react better than others, neoliberalism-as-free-market-utopianism does not necessarily deem these outcomes problematic. Abject misery, sickness, and death, in other words, do not constitute grounds for state action, either preemptive or responsive, in a neoliberal understanding. Does this mean that citizens should submit themselves to a regime of premature extinction when the political system ostensibly designed to protect their liberty and security is unavailable and unresponsive to them? What is to be done when government fundamentally fails to carry out the very assignments that give it reason for being? If government returns, or consigns, people to a state of nature, especially while bestowing lavish privileges of civilization on a very few, what options do they possess?

If the protagonists of *The East* seem radical or extreme (or worse) in their actions, attitudes, and way of life, does this comportment not mimic the disposition of their antagonists once the carefully crafted facade has been stripped away from the neoliberal order of things and its agents? Watching the film, it is virtually impossible not to empathize with the "terrorists" and feel that their victims have gotten their just deserts. If so, what are the implications for thinking about the questions of politics, violence, and responsibility the film raises? Benji, the leader of The East, slips away as the film concludes. He will not be brought to account for his activism – for his crimes against people and property – and this feels fitting, just. Jane, the undercover operative, opposes her nonviolence to his violence, but she will not detain him (or assist in his arrest). The actions he orchestrated may have been wrong, but they may also have been righteous – illegal but also legitimate. What's more, they may be needed again in the future.

Democracy flinches at the practice of self-assigned violence, however well-conceived and justified. But insofar as the ideals prohibiting it, such as the rule of law, deteriorate and implode, they effectively invite usurpations that can serve as reminders of their fragility and indispensability. If anything, given the ability of multinational corporations to counter-counterattack, The East's return should be anticipated, even welcomed. Jane's conversion and personal reform campaign produced definite but limited results. There is no indication that she is prepared for the larger, longer-term political dedication that membership in The East signals. For one thing, she takes no joy in her newfound work. There is a revelatory moment in the film when members learn that their champagne ruse succeeded brilliantly. The drug was removed from the market and a formal government investigation opened. We see members of The East dancing joyously in celebration. They cannot contain themselves. The violence they unleashed brought down a corporate empire and brutalized some of its lieutenants. How can this not feel good? The affect engendered by success energizes them. It enables them to carry on the difficult work of democratic violence and politics, just as Ransom Stoddard's killing of Liberty Valance set off dancing in the streets, launched a founding, and sustained a community for generations. Democracy and violence are not, contrary to Keane, anathema to one another.

What can constitutional patriotism contribute to the discussion on violence in democracy? Müller conceives constitutional patriotism as a source of civic empowerment that can take many forms, including dissent and civil disobedience. But the latter also constitutes limits for Müller. When constitutional patriots find themselves aligned with the state and its political imperatives, the traditional enemies of democracy can be addressed with force and violence if and when necessary. Antagonism toward parties or groups such as neo-Nazis that reject democracy, worship violence, and would use its institutions to destroy it poses few, if any problems. All too reminiscent of the historical circumstances that gave rise to constitutional patriotism, the full weight of the state may be brought to bear against them.

What, though, about forces who oppose democracy in any meaningful sense, are tactically prepared to tolerate its nominal or symbolic expression but otherwise seek to use democracy and its institutions to capture them for their own purposes regardless of the consequences to the demos? How does constitutional patriotism approach this kind of political enemy, one who privileges ideology and profit – as a matter of principle and policy – at the demonstrable expense of both democracy and life, especially when the state is unwilling or unable to respond? Given the violence that democratic constitutionalism daily allows and enacts, Müller's limitation of politics to dissent and civil disobedience seems incongruous. Dissent and civil disobedience can be effective, but the state has grown increasingly adept at containing, controlling, and domesticating them. Besides, people cannot stay in the streets forever, and as resistance drags on, the larger order may take less and less notice (or even tire) of them, at which point the state can move against people with relative impunity, citing all manner of safety and security concerns in the process. The state may even claim that those engaged in politics make it impossible for other citizens to exercise their rights to life and liberty, as happened with state repression of Occupy Wall Street across the United States. These claims are issued in bad faith, of course, but they may resonate in a depoliticized society. In any case, the state can outlast or outmuscle protestors. Not that citizens acting in concert can (or should think they can) win a violent confrontation with the state, but what might the people be able to induce or accomplish if they defy the state and channel their power toward soft targets, as do the protagonists of *The East*? Do we want the state to always be able to call the people's bluff when it comes to political struggle, to be able to attack, assault, and disperse citizens with impunity on any pretext or provocation?[120] Or is it essential that the state operate in a climate of uncertainty, thus with hesitancy, modesty, and respect? If citizen violence is disqualified categorically in advance, what kind of potential political advantage or leverage has been surrendered to the state? Müller emphasizes constitutional patriotism's reflexivity, its ability to adjust, modify, and correct itself, but can it or will it rethink the question of violence in an age marked by daily practices of it against citizens? Or is this impossible precisely because violence by definition violates its cardinal tenets?[121]

The question here is not whether to advocate or endorse violence since violence is already ubiquitous in democratic society, but whether to recognize its potential democratic value from new, unexpected sources – if on occasion. In short, we are talking about redistribution. Assume, for the moment, that democratic violence can play a productive role, that it can draw attention to crimes or injustices otherwise obscured, ignored, or denied and force meaningful remedial action, especially in instances where the state is complicit or responsible. A democratic society can respond in a variety of creative ways. Even if the state decided to hold responsible those who employed violence, it could do so in a manner that effectively ratifies it, especially if it could be claimed plausibly that the people themselves approved the results. In the tragic aftermath, in which evil has produced good (to borrow from

Weber), the democratic state could launch an investigation and issue a report. It could bring charges but not pursue them. It could conduct a prosecution and seek a symbolic penalty. It could find guilty and subsequently pardon any given "offenders." Or, invoking a credible claim of popular support, it could say that the people themselves have spoken and do nothing, in the interests of justice. Democratic violence, then, might be considered an ambiguous but contributive political practice when sanctioned by a respectable simulacrum of the democratic people on behalf of the ongoing project of democracy.

LET THE TRAGEDY BEGIN

It seems to be a tragic fact of life in democracy that violence, real or threatened, is inescapable. Necessary to bring democratic life into being (a lesson from *Liberty Valance* to Rousseau to the American founding), perhaps it is equally necessary to sustain or reclaim it. Constitutional patriotism and Machiavellian democracy reject violence, their virtual flirtation with it notwithstanding. A tragic democratic sensibility, on the other hand, can bring a different perspective to bear on the question of violence in democratic politics. Why intimate the readiness to use violence in the name of democracy as a grand gesture or bluff, as if there is everything to gain and nothing to lose? Why not deploy violence, however reluctantly, and delineate what needs to be done in the aftermath to become worthy of it? Constitutional patriotism and Machiavellian democracy entertain the first; a tragic democratic ethos envisions the second.

6

New Tragic Democratic Traditions

We must deal with all that lies before us. The future rests with the ones who tend the future. No more prayers now. For mortal men there is no escape from the doom we must endure.

Sophocles, *Antigone*

But crushing truths perish from being acknowledged ... I leave Sisyphus at the foot of the mountain! One always finds one's burden again.

Albert Camus, *The Myth of Sisyphus*

Democracy, the preceding chapters demonstrated, is conversant with violence. In the United States, violence is not only practiced, especially by the state, it is openly celebrated. The celebration, however, is not understood as such. Democracy is deeply invested in a peaceful, non-violent reputation and disavows the violence and damage it habitually dispenses. Rather, democracy understands itself as a locus of right and source of good in the world, leaving it vulnerable to enemies foreign and domestic who take advantage of it at moments of their choosing. Democracy is also devoted to confirming and consolidating its reputation through a network of national holidays, patriotic memorials, public rituals, commemorative ceremonies, and civic orations that attest to the wars it has fought for the ideals it symbolizes and the costs it has incurred as the last best hope on earth. Not surprisingly, then, the United States may have reached a new pinnacle regarding democracy's celebration of violence in the aftermath of the events of September 11, 2001.

Nevertheless, there is an opportunity here to re-cover and re-invent the communal machinery responsible for marking and honoring American ascendancy and triumphalism (victimization), sacrifice and loss (ressentiment), and resilience and perseverance (right of retribution). Following the example of Chapters 1 through 4, I introduce a new set of popular holidays, monuments, memorials, and commemorative occasions, including Democracy Day, September 11, which features three dedicatory odes that celebrate democracy as a daring political adventure and experiment ready to take chances on its own behalf free of existential bitterness in a world of tragic possibilities and opportunities: an Ode to Democracy, an Ode to the Enemy, and an Ode to Life Itself. I also propose Resistance Day, which affirms the spirit and practice of opposition as the hallmark of democratic life. Initially, however, there is need to rehearse, in order to leave behind, a number of problematic national political traditions that model the dangerous, destructive partnership between democracy and patriotism that a tragic democratic politics refuses and contests.

ANOTHER DAY THAT LIVES IN INFAMY

Think of it: At a moment of unprecedented national crisis, with an untold number of innocent lives on the verge of nasty, brutal, sudden extinction, and with no thought to their own well-being, a band of determined citizens convenes an impromptu "town hall" meeting on a jet plane hurtling toward the nation's capital to decide what to do – in defiance of their well-armed fanatical terrorist captors. Prepared to sacrifice themselves for the greater good, they decide to rush the cockpit, an action certain to be recorded for all posterity to honor and salute. It exceeds the stuff of Hollywood lore.

Welcome to the legend of United 93. It proves, first, that liberal democratic political principles perdure regardless of circumstances, and, second, that people are willing to knowingly forfeit their lives to enact and defend them. If Hollywood concocted the story from its own imaginative resources, moviegoers would likely shun, even denounce, it: people love horror stories, just not half-baked political ones. It's that good on the visceral register. There is just one potential problem: Hollywood may not have invented the fantastical story, but a democratic culture did fabricate it, and it works to subvert the dominant principles that inform, perhaps define, it. Patriotism is implicated here, but it should not be scapegoated for democracy's maladies, including the wars it wages on citizens, one of which we saw in Chapter 2.

Regardless, the events known as September 11, now inseparable from America's subsequent War on Terror, exhibit many signs of a tragedy: a once revolutionary democracy exercising and enjoying unparalleled global reach conducts its national and international affairs convinced of its virtue, standing, and entitlement, determined to represent freedom in the world. This leads not only to great confidence, status, and success but also to arrogance, cruelty, and, in a dramatic turnabout, comeuppance. What happens next to America's democracy? The political culture it spawned in September 11's aftermath can move in one of two directions. It can reflect and reinforce war-driven security imperatives in acts of unthinking patriotic insistence at irreparable cost to democracy and the world. It can also inaugurate, inspired by a vicious enemy's deadly assault, tragic democratic reinvention – not just by rededicating itself to necessary self-overcoming but also by making others a self-conscious subject of political and ethical concern. Once the horror within the *official* public story of September 11 has been revealed, a tragic democratic rendering of it can prove salutary and politically productive for a dying democracy. A polity that can see itself, in part, as the victim of its own hubris puts itself in position to see what that hubris has done not just to itself but also to others. Afterwards, democracy can (re)dedicate itself to principles of justice, equality, solidarity, and forbearance that flow not so much from a shared finitude or vulnerability but from the dark comedy of a commonly experienced tragic dynamic in a cosmos ignorant of any polity's claim to exceptionalism.

THE TENTH ANNIVERSARY

September 11, 2011, marked the tenth anniversary of al-Qaeda's coordinated attacks on the World Trade Center, the Pentagon, and Washington, DC. Commemoration in Shanksville, Pennsylvania, where United Airlines Flight 93 crashed on its way to the nation's capital, generated significantly more attention than in previous years. The increased regard may have been due to the progress made on the national memorial at the crash site (with phase one of the memorial then complete). It may have been due to the story that has been forged – thanks to national government reports, prior memorial tributes, and the release of a major Hollywood motion picture – in America's popular consciousness surrounding United 93.

The 9/11 Commission Report, formally known as the *Final Report of the National Commission on Terrorist Attacks upon the United States*, amounts to a kind of urtext regarding the events of late summer 2001 in the United States. Though it aspires to impartiality, it also understands itself to be a narrative production.[1] From the title of the first chapter ("WE HAVE SOME PLANES") to its ersatz real-time format to its overtly politicized language, *The 9/11 Commission Report* assumes two assignments: "to provide the fullest possible account of the events surrounding 9/11 and to identify lessons learned," and to articulate and confirm the country's dominant self-conception in a world filled with forces openly and aggressively hostile to it.[2] These commitments act as political twins.

Still, the *Commission Report*'s opening sections can take their toll on the unsuspecting reader. Each of the four hijacked planes receives alternating narrative attention – from boarding to takeoff to termination. At times the narrative proceeds minute by minute, and we accompany, textually speaking, the passengers on the plane until their phone connections are lost at impact. In fact, we listen in on individual phone conversations. It's as if we're losing someone we've just gotten to know. At the conclusion of each hijacking, the *Report* adopts a Vonnegut-like refrain: "All on board, along with an unknown number of people in the tower, were killed instantly." "All on board, along with an unknown number of people in the tower, were killed instantly." "All on board, as well as many civilian and military personnel, were killed." The narratives are structurally identical – with one exception: United 93. The chapter sections for the first three flights are rendered as hijackings ("The Hijacking of American 11," etc.). The chapter section for the plane downed in rural Pennsylvania is titled "The Battle for United 93." Though the planes that crashed into the World Trade Center and the Pentagon took such short flights that no passenger response was possible, the passengers on United Airlines Flight 175, the second plane from Boston to hit the Twin Towers, were discussing "storming the cockpit to take control of the plane away from the hijackers."[3] What would have happened, then, given time, on the first three flights did happen on United 93: resistance. Americans (even if the people on board these flights were not solely Americans) do not passively submit to terrorism.

Resistance notwithstanding, 9/11 commemoration poses considerable narrative challenges. How can public remembrance of lethal horror (a successful terrorist attack) do something more than remind people of a day in many respects best forgotten? The language of sacrifice (for freedom, for America) seems inapt for the 9/11 dead, but it has been routinely invoked nonetheless. Thus, it is regarding the fourth commandeered plane, United 93, that *narrative* intervention has achieved singular distinction and insistence.[4] This does not mean narration has proceeded smoothly. There is slippage between events as they purportedly happened, documented by *The 9/11 Commission Report*, and the story that we as a democratic people have decided to tell ourselves about those events, a story that begins with tensions contained within that very same *Commission Report*, as if the report must answer, even refute itself, at the moment of its publication. Make no mistake: in American hands, September 11 is a melodramatic tale of epic proportions.[5] This is one reason to retell it in tragic terms, which can appreciate the war being made on citizens in its telling. The problem is not (so much) that democracy endangers itself through its love affair with patriotism. Democracy is always endangering itself. The problem is that democracy needs a tragic public philosophy if it is going to put itself in position to forestall self-destruction. To make this argument clear, let's turn to the tenth anniversary events surrounding September 11, 2001.

SPEAKING NARRATIVE TO TRUTH

On September 10, 2011, at dedication ceremonies for the Flight 93 National Memorial in southwestern Pennsylvania, Vice President Joseph Biden and former Presidents George W. Bush and Bill Clinton offered moving orations. At the September 11 tenth anniversary ritual the next day, Tom Ridge (former Governor of Pennsylvania) and Tom Corbett (then Governor of Pennsylvania) spoke. Each reflected and reinforced the dominant narrative that has seized control of United 93's odyssey. While their respective remarks bear similarities suggesting coordination, no prior consultation was required.

Death, of course, governs the United 93 story. The fascination, even obsession, with death expresses itself with particular affective vehemence. The lives of United 93 passengers are no longer their own. Democracy takes rightful possession of them, exercising a kind of military eminent domain in the name of war. Democracy even wages narrative war against its own citizens. Not only do the passengers of United 93 meet with a grisly, horrific end. Not only are we told repeatedly that they knowingly and willingly sacrificed their lives so countless others could live at a moment when most people would have been paralyzed by fear and hesitation. The official story allows for no other understanding of United 93's trip. Death not only names the end of this flight. It also informs each and every moment leading to it. Since death was going to triumph in the end, the passengers of United 93, so the story goes, decided to make what would come last come first, their courage exceeded only by their innocence.

This places them in very good historical company. Joe Biden turns to Lexington, Massachusetts and the fabled start of the Revolutionary War:

None of them asked for what happened. They didn't go on that plane – they didn't board that plane to fight a war. But when they heard the news, when they found out what happened in New York, they knew ... it was the opening shot in a new war. And so, they acted. They acted as citizen-patriots have acted since the beginning of our country. They stood up and stood their ground. They thought, like Captain Parker said at Lexington, and I quote him, "If they mean to have a war, let it begin here."[6]

Bill Clinton, not to be outdone, appeals to the spirit of the Alamo, an equally famous battleground but one where defeat actually signals victory: "Why? Because those people knew they were going to die." For added inspiration, Clinton reaches into the archives and retrieves the Spartans at Thermopylae: "They all knew they were going to die. [The King of Sparta] told them that when they went." The difference, for Clinton, is that the passengers of United 93 were not soldiers. They "just happen[ed] to be on a plane."[7]

For George Bush, it is precisely the passengers' civilian status that stirs. Millions of Americans have joined the armed forces since 9/11 and thereby honored and "upheld the spirit of service shown by the passengers of Flight 93." Death was a foregone conclusion: "When the passengers and crew realized the plane had been hijacked, they reported the news calmly. When they learned that terrorists had crashed other planes into targets on the ground, they accepted greater responsibilities ... The choice they made would cost them their lives. And they knew it."[8]

Tom Corbett ups the sacrificial ante: "[The passengers] preferred to shorten the final minutes of their own lives." For Corbett, this makes comparisons to other American battlefields (Gettysburg, Pearl Harbor, the Alamo) inapt: "The truth is that this place is like no other, because the deeds aboard Flight 93 were like no others. There is nothing with which to compare the passenger uprising ten years ago. It has no companion in history." Pace Corbett, the story of American democracy, embodied in its citizens, is that it can always surpass its own exceptionalism.[9]

The passengers of United 93 distinguished themselves for a reason besides sacrifice. They enacted and thereby upheld the democratic principles that define the United States. In defiance of their captors (Bush's description), the passengers of United 93 convened a mock town hall meeting in the rear of the plane to consider their options. The democratic deliberation stands for a rejection of the violence being deployed against them. They even conducted a vote. As democracy itself was under attack, the passengers calmly affirmed its fundamental norms. No one panicked or invoked crisis as an excuse to impose his will on the rest. The spirit of equality prevailed, and the passengers, in consensus, united around a single course of action. The exercise in democracy made the forty passengers into one: e pluribus unum.[10]

The passengers of United 93, then, perfected democratic agency. Bush: "[W]ith their brave decision, they launched the first counteroffensive of the war on terror." Corbett: "They started their own battle when they realized they were in the hands of men intent on striking yet another public symbol of our nation." What were the results? For Corbett, there is no ambiguity: "They halted the final attack of 9/11 using their own blood. They put an end to the men who tried to steal our spirit." And even though (or perhaps precisely because) *The 9/11 Commission Report* concedes that the hijackers never lost control of the plane, "The Battle for United 93" narrative ends differently than the other hijacking accounts: "[Their] objective was to crash [the] airliner into symbols of the American Republic, the Capitol or the White House. [They were] *defeated* by the alerted, unarmed passengers of United 93." *The Report* surmises that the hijackers "must" have known the passengers were "only seconds" from taking control of the plane, which, in patriotic legend and legerdemain, amounts to the passengers actually having taken control of it – at least regarding the results achieved.[11]

The greatest narrative certainty of United 93 concerns the saving of lives. Nothing can be allowed to detract from the stunning achievement of the people on Flight 93, who morph from passengers to citizens to patriots to heroes to martyrs in a matter of moments. Bush signaled and saluted the transfiguration as passengers learned more and more about the day's events. These were no ordinary hijackings. They were suicide missions. The passengers, armed with this understanding, knew what it would mean to become "increasingly ready to defend democracy." The wait-and-see posture that characterized the initial response to the hijacking receded before the necessity of immediate, decisive action. This is the stuff of patriotic democracy, the ability to call on the spirit of lethal sacrifice at will. It is also critical to preempting a tragic account of the day's events.

American public discourse, having narratively dispensed with one deadly enemy, al-Qaeda, must address another threat to the status and standing of United 93's passengers – skepticism. *The 9/11 Commission Report*, in the concluding section of Chapter 1 ("What If?"), considers the possibility that American fighter jets scrambled to the area might have shot down United 93 rather than let it crash into Washington, DC. *The Report* works hard to discount this possibility, pointing out that the fighters were initially denied permission, perhaps in error, to shoot at the hijacked airliner. What would have happened if United 93 had not crashed in Shanksville cannot be known. This does not deter *The Report*, however, from reaching certitude on one question:

> NORAD officials have maintained that they would have intercepted and shot down United 93. We are not so sure. *We are sure that the nation owes a debt to the passengers of United 93. Their actions saved the lives of countless others*, and may have saved either the Capitol or the White House from destruction.[12]

The *Report* legitimately questions NORAD's conclusion about the ultimate fate of United 93, especially insofar as the conclusion seems unwarranted. History does not unfold twice so that comparisons can be made. However, the *Report* illegitimately takes the uncertainty inherent in the event and replaces one contestable assertion with an equally dogmatic claim. Let me be clear. This is not an issue about what the passengers of United 93 did or did not do. This is about *the story we tell about them to ourselves and the world in retrospect*. NORAD might be right. U.S. fighter jets might have downed United 93, which would render the actions of its passengers irrelevant since they were going to die no matter what they did. So they may or may not have actually saved "countless others." There is no way to know. Yet collective commemoration proceeds with the certainty (the product of sheer insistence) that *we do know*. The forced conviction testifies to patriotic democracy's commitment to sacrifice, especially to death in war, whether by soldiers or civilian airline passengers.

United 93's cockpit voice recorder reveals the perversity of this commitment. The recorder provides clues to the passengers' intentions. Assaulting the cockpit, the passengers meet with not just stiff resistance but also drastic countermeasures. Time was getting desperately short, which is why one passenger can be heard to yell: "In the cockpit. If we don't, we'll die." Contra Bush, Clinton, Biden, and Corbett, the passengers of United 93 were not trying to crash the plane – in an act of sacrifice – to save others. They were trying to take control of the plane in order to land it. One of the passengers was a trained pilot who possessed the skills required (with assistance from the ground). In other words, the passengers of United 93 wanted to live. Life – not sacrifice, not war, not death – was their first thought, perhaps their last. They wanted to live for themselves, their families, their loved ones. These were not patriots determined to martyr themselves for the greater good of the country and a secure place in history's pantheon. This does not make them any less brave. It may make them more human.

When the hijackers crashed the plane, they implicitly recognized the passengers' ambition. They understood the passengers better than the nation and people that seek to honor them. The attachment and commitment to life exhibited by the passengers of United 93 may disqualify them as patriots. They thought of themselves and their families first, a risk no patriot would dare take. How many (innocent) lives did they place in danger by such a selfish act? If they had taken control of the plane and landed it, such a feat would have generated applause *and suspicion*. What would they have been willing to do if the need to crash the plane had arisen? Would they have been willing to sacrifice themselves for the democracy? How could they prove their willingness to the satisfaction of a patriotic culture steeped in sacrifice conceived as death? Since they would not have died, nothing they might say in their defense could suffice. All things considered, death is the best outcome.

Ironically, when Tom Corbett proudly insists, as if trying to compliment the passengers, that "they preferred to shorten" the last few minutes of their lives, he sabotages the patriotic disposition he ostensibly enshrines. What does it mean for the official narrative for it to claim that the passengers of United 93 *sacrificed* themselves to save others *when they knew they were going to die regardless of what they did*? What happens to the virtue of such an act when people risk nothing, when they have nothing to lose because everything has already been taken from them? What, moreover, does the preference to shorten life signify? To project such intent onto United 93's passengers involves a struggle over the terms and timing of death and thus its rewards. What might the official story look like from the outside? Life has been forsaken. Thanks to the preference for immediate death, the passengers of United 93 become monstrous, mimicking the villains with whom they struggle. They had the chance to die, to choose death – and seized it, a nightmare come true. No wonder Tom Corbett claims this event has no precedent in American history.

George Bush also makes a distinct contribution to the Gothic character of the Flight 93 National Memorial dedication. Like the other speakers, Bush speaks of the day's events to reach the desired conclusion: "And with their brave decision, they launched the first counteroffensive of the war on terror." This assessment obviates the need to explain how the United States might bear responsibility for putting its citizens in the position of having to defend themselves against an enemy that hated it. While these citizens have every reason to be indignant, Bush prefers to speak of gratitude: "*But we do know this*: Americans are alive today because the passengers and crew of Flight 93 chose to act and *this Nation will be forever grateful.*" Bush's claim, however, cannot be vindicated, as I've already mentioned. It is not and cannot be known if the passengers saved (American) lives. What is known is that the nation is grateful for the opportunity to be grateful, to tell a heroic tale. For America, that United 93 crashed into southwestern Pennsylvania and became the subject of an inspiring narrative confirming the country's exceptionalism amounts to a happy ending. Ask Tom Ridge.

Ridge inadvertently captures and exposes the narrative fabrication at work in patriotic democracy's ceremonies. Saluting the heroism and corresponding humility of the passengers of United 93, he addresses them directly: "Now we suspect that you may not be comfortable when we call you heroes, *but humor us*, for you are heroes without a doubt." Ridge then makes the apparently hyperbolic claim that with the passage of ten years, "we are *even prouder* of you now" than we were in 2001. "*It is not a surprise to us*," Ridge adds.[13] Nor should it be: American democracy has been celebrating the passengers of United 93 for a decade. Ridge's declarations speak not to a fuller retrospective judgment of the events in question. They speak to the cumulative effect of commemorative concoction. Biden, too, disclosed the creative genius of repetition, making a comparison between what the residents of Washington, DC, suspected on September 11, 2001, and what *they now know to be true*, that a debt (an unpayable debt) is owed to the passengers of United 93. The truth is now known because it has been a truth ten years in the making through rituals like the one at which he speaks. Biden thus reveals American democracy's ugly secret, namely, that no event is beyond creative (re)appropriation. Despite the appearance of tragedy, "we" can "know, know with certitude that there is not a single, solitary [event] that America cannot overcome. There is not a single moment of hardship that cannot be transformed into one of national strength." Biden reverses and militarizes Nietzsche's ethic of self-overcoming. Rather than "what does not kill us makes us stronger," it becomes "what does kill (some of) us makes (the rest of) us stronger."

This spirit propels the United States into the wider geopolitical world. America must not isolate itself, as the events of 9/11 demonstrated.

Bolstered by the example of United 93, the country must finish the work those passengers started. The spirit of service they embodied can inspire new generations to action. Tyranny and bigotry recognize no national boundaries, which means those opposed to them must be willing to carry on the fight wherever they find it. The war may have begun here, but it will not remain here. As George Bush imagines a world where the principles of liberty, dignity, and hope reign, he insists: "the surest way to move toward that vision is for the United States of America to lead the cause of freedom." This is the same tragic dynamic that led to the events of 9/11, to which American democracy is blind – thanks in part to its collaboration with patriotism – and so now it uses 9/11 to go (back out) into the world to repeat the very pattern that led to the events that led to the commemoration calling for it.

GROUND ZERO, PENNSYLVANIA

The cultivation of new tragic democratic traditions from the ruins of September 11 might seem an unpromising political ambition likely to meet impassioned opposition. Nevertheless, the very extremity of 9/11 commemorations lends itself to, even encourages, tragic re-invention faithful to democracy's best creative possibilities. A tour through September 11 sites in southwestern Pennsylvania and New York City is needed.

In the American national monument complex, the Flight 93 National Memorial is relatively subtle. It consists of three parts: a long, low-standing black Memorial Plaza Wall to demarcate and cordon the crash area and field of debris; a white marble Wall of Names listing – one individual per slab – the passengers and crew of United Airlines Flight 93; and a boulder that indicates, more or less, the plane's crash point.[14] Compared, say, to the National World War II Memorial or the Korean War Veterans Memorial, the Flight 93 Memorial refuses traditional expressions of patriotic grandiosity or mawkishness. There is nothing supersized, celebratory, or particularly prideful about its memorial architecture. Insofar as Shanksville witnessed an episode of horrific violence, part of a larger sequence of barbarism, there is little need for the memorial to make a loud statement – hence the contrast between the bucolic setting and the understated memorial on the one hand and the jarring events of September 11 on the other.

Approaching the Arrival Forecourt, the spatial prelude to the memorial proper, the visitor is greeted by a number of information boards. These signposts betray a different ethos than the memorial. Tabloid-like, they provide the affective context within which the visitor is supposed to experience the memorial. This kind of framing device is not uncommon at memorial sites, of course, but it feels distinctly out of place here. This is not a memorial upon which one might stumble and need "educational" assistance. Rather, it is a memorial one must make a point of visiting. It is in a remote location (once on memorial grounds, visitors still have a three-and-a-half-mile drive to get there), and one would visit it already knowing the events that occasioned it.

The first sign announces, in capital letters, below a cloud of black smoke, "AMERICA ATTACKED!" It identifies United 93 as the fourth of four hijacked planes taken on September 11. The hijackings constitute "the deadliest attack on American soil by any foreign nation or terrorist group," references to Japan (Pearl Harbor) and Timothy McVeigh (Oklahoma City), respectively. It salutes the unarmed people on board for revolting quickly and decisively and for preventing the fight from reaching Washington, DC, and the United States Capitol, the likely target, where the House and Senate were in full session. Still, the day witnessed al-Qaeda's "unimaginable violence and destruction," as if to suggest the United States is exceptional even in the violence perpetrated against it – a presumption reflected in the usurpation of the "Ground Zero" designation from Hiroshima and Nagasaki to rename the World Trade Center site.

Visitors might think one such information board would suffice. They would be wrong. Political sentiment worth stating is worth reiterating. The second sign, below a map of the northeast United States that charts the doomed flight and lists the times of the other attacks, announces "MAYDAY!" – the alarm heard coming from the United 93 cockpit by Cleveland air traffic controllers. If the first sign provides context, the facts as *we* know them, the second sign puts the visitor inside the plane with the passengers and crew, as the hijacking begins. The first sign, then, maintains a discrete distance. It is an account of events from the outside, as it were. The second sign erodes that distance. It's an account moving within the events themselves. We are identified with our fellow citizens. It also reminds us of what we know, namely, that two planes have already struck the north and south towers at the World Trade Center. Soon, the Federal Aviation Administration will order all planes in American airspace to land, an unprecedented move in the country's aviation history. For the visitor, the first two signs combine to produce a sense of terror from without and terror from within. Things start to merge. We are not yet fully in Shanksville, Pennsylvania, however.

The third information signpost moves toward a denouement. It declares, "We're going to do something." It also rehearses the narrative of the first sign. Despite a bomb threat and instructions to sit quietly in the back of the plane, passengers and crew start making phone calls – the first act of resistance. They learn about New York City and the Pentagon. Though strangers, they deliberate, develop a plan, and vote to execute it. Enacting democracy's procedural norms, passengers and crew then assault the cockpit. The terrorists respond with extreme defensive measures, ultimately rolling the plane and crashing it into rural Pennsylvania at 563 miles per hour. The 7,000 gallons of jet fuel ignite, creating a fireball seen for miles. Most on board are instantly vaporized.[15]

A fourth sign, "Since September 11," returns us to the present. The terrorists wanted to induce fear and vulnerability, we are told, but America responded with unity and patriotism. Memorials both national and local have been built and "indelible memories of that day and those lost remain." Memory, of course, is not the passive phenomenon the signpost seems to suggest. Memories do not just remain. They are actively constructed through architectural performances such as the National Flight 93 Memorial, which pays tribute to the exceptional courage of forty everyday people, signified at the Wall of Names. Though indebted to Maya Lin's Vietnam Veterans Memorial, the white bulwark looms above ground, leaving little or no room for ambiguity. Each individual enjoys his or her own marble slab, but the slabs link one to another. The arrangement preserves the distinctiveness of each person but also reenacts their coming together in a crisis when the country needed their collective sacrifice. Each is one. Together, they are also one. Similarly, the memorial site tells us, "people from across the [country have] come together to create a national memorial." The patriotism reawakened by September 11 persists.

On the day (May 17, 2012) I visited the memorial, a National Park Service ranger gave a short prearranged talk to a small group of visitors. He emphasized the contrast between the scale of the memorial, especially its refusal of a representational form, and the violence that provided its backdrop. He first pointed to the gently sloping hill overlooking the memorial, which is the direction from which Flight 93 radically descended, as if emerging from nowhere, at breakneck speed. He then pointed to the debris field and mentioned that only 10 percent of the human remains deposited there had been recovered. Most of the plane, made of steel, disintegrated upon impact. You can imagine, he said, what that kind of force would do to a human being. If people were not imagining it before, they were doing so after his suggestion. With pride the ranger also informed the group that the terrorists who hijacked the plane were not recognized in any fashion at the site. The memorial constitutes an official burial ground, but only for (real) passengers and crew, not for those responsible for their deaths. This piece of information, previously well publicized, was met with verbal affirmations of "good." As Creon insists in *Antigone*, mortal enemies in life remain mortal enemies in death. Perhaps we would let vultures and dogs gnaw at their corpses, if we could.

The memorial's peaceful facade, then, belies a pungent politics circulating around it. Given the site's recreation and dissemination of horror, it appears that anger and hate for those responsible for mass death informs, even overwhelms, the tribute paid those who resisted. Given the site's cultivation of enmity as a framing device, which calls on visitors to confirm the reactive sensibility the memorial fosters, what kind of peace or hope does this "final resting place" offer to American democracy? After all, as one signpost reminds us, despite bin Laden's death, "the fight against the terrorists continues," a fight to which the Flight 93 National Memorial lends its material-cum-affective support. Accordingly, this is a site of death that does not allow for the recognition, let alone celebration, of life. Death receives priority and privilege. The memorial's official narrative, following the *9/11 Commission Report*, does not mention that passengers and crew were determined to take control of the plane and land it. They are saluted as figures of death alone; their courage takes shape in relation to death, not life. The story told ("FIGHTING BACK") presumes death was the only possible outcome, which is precisely what lends it grandeur. Life is denied any kind of significant presence. Death alone valorizes, commemorates, eternalizes. Hence the "obvious" decision not to acknowledge or recognize the four al Qaeda soldiers (it is a war, remember, our declared war) who brought down United 93. They give death a bad name. Their names and nationalities are known: Ziad Jarrah (Lebanon), Saeed al Ghamdi, Ahmad al Haznawi, and Ahmed al Nami (all from Saudi Arabia).[16] To accord them a place on this sacred site, so patriotic democracy's story goes, would be to admit they had succeeded in their monstrous task, namely, to attack "prominent symbols of the United States to create fear and a feeling of vulnerability in the American people." By refusing them burial recognition and formally erasing them from the site, it's as if they are denied agency in the attacks. The terrorists may have started this fight, but we finished it, and only the finish counts. This narrative fiction is critical to the story told, that passengers were

responsible for crashing United 93. The Flight 93 National Memorial is a
tribute to an American victory. Successful revolt "thwarts" the terrorists.
They are defeated. The memorial is a site of pain, anguish, and suffering –
but not defeat, not our defeat, anyway. It can't be. Democracy won't let
patriotism allow it.

Nevertheless, democracy suffers defeat not despite itself but because
of it. The memorial sign greeting visitors at the formal entrance to the
site, miles from the Wall of Names, quietly signals the democratic drive
governing this hallowed ground: "A common field one day, a field of
honor forever." The ordinary field becomes extraordinary because of
death. How is it that a democracy unthinkingly focuses on the moment
of impact but does not even mention the prior efforts of passengers and
crew to save their own lives and thus, perhaps, the lives of others? If
anything, the place of honor ought to be the airplane itself, in midair,
still intact. In it the passengers and crew demonstrated and vocalized,
according to the plane's cockpit voice recorder, a commitment to life.
Rather, Flight 93 National Memorial's design focuses attention on the
most horrific moment of the hijacking, its conclusion. The story told
here is not a recapitulation of events as they happened. The story told
is a narrative artifact that creates events – in the guise of recounting
them – in order to commemorate them later. The passengers and crew
of Flight 93 may have sacrificed themselves for the country, as the site
wills people to believe, or they may not have. But they have been narratively sacrificed, posthumously, to tell that particular story, told here
in ghastly fashion. Though not recruited, United 93 passengers were
drafted, placed at the front, and killed, as the American democracy
made war on them.

GOTHAM HORROR SHOW

The National September 11 Memorial opened on the tenth anniversary
of the 2001 attacks. It answered what the memorial's "official book"
refers to as the "instinct," "impulse," or "urge" to mark the slaughter.[17]
There was never any question that the site would one day house a memorial. Proposals were generated almost simultaneous to the crashes. The
design of the memorial prompted disputation, as all memorial proposals
do, but the idea of a memorial, including the suggestion that rebuild-
ing the towers exactly as they were would be the best tribute of all,
enjoyed consensus. In the immediate aftermath of al-Qaeda's assault,
the World Trade Center grounds were assigned sacrosanct status. The

country itself, for the ideals it embodies, was attacked – which of course confirmed its greatness. The smoldering site, renamed Ground Zero, would also be made sacred in self-conscious fashion, as if mass death were actually welcome given the memorial possibilities it opened for American democracy to express its self-love.

The memorial is titled "Reflecting Absence." It sits on the footprints of the former twin towers and features two reflecting pools with man-made waterfalls feeding them. Each of the reflecting pools, in turn, contains a square hole or void at its center toward which the flowing water slowly drifts and then disappears. The abstract design signifies loss and emptiness. For visitors approaching each of the pools, the sound of the water becomes deafening. It is difficult to talk to someone standing in close proximity. The waterfalls effectively eliminate the sounds of the city surrounding them.

The names of the nearly 3,000 people killed on September 11 are inscribed on bronze parapets framing the reflecting pools. The names are organized according to what the designers call "meaningful adjacencies." The names are not listed alphabetically or chronologically (by date of birth). Nor are they placed randomly. They are organized with precision. For example, the people who died on United Flight 93 are grouped together at the south pool. The principle applies to all victims, including the fire and police responders who perished trying to rescue them. People who died together thus live on together, in perpetuity, on the memorial. The contextualization, which tends to privatize and depoliticize public space, reflects the lives people actually lived. They did not live or die alone. They will not be remembered in isolation.

The National September 11 Memorial may not succeed in *overcoming* the day's horrors, enabling people to put them in some kind of perspective that allows life to continue by absorbing rather than obsessing over the day's events. It may succeed, however, in *reproducing* September 11's horrors, if on a smaller symbolic scale. This kind of effect fits American democracy well. The greatness of the horror confirms, in a way nothing else can, its exceptionalism, including the passionate belief that it is worthy of the zealous love citizens insist it deserves. Thus, on the September 11 Memorial website, in an informational section brimming with pride, one reads that the memorial honors "the largest loss of life resulting from a foreign attack on American soil and the greatest single loss of rescue personnel in American history."[18] Each death fact testifies to American democracy's status, at home and abroad. Enemies salute it by attacking and maiming it. Citizens honour it by sacrificing and dying for it. Death anchors the memorial. It must be incorporated, not transcended. The death of death would be fatal to American exceptionalism.

How does the National September 11 Memorial stage death? For visitors approaching the reflecting pools, the sound of the flowing water intensifies, bordering on assaultive. The roaring sound does not soothe, as ocean waves might, but consumes and rivets. It firmly locates the citizen in place – at a memorial, this memorial. The artificial character of the site is inescapable. From each pool's edge, the waterfalls manage to simulate the collapsing towers. The focus of the memorial is death, horrific death. This is especially true of the north pool when the wind gusts off the Hudson and the water streams not just downwards but sideways and diagonally, turning it from clean, clear, and orderly to messy, chaotic, and white. On one of the days I visited, spray (debris) forced people on the east side of the reflecting pool to run from their position. They scattered as the water suddenly, unexpectedly assaulted and inundated them. It's as if the climactic results of the attacks, replayed endlessly on television, could be experienced, witnessed, felt again, triggered by this corporeal water barrage. One could see and hear the buildings falling in the water. Consider it a commemorative reenactment of horror, an apocalyptic Gothic production.

The reenactment assumes more written form as well. The terms of the memorial design competition mandated the inclusion of the names of the day's victims from all three locations. Those killed in Virginia and Pennsylvania would also be listed on the New York City memorial (as would victims from the 1993 World Trade Center attack). The organizing principle for listing the names, "meaningful adjacencies," mentioned above, involves grouping people together on the memorial to mirror the precise location where they were killed: on a plane; in an office; on a specific floor; in a stairwell. It's as if the contingency and randomness of the day's deaths had to be addressed but denied. Unlike a Periclean funeral oration that speaks of the dead in general but mentions no one by name, not only are people named and affiliated; the groupings mean the precise circumstances of individual deaths can be imagined. He died from plane's impact; she died from gasoline fire; he was asphyxiated; she was crushed; he never saw it coming; she did see it coming; he might have jumped. Horror moves from abstract to concrete, which can produce an interesting effect on visitors. September 11 as a whole is not remembered. September 11 is experienced much like the day it unfolded, a series of surprise attacks coming in rapid succession accompanied by their heinous consequences. The inscriptions follow suit. People on the flights are grouped together, as are first responders: American Airlines Flight 77 from Boston, which hit the north tower; United Airlines Flight 175 from Boston, which hit the south tower; American Airlines Flight 73 from Chantilly, Virginia, which hit the Pentagon; United Airlines Flight 93 from Newark, which crashed in southwestern Pennsylvania; city police officers and firefighters, who died in the towers upon collapse. One day divided into six discrete events recalls the terror in its particularity. We relive each incident: the north tower struck; the south tower struck; the Pentagon hit; the south tower collapses; the north tower collapses; a crash in southwestern Pennsylvania.

At the memorial, of course, the recreated crash does not result in the destruction of building and dissemination of body that engulfed New York City. Here both are contained and re-circulated. That is, the water in each reflecting pool flows through a central void. It disappears only to reappear at the top of the waterfall and flow downward once more. The aquatic route cannot be seen in its totality. The void can only be glimpsed. It cannot be traced to the bottom of the memorial, enhancing the effect of loss and of nothingness. The recycled water feeds the infinite repetition of the simulation of the towers' collapse. Not only will September 11 be remembered. Here it cannot be forgotten. Visitors are effectively forced to watch, in silence, the simulation ad infinitum. The memorial can keep the trauma and injury it marks fresh and alive. It thus works to alleviate the architectural problem of transience, the inevitable invisibility and forgetting that await all monumental forms, perhaps especially those built as destinations.[19]

AN APOCALYPTIC GOTHIC MUSEUM IN GOTHAM CITY

The National September 11 Museum, which opened to controversy in May 2014,[20] functions as a political and affective continuation, even intensification of the National September 11 Memorial. Philip Kennicott, architecture critic of *The Washington Post*, considers the museum a "supplement" to Michael Arad's memorial pools but destructively so: it "overwhelms – or more literally undermines – the dignified power of [the] memorial by inviting visitors to re-experience the events in a strangely, obsessively, narcissistically repetitious way."[21] This is what makes the museum, in my judgment, a continuation of the memorial. That is, the museum, which is located directly beneath Ground Zero, does below ground what the memorial does above ground: it makes war on citizens. The museum recreates the horrors of September 11 in intimate, assaultive detail by targeting individuals – their memories, their experiences, their traumas.[22] The commemoration at work at the museum crystallizes America's self-understanding as an unrivaled source of right and good in the world and (nothing more than) an innocent victim on September 11, 2001. It thus formally denies, among other things, the violence and tragedy constitutive of its imperial democracy. Nevertheless, it was precisely the institutional structures of this violence and tragedy that were attacked or targeted on September 11. To acknowledge this, however, would be to acknowledge al-Qaeda's success on September 11, thereby showing respect for an enemy, an act of which America, not alone among democracies, is incapable.

What, more specifically, does it mean for the National September 11 Museum to make war on its citizens? Complementary to the kind of violence choreographed to make John Rambo and assorted animals fit for war, the ethic here is to overpower people with an awesome display of architectural and archaeological engineering, which perversely matches, even surpasses, al-Qaeda's 2001 assault. Apparently the world's leading democracy, feeling insecure not just about porous borders but also about its very identity, needed to prove itself superior to its deadliest enemy – regardless of the cost. What Terry Smith writes of the World Trade Center's and al-Qaeda's masterminds could be said of the museum's:

> To attempt creation or destruction on such an immense scale requires both bombers and master-builders to view living processes in general, and social life in particular, with a high degree of abstraction. Both must undertake a radical distancing of themselves from the flesh and blood of mundane experience "on the ground."[23]

Smith's claim might seem counter-intuitive regarding the museum, given its emphasis on the individual, but it simultaneously addresses everyone and no one, hence its air of abstraction.[24] Emanating from its own cavernous vacuum, the museum seems determined to induce a certain emotional-political sensibility in visitors, to break their morale and any possible resistance they might offer to its appalling yet impressive death-laden design. It is tempting to suggest that it may not matter if anyone visits the museum. For America's imperial democracy, it's enough that it was built.

Visitors enter the museum on the same level as the memorial. To access the museum proper, one first takes a long, descending escalator ride past one of the massive steel tridents that formed part of the World Trade Center façade. It is the first official ruin visible, a sign of both mass murder and indestructibility. It also serves, along with the other ruins, to make a point of political pride. The towers collapsed, intimating total destruction, but total destruction was not achieved. These are exceptional artifacts. The enemy did not succeed as it might first appear. The museum proper, so to speak, begins at the bottom of the escalator.

The museum's inexorable descent to bedrock seven stories below ground level, which somehow renders a sense of return to the surface (and life) problematic, if not quite doubtful, is reminiscent of the Vietnam Veterans Memorial wall on the National Mall, except this descent takes place entirely indoors on a much grander scale. Instead of virtually walking into a tomb from elsewhere, as in Washington, DC, one is always already in a tomb at the National September 11 Museum. This tomb is filled with thousands and thousands of still-unidentified remains of the day's victims. (The site is both a cemetery and the official repository of the dead.) It is also littered with ruins and debris from the day's attack: a roof antenna from one of the towers; an elevator motor; the last steel beam to be removed from the clean-up site; a fire truck damaged beyond repair during rescue efforts; twisted steel remnants from the floors that were struck. These substantial items look tiny in the immense surroundings of the underground mausoleum, which include the original slurry wall that held back the Hudson River. The visitor is made to feel puny.

Puniness reaches its climax beneath the north memorial pool, which can be circumnavigated. Here one encounters a small information sign. It reveals that some 1,200 feet above this very spot, "hijackers crashed American Airlines Flight 11 into the World Trade Center" and "tore a gash in the building more than 150 feet wide." What is the visitor to do now? How is she to react after reading this matter-of-fact fact? Look up and imagine the day's terrible events, the towers suddenly collapsing above and down upon her, winding up beneath 110 floors of compressed rubble? The inclusion on site of a composite of several floors of one of the towers flattened and fused suggests one answer. It is not enough to imagine the death of others. One must also imagine one's own. Vulnerability, susceptibility, contingency define life here.

In the museum's Memorial Exhibition, which highlights the identities of those killed in the day's attacks, the memorialization circle is closed. On a "Wall of Faces," there is a portrait photograph of (almost) each and every victim. This complements the names inscribed in the memorial directly above. On touch screen tables, visitors can call up the name of any victim and learn more about him or her.[25] Inside this memorial hall there is an inner chamber with benches lining the walls. The name of everyone killed is, sooner or later, projected onto opposing walls, followed by biographical information and, where possible, audiovisual reminiscences from family or friends. Visitors sit respectfully in the chamber, watching the parade of names relentlessly pass by, as if afraid to leave, which would seem rude given the solemnity of the space. The attacks that are recreated by the memorial waterfalls produce their offspring here.

The Memorial Exhibition aspires to pay tribute to the day's victims. To challenge this aspiration seems almost offensive by the time the museum's nadir is reached, especially after experiencing the room in the Historical Exhibition that documents those who jumped from the towers on September 11. Still photographs capture these horrific scenes, estimated at fifty to two hundred, accompanied by recollections of witnesses to the suicides who would not look away – for that would be to abandon people (though strangers) at the worst moment of their lives. It is a gut-wrenching alcove, one of several with a box of tissues at the ready and with a bench just outside it so people can sit and compose themselves afterwards. What is the point of this death-driven redundancy? Edward Rothstein speculates that the museum "is the site of their murder. And the attention to individuality presumably highlights the scale of the terrorist crime."[26] It also serves, as Rothstein notes, to distract. The museum signifies avoidance, even denial, of America's contradictory role in the world and its contributions to the circumstances that make 9/11 all too conceivable. The museum thus contributes to the impoverishment, through privatization, of public space.

At the National September 11 Museum, there is one prominent artifact that hails from elsewhere – a single, solitary brick from Osama bin Laden's house in Abbottabad, Afghanistan. It is proudly on display at bedrock and might be the museum's representative totem. There are two possibilities, the brick suggests: those who challenge the American-led global order of things will be reduced to this; those who align themselves with the American-led global order of things will also be reduced to a brick, a mere pillar of the global war on terror. Democracy may signify rule by the people but not in the war – not on terror but on citizens – waged in this museum.

AFFIRMATIONS OF THE TRAGIC DEMOCRATIC

In Athens's City Dionysia, a sequence of patriotic rituals preceded the formal presentation of the tragic plays. The city would pay elaborate tribute to its greatness before subjecting itself to often withering critique at the hands of tragic poets. As Simon Stow has argued, the patriotic display made the plays possible, and the plays made the patriotic ceremonies palatable.[27] In what follows I borrow from the Athenian tradition of civic scrutiny to develop a set of self-consciously tragic customs and exercises – not to reinvent patriotic occasions but, as far as possible, to leave them behind. The idea is not just to reverse the Athenian approach and offer critique before celebration to disclose the impropriety of self-glorification but also to double the critique by rejecting the self-idealization and resisting the projections typical of political orders. The idea, ultimately, is to articulate and develop a tragic political sensibility that, with luck, simultaneously reveals the impossibility of patriotic democracy and affirms the ambiguities inherent in democratic life. Rather than regard September 11 as Patriot Day, for example, it would be reinvented as Democracy Day. After all, what has come to be known in American political shorthand as 9/11 has provided cover for the forty-third and forty-fourth presidents of the United States to commit crimes against the Constitution and the world's peoples, the former launching a war of personal choice against another sovereign nation, the latter ordering drone strikes that have killed potentially hundreds of innocents and the assassination of American citizens. Democracy, it needs to be said, has become September 11's principal victim. American democracy does not need more patriotic occasions. It does need more democracy. Democracy Day commemoration would consist of three odes: an Ode to Democracy, an Ode to the Enemy, and an Ode to Life Itself.

DEMOCRACY DAY: OPENING CEREMONY

Democracy Day proceedings would begin not with prayers and libations but with a concession. (I developed another version of this ritual, Admission Day, in Chapter 2.) Democracy is not only imperfect. It is also cruel and unsparing. At its best, democracy routinely does wrong – often thanks to its best efforts. It inflicts untold harms and grave injuries. These flaws are structural features of democratic politics. For example, in a juridical setting, to see justice done not only risks but also guarantees injustice. Defendants may (or may not) be afforded superior procedural protections, but no matter how elaborate the protections might be, they always fail – sooner or later. Citizens wrongfully convicted of crimes regularly go to jail, as the Innocence Project has documented in excruciating detail. Nevertheless, nearly half of American states have no system of compensation available to the innocent finally freed from prison.

Colorado State Representative Angela Williams would like to remedy this situation in her state: "We have the responsibility to make this injustice a justice."[28] Williams's ambition is admirable, even if she overestimates the initiative's curative properties. Still, she has identified a constitutive dimension of democracy, not limited to the criminal justice system, that needs to be addressed. The admission of wrongdoing, then, is the occasion to articulate a capacious understanding of responsibility through which democracy embraces the consequences of its execution. Admission points to democracy's day of reckoning. While democracy bestows countless political gifts, it needs to widen its gift-giving and attend to the repercussions of its success. Insofar as democracy salutes its great legislators and political practitioners, it also needs to acknowledge those harmed in the conduct of politics. Democracy's victors and victims cannot be separated.

FIRST ODE

An Ode to Democracy highlights the symbiotic relationship between democracy's excellence and risk, its nobility and cruelty, its virtue and menace. Democracy is by definition a precarious undertaking. Yet this is not cause for alarm. Or, at least, this is no reason to sound an alarm. Life itself is beset by limitations, weaknesses, and vulnerabilities. For each of us it must end, eventually, in death. But the mere fact of finitude need not inform every move we make in life. Certainly it is no reason to narrow the parameters of our existence and privilege caution and safety, as if such measures would not only preserve and prolong life but also make it better. Such reduction too often entails impoverishment.

Democracy enjoys its own contingencies. The contestation, conflict, openness, and experimentation it institutionalizes – the competition enacted in a turbulent civil society, the limitations placed on the state's capacities to repress, the free flow of ideas and freedom of movement, the prospect of trying something new for an emergent constituency – can lead to heretofore unimagined breakthroughs and metamorphoses and leave it exposed and susceptible to any number of misfortunes, including attempted subversion and attack – from citizen and noncitizen alike. And if democracy entails a commitment to political life free of violence, it's because violence tends to characterize it. Democracy does not, in other words, presume a world friendly to its introduction, performance, or life. Yet democracy must proceed as if the norms and principles that constitute it already prevail. It must prefigure the world it would bring into being but cannot. Otherwise it is lost in advance. Nietzsche, as we saw in Chapter 2, argues that a commonwealth's strength can be discerned in its disposition to those who oppose or act against it – the greater the order, the more lenient its penal code. He envisions a commonwealth-to-come flushed with such a sense of self-assurance that its justice becomes self-canceling. It no longer concerns itself with "parasites." They are irrelevant.[29] Magnanimity is the kind of tragic affirmation that a democracy needs to cultivate, nurture, and internalize.

Tragic affirmations present challenges in the best of times. In times of emergency, they might seem impossible. Michael Ignatieff notes that following the September 11, 2001, attacks, American citizens felt betrayed and naïve. Al-Qaeda had successfully taken advantage of the country's freedoms, which, in turn, were no longer experienced as strengths but as weaknesses in need of correction. Strong majorities thus almost always support political elites who overreact in any crisis. Citizens turning against democratic traditions thereby reward those who attack them, giving them exactly what they want.[30] Ironically, Ignatieff contributes to the problem he diagnoses. He assumes the existence of evil that can, he insists, only be fought by evil means. He would like to stick to the lesser evil, which he considers an exercise in moral risk, but he does not think of democracy itself as a moral risk. This usually means that others will pay the price for our moral risk-taking, but we so-called democrats will not. Ignatieff advises democracies to find a way to see their vulnerabilities as strengths, but it comes too late. Commitment to the so-called lesser evil already signals its insufficiency.

To cultivate a tragic democratic ethos, a democracy would do well to recall and commemorate the self-possessed example of Patrick Henry at the Virginia State Ratifying Convention. Refusing, on principle, to attend the Philadelphia Convention and alarmed at the prospect of jettisoning the Articles of Confederation in favor of a Constitution that would unduly empower the national government, especially the executive, Henry not only extols the virtues of America's first constitution, which served the nation well as it fought and won a war of liberation against a great empire. He won't be frightened by what he sees as the fear-mongering tactics of the new Constitution's proponents.

On a fair investigation, we shall be found to be surrounded by no real dangers. We have the animating fortitude and persevering alacrity of republican [citizens], to carry us through misfortunes and calamities. [It is] the fortune of a republic to be able to withstand the stormy ocean of human vicissitudes. I know of no danger awaiting us. Public and private security are to be found here in the highest degree. Sir, it is the fortune of a free people, not to be intimidated by imaginary dangers.[31]

Admittedly, Henry's fair investigation slips from no real dangers to no dangers whatsoever to imaginary dangers, which suggests he is posing, but if he is posing, this self-conscious stance becomes more admirable, not less. He might believe, strictly speaking, that the republic faces many grave dangers (predatory European powers, Indian Nations, bitter internal divisions) – but dangers of some kind always confront a political community. And democracy has enemies. Yet Henry is not impressed by them and will not obsess over them. Democracy is uniquely positioned to negotiate the world but not by parroting antidemocratic regimes. Fear might intermittently, even frequently, disrupt the democratic order of things, resulting in damage to dominant principles, practices, and institutions – that is, to a way of life. But Henry's serene pose can contribute to a tragic appreciation of politics and thereby lessen the potential for self-inflicted harm.

SECOND ODE

An Ode to the Enemy would follow the Ode to Democracy. This might be the most important ethical-political project a democracy can undertake, a practice of forbearing and modesty that counters the will to exceptionalism and the ressentiment it engenders. Martin Luther King, Jr. offered an exemplary discourse for encountering the enemy in a stirring speech he gave at New York's Riverside Church in April 1967, the day before a massive antiwar march from Central Park to the United Nations to protest America's imperial aggression in Vietnam.[32] Conceding that it is never easy to speak against one's own government, especially during wartime, or to speak against majority opinion, King nevertheless felt compelled to raise his voice in opposition. Silence was not an option – not under such grave circumstances. While King did not want to speak directly to Hanoi, the National Liberation Front, Russia, or China, America's quartet of mortal communist enemies, he did want to speak for the enemy that could not speak for itself, not in America anyway. Much like Socrates and his beloved Athens, even reminiscent of Springsteen and his beloved America, King was concerned with America's well-being, fearing its democracy might be on the verge of self-inflicted spiritual death. The anti-Periclean speech he gave, then, could be considered a kind of preemptive funeral oration (part warning, possible eulogy) for the country he loved. If it did not reverse course, the United States would destroy itself – in which case the Vietnam War would figure prominently in its autopsy. King insisted, however, that the occasion demanded that he move beyond patriotic sentiments and national allegiances to speak as a citizen of the world. We must take care of more than our own.

Free of fear and resentment, King's speech embodies great admiration for the people of Vietnam, including those running the war against the United States. He understood that America was in the wrong. (As we saw in Chapter 2, even a reactionary film such as *First Blood* cannot help but admit, despite itself, that America was wrong.) Vietnam had been struggling for independence since (at least) the end of World War II and Japanese and French occupation. It appealed to the United States for assistance, borrowing from the Declaration of Independence to promote its cause. Vietnam did not want to emulate the United States or adopt its way of life. Essential differences would remain. Yet Vietnam appealed to us for help and thought we would offer it. Rather than side with a revolutionary movement, however, the United States decided to support French re-colonization. When this failed in 1954, America assumed the French mantle and denied the Vietnamese national independence and unification. The cost was staggering to every facet of Vietnamese life: family, village, land, water, culture. They suffered greatly for their political ideals and ambitions, and King compared America's military experimentation (of new weapons systems) on Vietnam with German experimentation on captive peoples in its concentration camps. Here the Ode to the Enemy dovetails with Admission Day.

King, following in the ministry of Jesus, would save the United States from itself and embrace the enemy. To do so he had to give the enemy voice. This might enable us to see that we were the real enemy Vietnam faced. It was imperative that America see itself as the other saw it. We had to see the destruction we brought to Vietnam. Perhaps by giving voice to its hopes and dreams this reversal of perspective could be achieved. King thereby revealed that we created an enemy for ourselves in Vietnam that need not have existed. He did not turn the enemy into a paragon of virtue to see the justness of their cause or to see that the United States was waging a perverted war that promised nothing so much as self-annihilation through genocide.

By giving voice to the enemy, King hoped to spur fellow citizens to action. Words and deeds must coincide: he advocated widespread conscientious objection to the war. Following one's conscience entailed taking risks. He also broached the subject of reparations.[33] The United States needed to atone for what it had done, compensating for the arrogance that led to intervention in the first place. The revolutionary spirit that once animated the West had been lost. It needed to recover its concern for justice and equality. Communism, then, needed to be reinterpreted as a sign of our own democratic failure to realize the political promise we once possessed. The enemy could remind us of the best in our political tradition. Racism, poverty, and militarism plagued us. Vietnam was an American war the burdens of which fell largely along class and racial lines. It was also an enemy of the American people. How we dealt with a foreign enemy governed democracy's prospects. The enemy was not a threat to democracy – we were. The enemy, however, could help us rescue democracy – from ourselves – and restore it.

King's oration suggests that one of life's ironies is that peoples create their own enemies. They might even choose them. They choose them as they articulate and define their identities and adopt principles, formulate policies, and take actions that express and enact them. "Choosing" enemies is an ordinary feature of political life, acknowledgment of which can inform, perhaps moderate, the affect accompanying it. Insofar as enmity is not just an inescapable but also a contingent dimension of politics, it is part of the order of things, no more a cause for anger or resentment, let alone hate, than the existential fact that life is finite, including the life of a democracy. An affirmation of enmity would require a sensibility free from moralization. We need our enemies. They have inherent value. They become worthy in their own right. We would not be who we are without them (for good and ill).

In Athens's Great Dionysia, the city marked its political superiority and dominance with a ritual affirming and consolidating its imperial power and prestige. The tribute it collected from "allies" was displayed on stage for citizens in attendance to appreciate – with representatives of those allies in the audience. Imagine if this kind of pride and arrogance were absent. Instead of treating enemies to a dose of humiliation, what if the enemy was invited to attend a tragically conceived ceremony as an honored, welcomed guest? In American politics, the State of the Union ritual includes presidents designating individual citizens as special invitees. They might have done something considered exemplary or heroic. They might have suffered some terrible loss. Presidents reference them for political purposes. Their stories might call attention to a grave problem the country refuses to acknowledge or perhaps spur the nation to necessary action. These guests have become an essential part of American political theater.

What if the United States eschewed narcissism and invited (a representative of) the enemy to its hitherto most solemn civic events? Why not start with Democracy Day? What if the survivors of the 9/11 hijackers were invited to attend as our guests? If this seems outlandish, what kind of precedent, if any, exists for treating September 11 militants with recognition and (at least) a modicum of respect?[34] Sophocles, whose literary genius was informed by extensive military experience, attended to the politics of Greek mourning practices. As Bonnie Honig argues, the struggle between Creon and Antigone over Polynices's body and burial represents a struggle between two rival forms of life, one democratic and egalitarian, the other Homeric and aristocratic. Until Creon's sudden, dramatic reversal toward the play's close, these deadly serious adversaries find themselves on the verge of an ancient version of mutually assured destruction.

What might a tragic democratic approach to Polynices entail? The circumstances surrounding the deaths of Eteocles and Polynices must be taken into account. Following Oedipus's death, the brothers, in some versions of the mythic tale, were supposed to share the throne, an arrangement Eteocles violated. This led to Polynices's exile where he married into a powerful family and raised an army to obtain what he believed rightly belonged to him. In the war that ensued, Thebes repulsed Argos and the brothers killed each other in hand-to-hand combat.

In the aftermath of war, Creon insists that Polynices was a traitor and should be treated as such. An enemy is an enemy – even in death. Antigone claims that Eteocles would not share Creon's assessment and argues that death demands the same mourning rites for all. Creon privileges the good of the city. Antigone privileges the gods and the uniqueness of her beloved brother. Ironically, perhaps they can both have their way – but also without getting fully what they want. Each can be vindicated by and dissatisfied with the outcome. Each can feel victorious – and that too much was surrendered to the other.

Why not bury Eteocles and Polynices together? They were brothers in life whose tragic ending reunited them in death. Let it remain such. This is not to say that distinctions cannot be made. Find a gently sloping hill. Place Eteocles above his brother, to honor the citizen who defended his homeland with his life, even at the cost of a beloved family member. Polynices receives the respectful treatment the gods demand, but he need not also receive the same ritual adulation. Eteocles can be praised for heroic service, though his ascension may have provoked a needless war. Polynices can be mourned for the ill-advised, desperate measures he felt he had to take at such great cost to his family and native land. Eteocles can be memorialized in stone with a patriotic inscription. Polynices's grave marker consists of his name alone. Eteocles was in the right, but this is not to say that he was necessarily blameless. Polynices was in the wrong, but this is not to say that he did not have a legitimate grievance or die for a principle in which he believed. Either way, Eteocles could not have become the revered citizen-soldier without Polynices, a status Polynices would, of course, challenge. The contest that they initiated in life thus continues in death, which seems altogether fitting for brothers-at-arms. They were both willing and able to take risks for what they believed. Whatever else divided them, this linked them. The joint burial plot provides a resolution bound to satisfy and antagonize, which is to say the conflict is by no means resolved. After all, the triumph of Creon and democratic Athens over Antigone and Homeric Greece comes with a steep cost. When a way of life requires the death of another, however justifiable, it ought to experience difficulty living with itself, as we saw in Chapter 1 through Ransom Stoddard. The defeat of Polynices made a democratic Thebes possible, and the debt thereby incurred could be paid, at least symbolically, with a ceremony disinterring the brothers' remains and reversing their positions on the gently sloping hill – for a time. We salute our enemies, too. We are rich enough for defeat.

A democracy at its best, then, especially in a tense, precarious postwar world, rises to the memorial occasion and practices the generosity, openness, and toleration it values – in the name of a domestic modus vivendi. Polynices was defeated, and his plot location signifies it, but there is no need to accentuate, let alone celebrate, his death. Eteocles may have reviled his brother in the end, but he cannot claim political purity for himself. He should have to reside next to him. Burying and mourning Eteocles and Polynices together signals to Thebes which brother receives priority, but privilege comes with a dose of doubt, even ambiguity. Enmity is real but not obsessive or all-encompassing. Democracy should never be too certain of itself, perhaps especially at memorial occasions, which brings us back to al-Qaeda.

America's three September 11 memorials contain a deliberate omission that doubles as a notable historical inaccuracy. Each undercounts the number of people killed. They undercount the dead because America refuses to recognize the hijackers who crashed the planes at the cost of their own lives as casualties of the day's horrors. The United States, however, was not attacked by a noun (terrorism). Flesh and blood human beings with reasons, interests, motives, beliefs, convictions, loves, passions, hatreds, and enmities of their own attacked it. America's recognition problem reflects a political sensibility driven by resentment toward a world capable of generating such savagery and blind to the contributions

America has made to it. The United States is responsible, in a Sophoclean sense, for the enemies it enjoys. Al-Qaeda could not exist without it.

Recognition of enemy dead at what so many consider sacred sites would represent a step toward the cultivation of a tragic democratic political ethos that runs counter to the country's dominant exceptionalist sensibility. What form might recognition take?[35] A single plaque, to be laid in the ground at the World Trade Center, the Pentagon, and Shanksville, Pennsylvania, in close proximity to the listings of "our" victims, would suffice (this one pertains to United 93):

This is the burial ground of the al-Qaeda insurgents (Ziad Jarrah, Saeed al Ghamdi, Ahmad al Haznawi, and Ahmed al Nami) who sacrificed themselves when they attacked the United States on September 11, 2001, on behalf of a cause they believed to be just.

We shall overcome … someday.

A democracy with any ambition to minimize the violence it practices as well as the violence committed against it must make the effort to see itself through the eyes of its enemies, as King argued regarding Vietnam. The location of the sign in the National September 11 Museum indicting the spot where American Airlines Flight 11 hit the north tower could become a site where Americans, when we look up and imagine the rubble falling, can understand what others have experienced at our hands – and thus what they see when they think of us. This is not just a question of self-induced estrangement to better understand and subsequently reinvent ourselves. It is a question of fostering, even as a conceit, a certain existential distance from events – as a counter to ressentiment. Regarding al-Qaeda, perhaps we recognize that they could not have done otherwise.

The United States did not deserve the September 11 attacks. No people deserve such a heinous crime. It is not surprising, however, that the United States might be targeted for retaliation given the history of its international conduct. Terry Smith offers the provocative claim that "Manhattan, it might be said, has always been at war." From colonial expropriation of Native Peoples in the seventeenth century to the destruction of Middle Eastern neighborhoods to make way for the World Trade Center complex in the twentieth, that is, to "a world increasingly dominated by the concerns of ruthless corporations, self-interested elites, and highly bureaucratized governments symbolized by buildings such as the WTC," the island has been the scene of repeated violence and destruction.[36] European conquerors and the colonial subjects that followed them have never been innocents. America has perpetrated massive violence on and from Manhattan. It has also suffered massive violence. Turnabout is part and parcel of politics. With this broader history in mind, commemoration of the events of September 11, 2001, might incorporate contrapuntal elements.

The commemorative burial plaque calls for self-overcoming. This project, however, is not an occasion for the enactment and celebration of American exceptionalism as the country transcends an atrocity committed against it, proving once again that it is ultimately the master of any and all circumstances or contingencies. Forget Joe Biden. Rather, self-overcoming signals the necessity for American democracy to address and redress the violence that has been characteristic of its political culture since its founding. We take the occasion of horrific violence committed against us to turn our gaze to the well-being of others. Magnanimity is the antidote to nihilistic killing.

Now let's reconsider September 11's tenth anniversary ceremonies in Pennsylvania. Ziad Jarrah was one of United 93's al-Qaeda hijackers and the likely pilot of the plane. Born in Lebanon, he was the product of a well-to-do Christian family. Jarrah moved to Germany to pursue higher education, first as a dental student, then in aircraft engineering. He had a serious relationship with Aysel Senguen, his girlfriend. Given frequent travels in and out of the United States in 2001, there is evidence that Jarrah might have been developing (as the date neared) second thoughts about his role in the attacks. This possibility was known to al-Qaeda.[37]

In Paul Greengrass's *United 93*, a 111-minute funereal tribute to (all of) the flight's passengers, Jarrah comes across as an ambivalent figure. Though he is the leader of the hijackers and sits in the front of the plane, as the pivotal moment arrives, he hesitates. To him, the timing for an assault on the cockpit never (somehow) seems quite right. His associates notice his reluctance and take action themselves. Jarrah, in short, is not the embodiment of evil America assumes him to be. (Nor are the other hijackers, who, despite their violence and demeanor, seem mostly frightened and young.) While prepared to sacrifice his life for a cause, he is not eager to do so. His life held other possibilities, and he, too, would leave survivors behind. Jarrah's parents lost a son, and Senguen lost a partner. They all have to live with the guilt-ridden knowledge of his participation in the mass murder of September 11, 2001.

Imagine Jarrah's family and loved ones in attendance at the 9/11 ceremonies in Shanksville, Pennsylvania – as invited guests. They would have to be recognized, their loss acknowledged. Jarrah would become a human being again, with a name and life of his own, through his survivors. He

could not be referred to as "the terrorist" given their presence. No ceremonial convention, not even a patriotic one, would condone such a violent insult. The mere attendance of these survivors, then, would broaden
the commemorative focus and counter the self-absorption that characterizes such events. It would also render calls for revenge, however implicit,
indecent and disrespectful. The departed should not be used for political
mobilization.

Inviting the enemy would affirm the norm that all lives, not just some
of them, are grievable.[38] All human lives count, and this includes, in the
United States, the lives of the al-Qaeda hijackers. As Bill Maher, then of
ABC News, asserted, the hijackers can be described in a number of ways,
but as cowards is not one of them. The truth of Maher's position is that
al-Qaeda operatives were carrying out an act of war against an enemy
of overwhelming might and perfidy. The United States does not have to
share this perspective, but it cannot deny that it, too, has been criticized
and condemned for criminal acts of war that cost civilians their lives – in
far greater numbers, many times over. Imagine how Americans would
react to Vietnamese calls for revenge, for bringing the perpetrators of
the American War to justice, or, failing that, for bringing justice to the
perpetrators. No one can be said to enjoy a monopoly on unconscionable
violence and we are not so dissimilar from our hated enemies – just ask
the Vietnamese or the Iraqis. We all too often become like them in the
course of fighting the good fight, blinded by the terms of our own political crusade. We level exactly this kind of charge against al-Qaeda, that
it defames the name of Islam on behalf of which it wages its perverted
brand of jihad.[39]

Democracy Day could be considered, in part, a sequel to the American
Dionysia proposed in Chapter 1, an occasion for self-reflection,
self-criticism, and the articulation of a noble political ethos. September 11
might seem ill-suited for such exercises, but it offers the United States
the Nietzschean chance to see if it is rich enough for defeat. There is a
film that might play a catalytic role on Democracy Day, especially in
the post-September 11 world. Kathryn Bigelow's *Zero Dark Thirty* is
another film through which America can see its enemies as something
other than embodiments of evil, in part because we can see ourselves as
they see us – as agents of brutality and violence.

Bigelow has been criticized for failing to provide historical context
in *Zero Dark Thirty*. Consider, then, the following scenario: an isola-
tionist democracy committed to freedom, equality, and justice assumes
center stage in international politics following its decisive role in a global

struggle against totalitarian (Nazi) terror. For the next half century the reborn democracy, unable to enjoy the peace it secured, leads a struggle against a new totalitarian enemy (the Soviet Union). A beacon of hope for oppressed peoples everywhere, it garners widespread applause and equal disapprobation. On freedom's behalf, it orchestrates a series of controversial proxy wars across the planet. In the process, it brings its citizens unprecedented wealth and power. It also requires numerous sacrifices and exposes them to considerable risks. Citizens revel in one and accept – with occasional dissent – the other. A stunning victory ensues from this second global struggle, but the problematic political and military architecture designed to win it remain intact despite their obsolescence. Once again, there is no peace to enjoy, no dividend to spend. A new enemy lurks on the horizon – one it actually helped usher into being during the prior global crusade. Now an unchallenged colossus governing the world, this imperial democracy's odyssey culminates in a series of horrific terrorist attacks from its latest enemy, which, ironically, tragically, lead to military and economic overreach and political self-mutilation.

Zero Dark Thirty, if read as a revenge tragedy, reveals the fraught character of American national identity, charts the dangers inherent in political action and responsibility, and closes the moral gap (allegedly) distinguishing mortal enemies. The film portrays an America informed by a sense of righteous victimization hell-bent on retaliation for wrongs done to it. It is indifferent to the consequences of retribution for others and blind to the predictable consequences for itself. Imperial prerogative animates *Zero Dark Thirty*'s two main characters, Dan and Maya. Operating in a culture of torture, they practice cruelty as a matter of course: results alone matter. Following the September 11 attacks, they presume torture's necessity and efficacy. The film also displays it as a reassertion of American power and mastery. We are entitled to the world. We will treat it as we please. We will take it back on our terms. We will enjoy the taking. Dan revels in the power torture expresses. It feels right, even good, following 9/11. This is not to say, however, that the film endorses what it depicts. Characters in a film may believe something to be true and act with conviction based on it – that, however, does not make it true. Nor does it make it the film's perspective.[40]

Torture, then, plays a prominent role in the film, but what does it mean to say that *Zero Dark Thirty* supports or justifies torture? This aspect of the film is particularly galling, so the argument goes, because torture played no role in locating and thus eliminating Osama bin Laden. To suggest otherwise is historically inaccurate, morally repellent, and politically dangerous. Nevertheless, whether the film effectively advocates the use of torture is not only difficult to answer; the question might obscure a more important point.

Advocates of torture rely, ultimately, on the coercive power of the ticking time bomb scenario. What is it permissible to do to prevent an imminent, unspeakable atrocity from taking place? What if torture alone can produce the knowledge necessary to stop such an event? Who would not agree to torture under these circumstances if it meant saving an untold number of innocent lives? Once agreement is exacted, it (supposedly) opens the floodgates to an otherwise forbidden practice. Even assuming that torture can be defended along narrow instrumental lines, proponents of torture do not justify it by claiming that if enough people are captured and subjected to criminal treatment, sooner or later a piece of information might be generated that, in turn, might prove useful at some later date, even ten years later, for another purpose altogether.

Yet that is the brutal, ugly scenario depicted in *Zero Dark Thirty*. The United States is spiraling out of control. Intelligence operatives question and torture a man, Ammar, who may or may not be a Saudi, regarding a matter having nothing whatsoever to do with Osama bin Laden. Moreover, torture does not actually get Ammar to talk. CIA agents trick him into believing he has talked (but has no memory of it), thus leading him actually to talk. True, they are clever enough to take advantage of torture's manifest failure, but it did fail. They seem surprised by this realization, but they do – because they must – adjust to it. The film thus depicts the corruption of two CIA case officers, standing in for America, who cannot see how far they have fallen. They can just as easily waterboard a person under their control as they can sit with, feed, and talk to him. In addition, throughout the film terrorists implement one successful terrorist attack after another – in London, Saudi Arabia, Islamabad, an American military facility – despite the widespread torture deployed to prevent it. Still, the torture continues.

At the close of the film, following bin Laden's assassination, Maya sits alone in a C-130, weeping. This follows a scene in which she confirms it is bin Laden who has been executed, a moment that brings her no apparent satisfaction, let alone joy, which is surprising since a great enemy has been terminated. What do the tears mean? Does Maya finally appreciate the cost of her ten-year mission-cum-obsession? The moral and political values she swore to uphold were repeatedly violated, perhaps destroyed, in the process. She has become uncomfortably similar to the enemy she hates. Does she sense this convergence and recognize that it was too high a price to pay, that her conduct and actions cannot be vindicated? Does she sense that as an act of revenge, the death penalty is unsatisfying, impotent even: it cannot undo bin Laden's spectacular 9/11 achievement? Nor can his assassination meaningfully enhance America's security. He will be replaced. In the end, bin Laden succeeded along another, more insidious dimension than the attacks themselves. He wanted to provoke the United States into a barbaric response, committing terrible deeds that revealed its true character. No one is in better position to see this than Maya is. Matt Taibbi suspects that *Zero Dark Thirty* celebrates America's response. I would argue it exposes it.[41]

Martin Luther King would undoubtedly have seen September 11 as another wake-up call for the United States. Rather than strike out against the world because an enemy struck us, we should affirm our democratic principles, resist the temptation to sacrifice them in the name of a hyperaggressive security, and work to remake ourselves and the world so that the conditions of possibility for terrorism do not prevail, conditions to which we previously contributed, however inadvertently. We would do this even if it might render us – at least initially – more vulnerable to attack.

THIRD ODE

Democracy Day ceremonies would conclude with an Ode to Life Itself. To affirm and embrace democracy's unrivaled risk requires fortitude; to affirm and embrace democracy's unsurpassed enemies requires magnanimity and generosity; each affirmation and embrace, in turn, pays respect to what makes our greatest triumphs and worst defeats possible – life itself. The world may be indifferent to us, but life defies its indifference. Sophocles suggests in the closing lines of *Antigone* that suffering teaches wisdom. If so, what kind of wisdom? This is not necessarily a question of what Sophocles's characters learn. Rather, it's a question of what can be learned from them. Following the ruinous confrontation with Antigone, Creon is left alive but wishing he were dead. He has lost both sons and his wife – one in war, two by suicide. He thinks he has lost everything. Unlike Eurydice, however, he does not kill himself. Not that it doesn't occur to him. Yet he can only pray for its end. Creon, apparently, is nothing if not resilient.

The leader of the chorus, while not unsympathetic to Creon's plight, tires of his death cries and more or less orders him to stop praying for death. They have civic obligations to meet. Life must be engaged. That is our condition. Despite the horrors that Creon has lived through, horrors for which he has assumed responsibility, life itself cannot be held responsible, blamed, or rejected. Nor should the thought be indulged that one has lived too long.[42] It would amount to an anti-tragic capitulation to contingency. The feeling is certainly understandable, especially after staggering loss, but the existential demands underlying it – for a world in which we feel at home, that is stable and predictable, that makes sense to us, that treats us fairly, in which we can form reliable expectations, where we won't lose everything – cannot be redeemed. The contest between Creon and Antigone is constitutive of (political) life, even if it seems particularly catastrophic. To affirm life is to affirm the perpetual presence of enmity and struggle – as well as their (many possible) ramifications. Creon acted on behalf of the city and thought he could anticipate and control Antigone's response to the power he wielded. He could not. Antigone acted on behalf of her brother and believed she would receive confirmation of her judgment from the gods. She did not. Precisely what we believe most fervently may be wrong. Lack of guarantee or warrant is part of the human condition. It can be viewed as a curse. It can also be taken up as a challenge constitutive of life itself – at once chastening and inspiring, terrifying and thrilling. Tragic actors recognize and respect limitations but do not succumb to them. Creon has suffered tremendous loss but not a catastrophic fall. He has lived, simultaneously, the glories and agonies life has to offer. It would be narcissistic of him to refuse life because of its doubled character. The world experiences it every day.

At the play's end, Creon takes responsibility for Antigone's, Haemon's, and Eurydice's deaths. He also forswears vengeance, which, as Bonnie Honig argues, marks a notable departure in Greek political life. What else might Creon undertake? The burials of Haemon and Antigone present him with distinctive opportunities – to do something new, something unexpected. In politics "we must deal with all that lies before us."[43] Creon now has the worldliness to take advantage of unforeseen opportunities, something he lacked when he first assumed power. In the beginning, he was a caricature of knee-jerk, bellicose patriotism. He was thoughtless. No more. Tragedy has made him interesting. Creon is not alone. He enjoys good company. In *Oedipus the King*, Oedipus learns that he not only killed his father, an unbearable truth, but also married and had children with his mother. The curse that he imposed on Laius' assailant as he launched the investigation of the late king's death must be brought down on him. Though he takes responsibility and blinds himself, the dreadful self-mutilation does not feel like a life-denying gesture. Unlike Jocasta, who committed suicide rather than continue living in the face of public pollution, Oedipus affirms life and, as always, endures its misfortunes. By the time he says goodbye to his children, he has regained his composure. He, too, is nothing if not resilient. How does he account for his decision to embrace life? He believes that he has been spared "for something great and terrible." If so, such a future would not only mimic the life he has already lived but also lay to rest the claim the chorus makes in *Oedipus at Colonus* that seems more than a little apt given Oedipus's near infanticide and subsequent travails: "Not to be born is best when all is reckoned in, but once a man has seen the light the next best thing, by far, is to go back, back where he came from, quickly as he can."[44] Creon mocks Oedipus for his resurrection, but *this* Creon does not understand that power doesn't make one "the master of all things," that, if anything, it means entanglement in life's inherent tragicomedy.[45] For Oedipus, killing Laius was the condition of possibility both of saving Thebes from the Sphinx and of damning it for regicide. For Oedipus, identifying himself as Laius's killer and abdicating the throne were the conditions of possibility for relieving Thebes of taint but also depriving the city of its finest leader. Oedipus's life has thus been an example of what it means to do something great and something terrible. They cannot be separated. The human estate does not allow for it. Rather, the human predicament demands to know how we are going to respond to it. If distinction can only be expressed in combinations of achievement and failure, the challenge is to create or discover a combination heretofore unknown. In this regard, Oedipus is not alone either. He, too, enjoys good company, at least in this book. It begins with Ransom Stoddard in Chapter 1, who was resilient enough to face down Liberty Valance when it looked like he was going to lose everything, overcome a flirtation with political suicide, and affirm creative destruction in the ambiguous world of politics. It continues with Bruce Springsteen's democratic rogues in Chapter 4, who are resilient enough to absorb every blow thrown at them without undue resentment, repay them in ironic kind without braggadocio, and disrupt an undemocratic present through violence on behalf of a more just, egalitarian future. It climaxes with *The East*'s radical environmental activists in Chapter 5, who are resilient enough to take on an unconquerable foe, neoliberalism, withstand the state's determination to hunt down and destroy them, and pursue a democratic vision that entails a tragic resort to cruelty.[46]

VIETNAM AT FIFTY

If September 11 can be reappropriated for democratic benefit, what other political events or legacies, if any, can profit from similar transformation? What other traditions might obstruct the introduction of a tragic political culture?

On Memorial Day 2012, President Barack Obama launched the fiftieth anniversary of the Vietnam War.[47] The Vietnam Veterans Memorial complex provided the institutional setting. The golden commemoration stems from the 2008 National Defense Authorization Act, designed, among other things, to honor and thank Vietnam veterans for the next decade – and more. What, exactly, marks 1962 as the starting point for American intervention in Vietnam? America recorded its first official fatality in 1959 (the date on which the names begin on Maya Lin's wall). The first American POW was captured in 1961. As Obama's Memorial Day remarks indicated, the anniversary is an act of calendrical fiat.[48]

Commemorating the Vietnam War, whatever the anniversary, poses distinct challenges. Apart from slavery and the Civil War, it may constitute the most divisive subject in American history. The war aroused great controversy (from geopolitical intent to military execution). In 1975, the Democratic Republic of Vietnam forced the United States to withdraw from the very country it created (South Vietnam), signaling not just departure but also defeat in the south. The last American helicopter left Saigon (immediately renamed Ho Chi Minh City) as Vietnamese troops reunited their country below. The United States also had to negotiate hard for the return of captured and tortured POWs, doubling the sense of humiliation felt by a country that took excessive pride in its (supposedly) perfect war record.

Obama proved equal to the commemorative challenge. He situated the story of Vietnam in America's larger political history. Invoking the Founders, Obama spoke of nation-building – "to form a more perfect Union." How does the Founding relate to the Vietnam War? The Constitution is the centerpiece of the nation, the basic framework that makes the republic possible. It embodies the common commitment to limited government and individual freedom. No part of the Constitution is more celebrated than the Bill of Rights, especially the fundamental political liberties protected by the first amendment. Nation-building, however, is not the work of a single generation. It is the work of each and every generation – the task is open-ended. The Founders believed in the possibility of steady progress but not ultimate perfection. Like Lincoln, Obama has no illusions about America's history. It includes many painful episodes, some of which are disgraceful and shameful. Yet America's past and its flaws can be overcome if the country continues to strive to meet its ideals. Those who gave their lives contributing to America's ongoing project of perfection serve as models of inspiration for the rest of us. This includes Vietnam veterans.

Obama cited Vietnam as "one of the most painful chapters" in American history. There were many events in the chapter, but he focused on the nobility of the citizen-soldiers who volunteered when called on to serve their country in "some of the most brutal conditions ever faced by Americans in war." Obama did not deny that "misdeeds" were committed by the American military, but he claimed these were the actions of a "few." The faithful service of the "many" should have been recognized, praised even. Celebration did not greet returning veterans, a grave mistake from an ungrateful country, especially the government. Obama spoke on this Memorial Day to "set the record straight," which is part of what it means to make a union more perfect. He insisted that debts must be recognized and paid. Those who served in Vietnam must be joined with those who served their country in the two prior centuries. America remembers Normandy and Iwo Jima. Now it must remember Hue and Khe Sanh. When it does, the Vietnam generation can take its place next to and with the greatest of generations.

Obama recovered not just the narrative of the war but also its politics. For most of the commemorative speech, he equated soldiers with patriots, privileging military service above and beyond any other form of democratic participation. He also cited the country's constitutional ideals as a critical aspect of the Vietnam story:

Let's resolve that in our democracy we can debate and disagree – even in a time of war. But let us never use patriotism as a political sword. Patriots can support a war; patriots can oppose a war. And whatever our view, let us always stand united in support of our troops, who we place in harm's way. This is our solemn obligation.

Obama was twice interrupted during this part of his talk, but not, noticeably, when he seemingly defended politics during war. Many believe that once a war starts, criticism stops. Patriots silence doubts. Obama's political ideal of contestation, however, did not move or inspire people – certainly not the projection that we are all patriots. The assembled crowd applauded only when Obama called for unity in supporting "our troops."

Support can even arrive, as Obama's speech demonstrated, forty or fifty years after the fact – through a thanksgiving narrative offered as a civic gift. We support our troops for their act of sacrifice, for it is in the act of service, of sacrifice – not the act of war – that glory is to be found. After all, "we hate war" and resort to it only when necessary for self-protection.

Obama's Vietnam narrative reveals the difficulties either critical or constitutional patriotism faces insofar as it relies on a patriotic culture for support. The Vietnam War is a problematic source from which to draw, and Obama's efforts to rewrite its history cannot keep discrepant elements from insinuating themselves into the new and improved official narrative. He not only approaches Vietnam with the kind of rhetorical insouciance characteristic of Richard Rorty but also revalues Vietnam in ways that disrupt the settlement to which he aspires. Appealing for Vietnam's battlefields to join the ranks of Normandy and Iwo Jima in the hearts and minds of Americans, Obama inexplicably includes "Rolling Thunder," a multiyear, arguably genocidal air campaign targeting northern Vietnam that produced immense civilian casualties, and "Hamburger Hill," the Pyrrhic struggle for a piece of real estate near the Laotian border with no strategic value whatsoever.[49] How can these military endeavors, one tantamount to a war crime, the other to suicide by combat, constitute sources of pride and thus inspire citizens to identify with and love democracy?[50]

Moreover, Obama admitted to military misdeeds but did not specify a single instance – not even My Lai, the atrocity of choice that functions in America's historical imagination as an exception to prove the rule of otherwise exemplary Vietnam (war) conduct. In other words, Obama would have the country believe, wrongly, that any misdeeds committed were performed by the few, thus making them by definition relatively rare. My Lai, however, was more rule than exception.[51] Nevertheless, according to Obama's redemptive narrative, all Vietnam veterans are "true heroes," an alchemical transformation that includes the likes of convicted war criminal William Calley.

Obama, unlike Martine Luther King, has no intention of speaking for the Vietnamese. He cannot admit that American national security was not at stake in Vietnam (a judgment even then in circulation) and that American troops fought for nothing. Candor here would belie his claim that Americans hate war and fight only when necessary. More importantly, Obama's revisionist history of the Vietnam War amounts to a denial of perhaps its most important truth, namely, that the United States, the world's leading democracy, placed its young men in a situation where they would have to murder civilians. (This is an ugly truth that even *First Blood* can indirectly admit, as I previously mentioned.) Obama concentrates on what the country did not do for its Vietnam veterans once they returned home. He thereby disregards and disowns what was done to them in the war itself by virtue of their service – by the very democracy that sent them there. Obama, it would seem, does not identify with the black funeral tradition. If he did, he might have felt compelled to deliver a speech that conceded democracy feeds on its young, with the hope that a public airing would make this dependence more difficult to sustain in the future, even at the risk of risking national security. Democracy should have to earn the right to go to war.[52]

Obama, in sum, hardly decries the Vietnam War. For America, he seems to proffer, like Biden in Pennsylvania, a banal version of Nietzsche's maxim that what does not kill us makes us stronger. Thus, whatever social, political, or cultural damage the Vietnam era inflicted on the country, the United States is, in the end, the better for it. "As any wound heals, the tissue around it becomes tougher, becomes stronger than before. And in this sense, finally, we might be able to see the true legacy of Vietnam … America is even stronger than before." Again, the narcissistic cruelty of this nationalist calculation, given the price that others (not just veterans) had to pay for reinvigoration, seems to escape Obama's notice. It discloses American exceptionalism's ability to recuperate anything in its optic. Vietnam, it turns out, was good for the country. Yet the very lessons Vietnam supposedly taught and in which Obama professes to believe have not been learned. American power is not used more wisely, as Bush's invasion of Iraq and his abandoned war in Afghanistan demonstrate, and American soldiers are treated with more disposability than ever. Obama's Vietnam simultaneously enhances the nobility and lessens the horror of war. Any good that might have resulted from Vietnam as a negative example has been lost. In short, we have created a past for ourselves that enables problematic commemoration of it, which, in turn, contributes to a political culture trapped in a pattern of self-destruction it cannot discern.

NIETZSCHEAN ARCHITECTURE

Obama's abysmal Memorial Day performance discloses the challenges facing a tragic public philosophy and culture. Still, how might Nietzsche's appreciation of enmity manifest itself in relation to Vietnam War commemoration? What architectural forms might aid and abet

Martin Luther King's Riverside Church anti-war oration on behalf of the enemy? As James Tatum wryly notes, "nations rarely build memorials to their enemy dead."[53] From a tragic perspective, however, the time has definitely come. What if a memorial pertaining to war, for example, tried to incorporate the perspective and experience of the enemy? What if it were required to include some kind of tribute or salute? Better, what if the enemy itself were allowed to contribute to a memorial design or, better still, design a counter-memorial in proximity to the original?[54]

There are numerous possibilities here. Several memorials Vietnam conceived in the aftermath of the American War offer inspiration. Consider, first, the monument in Hanoi to John McCain. It commemorates the day in 1967 that his airplane, along with nine others, was shot down on a bombing raid on the city. McCain parachuted to "safety" in Truc Bach Lake, was rescued, assaulted, and rescued again by local residents. Part of the monument depicts McCain on his knees, hands in the air above his head. It is a posture of abject surrender and humiliation, especially for a warrior. Inscribed next to McCain are the letters *U.S.A.F.* To perfect the reduction of status, McCain's name is deliberately misspelled: John Sney McGan. McGan was the son of a Navy admiral and high ranking official in the war.[55]

As the McGan Monument indicates, McCain is no hero. He may have been following orders, but those orders entailed raining death on Vietnam's capital and its civilian population – hence their outrage upon his capture. The Vietnamese people had every (good) reason to hate the likes of John McCain for murdering their families, friends, neighbors, and fellow citizens in a war of imperial aggression. No conception of heroism can accommodate such acts without denying or rewriting them. McCain's long captivity, likewise, cannot bestow heroic status on him. It can make him, in part, but only in part, a victim of victims (which the McGan Monument ironically captures). Again, McCain may have only been following orders, but not only is such a rationale suspect in the post-Nuremberg order; it also cannot alter his status as an agent of death and devastation. In this, the difference between John McCain and Lt. William Calley, architect of the My Lai slaughter, is negligible, perhaps nonexistent. Americans, of course, can only imagine McCain in a fighter plane, the Hanoi Hilton, or coming home. They cannot see him in the lake as the people of Vietnam saw him, the official representative of an imperial political-military apparatus bringing mass death to their people.[56]

There is a second possibility. Glenna Goodacre's *rejected* Vietnam Women's Memorial, the only shrine on the National Mall I know of that considered incorporating the enemy, a victim, into its design, resonates with a war crimes memorial built in Thuy Bo, Vietnam in 1977. For the Vietnamese it's called a Stone of Fury, self-consciously giving voice to an understandable hate. Placing Thuy Bo in the Vietnam Veterans Memorial complex would also position the United States to see itself through the eyes of the enemy against which it waged full-scale war for nearly a decade, a war with enormous civilian casualties.[57] This placement, in turn, would put pressure on American identity since it is the Vietnamese who appear to be exceptional.[58]

The Thuy Bo memorial "consists of a tall central Gothic tower and two horizontal wings that extend from the lower half of the vertical tower."[59] Each of the wings depicts wartime life. One wing portrays Vietnamese soldiers and civilians, both young and old, fighting the heroic fight against American imperialism. The other wing reproduces American atrocities committed against civilians. Women are shown "with the muzzles of carbines pointing to their necks." An American soldier, with a club in his hand and a grin on his face, is depicted dangling a baby by its leg. The Thuy Bo Memorial would remind American visitors that more than just 58,000 of their own citizens died in this war, and it would reveal what lies beneath the youthful innocence of Frederick Hart's The Three Servicemen sculpture. Hart's warriors represent not just names that might appear on Maya Lin's wall. They also represent the force that put countless Vietnamese names on memorial sites in Vietnam. These soldiers may be our own and they may have been serving their country, but they are also criminals, responsible for perpetrating, if not planning, the mass atrocity that was the Vietnam War, in which My Lai was the norm rather than the exception, as I mentioned previously.

Finally, the United States can look at another democracy for memorial inspiration. The character and implications of the American War may be denied in the United States, but in South Korea, America's crucial partner in the conflict that contributed 300,000 troops, some critical reckoning has taken place. Former ROK soldiers funded a memorial to the dead of Ha My, in recognition of their murder of 135 villagers.[60] This memorial differs from the Stone of Fury at Thuy Bo. It still incorporates an element of hate, but it also looks beyond the war to the better future that victory in the war made possible. Thus the names of the victims are listed on one side of the tombstone and a narrative of remembrance and forgiveness is inscribed on the other. This renders it a Stone of Spirit Consolation memorial.[61] The Vietnamese have not forgotten what the United States and its allies did to them during their war, but they seem to infer that enmity (and enemies) is inescapable in life, which means, ironically, that life need not revolve around, let alone dwell on it. An appreciation for enmity can also entail recognition that others pursue their interests and ideals blind to the consequences for others and themselves. They know not what they do. Is it surprising, then, that Vietnam was ready for formal diplomatic reconciliation with the United States long before the United States was ready?

Supplementing the Vietnam War Memorial complex with Thuy Bo's war crimes memorial (or the Ha My memorial to the dead) would not only call the entire space into commemorative question. It would also expose and challenge democracy's complacent self-conception. Democracy is a purveyor of war, crime, injury, violence, and death as much as the rival political systems it scorns – not because of the inevitable shortcomings of any system but thanks to the ordinary, everyday unfolding of its highest ideals and principles. The only failing to which the United States can admit, even forty years after Saigon's liberation, involves the mistreatment of returning veterans, which is the only political lesson it seems to have "learned."

KENT STATE

Democracy's patriotism addiction pushed to its extreme reveals tragic democratic possibilities. As I did in relation to September 11, Vietnam can be placed within a tragic geo-political context in which the United States destroys itself at home as it promotes its universal values and projects itself abroad. Not surprisingly, as Obama remembers and salutes one class of Vietnam service members, he forgets and disrespects another class of the same generation. The forgotten, however, remain. They cannot be erased. Obama, as mentioned, criticized America for its shabby treatment of the citizens it sent to war. Long after the fact, then, he welcomes them home. He also needed to welcome home, as it were, an equally courageous group of citizens who suffered – who continue to suffer – the country's angry treatment for their Vietnam-era bravery. Obama called on Americans to "never forget the costs of war," including the "loss of innocent civilians" in Vietnam (which he called terrible). It did not occur to Obama that Americans who opposed the war on college campuses across the country also served their country. Through their determined political action they helped bring about the end of a tragically misguided war. This generation of Vietnam veterans receives no tribute – only derision. And those who were slaughtered for opposing the war do not count in the loss of innocent civilian life – for example, the students at Kent State and Jackson State found no place in the president's remarks.

Thus, I propose May 4 as a national holiday, part of a new tragic democratic tradition. Call it Resistance Day. It would pay tribute to the thirteen students – accompanied by hundreds, perhaps thousands, more – who were gunned down by Ohio National Guardsmen for enacting their democratic citizenship in 1970. Not only were they protesting the war and its criminal expansion into Cambodia. They were also objecting to the presence of Ohio National Guard troops on campus to forcibly silence them – to silence democracy itself – as they were demonstrating on behalf of life. The university had banned rallies on campus. The students defied the order and performed their democratic obligations, especially resistance. As a result, National Guardsmen opened fire: four were killed; another nine were wounded, one of whom was permanently paralyzed. Not every victim was even participating in the anti-war demonstration (at least one was just going to class). Those who did participate were unarmed. They were dissenting on behalf of life. They wanted the mass killing in Vietnam and Southeast Asia stopped. Though they would not have their lives sacrificed for a stupid, illegitimate war, they had no expectation that their lives would be taken from them for exercising political rights (presumably they did understand they were placing themselves in harm's way, facing a state capable of great violence against civilians). Hence one of the war's tragedies: as the United States (ostensibly) defends democracy abroad, it destroys it at home.

Commemoration took fifteen years to materialize. With the May 4 Memorial at Kent State on the verge of becoming a reality in the mid-1980s, the Ohio branch of the American Legion passed a unanimous resolution denouncing the memorial as "an insult to patriotic veterans." The Legion initially titled its proclamation "Kent State Memorial to Terrorists."[62] It was particularly offended by the students' civil disobedience, signaling an ignorance of the American political history they invoked to condemn the students. In his Memorial Day speech, Obama does not exactly mimic the American Legion, but his silence regarding students bolsters the traditional patriotic sensibility he ostensibly seeks to re-cover. For Obama, unlike Richard Rorty, there is no shame, let alone indignation, regarding what America did in Vietnam. Nor is there shame or indignation regarding what America did to its citizens who protested the war and thus to its own democracy. If anything, Obama's quick embrace of America's commitment to debate minimizes its place in the American political tradition.[63] Besides, dogmatic insistence on "supporting the troops" circumscribes the dissent Obama appears to endorse. In sum, Obama's celebration of America – it may have been Memorial Day, but this was a celebration – did not enable meaningful criticism, and the so-called criticism offered did nothing to make the celebration palatable.[64]

The United States, if it learned anything from Vietnam, should not be celebrating the fiftieth anniversary of its "initial" commitment to an indefensible war. It should be planning a fiftieth anniversary celebration of the war's termination in 2025, saluting those citizens who brought it to a halt through their democratic agency, perhaps especially those citizens whose lives were stolen from them for doing so. They died. The democracy then dissolving lived. The students at Kent State were not on the commons staring down armed troops with visions of prior patriotic martyrdom in their minds, a tragic democratic truth to which the May 4 Memorial, honoring the nobility of democratic citizens, pays homage.[65] It consists of four polished black granite disks laid to rest on the earth leading to four granite squares. They watch over American democracy. The names of those killed formed no part of the original memorial. The absence diverts focus from the students themselves to the greater good they served. They were not seeking attention for themselves. The cause they served was greater than self. The 58,000 daffodils, symbolizing rebirth and new beginnings, which help compose the memorial, point to their principal concern.[66] To hold a democracy to its principles often enrages and threatens those who cannot admit it capable of violating them. In politics, holding to account can lead to an existential identity crisis. The most acute crisis, in turn, flows from the anxiety generated by questions of security and war. One of the many tragedies of democratic politics, then, is that citizens will, at times, pay a violent price for exercising their rights on behalf of democracy. Democracy needs to recognize this uncomfortable truth, as it is recognized at Kent State, for democracy is an expression of life and a commitment to resistance. Not even Memorial Day, Obama's dismal performance notwithstanding, needs to be consumed by patriotic pieties of sacrifice and death. A tragic democratic mantra on behalf of life works better: next year at Kent State.

Conclusion

Democracy's Tragic Affirmations

> There are two tragedies in life. One is not to get your heart's desire. The other is to get it.
>
> George Bernard Shaw, *Man and Superman*

Contrary to *The Man Who Shot Liberty Valance*, *Shane* enjoys a secure place in American cinematic history, at least in the popular imagination. In 1998 it appeared on the American Film Institute's 100 best American movies list, ranked sixty-ninth. Nine years later, in a second polling, it ranked forty-fifth. In 2003 Shane (the character) appeared on the Institute's list of fifty greatest heroes, ranked sixteenth.[1] In the Institute's 2008 genre poll, *Shane* ranked as the third greatest western, behind *The Searchers* and *High Noon*. The first category carries the most prestige; fifteen hundred leading figures in the industry picked *Shane* from among four hundred nominated films based on critical recognition, cultural significance, historical impact, enduring popularity, and awards won.[2]

It might seem unduly contrarian to disagree with an American cultural consensus, but what if *Shane* rightly appears on the best one hundred list for the wrong reasons? Here Shane's place on the greatest heroes list might be telling. It suggests the film is to be approached through a romantic frame, as a story at once moving and inspiring, touching and uplifting, in which good defeats evil, justice prevails, and, despite a few rocky moments, all ends well. Not that *Shane* can't be read this way, but it exacts a stiff price by compromising its possible status as a democratic tragedy on a par with ancient Greek classics. At its most politically problematic, *Shane* also contains resources for a democratic approach to the constitutive role violence plays in democracy. Do not look to the leading man, though. As with *Valance*, look to the quiet man who shuns the spotlight and appears to be nothing more than a supporting actor.

Shane is a political story of founding. This alone suggests it cannot be fully appreciated through a romantic frame. A founding may conclude successfully, but this means it also produces considerable costs, and in this regard *Shane*, like *Valance* and Rousseau's republic, is no exception. It tells the story of a group of homesteaders in Wyoming locked in mortal struggle with a cattle baron for control of open range land. Told largely through the eyes of a young boy named Joey, the son of the leading homesteader (Joe Starrett), it favors the family farmers. Still, key details of the film also work against the dominant trajectory of the heroic (romanticized) narrative.

The homesteaders have settled legally on government land with the intent, ultimately, to own it. To Rufus Ryker, the local cattle rancher, they are nothing more than squatters on his land. From the film's opening, the audience witnesses Ryker alternately bullying, cajoling, and threatening the homesteaders. Moreover, Ryker, his brother, and his men have skills and experience with guns that put the homesteaders in a decidedly inferior position. They equal or even exceed the Rykers in sheer numbers, but they do not possess the competence, let alone ruthlessness, necessary to contest them. As the film opens, tensions mount as Ryker informs the homesteaders, Starrett in particular, that he needs all of the range land in "dispute" because of a government cattle contract.

Into this fraught situation rides Shane, an elegant, stylish gunfighter passing through Starrett's land on the way to nowhere (reminiscent of Oedipus). Recognizing a mismatch when he sees one, Shane decides to linger. While he appears ready to bracket his old ways and reinvent his life, circumstances do not allow Shane to settle down as a hardworking farmhand. They continually pressure him to intervene, pressure he can resist temporarily at best. Assuming he wants to, of course. As with Oedipus, the world elicits his abilities.

As the film moves toward its inevitably violent conclusion, the homesteaders mark and celebrate the Fourth of July (which the Ryker brothers conspicuously ignore). The festivities link the homesteaders to Jefferson's yeoman farmers as the true possessors of the land and perhaps even identify them as the true American patriots. At the end of the day's celebration, the Starretts and Shane return home where the Rykers are waiting for them. The midnight menace is palpable. It might be an ambush in the dark, but Ryker has come to make Starrett a generous financial offer to work for him. Ryker, surprisingly, seeks compromise. The compromise would be on his terms, of course, but Ryker makes the offer based on the assumption that there must be winners and losers in this struggle given the limits (land, water, etc.) in play. Starrett rejects the offer, in part because the rest of the homesteaders would be excluded from the settlement. Ryker's demise would be unproblematic but not theirs. Ryker, ironically, exhibits a feel for the tragic, not Starrett.

In the conversation that ensues, contrary to the dominant narrative of the film, the audience learns Ryker's history, which also means that for the first time the tragic character of the struggle can be discerned, a tragedy that marginalizes Shane – for the moment, anyway.[3] Ryker considers himself, not without good reason, the founder of this land. Facing resistance from Native Americans (themselves victims of violence the film ignores) and brutal climatic conditions, he settled it with blood, sweat, and courage decades ago – when Starrett was still a young boy. Like the veteran of a war, Ryker bears the scars of his battles, including a Cheyenne arrowhead lodged in his shoulder, a daily reminder of the past and its pains. The sacrifices that Ryker made to tame and domesticate the land, ironically, enabled the homesteaders to settle on it years later. Ryker believes he made this land his own with his life and labor.

Starrett formally acknowledges Ryker's claim but nonetheless challenges and even dismisses it and then opposes it with one of his own. The film ultimately privileges Starrett's story insofar as he represents both progress and the future. In this *Shane* mimics *Liberty Valance*. Ryker's approach to raising cattle and land use is antiquated, thus inefficient and unproductive. He represents the past. Starrett and the other homesteaders, who will also build something more than the mere shell of a town and community, stand for what might be. In short, Ryker's day has come and gone, as Shane points out in the film's denouement. Ryker is history's relic, and his demise is no cause for regret. Starrett represents refounding. Nevertheless, Ryker's claim to the land rivals (or even exceeds) Starrett's. Starrett's position is also legitimate. He has done exactly what the government has mandated and has every reason and right to expect the land will one day be his. Alas, there is no independent position from which to settle this struggle. The people themselves must resolve it, and the ways of life the contending factions represent are incommensurable. One has to give way. Violence is thus inescapable.

The impasse poses no problems – ethical, political, or otherwise – for Ryker, who turns to a professional gunfighter to counter Shane's presence. Unfortunately for Ryker, he underestimates Shane's skills – badly.

After failing to lure Starrett into a trap, Ryker must contend with Shane instead. Though determined to retire his gun, Shane straps it on again because he believes Starrett is no match for a professional. Shane comes to the conclusion, if reluctantly, that he must stand for right where legal institutions cannot guarantee it. He has no doubt he is in the right. He also resorts to violent trickery to prevent Joe from, in his view, effectively committing suicide to defend the incipient community. Again, he knows he is doing the right thing. Shane eliminates Jack Wilson and the Ryker brothers and then rides way – never to return. Joey, who witnessed the gunfight and Shane's killer expertise, begs him to stay. Shane insists that staying is impossible and asks Joey to assure his mother that "there are no more guns in the valley." Shane's resort to violence has supposedly cleansed the valley of weaponry, his own included. He has created the conditions in which a democratic community can flourish while making it impossible for him to live in it as an equal. He must go. Otherwise, he would threaten the community he has founded and one day destabilize and destroy it.[4]

Where does this leave the homesteaders? Bonnie Honig argues that Shane's intervention subverts the democratic agency of the community he makes possible.[5] As with Rousseau's republican citizens following the departure of the Legislator, once Shane leaves, can the people left behind govern themselves? In keeping with a world of tragic possibilities and outcomes, not even the people themselves know what they are capable of left to their own devices. Following Ryker's demise, the community can assure itself of its just origins and foundations. Ryker's comeuppance was his due. Not only did he thwart the will of the democratic people; he did so through violence. Ryker was doubly illegitimate. What's more, the figure responsible for violence has left, and he was not a true part of the community anyway. It will govern itself according to strictly democratic norms and principles, which it has already been rehearsing, led by Joe Starrett. The founding moment was exceptional and need not trouble the community to come.

This triumphal narrative erases the violence done to Ryker and the form of life he represented (Ryker anticipates *Liberty Valance*'s cattle interests). The tragic dynamic operative at the founding, however, recurs, if obscured, throughout the lifetime of a political community. The newborn polity has yet to create anything together. Rather, it has fended off the threat to what it might create. Now that the community no longer has Ryker to unite and keep it together, differences and disagreements previously ignored or suppressed for tactical reasons are free to emerge.

Fragmentation is likely to ensue. The people might not resort to violence to settle it, but this does not mean the settlements they reach will not entail injuries, injustices, and cruelties, as in Rousseau's republic. Losers – thus victims – will find themselves in Ryker's position. Moreover, Shane did not eliminate all the guns in the valley – he eliminated all but Joe's and the other homesteaders' guns.

Perhaps Starrett and the other citizens have been underestimated. As Honig argues, perhaps they are not weak at all. Perhaps they are quite powerful and have fabricated an origins story in which Shane is scapegoated for the violence they themselves performed in an effort to absolve themselves of responsibility.[6] If so, then perhaps they also have the strength to discard their cover story, embrace responsibility, and deal with the tragic aftermath of the violence required to bring their just community into being – and to maintain it. After all, as Honig observes, "bullies and bandits surface all the time while powerful rescuers do not."[7] What if the founding were treated as an event to be both celebrated and mourned, at once a stellar accomplishment and a crime, an embodiment of the community's values as well as their defeat? The ambiguity of the founding could serve as a warning about the conduct of politics henceforth, something for the new regime to remember and keep in mind lest it routinely resort to violence when things get difficult or dicey. Although circumstances at the founding dictated the use of force, this does not mean that violence is either incidental or external to the life and times of liberal democracy. If Starrett and the others keep to their cover story and deflect responsibility, however, they are bound to reproduce the troubles that marked the founding deed and disavow their consequences.

If *Shane* were fifteen minutes longer, would the "day after" resemble the film's opening scene, with the Starretts hard at work on their farm content in the knowledge that the Ryker brothers were dead? Or might the community hold its first official funeral? What would it mean to mourn (for) the Rykers? Mourning would not only salute an opponent defeated in contest for a revered prize but also acknowledge a debt to an enemy whose very defeat made everything possible. Not surprisingly, Ryker and Starrett were in many ways alike. Each was self-reliant. Each pursued his self-interest with zeal. Each made sacrifices for his preferred way of life, absorbing considerable cost in the process. Starrett embodies a version of an ideal first made manifest in men such as Ryker. Starrett follows in his footsteps. Ryker, in the end, dies, which means that Starrett, his family, and the other homesteaders can fully realize their form of life. The new community must find a way to become worthy of Ryker's sacrifice, of Ryker being sacrificed. Worthiness is an aspiration that cannot be accomplished in any imaginable present. After all, Starrett and the others may squander the opportunity Ryker's killing affords them – an outcome that may not become apparent until much later. Judgment of the founding awaits the success of the democracy (always?) to come, and success depends, in part, on democracy's ability to address its haunted past. Tragically, the community would be well advised to postpone any final judgment, not only so that it always aspires to worthiness but also because it continually gives itself new reasons for congratulations and regret in the meantime. The drive to settle political accounts risks complacency, indifference, forgetting, and callousness.

Let's return to *The Man Who Shot Liberty Valance*. Joe Starrett finds himself, post-founding, in a position similar to Ransom Stoddard's. What might the figure of Stoddard suggest about the possibilities of democratic agency? Scorning a threat issued by Valance, Stoddard summoned Liberty to the street. We knew Stoddard was capable of violence. Not only had he assaulted Tom following Doniphon's practical joke with the paint cans. He had also been secretly practicing his aim for weeks in preparation for this very moment. More importantly, following the murder of Valance, Stoddard possessed the Weberian fortitude to live with the foul deed and not let its repugnance derail the drive for statehood. It was Tom Doniphon who lacked the moral resources, the integrity, to live with his crime. He saved Stoddard but was destroyed because of it. He could not live with his violation of one of the West's taboos. Following Valance's shooting Doniphon made a beeline for the local saloon and started drinking heavily. Once back at the ranch, he set fire to his house with the intent to perish in the flames. Since he had effectively killed himself when he gunned down Valance like a rabid dog, why not make it official? Doniphon flouted a respected civic convention and violated his personal code of conduct on behalf of the greater good. Doniphon could not tolerate this doubling. Stoddard alone found the strength to straddle two worlds, one of legend, the other of fact. Stoddard may not have killed Liberty Valance, but he did force the situation when no one else would and thereby made a refounding possible.

Joe Starrett seems to possess Stoddard's civic courage. When informed by Shane that he would be no match for Wilson, Starrett does not deny it. He suggests he will outlast him. In other words, he will find a way to overcome his limitations. Life is unpredictable; action is contingent. Outcomes are not predetermined. *Shane*, of course, privileges its hero's every move. As Richard Slotkin notes, "the underlying message of the narrative is…: a 'good man with a gun' is in every sense the best of men – an armed redeemer who is the sole vindicator of the 'liberties of the people,' the 'indispensable man' in the quest for progress."[8] Even Joey, who watches Shane beat his father – and hates him for it – believes in Shane's virtue. Yet Joey's (initial) denunciation of Shane is worthy of attention. His father not only refused to abide Shane's interference but also attacked Shane and demonstrated he was more than a match for him. Slotkin describes this moment in epic terms: "When the principal males in the story are in troubled thought, the skies darken; when they fight, the animals in the corral go crazy, leaping over fences as lightning flashes in the sky – as if they were Homeric demigods and Nature itself were responsive to their powers."[9] Slotkin's marvelous characterization inadvertently equalizes Shane and Starrett. This is not god versus mere mortal, however exceptional or admirable the mortal. This is a struggle between divinities. The Joe Starrett introduced at the beginning of the film is gone, replaced by his own double, the realization of which the film charts. Shane has been the catalyst for Joe's emergence, and Joe was on the verge of defeating his "better" and thus facing Wilson when Shane resorted to foul means to incapacitate him. Not deferring to Shane, Joe proved himself capable of something that no one expected, including himself. And Joe challenged Shane knowing their fistfight might well escalate and spiral out of control.[10] Either could have pulled his gun. This gives substance to Joe's claim that while he might not be a match for Wilson's speed, he might outlast him (just as he outlasted Shane). We'll never know, of course, an undecidability the film refuses to take seriously. We're supposed to assume, without doubt, that Shane was right and Joe would have been killed. Yet why assume Joe would simply stand toe-to-toe against Wilson? Joe was no Torrey.[11]

If anything, Shane takes the easy way out. We're supposed to admire Shane for his noblesse oblige, but he does not have to live with the repercussions of his "success" and assume responsibility for them. Like Doniphon, Shane is unaccountable, which the film celebrates, but nonresponsibility also represents a serious democratic shortcoming. Anyone can kill and leave town (or drink himself into oblivion). The truly difficult work follows the killing. Still, it is Joe (like Stoddard) who decides to bring matters to a conclusion while Shane initially seems determined to remain aloof, to respect Joe's autonomy and sense of communal conviction and responsibility. Shane changes his mind, of course, though he does so confident that Joe will be able to take advantage of the opportunity Shane provides, the difficult quotidian work that exceeds Shane's talents. As Slotkin characterizes Shane, he "is better than those he helps and is finally not accountable to those for whom he sacrifices himself."[12] Yet the lack of accountability might also mean that he is not the better man. He will not have to make himself worthy of his deed. His action thus comes with no moral or political price attached to it. This is Joey's (a child's) view of heroism, but to grow up is to realize that Joe Starrett is the figure to be admired, not the handsome, magnetic, charismatic transient. When Shane insists that there is no living with a killing, he is wrong. There is no *not* living with a killing. There is no choice.

Without our knowing it, Joe signaled early on that he was a democratic force. At the first "town meeting" in Joe's house, the inevitably of violence is already evident. Joe's hesitation and delay regarding what action the community ought to take in response to Ryker are thus admirable. It is not that he is incapable of violence. In the bar brawl in which he rescues Shane, Joe wields an axe handle with devastating ferocity and effectiveness. Rather, Joe understands that a democracy, including an incipient one, proceeds with caution, knowing that it will inflict damage as it acts for the greater good – and even as it realizes that good. When Joe refuses Ryker's buyout offer to protect the other homesteaders, he indicates that someone will have to pay to resolve this conflict – that someone is and must be Ryker (who also understands the zero-sum circumstances at work).[13] Joe insists that he and the homesteaders have been in the right all along, but this is a partial truth, which can be vindicated, if at all, only in retrospect. Ryker's counterstory disabuses Starrett's easy moralizing. The homesteaders may be right but they must definitely do wrong. Joe's ability to pursue and potentially consummate a vision of democratic good while living with the ambiguity of its results suggests a Weberian strength worthy of a tragic world in which democracy lives on the precipice of chance. Joe Starrett (dead or alive) is not a romantic figure, but he represents a tragic democratic politics – like Ransom Stoddard who returns to the convention hall to launch a thorny political career; like John Rambo who walks back to Hope ready to take his democratic rights; like the animals who resist military appropriation as an expression of life; like Rousseau's malefactors who knowingly defy the general will on principle; like Bruce Springsteen's well-armed anti-hero who exacts equality and street justice for a society yet to come; like the members of The East who serve democracy, justice, law, the earth, and its creatures through extra-legal violence; like the passengers of United 93 who aspire to take the cockpit and land United 93 in the name of life; like the students at Kent State who refuse a war and state repression on behalf of democracy and life itself. These figures epitomize the tragic constitution of democratic life – its possibilities, its achievements, its violence, its responsibilities, its greatness, and its terribleness.

Notes

1 Daniell Allen explores this theme regarding sovereignty, though not in a
   tragic framework. See Allen, *Talking to Strangers: Anxieties of Citizenship
   since Brown v. Board of Education.*
2 To cite one example, Bonnie Honig, employing Bernard Williams, pursues
   tragic reflections on the question of torture in a democracy. See Honig,
   Emergency Politics: Paradox, Law, Democracy, 4–11.
3 Here I borrow and recover Walter Kaufmann's notion of tragic responsibility, which presupposes a lack of moral fault or blame (he is thinking about
   Oedipus in *Oedipus the King*). For Kaufmann, it is precisely in a context
   of innocence (ignorance) that tragic responsibility can (and ought to) be
   taken: "Pride can mean that we accept high standards and feel that behavior
   and accomplishments considered satisfactory by others will not do for us.
   Similarly, responsibility can be free of guilt feelings and can mean that we
   define our field of action. Thus pride and responsibility can be future-oriented
   and, as it were, two sides of the same outlook." Kaufmann, *Tragedy and
   Philosophy,* 210. Democracy, however, unlike Oedipus, cannot claim
   innocence (or ignorance) regarding its actions. There is moral fault, of a
   tragic kind.
4 Allen pursues this line of thought along racial lines, but, again, not in
   tragic terms.
5 See Honig's splendid *Democracy and the Foreigner,* specifically her reflections on democracy and genre (110, 120). I am also indebted to Mark
   Edmundson's *Nightmare on Main Street: Angels, Sadomasochism, and the
   Culture of Gothic.*
6 Kateb, *Patriotism and Other Mistakes,* 3.
7 Ibid., 4.

8 Patriotism should be considered democracy's underlaborer, its junior partner in political crime. Subject to potential scapegoating, patriotism is not democracy's primary antagonist. Ironically, it may turn out to be the least of democracy's problems.

9 Patriotic sacrifice and obligation, on the other hand, operate with a presumption that everything has its price, the price must be paid, and patriots willingly, even gladly, pay it, which is why sacrifice poses no special set of political or ethical problems in need of further response. Patriotism revels in sacrifice. It is angry and righteous. It demands recognition of and respect for the sacrifice it extols. Death, patriotism insists, sustains the polity, trapping it in a virtuous circle of pain and suffering. In patriotism's imaginary, the polity could feed on killing and death happily, without end, regardless of its depressive, destructive effects.

10 See, for example, Goldhill, "The Great Dionysia and Civic Ideology," and *Love, Sex & Tragedy: How the Ancient World Shapes Our Lives.*

11 This revision of the City Dionysia might strike some as anachronistic or fanciful. Recall, however, that Pericles, in his funeral oration, refuses to commiserate with Athenian parents on the loss of their children. He insists they should be pleased their sons died honorable deaths – what greater glory could there be than to die for the city? He doubts he can convince parents of this patriotic truth. Pericles's refusal and doubt suggest not only the multiple and precarious affects in play among the city's various constituencies but also the alternative democratic political possibilities lodged in any ritual. Many Athenians might be receptive to the revised commemoration I have in mind insofar as it gives voice to the anger, hate, and indignation that love of homeland must suppress to sustain itself. In suggesting a new Dionysia, in which the ambiguities attending democratic political life would be prioritized against the backdrop of quotidian commitment, allegiance, and loyalty, I take Athens to be one model of the tragic, but not *the* model of the tragic. As Nietzsche counseled, "we must overcome even the Greeks!" Why follow Nietzsche's instruction? The Greeks' flirtation with tragedy relied on a patriotic safety net. Nietzsche, *The Gay Science*, #340, 272.

12 Nietzsche, *The Gay Science*, #109, 168.

13 Connolly, *Capitalism and Christianity, American Style*, 120.

14 White, *The Ethos of a Late-Modern Citizen*, 38–39.

15 Ibid., 37.

16 Ibid., 40, emphasis mine.

17 Ibid., 41.

18 Mouffe, *Agonistics: Thinking the World Politically*, 13.

19 White, *The Ethos of a Late-Modern Citizen*, 87–88.

20 Honig, *Antigone, Interrupted*, chapter 4.

21 Mouffe, 13. Mouffe insists that her recognition of the ineradicability of antagonism distinguishes her conceptualization of agonism from Arendt's, Connolly's and Honig's, though it might be more accurate to argue that Mouffe has a different threshold for marking and responding to it as such.

22 Honig, *Antigone, Interrupted*, 2, 7–8, 19.

23 Ibid., 6.

24 "There Will Be Blood" seems a fitting title for the Introduction. Paul Thomas Anderson's film depicts a world, exemplified by southern California in the early twentieth century, indifferent, perhaps antipathetic to human aspirations and projects. We may appear to be lords and masters of the planet, but the impression is illusory. To eke out a hardscrabble living in this desert, Daniel Plainview, an entrepreneur with grand ambitions for himself and civilization, risks life and limb beneath and above the ground through body-breaking labor and techniques. The violence required to extract raw materials necessary to life returns to take its toll on those who unleash it. This outcome is no ground for complaint, however, merely the condition of possibility for all manner of human enterprise, the prospects of which are at best uncertain. What is certain is that the violence inherent in life renders it risky and dangerous. It cannot be controlled or contained. It also fosters tragedy: Plainview's employment of various evils produces much good, and the good produced in turn results in new evils. As with John Ford's classic western *The Man Who Shot Liberty Valance*, *There Will Be Blood* demystifies the American democratic success story and reveals the enormous price to be paid, by one and all, for the unprecedented achievement it claims to represent but can only deliver with ambiguity.

25 Mansfield, "Derrida, Democracy and Violence."

26 Rousseau, *On the Social Contract*, 100, 102. This is a close paraphrase of Rousseau.

I AMERICAN DIONYSIA

1 See Connolly, *The Ethos of Pluralization, Pluralism*, and *Capitalism and Christianity, American Style*; Berlin, *The Crooked Timber of Humanity*; and Mouffe, *The Democratic Paradox*.

2 Eagleton, *Sweet Violence: The Idea of the Tragic*, 3.

3 Camus, "On the Future of Tragedy," 296–298

4 Ibid., 295.

5 Ibid., 306.

6 Steiner, "Tragedy, Pure and Simple," 535–536.

7 Nietzsche, *Twilight of the Idols*, 54; Connolly, "Democracy and Normalization," 12–13.

8 Machiavelli, *The Prince*, 84–87.

9 Ibid., 20.

10 Honig, *Political Theory and the Displacement of Politics*, 70–71.

11 Machiavelli, *The Discourses*, 1, 4, 5, 7, 8. Machiavelli likewise praises the Roman dictatorship, a necessary but fraught institution that might prove lethal. See also Wolin, *Politics and Vision*.

12 Ibid., 7.

13 Honig, *Political Theory and the Displacement of Politics*, 70.

14 Ibid., 71.

15 Ibid., 111. Honig argues that "Machiavelli believed that the durability of republics was due to the inner diversity that provided them with more

resources than any other form of regime to adapt to changing circumstances." The durability of republics was also due to the ability and readiness of citizens to wage political violence on behalf of liberty. Ibid., 112.

16 Nietzsche, *The Genealogy of Morals*, 228, 219. Cf. Honig, *Political Theory and the Displacement of Politics*, 69–73.
17 Nietzsche, *Twilight of the Idols*, 44.
18 Honig, *Political Theory and the Displacement of Politics*, 69–75.
19 Nietzsche, "Homer's Contest," 35, 36–37.
20 White, *The Ethos of a Late-Modern Citizen*, 40–41.
21 Nietzsche, *The Genealogy of Morals*, 205.
22 Nietzsche, *The Gay Science*, #303, 244.
23 Weber, "Politics as a Vocation," 117.
24 Ibid., 121–122.
25 Villa, *Socratic Citizenship*, 187–188; 192; 201–202; 211; 214; 216; 220; 224; 227; 228; 228–229.
26 Euben, *Platonic Noise*, 35–37.
27 Though not included in the minor tradition of tragic political thought elaborated here, Rousseau's democratic theorizations might be read to suggest
that while the general will is always right, it can still live in the wrong.
Though Rousseau struggles to save democracy from its routine operations,
not even the best laws can always benefit or burden, obligate or favor all
citizens equally, as he claims they must. Call it democratic tragedy. Present
but also denied in Rousseau's idealized republic, tragedy can illuminate the
Hobbesian elements of cruelty to be found in its institutions. Though fundamental decisions can always be reconsidered, revised, or reversed, none
of these options lessens the damage already done and the effects likely to
outlive any changes made. Rousseau, *On the Social Contract*, 63, 110; see
Johnston, *Encountering Tragedy*.
28 Cavell, *Cities of Words*, 1–3, 6.
29 Steiner, *The Death of Tragedy*, 8, 4.
30 Consider the founding of the United States or Israel.
31 Consider abortion or affirmative action politics in the United States.
32 Machiavelli, *The Discourses*, 121, 505–506.
33 Schaar, 'The Case for Patriotism,' 286.
34 See Johnston, *The Truth about Patriotism*, chapters 5 and 6.
35 Morgan, *American Slavery, American Freedom*.
36 Goldhill, *Reading Greek Tragedy*, 76–77; see Stow, 'Pericles at Gettysburg and Ground Zero,' 198.
37 Ibid., 77.
38 Ibid., 76.
39 Stow, "Pericles at Gettysburg and Ground Zero" 198–199.
40 Robert Pippin puts it neatly: "there can be no law unless the lawless are eliminated, controlled, but given what the lawless are willing to do, this violent
elimination cannot itself be just or fair, cannot play by the rules ... [I]t seems
that a civilized order must view itself as founded by heroic and unproblematic violence, so this truth about founding must be hidden by a lie." Pippin,
Hollywood Westerns and American Myth, 80–81.

41 Hauke Brunkhorst argues that once Liberty Valance and his associates attend
    Shinbone's delegate election, the procedural integrity of which is secured by
    the threat of violence, they "are but being *forced* to respect the rules of a fair
    discussion and vote, which they want to participate in. The point here is only
    that they want to participate, and not in which intention they want to do
    so, even if this intention is as sinister as obvious." Once they "enter the legal
    community that is still under construction, thus legitimizing it to exert con-
    stituent power in the first place ... the threat of violence serves the one and
    only purpose of ensuring the free and equal self-determination of *all* affected
    protagonists." Brunkhorst describes this constituent power as "*founding
    power*. It is founding instead of merely destroying in a double sense. It pro-
    duces a libertarian legal order and can do so *without* doing constitutive dam-
    age to the liberty that is to be established because it is performed not only
    factually, but with *reasons* all participants can agree to, if out of different
    motivations, and in this case even have agreed on." Brunkhorst's analysis
    drains the conflict between the cattle ranchers and the small farmers and
    townspeople of its tragic dimensions by denying its incommensurability. Do
    the cattle interests want to participate in politics? Or do they recognize that
    in the United States they already have no choice but to participate in politics?
    Rousseau contends in *On the Social Contract* that the legitimacy of major-
    ity rule as a governing principle presupposes a prior instance of unanimity.
    Otherwise, majorities have no right to impose their will on minorities. In
    short, the vote in Shinbone would be representative of a fair process ensuring
    the equal right to freedom of all if only Shinbone residents were involved.
    Brunkhorst, "From avenging to revolutionary force: John Ford's *The Man
    Who Shot Liberty Valance*," 696, 698 (emphases original).

42 For a comprehensive list, see Ray, *A Certain Tendency in the Hollywood
    Cinema*, 220.

43 Pippin writes: "Ranse's own confrontation with Valance is not itself accom-
    panied by any rhetoric of politics." Stoddard does proceed in silence, but
    prior to Peabody's beating, an act of political repression in which Valance
    forces him to eat the newspaper that exposed and denounced his politically
    motivated murders, Doniphon had warned Peabody, in front of Stoddard,
    that if he printed the article he would be signing his own death warrant.
    Stoddard knows exactly why Valance tried to kill Peabody – retaliation
    for what amounts to a courageous civic-political act. At this point in the
    film, Valance is a hired assassin for the cattle barons. Pippin, *Hollywood
    Westerns and American Myth*, 92.

44 Joshua Dienstag romantically posits eros as "the force that binds" Tom,
    Ransom, and Hallie [Tom's unofficial fiancé] together and "through them,
    the community." Moreover, "this presentation of eros transforms our per-
    ception of 'power' and 'law' so that they do not appear to be opposite
    forms of social organization ... [I]t is only when we see law and power not
    as originary and opposite forces but as two halves of an erotic whole that
    we can understand the foundation of the state as an act worth remember-
    ing and acknowledging, with all its attendant costs and sacrifices." Hallie
    becomes the key to Dienstag's reading: "For it is her relationship with both

men that ensures, for everyone else in town, that they have not acted self-
ishly, for their own motives (to become powerful or famous, etc.), that is,
that the shooting has the proper meaning – that it means the establishment
of law and not just, as it could, the continuation of rule by the gun. It is
the *story* of the death of Liberty, not the bullet that kills him, that ensures
the state of law continues past its founding moments" (emphasis original).
Dienstag, accordingly, insists that Stoddard "has realized that he cannot
bear to leave Hallie or the town." Yet, despite Dienstag's story, Doniphon
and Stoddard have a relationship with each other prior to and independent
of Hallie – through Valance. There is more than one triangle in the film.
Valance, Stoddard, and Doniphon are linked from the beginning through
violence, which Valance celebrates, Doniphon reveres, and Stoddard ultimately learns to appreciate. What's more, Dienstag, unlike Pippin, ignores
the beating of Mr. Peabody as the trigger that leads Stoddard to the street
to face Valance. Stoddard seeks to avenge Peabody's mauling – and by
extension his own beating when he first arrived in Shinbone. In calling out
Valance, he intends to shoot him dead, to murder him. The drive to statehood receives a critical push from the desire for revenge. Moreover, there
is little cinematic suggestion that Stoddard cannot bear to leave Hallie or
the town. At the territorial convention, Stoddard, ashamed of his newfound notoriety, decided to return east where he supposedly belonged, not
giving one thought either to Hallie or the town. Thus, contrary to Joseph
McBride and Michael Wilmington's claim that "the most remarkable dis-
covery the viewer makes after close study of the film is that it is Hallie, not
Tom or Ranse, who makes every important decision," it is actually possible to imagine the film without her. Dienstag also ignores the symbolism
of Stoddard tearing down the remains of his shingle outside the newspaper office before facing Valance. He discards his standing as an officer of
the law before usurping it. In addition, after (apparently) killing Valance
Stoddard does not drop his gun in the street in an official act of repudiation, but leaves the street with it prominently displayed while nursing his
wounded right arm. He took a bullet and then he delivered one. There is
a new gun in town. Stoddard may or may not represent rule by the gun,
but it is rule with a gun. It is only when Stoddard returns "home" that he
drops it, unseen by the town. See Dienstag, "A Storied Shooting: Liberty
Valance and the Paradox of Sovereignty," 306–307, 310, and McBride
and Wilmington, *John Ford*, 185.

45 Mark Roche and Vittorio Hosle insist that "Peabody tells the truth and does
not speak of legends ... The legend exists only for the modern consciousness,
which looks back on the West ... The legend exists not in the West itself
..." Nevertheless, when Peabody and Stoddard first arrive in Capitol City
for the statehood convention, no sooner has Stoddard stepped off the stagecoach than a prominent political fixer, Handy Strong, gawks at him and
asks Peabody, much like a star-struck youth: "Is that him?" Peabody also
refers to Stoddard in his convention speech as someone who has "come to
be known" across the territory "as a great champion of law and order." He
was an instant folk hero and legend. The West was full of them. Roche and

Hosle, "Vico's Age of Heroes and the Age of Men in John Ford's Film 'The Man Who Shot Liberty Valance.'"

46 Dienstag refuses to consider *The Man Who Shot Liberty Valance* a tragedy. He claims, pace Pippin, that thinking of *Liberty Valance* as a tragedy makes the film "Doniphon's story where in fact it is the story of a would-be democratic society and its enemy, unbounded Liberty." Ironically, Dienstag proceeds to describe the film in tragic terms. One example: "If the only loss, in establishing a sovereign community of law, were the death of an obnoxious villain like Valance, the choice would be a relatively easy one. But ... Valance is not the only one who pays. In this film, more plausibly, civic freedom comes with a visible and continuing cost – one paid not only by those excluded but by all who participate in the act of exclusion as well." Grand achievement paired with notable loss: Is this not a tragic dynamic? Besides, Doniphon and the would-be democratic community cannot be separated. He is one of its founders. At the meeting to send delegates from Shinbone to a statehood convention, it is Doniphon who brings it to order and appoints Stoddard to run it. Later, he not only seconds Stoddard's nomination, he preserves and protects the election from Valance's efforts to capture and negate it. Force defeats force. Doniphon may not want to be a politician, but he acts as a democratic political agent on behalf of the democracy to come and pays a horrific price for his efforts. More importantly, perhaps, for the question of tragedy, Dienstag's account seems blind to the legitimacy of the cattle interests who oppose statehood. They stand for a way of life that has flourished for generations, a life Tom Doniphon, in some ways, embodies on a smaller scale. Dienstag notes that Valance is "paid by the ranchers who oppose statehood," but not that Valance was paid to derail it. Valance is also a political agent. As mentioned, the ranchers turn to Valance because the electoral process to determine statehood, exemplified by Shinbone, is designed to produce an outcome favored by one side in the contest. Dienstag seems to assume reading the film as a tragedy would lead to political delegitimation, resignation, and paralysis, but none of these conclusions follows. For other examples of Dienstag's tragic formulations, see, "A Storied Shooting: Liberty Valance and the Paradox of Sovereignty," 292, 293, 294, 295, 307, and 310.

47 Gilberto Perez argues that "print the legend" is certainly not Ford's position. "He would not let men like the editor of the *Shinbone Star* decide for us what we are and are not to know." Perhaps, but Scott's decision is confirmed by Shinbone's Mayor Winder and even by United States Senator Ransom Stoddard himself, two representative democratic figures who routinely make decisions for the people. Perez, "House of Miscegenation," 25.

48 Ford's cinematic sleight of hand illuminates the film's closing presumption that the audience agrees with the decision to conceal the truth. And why would we not agree with a truth we already know? The second flashback spurs reconsideration of the initial presentation of the shootout. As Valance toys with Stoddard, we have to wonder, where is Doniphon? Nearby in such a small town, he should have intervened by now. The riddle goes more or less unnoticed, certainly unanswered. Think back, however, to the manner

of Valance's death: Valances's body recoils sharply from the kill shot with a force that Stoddard's "pop gun," so dubbed by Doniphon earlier in the film, could not have generated. We know at some level that Stoddard could not have produced the lethal result. His confession confirms our guilty visceral knowledge. As we agree with the decision to bury the truth, is it not because we have been complicit all along? The claim cannot be proven, but I believe it is folded into the film's structure as a possibility. We the people know that our myths bear disconcerting truths. We prefer not to know – not too much anyway. Perez, on the other hand, asks: "Yet how can the people, once apprised of the truth, decide in favor of the myth? Isn't it impossible to go on believing in a legend that has been exposed as false? 'You can't make yourself believe something,' as Pippin says, just because you believe that it's good for the country to believe it." I wonder. People make themselves believe something all the time because it makes the country good, which they already believe. Thus Tom's "cold-blooded murder" becomes justifiable homicide, merely saving a friend, or killing a rabid animal. People will not necessarily share Tom's characterization or assessment of his own act. Perez argues: "You can, however, find Tom guilty of murder and Ranse of mendacity and still think they did the right thing for the country – this is the real issue, the national rather than the individual story." Precisely because people conclude they did the right thing for the country, the acts themselves can partake in rightness. As Mr. Peabody bellowed on the statehood convention floor in response to Cassius Starbuckle's dissection of Stoddard's legend-in-the-making, which featured killing a man: "You call Liberty Valance a man?!"

49 No doubt thinking of Jason, the train conductor who genuflects in the presence of Senator Stoddard and who works twice as hard to make his train run not just on time but ahead of schedule, Pippin writes, "Our newspaper editor is not wrong to worry about Shinbone, so clean and empty and quiet, without its legends. What kind of dedication and commitment could that way of life inspire on its own?" One might also recall that in the immediate aftermath of Valance's killing, residents of Shinbone were singing and dancing in the streets. Yet isn't it the figure of Ransom Stoddard himself that indicates that we do not necessarily have to worry along with the editor? Stoddard, after all, was an ordinary man before he became involved in politics. Similarly, Roche and Hosle note: "the film closes with the Senator being heralded not for his government service but for his supposedly having shot Liberty Valance, that is, for the old morality, which lives on in the people and which the Senator has worked to replace. The structure is ironic, for Ranse has been successful in his overarching goal of bringing democracy and good government to his people, but he is recognized not for his democratic service but for the old morality to which he owes his success and which he has knowingly worked to replace." The problem here is overstated and obscures Stoddard's success subsequent to the shooting. In the film's opening sequence, the Stoddards arrive in Shinbone by train. A young reporter hanging about the tracks does not recognize them and asks Jason to identify them. Jason rebukes

him and says, "That's Senator Stoddard and his wife. Why you could fill your newspaper with stories about them." He is *Senator* Stoddard and neither Valance nor the killing is mentioned. The stories would be political stories and the reporter leaps at the chance to interview Stoddard. Likewise, when Scott recounts Stoddard's long political career, he omits Valance. Pippin, *Hollywood Westerns and American Myth*, 101; Roche and Hosle, "Vico's Age of Heroes and the Age of Men in John Ford's Film 'The Man Who Shot Liberty Valance.'"

50 Shapiro, *Methods and Nations*, 146–150. See also Shapiro, *Deforming American Political Thought*, Chapter 3.

51 As Robert Ray, *A Certain Tendency in the Hollywood Cinema*, argues (236), *Liberty Valance* presents a fundamental ambiguity in "almost every image, issue, action, and character." The "inherent equivocalness" between the contending sets of values represented by Doniphon and Stoddard makes any choice between them not only "treacherous," to borrow Ray's formulation, but tragic. The film, alas, ultimately obviates the need for choice. Doniphon's death requires silence, which means forgetting and, in effect, denial. Scott's question at the beginning of the film, "Who was Tom Doniphon?" becomes retroactively unasked. There was no Tom Doniphon, which also means there was no cost to founding.

52 Pippin writes: "We also need to take fully on board the fact that Ranse, for all his high-mindedness, is willing, without much visible struggling with his conscience, to build his life on a lie. In a simple word, this is dishonorable, and there is no question that Ford wants us to see that it is dishonorable, even if it is also excusable." Perez challenges this damning conclusion about Stoddard. Not that it is necessarily wrong, but it may occlude other interpretive possibilities. Pippin's judgment presumes Stoddard's long-standing fame and fortune and thus seems temporally compromised. When Stoddard reenters the statehood convention, it cannot be known – certainly not by Ranse – what it might mean to build a life on a secret founding crime or if it can even be done. If the Stoddard who returns to the convention hall retains any of the integrity of the Stoddard who left it, then the kind of politics he would practice would likely be *responsive* to the destruction success entails. Pippin's conclusion also ignores Doniphon's order that Stoddard accept the nomination and become worthy of it. Pippin, *Hollywood Westerns and American Myths*, 93; Perez, "House of Miscegenation," 25.

53 Williams, *Moral Luck*, 74. Likewise, Simon Critchley writes: "what I would like to question, is the thought that in tragic action the subject can achieve authenticity in its confrontation with finitude." Critchley, *Infinitely Demanding*, 76.

54 It could be argued that Stoddard killed Doniphon insofar as he, like the young Oedipus, could not begin to imagine the possible consequences of what he was doing.

55 Ray writes: "That Ranse's rise came at Tom's expense suggested the historical impossibility of outlaw and official values. Even more pessimistically, the film suggested Tom's fall had been inevitable and, in fact, accomplished by his own hands. For in killing Valance, Doniphon destroyed the very

conditions that made him, rather than Stoddard, a hero." This dynamic is worthy of Greek tragedy. Ray, *A Certain Tendency in the Hollywood Cinema*, 229.

56 McBride and Wilmington, Roche and Hosle, and Pippin (as mentioned earlier) are troubled by Stoddard's return to the convention hall after learning that he did not kill Valance. McBride and Wilmington insist, wrongly, that "Stoddard *sought* his title, even if he has not really earned it." Roche and Hosle condemn him for opportunism and hypocrisy. This is much too harsh. Pippin, on the other hand, suggests that Stoddard has come to "a more sober and pragmatic realization of the necessity of … moral compromises." I would revise Pippin's formulation and argue that Stoddard's realization is tragic. Having arrived in Shinbone following Valances's stagecoach robbery, Stoddard asks: "What kind of community have I come to?" By the close of the second flashback, Stoddard no longer needs to ask. He can return to the convention floor to accept the nomination because he has been given a slow civic education in tragedy, which has finally produced an epiphany. Politics entails the continuation of violence – and not always by other means. Stoddard initially rejected the gun as the appropriate response to Valance, but not ultimately. He now knows the kind of world in which he lives (this is not just about life in Shinbone). Returning east where he supposedly belongs can't work. It would, somewhat pathetically, match Doniphon's descent into drink and homelessness. As McBride and Wilmington note, "What we are really seeing is not the building of a legend but a gradual stripping away of Stoddard's illusions. We are constantly taken 'backstage,' a motif introduced before the flashback even begins, when Stoddard leaves the room with the coffin to tell his story in the anteroom." Pippin, *Hollywood Westerns and American Myth*, 84; McBride and Wilmington, *John Ford*, 181.

57 McBride and Wilmington write: "Ford is not suggesting that the lie has become truth – after all, as Peter Bogdanovich notes, 'Ford prints the fact' – but instead that the lie was part of history, and the *symbol* of Stoddard the hero has become a fact. Law triumphed over anarchy; the wilderness did become a garden. To expose the symbol as a lie would be to deny the meaning of history." The symbol can be exposed, but it cannot be exposed as a mere lie. After all, Stoddard did face Valance on the street and exchange gunfire with him and who knows where his bullet landed. Doniphon claims to have killed Valance and believes it, but what makes him right? Also, history's meaning is more complicated than these alleged transformations (law over anarchy, etc.) suggest. Stoddard's career is filled with accomplishments, but they too necessarily come with a cost. Stoddard's career, then, reflects the ambiguity of its launch (the founding). He has become more than a symbol of heroism given his political work over decades. When Jason assures the Senator as he leaves Shinbone that there is no need to thank him for all the courtesy shown him because nothing is too good for the man who shot Liberty Valance, he insults him. Stoddard can no longer be reduced to a one-act legend. McBride and Wilmington, *John Ford*, 189.

58 On the question of cost, Dienstag is strategic but perhaps shortsighted in focusing on the founding alone: "Both fact and legend, the narrative of *The*

Man Who Shot Liberty Valance creates us as the inheritors of a violent past that we can choose to acknowledge or, like the editor, choose to ignore. We cannot undo the violence that has created and sustained the democracy we enjoy, neither can we legalize it – any more than the original participants could – but perhaps we can *bear* to live with its memory if we come to believe that its origin was not selfish but shared and burdensome to those who perpetrated it. Not just an arbitrary decision to exclude but a creative and collective act of union" (emphasis original). Here Dienstag's re-narration of *The Man Who Shot Liberty Valance* comes into play. He refers throughout most of the essay to the "killing" or "death" or "demise" of Liberty Valance, but the killing was something else altogether, namely, a "cold-blooded murder" (Doniphon's words). To refer to Valance as an "obnoxious villain" depoliticizes him and works to erase the cattle ranchers as one contestant in what amounts to a political struggle between incommensurable forms of life. In short, Dienstag's re-narration provides us with a past with which we can live. He has effectively become the fourth man to shoot Valance. Thus, insofar as Dienstag's story is a story about the (mere) death of Liberty, the question becomes whether we can "bear" our own narrative fabrication, the one designed to produce such a result. How could the answer be anything but yes? In short, Dienstag has come to believe what he has re-narrated. His position is much closer to the editor's than he realizes. He later writes: "The state is depicted as the bittersweet constitutive merging of law and power enacted by humans bound together by erotic forces. Whether it was worth it is a question always to be answered in the present by an audience that receives this state as a narrative inheritance and has to decide whether to reprint it." Dienstag knows his answer, but the question exceeds the founding moment. That is, the kind of tragic dynamic present at the founding recurs throughout the life of a democratic society. Those in the present can never fully answer the question – nor should they aspire to do so. It would affect (limit, impair) their sense of responsibility, a tragic understanding of which pertains not just to what they have inherited but also to what they are always in the process of creating for themselves and passing on to future generations. In the present, polities always lack the perspective from which they can make any definitive assessment of what they have done – hence Stoddard must return to the convention hall and accept the nomination. He both can and cannot bear the memory and cost of politics because he is not (yet) in position to believe a truth (politics is definitely worth the cost) convenient to him now. It's too early. It's always too early. Ask Oedipus. Dienstag, "A Storied Shooting: Liberty Valance and the Paradox of Sovereignty," 309, 311.

59 Roche and Hosle rebuke Stoddard for putting Doniphon in an impossible position, holding Stoddard "even more guilty for having morally obliged another person to commit a cold-blooded murder." Pippin, for one, notes the calculated character of Doniphon's decision, meaning that he had more than one option. In the end, he chose to murder Valance. It is also worth noting that Doniphon put Stoddard in an impossible position. He catapulted Stoddard into an official political position, preserving and protecting

Shinbone's election, but refused to secure the results. When Valance, having failed to commandeer the election, calls out Stoddard he also warns off Doniphon, telling him that Stoddard has been "hiding behind" his "gun long enough." Doniphon duly backs down, perhaps assuming that Stoddard will leave town, but why accede to a dictate that amounts to sanctioning Stoddard's murder? Why take orders from Valance and why now? After all, more than Stoddard's life is at stake, namely, the statehood Doniphon supports, despite his refusal to participate directly in it. The tragic responsibility belongs to both Doniphon and Stoddard. Roche and Hosle, "Vico's Age of Heroes and the Age of Men in John Ford's Film 'The Man Who Shot Liberty Valance"; Pippin, *Hollywood Westerns and American Myth*, 89.

60 Richard Rorty's account of the United States, the Cold War, and Vietnam, a subject addressed in the next chapter, exemplifies this danger. Rorty, *Achieving Our Country*, 32.

61 Beckett, *Worstward Ho.*

62 Perez, "House of Miscegenation," 24, 24–25.

63 Pippin, *Hollywood Westerns and American Myths*, 98.

2 DEMOCRACY AT WAR WITH ITSELF: CITIZENS

1 For a brilliant study of melodrama and democracy, see Anker, *Orgies of Feeling: Melodrama and the Politics of Freedom.*

2 The Greeks, too, have their patriotic horror shows, thanks to Sophocles's *Ajax* and *Philoctetes.*

3 Stow, "Pericles at Gettysburg and Ground Zero: Tragedy, Patriotism, and Public Mourning," 195–196.

4 Raddatz, "Obama Reflects on 9/11, War That Followed."

5 Wilson, "Sept. 11 Steel Forms Heart of Far-Flung Memorials."

6 The Associated Press, "On 9/11, Day of Mourning Becomes Day of Service."

7 Kateb, *Patriotism and Other Mistakes.* Given Kateb's trenchant analysis, patriotism feels more like a moral offense than a mistake.

8 Ibid., 3

9 For the danger to democratic politics, see Johnston, *The Truth about Patriotism.*

10 I am deeply indebted to Michaele Ferguson for suggesting that I think in terms of genre and to Bonnie Honig's provocative theorizations on democracy and genre in *Democracy and the Foreigner.*

11 Honig, Democracy and the Foreigner, 120.

12 Edmundson, *Nightmare on Main Street*, 4, 5, 7, 23.

13 Ibid., 5, 28.

14 Ibid., 23. In terror Gothic, the individual is stalked.

15 Descartes, *Discourse on Method*, 35.

16 Shelley, *Frankenstein*, 52–53.

17 Ibid., 135.

18 Ibid., 145, 147.

19 Ibid., 164.

20 Ibid., 189.

21 Ibid., 204.

22 For a fuller treatment of Rorty and patriotism, see Johnston, *The Truth about Patriotism*, chapter 2.

23 Rorty, *Achieving Our Country*, 32.

24 Here Honig's account of Rorty is indispensable. See *Democracy and the Foreigner*, 94–95.

25 Honig, *Democracy and the Foreigner*, 117; Rorty, *Achieving Our Country*, 22.

26 Rorty, *Achieving Our Country*, 67–69.

27 American democracy did not realize Rorty's Vietnam nightmare, but can the same be said for its citizen-veterans?

28 See, for example, Schell, *The Time of Illusion*.

29 Stow, "Pericles at Gettysburg and Ground Zero," 198, 200. Of course, it might just be one more reason to celebrate the city.

30 Ibid., 200.

31 Here Stow needs to clarify what it means to affirm a political good that is ambiguous, that is, one that involves the horrific.

32 Thucydides, *The Peloponnesian War*, 161.

33 Ibid., 160.

34 Ibid., 162, emphasis added.

35 Ironically, Pericles might have successfully invoked Sparta, the Athenian rival disparaged in the Funeral Oration, as an example worthy of emulation. Spartan warriors fought bravely for days against astronomical odds at Thermopylae before finally succumbing to superior Persian numbers following an act of treason that compromised their position. Still, Spartan soldiers knowingly and willingly sacrificed their lives to resist foreign encroachment and domination. That the battle itself was inconsequential in the larger war makes no difference. Death trumped life.

36 Stow's aspiration for a more balanced or critical patriotism strikes me as problematic – because it is not tragic. A balanced patriotism suggests that the political reason for being of the tragic festival revolved around, in the end, domesticating or normalizing self-criticism and privileging, if by implication, moderate possibilities of reform. It seems to me that the tragic conditions of life call for something more radical and far-reaching.

37 Rambo's homelessness does not find a place in Cynthia Enloe's militarized account of *First Blood*. See Enloe, "Beyond Steve Canyon and Rambo," 123.

38 American popular culture is taken with democracy's crimes against and by its citizen-soldiers. Consider a small sample over the decades. A 1970 episode of *The Mod Squad* titled "A Far Away Place So Near" tells the story of a handful of soldiers cut off from their platoon who murder a large number of civilians. (My Lai was no exception.) The initial shooting of an old man is driven by fear and drugs (to numb the reality of the war they're fighting). The shootings of those who come to the old man's aid are designed to cover-up the first killing. An act of criminal malfeasance thus turns into a war crime. When one of the soldiers breaks ranks and threatens exposure, he, too, is murdered. The fratricide requires more killing in the United States to maintain the cover-up when the soldiers return on leave and face questions, bringing the war back home. Ultimately, the supposed ringleader

of the sequence of crimes is held responsible, but this act of scapegoating also means he is forgotten as one of the war's victims. A 1990 episode of *Star Trek: The Next Generation* titled "The Hunted" tells the story of a foreign people in the midst of a self-made crisis. Idealistic young men who volunteered to serve in a war to protect their society's way of life sacrificed their place in that way of life in the process. The training, conditioning, and physical alterations imposed on them to fight and win the war coupled with actual war experience rendered them unfit to return home and resume their prior lives. Surviving veterans were resettled on another planet and provided with a comfortable existence. They reject segregation, however, and escape, demanding reintegration in the homeland. The Enterprise crew believes the failure of reincorporation to be a problem of political will. They insist that the democracy meet its responsibilities and help its veterans, a neat solution that betrays a narcissistic ontology, namely, the presumption of a world at our disposal. The leaders of the democracy, however, do not naively assume that what they have done to their soldiers can simply be undone. They made these men into super-soldiers, but this does not mean they can be restored to their former selves. When asked if they have even tried, they do not respond, which seems like a damning silence, but it may also mean that they actually know there is nothing to be done – and that they knew it all along. What's more, the price of restoration, even if possible, may pose undue risks or prove unaffordable. The veterans, a vital resource, may have to be pressed into future military service for a democratic community that cannot defend itself. Finally, a 2007 episode of *Criminal Minds* titled "Distress" tells the story of a soldier that served in Mogadishu reliving the Ethiopian war on the streets of Houston. Plagued by PTSD (largely from having to kill children), he must be put down by the state, but not before murdering a number of unsuspecting fellow citizens in what he believes to be self-defense.

39 Here I depart from Jeffords's reading of *First Blood*. She claims, "Rambo fights only when goaded," but this reading of Rambo ignores his refusal to accept any responsibility for the violence he unleashes (he had ample opportunity both to surrender and to escape from Hope). Rambo is more than a victim; he is also an agent. See Jeffords, *The Remasculinization of America: Gender and the Vietnam War*, 128.

40 Many thanks to Michaele Ferguson for noting that *First Blood* can be quite funny.

41 Jeffords's account of hard bodies defining Reagan Era masculinity is relevant here. Rambo's freakish musculature contributes to his monsterlike qualities. Jeffords, *Hard Bodies: Hollywood Masculinity in the Reagan Era*, 30–34.

42 Once again, I depart from Jeffords, who insists that "The close of the film freezes Rambo's status as a victim" (Jeffords, 128). Rambo also leaves Hope a proud, defiant victor standing over the humiliated, defeated, prostrate sheriff and the town he ruled.

43 A video of the (hilarious) scene is no longer available on YouTube.

44 On Thursday, March 27, 2014, 1892 American flags were planted on the National Mall between the Capitol and the Washington Monument. The

flags corresponded to the number of veteran suicides in the first three months of 2014. This amounted to twenty-two per day. As of July 14, there were 161 known suicides of military personnel on active duty, a slight increase – at the time – from 2013. See Smith, "Using Flags to Focus on Veteran Suicides," and Associated Press, "Military suicides up a bit among active duty in 2014; But more seek help via hotlines."

45 Ajax was the product of a warrior culture that pitted him in competition against a hated opponent for the greatest of prizes, Achilles's armor. He lost and could not live with the outcome. This is part of what made him a great warrior. The comportment that made him an indispensable soldier, placed in another context, made him a crazed animal bent on implementing a heinous plan to torment and murder the enemies who denied him his due. Rambo won his country's highest award, the Medal of Honor, but he was denied the status and standing meant to accompany it. The country's rejection effectively stripped Rambo of his medal. Fittingly, it is not among his few possessions. Why carry a gold medal when it's really just a piece of bronze?

46 For a patriotism-free answer to the question, see Solnit, *A Paradise Built in Hell.*

47 The American Veterans Disabled for Life Memorial opened in October 2014. In many respects, it constitutes a rebuke to the national World War II Memorial, which celebrates the triumph and ascendancy of American power and freedom, but, while paying lip service to the idea of debt, devotes little architectural attention to the human costs of war. The American Veterans Disabled for Life Memorial tries to right this wrong. Among other things, the visitor can see, in bronze, the lost limbs of soldiers. The memorial salutes the bravery of American democracy's veterans disabled for life and what it represents: "the hope that springs from perseverance in the face of adversity." Inscriptions from George Washington and Dwight Eisenhower attest to the permanent scars and deformities America's veterans necessarily bear, that is, to the bodily signs of war's horrors that tend to remain hidden from public view. No more. Invisibility is injustice. At the same time, the inscriptions from America's two most famous generals are deployed to place the signs of war in a patriotic frame that renders service to democracy always honorable, always worthwhile. Whether the memorial, in its totality, can mitigate the unthinking work of the inscriptions and convey the difficult truth that democracy often sends its soldiers off to die for nothing, or in criminal wars, and thus make service a contestable practice and war more difficult to wage, remains to be seen. Either way, the American Veterans Disabled for Life Memorial sets an example for the shape a monumental complement to Admission Day *might* take. At its best, a disabled veterans memorial in a democracy would recognize that other peoples' veterans (and civilians) suffer(ed) similarly. The veterans acknowledged here not only suffer(ed) great harm. They also inflicted it on others. Remember both. See American Veterans Disabled for Life Memorial website, Design, Design Concept.

3 DEMOCRACY AT WAR WITH ITSELF: ANIMALS

1 Cramer, "They Were Heroes Too."
2 War dogs were ultimately honored with a stamp.
3 For a list of memorials, see the Vietnam Dog Handler Association's compilation on its website.
4 Putney, *Always Faithful*, xi.
5 Lemish, *War Dogs*, 45.
6 Ibid., 242. With the wars in Afghanistan and Iraq, the use of dogs in war spiked. They face dangers similar to those faced in Vietnam but also new ones, thanks to improvised explosive devices (IEDs). The logic of use, however, remains inexorably the same: we "need" dogs; dogs will be used as we see fit. See Maria Goodavage's *Soldier Dogs*, in which she writes (4): "IEDs are the top killer in Afghanistan – even with the highest technology, the best mine-sweeping devices, the most sophisticated bomb-jamming equipment, and the study of 'pattern of life' activities being observed from remote piloted aircraft. But there is one response that the Taliban has no answer for: the soldier dog ..."
7 Ibid., 53–59, 88–90.
8 Ibid., 216.
9 Lemish, *War Dogs*, 142; Putney, *Always Faithful*, 25, 29, 42; the quote is from Putney, 42.
10 O'Donnell, "*None came Home.*"
11 United States War Dog Association, K-9 Wall of Honor.
12 Lemish, *War Dogs*, 36, emphasis added.
13 Ibid., x–xi.
14 Ferguson, "I ♥ My Dog," 373–395.
15 Ibid., 375
16 Ibid., 376–377.
17 Ibid., 376.
18 Cooper, *Animals in War*, 75; Lemish, *War Dogs*, 47.
19 Ferguson, "I ♥ My Dog," 380, 384.
20 Cooper, *Animals in War*, 75.
21 Ferguson, "I ♥ My Dog," 375.
22 See Hart's own description on the Vietnam Veterans Memorial Fund website.
23 For photographs, see Langley. Emphases added.
24 The memorial's official website informs the visitor that "British, Commonwealth, and Allied forces enlisted many millions of animals to serve and often die alongside their armies." The verb "enlist" hovers between the transitive and intransitive, obscuring the command nature of the relationship between human and animals. See Animals in War Memorial website, History.
25 Edkins, *Trauma and the Memory of Politics*, 64.
26 Young, *The Texture of Memory: Holocaust Memorials and Meaning*, chapter 1.
27 See: Hornaday, "Spielberg pays homage to a pal, Joey"; Stevens, "All the Weepy Horses"; Tookey, "Spectacular, tear-jerking, uplifting; *War Horse* is

a Spielberg masterpiece;" Scott, A.O., "Innocence is Trampled, but a Bond Endures."

28 See Schickel, "A 'War Horse' and his Boy."

29 Ibid.

30 Stevens, "All the Weepy Horses."

31 See YouTube, Riverside War Dog Memorial.

32 Cooper, *Animals in War*, 32, 48–49, 62.

33 Ibid., 103.

34 Ibid., 199–200.

35 Ibid., 95.

36 The history of animal use is nothing if not creative. Richard Wrangham writes: "According to Marco Polo, Mongol warriors of the thirteenth century supposedly rode for ten days at a time without lighting a fire. The riders' food was the raw blood of their horses, obtained by piercing a vein." This kind of human parasitism saved time and provided security. Wrangham, *Catching Fire*, 15.

37 Cooper, *Animals in War*, 139, 154, 36, 62–63, 65.

38 Lemish, *War Dogs*, 29.

39 Cooper, *Animals in War*, 186.

40 Ibid., 123.

41 Or living next door to us: at the outset of World War II, people in the London area killed several hundred thousand dogs and cats in anticipation of the fighting (ibid., 86).

42 Ibid., 137.

43 Lemish, *War Dogs*, 224–225. An animal's useful military life does not expire with death. Washington's National Museum of American History exhibits a stuffed dog and pigeon, both considered heroes, from World War I. These animals, which would have been awarded purple hearts if human, saved lives under fire, with Cher Ami, the pigeon, losing a leg in the process. Apparently, placing the animals on display proves that nature, perhaps the world itself, was on democracy's side. No one I know of has suggested placing the remains of, say, Sergeant Alvin York, America's quintessential World War I hero, on similar display. See Smithsonian, National Museum of American History, "The Price of Freedom: Americans at War."

44 Nietzsche, *The Will to Power* and *Twilight of the Idols*; and Connolly, *Political Theory and Modernity*.

45 Calarco, *Zoographies*.

46 Cooper, Animals in War, 134, 130, 142, 131.

47 *Ibid.*, 130, 142.

48 Thanks to Andy Smerdon.

49 Rousseau, *The First and Second Discourses*, 114–115.

50 Cooper, *Animals in War*, 145.

51 Moreover, patriotic logic means animals killed because they would/could not serve human purposes receive no recognition, let alone memorialization. They – their lives – have been doubly erased.

52 Ibid., 75–76.

53 See Price, "They served and suffered for us," where Princess Anne, patron of the fund that built the Animals in War Memorial, makes such a claim.

54 Lemish, *War Dogs*, 141.

55 Cooper, *Animals in War*, 73. Cramer prefers a more subtle approach. Following Pearl Harbor, he writes, "canine combatants were recruited just as men were. But no draft was required." A few owners may have been unloading unwanted pets, "but most were patriots who sent a dog off to war just as they would a son." Here dogs bask in human equivalence and absorb the patriotic glow of their owner-parents, as if to suggest that no draft was needed for dogs because dogs, who act out of love, were ready and waiting to serve. Cramer, "They Were Heroes Too."

56 *Ibid.*, 47.

57 Ibid., 192.

58 In World War II, the Marines developed a certificate of discharge for dogs to instill an "esprit de corps" in them. See Lemish, *War Dogs*, 60–61.

59 Cooper, *Animals in War*, 79; Lemish, *War Dogs*, 19–20. Consider also Winkie, the damaged pigeon that flew 129 miles from the North Sea to Scotland, triggering the rescue of an otherwise doomed World War II bomber crew. The courage of this little bird, quite proud when duly honored and toasted at a dinner held in her honor, might be doubted, but given the number of pigeons who prefer to dally, this would be a mistake and an injustice. Cooper, *War Dogs*, 105–107.

60 Cooper, *Animals in War*, 211.

4 FORCING DEMOCRACY TO BE FREE: ROUSSEAU TO SPRINGSTEEN

1 I have addressed contemporary patriotic thinkers in Johnston, *The Truth about Patriotism*.

2 Rousseau, *On the Social Contract*, 52, 96, 110. Admittedly, Rousseau occasionally provides a glimpse of tragedy ("if the abuses of this new condition [the civil state] did not often degrade him beneath the condition he left [the state of nature], he ought ceaselessly to bless the happy moment that tore him away from it forever"), but he does not thematize it.

3 Rousseau, *Considerations on the Government of Poland*, 186.

4 Rousseau, *On the Social Contract*, 64.

5 Ibid., 64–65, 131.

6 Rousseau writes: "as long as a people is constrained to obey and does so, it does well; as soon as it can shake off the yoke and does so, it does even better." Rousseau, *On the Social Contract*, 46.

7 Ibid.

8 Hobbes, *Leviathan*, 238.

9 Rousseau, *On the Social Contract*, 52.

10 Cf. Cranston, *The Noble Savage*, 307.

11 Rousseau, *On the Social Contract*, 56.

12 Ibid., 69.

13 Honig, *Democracy and the Foreigner*, 32.

14 Ibid., 23–24.

15 Ibid., 35–37.

16 Ibid., 37.

17 Rousseau, *On the Social Contract*, 110.

18 Ransom Stoddard in the convention hall wears a sling on the arm where Liberty Valance shot him.

19 This is the democratic norm that the figure of Ransom Stoddard challenged in *The Man Who Shot Liberty Valance*, though the polity was in no position to recognize, let alone appreciate, the counter-ethos of responsibility the character practiced insofar as Stoddard concealed the murder of Valance. The losers were consigned to history's dustbin in good Rousseauean fashion and forgotten.

20 Rousseau, *Geneva Manuscript*, 162.

21 Ibid., 111.

22 Rousseau's approach to politics is conservative. Democracy cannot be instituted given unfavorable conditions. It would generate the very violence democracy rejects. The reach of politics is thereby restricted. Yet Rousseau's well-known preconditions of democracy did not emerge through a slow evolutionary process rendering a people fortunate enough to profit from them. Rather, they had to be the product, to some extent, of an original constitutive violence. The making, however incomplete, of a people on a given territory is never benign.

23 Ibid.

24 Ibid., 76.

25 Ibid., 69.

26 Ibid., 99.

27 Ibid., 108.

28 Ibid., 98–99.

29 Ibid., 100.

30 Honig, *Emergency Politics*, 18.

31 Rousseau, *On the Social Contract*, 99.

32 Ibid., 110.

33 Ibid., 110–111.

34 Ibid., 111. Rousseau, as we saw above, effectively admits voting requires a leap of faith about majority possession of the general will.

35 Ibid., 63.

36 Ibid., 110.

37 Ibid.

38 Ibid.

39 Ibid.

40 Ibid.

41 Ibid.

42 See Springsteen interview.

43 Smith & Wesson no doubt cringes at the free publicity Springsteen furnishes its famous .38 caliber handgun on "Easy Money," converted by Springsteen into an instrument of democratic street justice.

44 *Wrecking Ball* represents something of a departure for Springsteen despite the uncompromising candor of *Nebraska* and *Born in the U.S.A.* (at least on

the title track). While songs on these recordings address the violence endemic to American life, they also remain at a distance from it. Geoffrey Himes insists that on "Born in the U.S.A." Springsteen suggests that it's finally time to "stand and fight back," though the song's narrative lacks any kind of action taken. This is not to deny the record's rhetorical defiance. Himes firmly locates Springsteen in what he calls the "mature patriotism" camp, which is reminiscent of Simon Stow's balanced patriotism, seen in Chapter 2. The American Dream may not be true, but it is a necessary fiction – an "indispensable lie" that keeps hope alive, as Richard Rorty recommends. Yet for Himes, we must love our country, in the end, no matter what, despite any flaws it possesses. The unconditional commitment makes Springsteen's patriotism mature, as in a "mature romantic relationship." The patriotic imperative, however, tends to forgive the violence Springsteen's songs reveal, largely because patriotism eschews reciprocity. We love our country; it does not love us. See Himes, *Born in the U.S.A.*, 22–23, 24, 6, 29. The characters that dominate *Nebraska* do not involve themselves with political action either. Those suffering from the carnage of brutal class warfare may turn to a life of crime to get by, but on songs such as "Atlantic City," the politics is implicit at best. For an astute reading on the apolitical violence of the characters on this album (as opposed to the album itself), see Burke, *Heart of Darkness*, 71–84.

45 The song sung in concert fell flat. On the studio recording, the much ballyhooed Springsteen anger never materializes, and the song lacks the dissonance associated with, say, "Badlands" or "Born in the U.S.A."

46 Springsteen interview.

47 Ibid.

48 Likewise, Springsteen considers the assassination of Osama bin Laden to be one of Barack Obama's great achievements (alongside saving General Motors). This reveals another meaning to the phrase "we take care of our own." The United States does not allow those who attack it to go unpunished. Violence will be met with violence. We will finish what others (foolishly) start. Springsteen thus compliments Obama for his mission accomplished – something that eluded his detested (by Springsteen) predecessor, George W. Bush.

49 Chinen, "The Boss Roars Tough and Tender," covered Springsteen's New Jersey concert two days later, noting the alternations between "hope and despair," the emotional "peaks and valleys," and the "whiplash" he generated. Chinen did not, however, explore the ultimate effect produced by Springsteen's three-hour concert of "disjunctions."

50 Springsteen interview.

51 Himes writes of Springsteen: "Bruce Springsteen is best known for his most public acts. It's in the concert hall – more than on the stereo or the screen – that he engages his audience as few other performers ever have. It's on the stage that he makes his deepest impression, not only singing his hits, but also telling stories, digging out forgotten songs, shouting like a preacher, clowning like a vaudevillian, whispering like a confessor and leaping about

in flagrant disregard for his own safety. From the seats, his fans respond with almost equal fervor until each show, larger than life and longer than a football game, reaches its climax of happy, communal exhaustion." Himes is right about happy, communal exhaustion. and that is precisely the short-coming I am highlighting here. Himes, *Born in the U.S.A.*, 1.

52 Allen writes: "An honest account of collective democratic action must begin by acknowledging that communal decisions inevitably benefit some citizens at the expense of others, even when the whole community generally benefits. Since democracy claims to secure the good of all citizens, those people who benefit less than others from particular decisions, but nonetheless accede to those decisions, preserve the stability of political institutions. Their sacri-fice makes collective democratic action possible. Democracy is ... a political practice by which the diverse negative effects of collective political action, and even of just decisions, can be distributed equally, and constantly redis-tributed over time, on the basis of consensual interactions. The hard truth of democracy is that some citizens are always giving things up for others. Only vigorous forms of citizenship can give a polity the resources to deal with the inevitable problem of sacrifice." Allen's take on democracy as a practice, absent mechanisms for securing it, seems just as fantastic as Springsteen's faith in the American Dream. Allen, *Talking to Strangers*, 28–29.

53 Ibid., 22–23, 27, 41.

54 Ibid., 39–42.

55 Ibid., 41.

56 Ibid., 140.

57 Ibid., 129, 133, 165.

58 Ibid., 45, for example.

59 Ibid., 109–110.

60 Ibid., 110–111.

61 Ibid., 117–118.

62 Ibid., 150.

63 Ibid., 38.

64 Honig, *Democracy and the Foreigner*, chapters 3 and 4.

65 Krugman, "The Twinkie Manifesto."

66 Again, this renders *Wrecking Ball* at least something of a departure for Springsteen. Greil Marcus is ambivalent – critical but understanding – toward Springsteen's characters on *Nebraska* "because [their] only acts of rebellion ... are murders. They are nihilistic acts committed in a world where social and economic functions have become the measure of all things and have dissolved all values beyond money and status. In that context, these acts make sense." Making sense, however, does not put serious pressure on the order of things. Isolated, alone, these characters cannot give their lives a "public dimension." And Springsteen only gives their lives a limited civic dimension insofar as he confines their "resistance" to criminal acts that lack an overtly democratic political component. Marcus, *Ranters & Crowd Pleasers*, 238, 237.

67 Rousseau, *On the Social Contract*, 74.

68 Connolly, *Capitalism and Christianity, American Style*, 121.

5 TWO CHEERS FOR DEMOCRATIC VIOLENCE

1 Müller, *Constitutional Patriotism*.
2 See Habermas, "Citizenship and National Identity."
3 Bloodless can refer to either a lack of passion or a lack of violence. It is noteworthy that constitutional patriotism's advocates do not specify the meaning to which they object.
4 Müller, *Constitutional Patriotism*, 48.
5 Ibid., 84.
6 Viroli, *For Love of Country: An Essay on Patriotism and Nationalism*.
7 Schaar, "The Case for Patriotism."
8 Canovan, "Patriotism Is Not Enough."
9 Kateb, *Patriotism and Other Mistakes*.
10 Müller, *Constitutional Patriotism*, 85.
11 Ingram, "Constitutional patriotism," 1–3.
12 Müller, 10–11.
13 The irony that speech might be limited in order to secure its flourishing is not unique to the West German context. See Fiss, *The Irony of Free Speech*.
14 Müller, 21–22.
15 Ibid., 23.
16 Ibid., 22–25.
17 Ibid., 11, emphases added.
18 Ibid., 13.
19 Hayward, "Democracy's Identity Problem: Is 'Constitutional Patriotism' the Answer?"
20 See, for example, Müller, *Constitutional Patriotism*, 66–67, on McCarthyism.
21 Hayward, "Democracy's Identity Problem: Is 'Constitutional Patriotism' the Answer?" 182–183.
22 Ibid, 184.
23 Ibid.
24 Ibid., 185.
25 The phrase is Markell's, "Making Affect Safe for Democracy? On 'Constitutional Patriotism,'" 40, 50–51, for example.
26 What makes reconciliation possible, even desirable? Patriotism brings together former enemies who share a mutual commitment to sacrifice, that is, to killing and dying on behalf of country. Patriotism allows for, perhaps requires, a certain generosity toward enemies. They also do whatever it takes to serve the country they love. As a country overlooks the crimes its enemies perpetrated in order to embrace them, perhaps it overlooks the crimes of which it is guilty: reconciliation as an unconscious confession of patriot crime.
27 On slavery and the civil war, see Dew, *Apostles of Disunion*.
28 Savage, "The President and the Confederacy."
29 Müller, *Constitutional Patriotism*, 83.
30 Ibid., 161.
31 Ibid.
32 Ibid., 84.

33 For a fuller account of Rorty, see Johnston, *The Truth about Patriotism.*

34 Ibid., 85.

35 Ibid., 66, 64.

36 Hayward writes of the political principles of constitutional patriots: "They define illiberal and anti-democratic others, along with others who are insufficiently acculturated to the beliefs, norms, and values that constitute the polity's politically particular civic bond." Hayward, "Democracy's Identity Problem: Is 'Constitutional Patriotism' the Answer?" 189.

37 Constitutional patriotism's self-subverting dynamics lead Dora Kostakopoulou to argue that it seeks to counter and contain nationalism by taming and civilizing "inherited particularistic loyalties." Can this work? She seems to think so: "By situating these [constitutional] principles within the horizon of the history of the nation, that is, of a prepolitical community with its own cultural horizon of shared memories and historical experiences, Habermas recuperates nationalism under a civic mode." Kostakopoulou, "Thick, Thin, and Thinner Patriotisms: Is This All There Is?," 75–77.

38 Markell, "Making Affect Safe for Democracy? On 'Constitutional Patriotism,'" 38–63.

39 Ibid., 39, emphasis original.

40 Ibid., 41–44.

41 Ibid., 43.

42 For a riveting challenge to the "commonality thesis," see Ferguson's *Sharing Democracy.*

43 Markell, "Making Affect Safe for Democracy? On 'Constitutional Patriotism,'" 39, 40.

44 Ibid., 40.

45 Ibid., 61.

46 Ibid., 53.

47 Ibid., 56, emphasis in the original.

48 See, for example, Collins and Skover, *On Dissent.*

49 Canovan, "Patriotism Is Not Enough," 431.

50 Canovan, *Nationhood and Political Theory.*

51 Ibid., 95.

52 Ibid., 92.

53 Jennet Kirkpatrick broaches the subject of democratic violence in *Uncivil Disobedience.* She opens with a discussion of the Anthony Burns affair in 1854, when Boston citizens acting in concert (Kirkpatrick prefers the language of the mob) tried to prevent, through violence, the state from enforcing the Fugitive Slave Act. A United States marshal was killed in the process. This seems to be a promising theoretical beginning. Unfortunately, Kirkpatrick quickly moves away from potentially tragic cases to focus on "indiscriminate violence toward uninvolved individuals." There are certain (tragic) places she apparently does not wish to go: "Even uncivil disobedience that avoids this type of violence has been harmful to American democracy and dangerous to some of its central precepts. Certain acts of uncivil disobedience might be legitimate nonetheless. In this respect the Burns case

gives us much to think about. Was the storming of the courthouse to rescue Burns legitimate? These are questions of great consequence. To address them sufficiently requires a different kind of analysis than I undertake here." A few pages earlier Kirkpatrick had effectively dispensed with the Burns example: "The passionate call for liberty and the participatory democratic ideas elucidated by the Boston mob may have been commendable, but its results – violence and killing – were not." This reductive account appears to drain the Burns affair of its inherent ambiguity. *Uncivil Disobedience*, 14, 5.

54 Keane, *Violence and Democracy*, 1.
55 Ibid., 4.
56 Ibid., 2.
57 Ibid, 5.
58 Ibid., 142, 158.
59 Ibid., 143–147.
60 Ibid., 139.
61 Ibid. 161.
62 Ibid., 139–140.
63 Ibid., 20.
64 Žižek, *Violence* (New York: Picador, 2008).
65 Keane, *Violence and Democracy*, 36–37.
66 Ibid., 100–101.
67 Ibid., 100; 141–142; 143–144;146–147; 160–161.
68 Ibid., 158; 161, 154.
69 Ibid., 160.
70 Ibid., 161. Stoddard's confrontation with Valance and the latter's killing might well have brought about a civil war with the cattle interests.
71 Ibid., 158.
72 Ibid., 191.
73 Maier, *From Resistance to Revolution*.
74 Ibid., 4.
75 Ibid., 9.
76 Ibid., 26.
77 Ibid., 31–35.
78 Ibid, 41–42.
79 Ibid, 42–43.
80 Ibid, 51–52.
81 Ibid, 54, 57, 62.
82 Feldberg, *The Turbulent Era*, 64.
83 Ibid., 64–71.
84 Cobb Jr., *This Nonviolent Stuff'll Get You Killed*, 6.
85 McCormick, *Machiavellian Democracy*.
86 McCormick also notes that *The Prince* contains democratic elements. On this theme one might consult Wolin's *Politics and Vision* and Viroli's *Redeeming "The Prince."*
87 McCormick, *Machiavellian Democracy*, 4–5.
88 Machiavelli, *The Discourses*, 113–114.
89 Ibid.

90 Ibid., 124–127.
91 Ibid., 68, 117.
92 Ibid., 124–127.
93 McCormick, *Machiavellian Democracy*, 68, 68–69.
94 Ibid., 182.
95 Bouie, "Republicans Admit Voter ID-Laws Are Aimed at Democratic Voters."
96 Among other things, I have (at least) three Roberts Court decisions in mind: *Shelby County v. Holder, McCullen v. Coakley*, and *Citizens United v. Federal Elections Commission.*
97 Robin, *The Reactionary Mind.*
98 The information on Roberts is available publicly (online) thanks to Montgomery County, Maryland's tax records.
99 Roberts, of course, presumes his position of power to be a lifetime post immune to democratic influence. Targeted pressure on him at home (and elsewhere) might enable, even force, him and the Court to (re)consider the implications of various decisions and the role of the Supreme Court in American political life (as certain justices of the Court did following Franklin Roosevelt's catalytic scheme to expand its membership). Ideally it might force Roberts out of office altogether, an informal version of the Greek practice of ostracism, which sent into exile unduly influential political figures who threatened the viability of democracy.
100 White, *The Ethos of a Late-Modern Citizen*, 88.
101 Ibid., 40–41.
102 McCormick, *Machiavellian Democracy*, 2.
103 Ibid., 6.
104 Ibid., 33.
105 Ibid., 34.
106 Ibid., 171ff.
107 Ibid., 172.
108 In 2008 Turner Network Television aired the Robin Hood-inspired *Leverage*, an hour-long weekly drama about the justice-driven exploits of a group of con artists who "like to think of [what they do] as picking up where the law leaves off." Not only do they make those injured by the rich and powerful whole again; they also generally humiliate the latter as they bring them down, putting them in their proper place. On occasion the *Leverage* team turns to the state for assistance, but the presumption of the show is that the state is compromised or helpless. The schemes they concoct, while brilliantly conceived, invariably rely on violence, sometimes including death. The show ran for five years.
109 West Virginia, a state notorious for its lack of environmental regulation and safeguards, suffered two chemical spills with eerie similarities to one of the ecological crimes depicted in the film. See Bratu and Austin, "West Virginia Chemical Spill Cuts Water to up to 300,000, State of Emergency Declared," and Delmore, "Another Chemical Spill in West Virginia."
110 In 1968 Barrington Moore, Jr. argued that a "limited degree of violence, even in the form of black riots directed at what wide sections of the white

community regard as specific injustices – for example, unprovoked police brutality – could have some effect in putting more steam behind respectable opposition to prevailing injustice." Moore, "Thoughts on Violence and Democracy," 7.

111 Keane, *Violence and Democracy*, 4, 155; Arendt, *On Violence*, 80, 4.

112 The East embodies and practices many of the virtues Thoreau attributed to John Brown in his admirable, if also problematic, resistance to slavery. Here I am deeply indebted to Chip Turner's first-rate article "Performing Conscience: Thoreau, Political Action, and the Plea for John Brown."

113 On gratitude and abundance, see the work of Connolly, perhaps especially *Capitalism and Christianity, American-Style*; *A World of Becoming*; and *The Fragility of Things*.

114 Arendt, *On Violence*, 64.

115 Zizek, *On Violence*, 2. For their democratic trouble, members of the East find that the state has declared war against them.

116 Krugman, "Rich Man's Recovery."

117 For a brief account of Francis's "papal exhortation" on, among other things, the "new tyranny" of capitalism, see Rosenthal, "The Pope's Take on Capitalism."

118 Krugman, "Rich Man's Recovery."

119 Stuckler and Basu, "Europe's public health disaster: How austerity kills"; Tavernise, "Life Spans Shrink for Least-Educated Whites in the U.S."

120 Democracies spend whatever it takes (money, resources, labor, personnel) for national security and war. The value of each is considered indispensable and beyond question. Ironically, democracies do not approach politics in the same way. When faced with democratic tumult or uprising, they will not hesitate to send robustly armed police, even military forces, onto the streets to establish law and order and restore peace and quiet, often a cover to protect the sanctity of private property, despite the harm, literal and figurative, done in the process to what should be valued most, the enactment of democratic citizenship, that is, freedom. Democracies as a normative principle should comport themselves with equanimity to the reality that the exercise of politics can, at times, turn violent, destructive, and messy, and accept its costs and consequences as an integral part of democratic life. Democracies allocate funds to a wide range of necessary activities. How is this not one of them? Might this encourage people to embrace their citizenship more fully, perhaps problematically? Yes, that is the point.

121 Habermas, *The Inclusion of the Other*, 225–226.

6 NEW TRAGIC DEMOCRATIC TRADITIONS

1 *The 9/11 Commission Report: Final Report of the National Commission on Terrorist Attacks upon the United States*, xv.

2 Ibid., xvi.

3 Ibid., 8.

4 The act of narration, of course, cannot be acknowledged. After recounting events at the Pentagon, President Bush said: "Then there *is the extraordinary story we commemorate* here," as if the story speaks itself and Bush is merely the medium.

5 For a lucid account of melodrama, see Anker, *Orgies of Feeling.*

6 Biden, "Remarks by Vice President Joseph Biden at Dedication of Flight 93 Memorial."

7 Sheppard, "Bill Clinton's Flight 93 Memorial Dedication Speech." Clinton's choice of the Alamo conveniently ignores America's role as imperial aggressor in the Mexican-American War.

8 Sheppard, "George W. Bush's Flight 93 Memorial Dedication Speech."

9 Corbett, September 11 10th Anniversary Speech, Shanksville, PA. Corbett mimics Biden: "They did not choose to go into battle when they boarded that jetliner."

10 *The 9/11 Commission Report*, 13. "At 9:57, the passenger assault began. Several passengers had terminated phone calls with loved ones in order to join the revolt. One of the callers ended her message as follows: 'Everyone's running up to first class. I've got to go. Bye.' "

11 The transfiguration of United 93's passengers from ordinary people to extraordinary patriots overshadows the inconvenient truth that the hijackers remained in control of the plane and crashed it themselves, which is also noted on the National Park Service website for the United 93 Memorial. The official story, as mentioned, credits the crash to the passenger uprising and revolt. On this account it doesn't matter that the hijackers crashed it, for it (supposedly) foiled their plan to strike, it is believed, the United States Capitol. The hijackers, however, not only had a primary objective. They also allowed for multiple possibilities. If the designated target could not be reached, for whatever reason, the plane was to be crashed into a target of choice, including the ground, which would still be considered a great victory for them and a devastating defeat for the United States. In short, with any crash they would win.

12 Ibid., 45. Imagine that the passengers of United 93 did not contribute to its premature crash. Imagine instead that fighters from Langley shot it down. Would the Air Force pilots be celebrated for (their) heroic actions? Would they be celebrated for saving countless innocent lives? Think of the fortitude required to fire on and kill not just anonymous strangers but also fellow citizens. Would the pilots need to be doubly celebrated? Wouldn't their heroism require a special kind of recognition? Wouldn't it be said on behalf of the passengers shot down that they approved of the pilots' actions?

13 Ridge, September 11 10th Anniversary Speech, Shanksville, PA.

14 The Congressional legislation authorizing a national memorial in Pennsylvania refused the hijackers official memorialization on the site. They cannot be included in or counted among the September 11 dead. This effectively erases their deaths from the memorial, which means that only "our patriots" died in the fields of Somerset County on September 11 – only patriots can die in such fashion.

15 Seelye, "In Pennsylvania, a Wall of Names."

16 National Park Service, Flight 93 National Memorial.

17 *A Place of Remembrance: Official Book of the National September 11 Memorial.*

18 9/11 Memorial, About the Memorial.

19 When I first visited the memorial, the World Trade Center complex was a working construction site, which meant accessing it was complicated. It was not a question of procuring tickets for a specific day and time or tolerating gratuitous security procedures. One followed a long, circuitous path around much of the site before arriving on the memorial plaza. The security protocols felt tedious and unnecessary, but they contributed to the memorial experience by reminding people of the omnipresent dangers of terrorism. Ground Zero is now an open public space. World Trade Center reconstruction remains incomplete, but anyone can approach the memorial site unsearched, unscanned. As a result, the memorial might suffer, perhaps prematurely, from a kind of invisibility. Ease of access may inadvertently contribute to the kind of forgetting the memorial is designed to preempt. Forgetting may also be abetted by the bland character of the plaza itself, which looks and feels very much like a bank concourse with tidy rows of expensive trees and square blocks on which people can sit in the shade. One could traverse the space and pass the reflecting pools without noticing them.

20 See the press coverage by Kandell and Edelman.

21 Kennicott, "The 9/11 Memorial museum doesn't just display artifacts, it ritualizes grief on a loop."

22 Edward Rothstein captures the individual rather than civic character of the museum brilliantly in "A Memoir to Personal Memory."

23 Smith, *The Architecture of Aftermath*, 122.

24 The abstraction may peak in the first-floor gift shop where 9/11 knickknacks are sold.

25 The flight skills of Donald Greene, who might have piloted United 93 to safety, are not mentioned.

26 Rothstein, "A Memoir to Personal Memory."

27 Stow, "Pericles at Gettysburg and Ground Zero."

28 Healy, "Wrongfully Convicted and Seeking Restitution."

29 Nietzsche, *The Genealogy of Morals*, 205.

30 Ignatieff, *The Lesser Evil*, 58, 80.

31 *The Anti-Federalist*, 306–307.

32 King, Jr., "Beyond Vietnam," 139–164.

33 Here it can be seen that the reparations apparatus outlined in Chapter 4 might need to address other peoples.

34 Honig, "Antigone's Laments, Creon's Grief." See also, Honig, *Antigone, Interrupted.*

35 Recognition of an enemy at national memorial sites is improbable, which is one reason to advocate for it. The idea, however, is not unheard-of. Glenna Goodacre's Vietnam Women's Memorial proposal – which was not the design first chosen – incorporated a dead Vietnamese baby cradled by a kneeling American nurse into its original composition. When Goodacre's

vision ultimately prevailed, she was asked to rework the proposal and eliminate the baby (it was replaced by a helmet). She consented. Goodacre did not conceive the depiction of Vietnamese dead, not even an infant, as a moral or political gesture. It conveyed a reality of war. Ironically, the United States has no trouble recognizing and honoring its soldiers for what the Vietnamese (and others) consider a genocidal imperial war. Yet America cannot appreciate how the Vietnamese might assess our commemoration. The United States knows well what the Vietnam War cost America, but not what it cost Vietnam. Goodacre's inspiration could be extended. The Women's Memorial portrays the aftermath of battle. Nurses tend to a wounded American soldier, the centerpiece of the sculpture, while waiting (or hoping) for a medevac helicopter. Instead of letting the imagination drift skyward with the gaze of one of the nurses, ask instead, where is the visitor effectively standing? What is the setting for this Pietàlike melodrama? The answer is the Vietnamese countryside. And what does this countryside look like? Simply put, it looks nothing like the well-manicured Washington Mall. To supplement Goodacre's original conception, the space surrounding the wounded soldier could be converted into a bombed-out, barren landscape featuring a barrel of Agent Orange, the cancerous defoliant deployed to deny Vietnamese guerrillas military cover and food. This is the American War that the United States has been unable to confront in its political culture. It cannot admit what it did to another people as it pursued its national interests. If the Women's Memorial were redesigned as suggested, the suffering of the Vietnamese would complement the reflective aspects of the Vietnam Veterans Memorial wall and the narcissism of the latter would recede. Goodacre's original design conception, then, reveals the limited dialectical parameters of the Vietnam complex, something I did not fully appreciate in *The Truth about Patriotism*.

36 Smith, *The Architecture of Aftermath*, 100–101, 111.

37 *The 9/11 Commission Report*, 163.

38 Butler, *Precarious Life*.

39 The United States and the West once embraced this approach when fighting the Cold War. We were proud to play and beat the Soviets at their own game. John le Carré's *The Spy Who Came in from the Cold* reveals the moral damage we inflicted on ourselves in the process: we became indistinguishable from the enemy we fought. Is there a John le Carré for the post-September 11 world?

40 Alex Gibney insists that "Maya is a glamorous heroine [and] we identify with her." This may or may not be true, but it isn't necessarily problematic given the film's conclusion. Gibney, "*Zero Dark Thirty*'s Wrong and Dangerous Conclusion."

41 Matt Taibbi rejects reading *Zero Dark Thirty* as an exposé and does so, oddly enough, because it supposedly reads into the film a perspective that isn't explicitly developed. According to Taibbi, *Zero Dark Thirty* needed to condemn torture in no uncertain terms. Audiences cannot be trusted to do difficult interpretive work, to discern the tragedy (the self-destruction) unfolding before them and their own implication in it. But isn't that approach, which

lets us come to a realization on our own rather than through another's moralizing, the one most likely to prevent future self-inflicted disasters? See Taibbi, "*Zero Dark Thirty* Is Osama Bin Laden's Last Victory over America."

42 Emily Wilson argues that "there is a central thread in the tragic tradition that is concerned not with dying too early but with living too long, or 'overliving.' Lives do not always end at the expected time. Sometimes people go on living even after the moment when they or others feel they should have died ... Tragedies of overliving disturb the audience or reader by reminding us that life may feel too long and endings may seem to have come too late." Insofar as Wilson is right about the audience or reader, Sophocles's art can be understood as a necessary education in tragedy for both – or what they take to be tragedy. In other words, there is no such thing as overliving. Wilson, *Mocked with Death*, 1–2.

43 Sophocles, *Antigone*, 1455.

44 Sophocles, *Oedipus at Colonus*, 1390.

45 Sophocles, *Oedipus the King*, 1597, 1675.

46 Democracy Day draws inspiration from the practice of African-American mourning, which includes honoring and celebrating the lives of the dead but also throwing down a gauntlet at the living who survive them. We know what they did. What, now, are you going to do? Think of this not as a patriotic exercise that demands to know for what citizens are willing to die. This is a democratic challenge that encourages citizens to show gratitude for life through the public good they can create. See Stow's indispensable, "Agonistic Homegoing."

47 Obama, "Remarks by the President at the Commemoration Ceremony of the 50th Anniversary of the Vietnam War." All quotes are from this speech.

48 Obama claimed, in passing, "that, even now, historians cannot agree on precisely when the war began." No doubt he refers to American historians. Vietnamese historians may not have trouble dating the military interventions of foreign aggressors.

49 Also on Memorial Day 2012, Obama delivered remarks at another sacred site, the Memorial Amphitheater at Arlington National Cemetery, home to the Tomb of the Unknowns. Surrounded by acres of white crosses and interred patriots, Obama saluted the many generations of soldiers separated by hundreds of years but united by an all-consuming love of country. This love transcended a potential rival – love for "life itself." Obama intended this as a compliment, but what does it mean to love American democracy more than life itself? A citizen can willingly place him- or herself in harm's way (volunteering in war, for example) knowing full well that it *may* lead to death. This is not the kind of sacrifice Obama lauds. The commitment it expresses is too thin. To love country more than life itself means to be able to sacrifice it for no reason, *ultimately*, except to prove that such sacrifice is possible ("Hamburger Hill"), or it means to be able to destroy the conditions of possibility of life to win a war ("Rolling Thunder"). In other words, to love the country and everything it stands for translates into loving to stand for the country (read: kill, die, and sacrifice). From a tragic perspective, life and death situations will be

encountered, but when sacrifice becomes necessary, it will not be loved. It will be hated, as it should be.

50 The limits to setting the record straight and perfecting the Union call the enterprise itself into question. The United States recently began a minor clean-up of Agent Orange in Vietnam, yet it still refuses to take responsibility for the spraying and its devastating consequences. It provides "assistance regardless of cause." See Fuller, "4 Decades on, U.S. Starts Clean-up of Agent Orange in Vietnam."

51 See the prize-winning series of stories by the *Toledo Blade*.

52 Obama is not without sympathy. He does bemoan the treatment of returning veterans suffering from exposure to Agent Orange. Still, this cheap rhetorical move practically begs for a comparative judgment to be made. That is, to raise the cancerous presence of Agent Orange in the lives of returning vets is to indulge the psychological underpinnings of American exceptionalism: narcissism. After all, whatever consequences American troops suffer(ed) from spraying, they pale in comparison to the suffering of the Vietnamese people who, after all, were the intended targets of exposure. The defoliant campaign in Vietnam invoked a military rationale – to make it impossible for the Vietnamese to fight a guerrilla war. To achieve this aim, the United States attacked the very possibility of life itself in Vietnam (and not just human life). The tragic irony is that the commission of a war crime by the United States came back to haunt its perpetrator.

53 Tatum, *The Mourner's Song*, 21.

54 This architectural ambition could be realized in lesser form if war memorial design competitions folded (at least) two critical requirements into their selection criteria. Do death and its horrors, which treat victims uniformly, receive adequate recognition? Is the enemy treated in Homeric terms, that is, with honor and respect as an equal? Would the enemy, in other words, be able to recognize and affirm itself in the composition?

55 Ibid., 25.

56 Adding Hanoi's McGan Monument to the Vietnam complex would formally dissolve the American-centric focus of the site. The double foreignness of the memorial – it hails from Vietnam and embodies a socialist realist aesthetic – would allow America to see its own commemorative practices anew. Not surprisingly, the crudeness and brutality of the McGan Monument would complement America's architectural narcissism, whether expressed through heavy-handed professions of innocence or self-pity – The Three Servicemen and Vietnam Women's Memorial, respectively. The juxtaposition, ideally, would startle visitors, who would be transfixed by the absurdity, even obscenity, of commemorative competition: memorialization as the continuation of war through artistic means. It would suggest that war must not be an occasion for memorial self-celebration, however muted.

57 The Vietnamese, ironically, allow – perhaps force – us to see what American democracy did to its own soldiers.

58 To incorporate the perspective and experience of the enemy, one might also consider the memorial to the My Lai massacre, which depicts defiant

Vietnamese civilians cradling and covering their murdered beloved. America may have slaughtered us, it proclaims, but we prevailed. If anything, the slaughter doubled our determination to prevail. Victory trumps life. Tatum, "Memorials of the American War in Vietnam," 666–667.

59 Kwon, *After the Massacre*, 139.

60 Ibid., 143.

61 Ibid., 141.

62 Greene, "Legion Condemns Kent State Memorial."

63 Obama might have downplayed the significance of his words supporting disagreement during war to heighten their effect, a rhetorical strategy Lincoln deployed at Gettysburg. See Stow, "Pericles at Gettysburg and Ground Zero," 202; for Stow's account of a similar rhetorical move in Pericles's funeral oration, see 200.

64 Stow, "Pericles at Gettysburg and Ground Zero," 200.

65 Predictably, the *May 4 Memorial* enjoys few architectural friends. In late 2014, however, the Austrians unveiled a World War II memorial to deserters. Though not located in Heroes Square, home to Austria's national war memorials, it was placed in the center of political Vienna across from the presidential palace and federal chancellery. The X-shaped monument with the words "all alone" emblazoned on it, designed to convey anonymity, honors the courage and fortitude of the roughly 20,000 soldiers who refused or discarded service in Hitler's army. Nazi Germany, of course, criminalized this political resistance to its perverted regime and illegitimate war, and executed some 1,500 as traitors. The Austrian Veterans' Association opposed the memorial and the normalization of the deserters. Bell, "Austria unveils World War Two deserters' memorial."

66 Memorial supplements include a simple plaque and more elaborate markings where the students fell after being shot. These additions identify and directly honor the four killed but do not necessarily contribute to the democratic character of the memorial. See Kent State University Library, Special Collections and Archives, *May 4 Memorial*.

CONCLUSION: DEMOCRACY'S TRAGIC AFFIRMATIONS

1 Joe Starrett, Tom Doniphon, and Ransom Stoddard did not make the list – though Lassie did.

2 Bosley Crowther wrote, "With 'High Noon' so lately among us, it scarcely seems possible that the screen should so soon again come up with another great Western film. Yet that is substantially what has happened in the case of George Stevens' 'Shane,' which made a magnificent appearance at the Music Hall yesterday."

3 Contrary to Bonnie Honig and Kiku Adatto, I do not assume Ryker's villainy. Honig, *Democracy and the Foreigner*, 21–22; Adatto, *Picture Perfect*, 191–192.

4 Honig, 21–22.

5 Ibid., 21–22.

6 Ibid., 35–36.

7 Ibid.

8 Slotkin, *Gunfighter Nation*, 396.

9 Ibid., 397.

10 It is also worth recalling that in the film's opening sequence, Joe successfully bluffed Shane with an unloaded rifle, effectively forcing Shane to leave his property. Joe had mistakenly assumed that Shane was an advance man for the Rykers. At the film's close, when Shane decides to intervene, he seems to assume that the mere sight of his fancy buckskins and sparkling pistol will put Joe in his place. He was wrong, underestimating Joe again, who, as I mentioned, suddenly attacks Shane to land the first strike and seize the advantage. Apparently Joe understands that doing the right thing and what is best for the community will entail costs – to himself, to his friend, and to their friendship as well. Joe is ready to absorb them.

11 For one thing, Joe devised collective forms of action. The homesteaders traveled to town together to gather supplies, thereby converting women and children into democratic citizens who bear risk and responsibility. This tactic stymied the Rykers. It also showed that he was not above deploying dubious means for good ends.

12 Ibid., 400.

13 Honig's astute reading of Shane as Joey's fantasy, a projection that enables him to domesticate his father's frightening power and violence, also suggests democracy's weakness, that it cannot address its lethal flaws. It, too, prefers legends.

Bibliography

A Place of Remembrance: Official Book of the National September 11 Memorial (Washington, DC: National Geographic, 2011).

Adatto, Kiku, *Picture Perfect: Life in the Age of the Photo-Op* (Princeton: Princeton University Press, 2008).

Allen, Danielle, *Talking to Strangers: Anxieties of Citizenship since Brown v. Board of Education* (Chicago: University of Chicago Press, 2004).

American Veterans Disabled for Life Memorial website, Design, Design Concept, http://www.avdlm.org/design-concept.

Animals in War Memorial website, History, http://www.animalsinwar.org.uk/index.cfm?asset_id=1375.

Anker, Elisabeth R., *Orgies of Feeling: Melodrama and the Politics of Freedom* (Durham: Duke University Press, 2014).

Arendt, Hannah, *On Violence* (New York: Harcourt, 1970).

Associated Press, The, "Military suicides up a bit among active duty in 2014; But more seek help via hotlines," July 22, 2014.

Associated Press, The, "On 9/11, Day of Mourning Becomes Day of Service," September 10, 2009.

Beckett, Samuel, *Worstward Ho* (New York: Grove, 1984).

Bell, Bethany, "Austria unveils World War Two deserters' memorial," 24 October 2014, http://www.bbc.com/news/world-europe-29754386

Benjamin, Walter, "Critique of Violence," in *Reflections*, tr. Edmund Jephcott (New York: Schocken, 1986).

Berlin, Isaiah, *The Crooked Timber of Humanity: Chapters in the History of Ideas* (New York: Vintage, 1992).

Bratu, Becky and Henry Austin, "West Virginia Chemical Spill Cuts Water to up to 300,000, State of Emergency Declared," January 10, 2014, NBC News, http://usnews.nbcnews.com/_news/2014/01/10/22245996-west-virginia-chemical-spill-cuts-water-to-up-to-300000-state-of-emergency-declared?lite.

Bouie, Jamelle, "Republicans Admit Voter ID-Laws Are Aimed at Democratic Voters," *The Daily Beast*, August 28, 2013, http://www.thedailybeast.com/articles/2013/08/28/republicans-admit-voter-id-laws-are-aimed-at-democratic-voters.html.

Bernstein, Richard, *Violence: Thinking without Banisters* (Cambridge, MA: Polity, 2013).

Biden, Joseph, "Remarks by Vice President Joseph Biden at Dedication of Flight 93 Memorial," September 10, 2011, http://www.whitehouse.gov/the-press-office/2011/09/10/remarks-vice-president-joseph-biden-dedication-flight-93-memorial.

Brown, Wendy, "Political Idealization and Its Discontents," Brown, *Edgework: Critical Essays on Knowledge and Politics* (Princeton: Princeton University Press, 2005).

Brunkhorst, Hauke, "From avenging to revolutionary force: John Ford's *The Man Who Shot Liberty Valance*," *Philosophy and Social Criticism* 34:6, 2008.

Burke, David, *Heart of Darkness: Bruce Springsteen's Nebraska* (London: Cherry Red Books, 2011).

Butler, Judith, *Precarious Life: The Powers of Mourning and Violence* (London: Verso, 2004).

Calarco, Matthew, *Zoographies: The Question of the Animal from Heidegger to Derrida* (New York: Columbia University Press, 2008).

Camus, Albert, "On the Future of Tragedy," in *Lyrical and Critical Essays, ed.* Philip Thody, tr. Ellen Conroy Kennedy (New York: Knopf, 1969).

Canovan, Margaret, *Nationhood and Political Theory* (Cheltenham, UK: Edward Elgar, 1996).

"Patriotism Is Not Enough," *British Journal of Political Science* 30:3 2000.

Cavell, Stanley, *Cities of Words: Pedagogical Letters on a Register of the Moral Life* (Cambridge, MA: Harvard University Press, 2004).

Chinen, Nate, "The Boss Roars Tough and Tender," *New York Times*, April 4, 2012, http://www.nytimes.com/2012/04/05/arts/music/bruce-springsteen-and-the-e-street-band-at-the-izod-center.html.

Cobb Jr., Charles E., *This Nonviolent Stuff'll Get You Killed: How Guns Made the Civil Rights Movement Possible* (New York: Basic Books, 2014).

Collins, Richard and David Skover, *On Dissent: Its Meaning in America* (Cambridge, MA: Cambridge University Press, 2013).

Connolly, William E., "Democracy and Normalization," in *Politics and Ambiguity* (Madison: University of Wisconsin Press, 1987).

Political Theory and Modernity (Oxford: Basil Blackwell, 1988).

The Ethos of Pluralization (Minneapolis: University of Minnesota Press, 1995).

Pluralism (Durham: Duke University Press, 2005).

Capitalism and Christianity, American Style (Durham: Duke University Press, 2008).

Cooper, Jilly, *Animals in War: Valiant Horses, Courageous Dogs, and Other Animal Heroes* (Guilford: Lyons Press, 2002).

Corbett, Tom, September 11 10th Anniversary Speech, Shanksville, PA, https://www.youtube.com/watch?v=OyhdyN_-n2U.

Cramer, Richard Ben, "They Were Heroes Too," *Parade Magazine*, April 1, 2009, http://northwestvets.com/spurs/k9htm.

Cranston, Maurice, *The Noble Savage: Jean-Jacques Rousseau, 1754–1762* (Chicago: University of Chicago Press, 1991).

Critchley, Simon, *Infinitely Demanding: Ethics of Commitment, Politics of Resistance* (London: Verso, 2007).

Cronin, Ciaran, "Democracy and Collective Identity: In Defence of Constitutional Patriotism," *European Journal of Philosophy* 11:1, 2003.

Crowther, Bosley, "High Noon," *The New York Times*, July 25, 1952, http://www.nytimes.com/1952/07/25/arts/high-noon-oscars.html.

Delmore, Erin, "Another Chemical Spill in West Virginia," MSNBC, February 11, 2014, http://www.msnbc.com/all/another-chemical-spill-west-virginia.

Descartes, René, *Discourse on Method*, tr. Donald Cress (Indianapolis: Hackett Publishing, 2008).

Dew, Charles B., *Apostles of Disunion: Southern Secession Commissioners and the Causes of the Civil War* (Charlottesville: University of Virginia Press, 2001).

Dienstag, Joshua, "A Storied Shooting: Liberty Valance and the Paradox of Sovereignty," *Political Theory* 40:3, June 2012.

Dolan, Frederick M., *Allegories of America: Narratives, Metaphysics, Politics* (Ithaca: Cornell University Press, 1994).

Doss, Erika, *Memorial Mania: Public Feeling in America* (Chicago: University of Chicago Press, 2010).

Eagleton, Terry, *Sweet Violence: The Idea of the Tragic* (Oxford: Blackwell Publishing, 2002).

The East, Batmanglij, Zal (2013).

Edelman, Susan, "The 9/11 museum's absurd gift shop," *New York Post*, May 18, 2014, http://nypost.com/2014/05/18/outrage-over-911-museum-gift-shops-crass-souvenirs/.

Edkins, Jenny, *Trauma and the Memory of Politics* (Cambridge, MA: Cambridge University Press, 2003).

Edmundson, Mark, *Nightmare on Main Street: Angels, Sadomasochism, and the Culture of Gothic* (Cambridge, MA: Harvard University Press, 1997).

Enloe, Cynthia, "Beyond Steve Canyon and Rambo: Feminist Histories of Militarized Masculinity," in John R. Gillis, ed., *The Militarization of the Western World* (New Brunswick: Rutgers University Press, 1989).

Euben, J. Peter, *Platonic Noise* (Princeton: Princeton University Press, 2003).

Feldberg, Michael, *The Turbulent Era: Riot and Disorder in Jacksonian America* (Oxford: Oxford University Press, 1980).

Ferguson, Kennan, "I ♥ My Dog," *Political Theory* 32:3, June 2004.

Ferguson, Michaele, *Sharing Democracy* (Oxford: Oxford University Press, 2012).

First Blood, Kotcheff, Ted (1982).

Filkins, Dexter, "The Long Road Home," *The New York Times*, March 6, 2014, http://www.nytimes.com/2014/03/09/books/review/redeployment-by-phil-klay.html.

Fiss, Owen, *The Irony of Free Speech* (Cambridge, MA: Harvard University Press, 1998).

Flags of Our Fathers, Eastwood, Clint (2006).

Fuller, Thomas, "4 Decades on, U.S. Starts Clean-up of Agent Orange in Vietnam," *The New York Times*, August 9, 2012, http://www.nytimes.com/2012/08/10/world/asia/us-moves-to-address-agent-orange-contamination-in-vietnam.html?pagewanted=all.

Gibney, Alex, "*Zero Dark Thirty*'s Wrong and Dangerous Conclusion," www.huffingpost.com, December 21, 2012.

Goldhill, Simon, *Reading Greek Tragedy* (Cambridge, MA: Cambridge University Press, 1986).

"The Great Dionysia and Civic Ideology," in John J. Winkler and Froma I. Zeitlin, eds., *Nothing to Do with Dionysos* (Princeton: Princeton University Press, 1990).

Love, Sex & Tragedy: How the Ancient World Shapes Our Lives (Chicago: University of Chicago Press, 2004).

Goodavage, Maria, *Soldier Dogs: The Untold Story of America's Canine Heroes* (New York: Dutton, 2012).

Graeber, David, *Revolutions in Reverse: Essays on Politics, Violence, and Imagination* (Brooklyn: Autonomedia, 2011).

Greene, Robert, "Legion Condemns Kent State Memorial," July 12, 1986, http://www.apnewsarchive.com/1986/Legion-Condemns-Kent-State-Memorial/id-eb086c9ca722b155559f8783bc449630.

Habermas, Jürgen, "Citizenship and National Identity," *Between Facts and Norms: Contributions to a Discourse Theory of Law and Democracy*, tr. William Rehg (Cambridge, MA: MIT University Press, 1996).

The Inclusion of the Other: Studies in Political Theory (Cambridge, MA: MIT University Press, 2000).

Hayward, Clarissa Rile, "Democracy's Identity Problem: Is 'Constitutional Patriotism' the Answer?" *Constellations* 14:2, June 2007.

Healy, Jack, "Wrongfully Convicted and Seeking Restitution," *New York Times*, March 13, 2013, http://www.nytimes.com/2013/03/14/us/prisoners-seek-restitution-for-wrongful-convictions.html?hpw.

Himes, Geoffrey, *Born in the U.S.A.* (New York: Continuum, 2005).

Hobbes, Thomas, *Leviathan* (New York: Penguin, 1968).

Honig, Bonnie, *Political Theory and the Displacement of Politics* (Ithaca: Cornell University Press, 1993).

Democracy and the Foreigner (Princeton: Princeton University Press, 2001).

"Antigone's Laments, Creon's Grief: Mourning, Membership, and the Politics of Exception, *Political Theory* 37:1, February 2009.

Emergency Politics: Paradox, Law, Democracy (Princeton: Princeton University Press, 2009).

Antigone, Interrupted (Cambridge, MA: Cambridge University Press, 2013).

Hornaday, Anne, "Spielberg pays homage to a pal, Joey," *The Washington Post*, December 23, 2011, http://www.washingtonpost.com/gog/movies/war-horse,1163207.html.

"'A manhunt won by the little people,'" January 11, 2013, www.washingtonpost.com.

Ignatieff, Michael, *The Lesser Evil: Political Ethics in an Age of Terror* (Cambridge, MA: Harvard University Press, 2004).

Ingram, Attracta, "Constitutional patriotism," *Philosophy and Social Criticism* 22:6, November 1996.

Jeffords, Susan, *The Remasculinization of America: Gender and the Vietnam War* (Indianapolis: Indiana University Press, 1989).

   Hard Bodies: Hollywood Masculinity in the Reagan Era (New Brunswick: Rutgers University Press, 1993).

Johnston, Steven, *Encountering Tragedy: Rousseau and the Project of Democratic Order* (Ithaca: Cornell University Press, 1999).

   The Truth about Patriotism (Durham: Duke University Press, 2007).

   "American Dionysia," *Contemporary Political Theory* 8:3, August 2009.

   "Animals in War: Commemoration, Patriotism, Death," *Political Research Quarterly* 65:2, June 2012.

Kandell, Steve, "The Worst Day of My Life Is Now New York's Hottest Tourist Attraction," http://www.buzzfeed.com/stevekandell/the-worst-day-of-my-life-is-now-new-yorks-hottest-tourist-at.

Kateb, George, *Patriotism and Other Mistakes* (New Haven: Yale University Press, 2008).

Keane, John, *Violence and Democracy* (Cambridge: Cambridge University Press, 2004).

Kent State University Library, Special Collections and Archives, May 4 Memorial, http://speccoll.library.kent.edu/4may70/exhibit/memorials/m4mem.html.

King Jr., Martin Luther, "Beyond Vietnam," in *A Call to Conscience* (New York: Warner Books, 2002).

Kirkpatrick, Jennet, *Uncivil Disobedience: Studies in Violence and Democratic Politics* (Princeton: Princeton University Press, 2008).

Klay, Phil, *Redeployment* (New York: Penguin Press, 2014).

Kaufmann, Walter, *Tragedy and Philosophy* (Princeton: Princeton University Press, 1968).

Kennicott, Philip, "The 9/11 Memorial museum doesn't just display artifacts, it ritualizes grief on a loop," *The Washington Post*, June 7, 2014.

Kerrigan, John, *Revenge Tragedy: Aeschylus to Armageddon* (Oxford: Clarendon Press, 1996).

Kostakopoulou, Dora, "Thick, Thin, and Thinner Patriotisms: Is This All There Is?" *Oxford Journal of Legal Studies* 261, Spring 2006.

Krugman, Paul, "The Twinkie Defense," *The New York Times*, November 18, 2102, http://www.nytimes.com/2012/11/19/opinion/krugman-the-twinkie-manifesto.html?_r=0.

   "Rich Man's Recovery," *New York Times*, September 12, 2013.

Kwon, Heonik, *After the Massacre: Commemoration and Consolation in Ha My and My Lai* (Berkeley: University of California Press, 2006).

Langley, Carolynn, *Animals in War Memorial* photographs, http://www.roll-of-honour.com/London/AnimalsInWarMemorial.html.

Lemish, Michael G., *War Dogs: A History of Loyalty and Heroism* (Washington, DC: Potomac Books, 2008).

Letters from Iwo Jima, Eastwood, Clint (2006).

Machiavelli, Niccolò, *The Discourses*, ed. Bernard Crick (New York: Penguin Books, 1970).

The Prince, eds. Quentin Skinner and Russell Price (Cambridge, MA: Cambridge University Press, 1988).

Maier, Pauline, *From Resistance to Revolution: Colonial radicals and the development of American opposition to Britain, 1765–1776* (New York: W.W. Norton, 1991).

The Man Who Shot Liberty Valance, Ford, John (1962).

Mansfield, Nick, "Derrida, Democracy and Violence," *Studies on Social Justice* 5:2, 2011.

Marcus, Greil, *Ranters & Crowd Pleasers: Punk in Pop Music 1977–1992* (New York: Anchor Books, 1993).

Markell, Patchen, "Making Affect Safe for Democracy? On 'Constitutional Patriotism,'" *Political Theory* 281, February 2000.

McBride, Joseph and Michael Wilmington, *John Ford* (New York: Da Capo Press, 1975).

McCormick, John P., *Machiavellian Democracy* (Cambridge: Cambridge University Press, 2011).

Minder, Raphael, "Swiss Voters Approve a Plan to Severely Limit Executive Compensation," *The New York Times*, March 3, 2013, http://www.nytimes.com/2013/03/04/business/global/swiss-voters-tighten-countrys-limits-on-executive-pay.html?_r=0.

Moore, Barrington, "Thoughts on Violence and Democracy," *Proceedings of the Academy of Political Science* 29:1, 1968.

Morgan, Edmund, *American Slavery, American Freedom: The Ordeal of Colonial Virginia* (New York: W.W. Norton, 1975).

Mouffe, Chantal, *The Democratic Paradox* (London: Verso, 2000).

Agonistics: Thinking the World Politically (London: Verso, 2013).

Müller, Jan-Werner, *Constitutional Patriotism* (Princeton: Princeton University Press, 2007).

National Park Service, Flight 93 National Memorial, Sources and Detailed Information, http://www.nps.gov/flni/historyculture/sources-and-detailed-information.htm.

Nietzsche, Friedrich, "Homer's Contest," in *The Portable Nietzsche*, tr. and ed. Walter Kaufmann (New York: Viking Press, 1954).

The Birth of Tragedy and The Genealogy of Morals, tr. Francis Golffing (New York: Anchor Books, 1956)

The Will to Power, trs. Walter Kaufmann and R.J. Hollingdale (New York: Vintage Books, 1968).

Twilight of the Idols and The Anti-Christ, tr. R.J. Hollingdale (New York: Penguin, 1968).

The Gay Science, tr. Walter Kaufmann (New York: Vintage Books, 1974).

The 9/11 Commission Report: Final Report of the National Commission on Terrorist Attacks upon the United States (New York: W.W. Norton, 2004).

9/11 Memorial, About the Memorial, http://www.911memorial.org/about-memorial.

Obama, Barack, "Remarks by the President at the Commemoration Ceremony of the 50th Anniversary of the Vietnam War," http://www.whitehouse.gov/the-press-office/2012/05/28/remarks-president-commemoration-ceremony-50th-anniversary-vietnam-war.

O'Donnell, Sgt. John E., *None Came Home: The War Dogs of Vietnam* (1st Books Library, 2001).

Pale Rider, Eastwood, Clint (1985).

Perez, Gilberto, "House of Miscegenation," *London Review of Books*, November 18, 2010.

Pippin, Robert, *Hollywood Westerns and American Myth* (New Haven: Yale University Press, 2010).

Price, Eluned, "They served and suffered for us," *Telegraph*, November 1, 2004, http://www.telegraph.co.uk/culture/3626468/They-served-andsuffered-for-us.html.

Putney, William W., *Always Faithful: A Memoir of the Marine Dogs of WW II* (Dulles: Potomac Books, 2003).

Raddatz, Martha, "Obama Reflects on 9/11, War That Followed," abcnews. go.com, September 11, 2009.

Ray, Robert, *A Certain Tendency in the Hollywood Cinema* (Princeton: Princeton University Press, 1985).

Ridge, Tom, September 11 10th Anniversary Speech, Shanksville, PA, https:// www.youtube.com/watch?v=a9tLJorURo8.

Riverside War Dog Memorial, http://www.youtube.com/watch?v=R3dQSdR5LwA.

Robin, Corey, *The Reactionary Mind: Conservatism from Edmund Burke to Sarah Palin* (Oxford: Oxford University Press, 2011).

Roche, Mark and Vittorio Hosle, "Vico's Age of Heroes and the Age of Men in John Ford's Film 'The Man Who Shot Liberty Valance,'" *Clio* 232, Winter 1994.

Rorty, Richard, *Achieving Our Country* (Cambridge, MA: Harvard University Press, 1998).

Rosenthal, "The Pope's Take on Capitalism," *The New York Times*, November 26, 2013, http://takingnote.blogs.nytimes.com/2013/11/26/the-popes-take-on -capitalism/?hp&rref=opinion.

Rothstein, Edward, "A Memoir to Personal Memory: Recalling Sept. 11 by Inverting a Museum's Usual Role," *The New York Times*, May 22, 2014.

Rousseau, Jean-Jacques, *The First and Second Discourses*, ed. Roger Masters (New York: St. Martin's Press, 1964).

    On the Social Contract with Geneva Manuscript and Political Economy, ed. Roger D. Masters, tr. Judith R. Masters (New York: St. Martin's Press, 1978).

    Considerations on the Government of Poland, in *Political Writings*, tr. and ed. Frederick Watkins (Madison: University of Wisconsin Press, 1986).

Schaar, John, "The Case for Patriotism," *Legitimacy in the Modern State* (New Brunswick: Transaction Publishers, 1989).

Savage, Kirk, *Monument Wars* (Berkeley: University of California Press, 2009).

    "The President and the Confederacy," *The Washington Post*, May 23, 2009.

Schell, Jonathan, *The Time of Illusion* (New York: Vintage, 1976).

Schickel, Richard, "A 'War Horse' and his Boy," Truthdig, December 24, 2011, http://www.truthdig.com/arts_culture/item/a_war_horse_and_his_boy_ 20111224.

Scott, A.O., "Innocence is Trampled, but a Bond Endures," *The New York Times*, December 22, 2011, http://www.nytimes.com/2011/12/23/movies/war-horse-directed-by-steven-spielberg-review.html.

Seelye, Katharine Q., "In Pennsylvania, a Wall of Names," *The New York Times*, September 11, 2011, http://www.nytimes.com/2011/09/12/us/12shanksville.html?pagewanted=all.

Shane, Stevens, George (1953).

Shapiro, Michael, J., *Methods and Nations: Cultural Governance and the Indigenous Subject* (New York: Routledge, 2004).

Shapiro, Michael J., *Deforming American Political Thought: Ethnicity, Facticity, and Genre* (Lexington: The University of Kentucky Press, 2006).

Shelley, Mary, *Frankenstein* (New York: Barnes & Noble Classics, 2003).

Sheppard, Noel, "George W. Bush's Flight 93 Memorial Dedication Speech," September 10, 2011, http://newsbusters.org/blogs/noel-sheppard/2011/09/10/george-w-bushs-flight-93-memorial-dedication-speech.

   "Bill Clinton's Flight 93 Memorial Dedication Speech," September 10, 2011, http://newsbusters.org/blogs/noel-sheppard/2011/09/10/bill-clintons-flight-93-memorial-dedication-speech.

Slotkin, Richard, *Gunfighter Nation: The Myth of the Frontier in Twentieth-Century America* (New York: Harper Perennial, 1992).

Smith, Jada F., "Using Flags to Focus on Veteran Suicides," *The New York Times*, March 27, 2014, http://www.nytimes.com/2014/03/28/us/using-flags-to-focus-on-veteran-suicides.html.

Smith, Terry, *The Architecture of Aftermath* (Chicago: University of Chicago Press, 2006).

Smithsonian, National Museum of American History, "The Price of Freedom: Americans at War," http://americanhistory.si.edu/militaryhistory/exhibition/flash.html.

Solnit, Rebecca, *A Paradise Built in Hell: The Extraordinary Communities that Arise in Disaster* (New York: Viking, 2009).

Sophocles, *The Three Theban Plays: Antigone, Oedipus the King, Oedipus at Colonus*, tr. Robert Fagles (New York: Penguin Classics, 1984).

Springsteen, Bruce, *Guardian* interview, February 17, 2012, www.guardian.co.uk/music/2012/feb17/bruce-springsteen-wrecking-ball/print.

Steiner, George, *The Death of Tragedy* (New Haven: Yale University Press, 1996).

   "Tragedy, Pure and Simple," in M.S. Silk ed. *Tragedy and the Tragic: Greek Theater and Beyond* (Oxford: Oxford University Press, 1996).

Stevens, Dana, "All the Weepy Horses," Slate, December 23, 2011, http://www.slate.com/articles/arts/movies/2011/12/war_horse_review_steven_spielberg_s_corny_equine_drama_breached_my_emotional_defenses_.html.

Storing, Herbert J., ed., *The Anti-Federalist* (Chicago: University of Chicago Press, 1985).

Stow, Simon, "Pericles at Gettysburg and Ground Zero: Tragedy, Patriotism, and Public Mourning," *American Political Science Review* 101:2, May 2007.

   "Agonistic Homegoing: Frederick Douglass, Joseph Lowery, and the Democratic Value of African American Public Mourning," *American Political Science Review* 104: 04, November 2010.

Stuckler, David, and Sanjay Basu, "Europe's public health disaster: How austerity kills," CNN.com, September 9, 2013.

Taibbi, Matt, *"Zero Dark Thirty"* is Osama Bin Laden's Last Victory over America," www.rollingstone.com, January 16, 2013.

Tatum, James, "Memorials of the American War in Vietnam," *Critical Inquiry* 224, Summer 1996.

The Mourner's Song: War and Remembrance from the Iliad to Vietnam (Chicago: University of Chicago Press, 2003).

Tavernise, Sabrina, "Life Spans Shrink for Least-Educated Whites in the U.S.," *The New York Times*, September 20, 2012.

There Will Be Blood, Anderson, Paul Thomas (2007).

Thucydides, *The Peloponnesian War* (New York: Penguin Books, 1954).

Thoreau, Henry D., *The Higher Law*, ed. Wendell Glick (Princeton: Princeton University Press, 2004).

Toledo Blade, http://www.toledoblade.com/special-tiger-force.

Tookey, Chris, "Spectacular, tear-jerking, uplifting; *War Horse* is a Spielberg masterpiece," Mail Online, January 13, 2012, http://www.dailymail.co.uk/tvshowbiz/article-2085885/War-Horse-film-review-A-Steven-Spielberg-masterpiece.html.

Turner, Jack, "Performing Conscience: Thoreau, Political Action, and the Plea for John Brown," *Political Theory* 33: 4, August 2005.

United States War Dog Association, The, K-9 Wall of Honor.

Vietnam Dog Handler Association, History, http://vdha.us/memorials/.

Vietnam Veterans Memorial Fund website, http://www.vvmf.org/index.cfm?SectionID=103.

Villa, Dana, *Socratic Citizenship* (Princeton: Princeton University Press, 2001).

Viroli, Maurizio, *For Love of Country: An Essay on Patriotism and Nationalism* (Oxford: Oxford University Press, 1997).

Redeeming "The Prince": The Meaning of Machiavelli's Masterpiece (Princeton: Princeton University Press, 2013).

War Horse, Spielberg, Steven (2011).

Weber, Max, "Politics as a Vocation," in *From Max Weber: Essays in Sociology*, tr. H.H. Gerth and C. Wright Mills (New York: Oxford University Press, 1958).

White, Stephen, K., *The Ethos of a Late-Modern Citizen* (Cambridge, MA: Harvard University Press, 2009).

Williams, Bernard, *Moral Luck* (Cambridge: Cambridge University Press, 1981).

Wilson, Emily, *Mocked with Death: Tragic Overliving from Sophocles to Milton* (Baltimore: The Johns Hopkins University Press, 2004).

Wilson, Michael, "Sept. 11 Steel Forms Heart of Far-Flung Memorials," *The New York Times*, September 7, 2009.

Wood, Gordon S., *The American Revolution: A History* (New York: The Modern Library, 2003).

Wolin, Sheldon, *Politics and Vision: Continuity and Innovation in Western Political Thought* (New York: Little Brown, 1960).

Wrangham, Richard, *Catching Fire: How Cooking Made Us Human* (New York: Basic Books, 2009).

Yack, Bernard, "The Myth of the Civic Nation," *Critical Review* 10:2, Spring 1996.

Young, James E., *The Texture of Memory: Holocaust Memorials and Meaning* (New Haven: Yale University Press, 1993).

Zero Dark Thirty, Bigelow, Kathryn (2012).

Žižek, Slavoj, *Violence* (New York: Picador, 2008).

Index

Made in the USA
Middletown, DE
26 August 2016